Financial Modeling for Decision Making

Financial Modeling for Decision Making: Using MS-Excel in Accounting and Finance

Ron Messer

Kwantlen Polytechnic University, Canada

Accounting is About More than Just Numbers
... it's About Making Better Decisions

United Kingdom – North America
Japan – India – Malaysia – China

Emerald Publishing Limited
Howard House, Wagon Lane, Bingley BD16 1WA, UK

First edition 2020

Reprints and permissions service
Contact: permissions@emeraldinsight.com

British Library Cataloguing in Publication Data
A catalogue record for this book is available from the British Library

ISBN: 978-1-78973-414-0 (Print)
ISBN: 978-1-78973-413-3 (Online)
ISBN: 978-1-78973-415-7 (Epub)

Printed and bound by CPI Group (UK) Ltd, Croydon, CR0 4YY

ISOQAR certified
Management System,
awarded to Emerald
for adherence to
Environmental
standard
ISO 14001:2004.

Certificate Number 1985
ISO 14001

INVESTOR IN PEOPLE

I dedicate this book to the memory of my late brother,
Martin Oscar Messer, who left this world much too soon.

Contents

About the Author

Snapshot

Ron Messer is a faculty member of the School of Business at Kwantlen Polytechnic University whose research interests focus broadly on management accounting and decision making. A graduate of six universities, Ron holds undergraduate and graduate degrees in both public and business administration. He is a CPA, a Chartered Accountant, and a Certified Management Accountant with 25 years of working experience in accounting, finance, and information systems. His essays have appeared in publications in Canada, the United States, and the United Kingdom.

Key Research

Ron Messer's primary areas of interest include organizational strategy, financial planning, and supply chain management (with an emphasis on logistics). To this end, he has published in peer-reviewed academic journals (14 essays), industry-specific journals (six articles), chapters in authoritative texts (four chapters in four books), and business case studies (two teaching cases).

Organizational Strategy

Based on his strategy research, Ron developed a method for charging airport landing and terminal fees that optimizes the social welfare for both the traveling public and private sector operators. In conjunction with this work, Ron also proposed a pricing framework for private sector airports. With respect to the public sector, he suggested a renewed focus on organizational vision, whereby the government adopts private sector values in the delivery of its services.

Financial Planning

In the area of financial planning, Ron proposed a budgeting method that eliminates many of the problems encountered when companies prepare their annual financial plan. He also created a process for identifying budget "cheaters," which allows for the creation of more realistic business plans and avoids the inefficient allocation of corporate capital.

Supply Chain Management

In an essay written almost two decades ago ("Airports, Air Cargo and the Internet"), Ron outlines the possible effects of e-commerce on airports as logistics hubs in the supply chain. In this paper, Ron predicts that Internet-enabled business models will lead to increased air cargo and possible on-airport manufacturing facilities. Recent evidence surrounding the development at Indian airports (with the production of off-patent pharmaceuticals), the United Parcel Services aviation group (servicing laptop computers), and the many "fulfillment" centers under construction at, or near, airports (Amazon) provides evidence to support this hypothesis.

Impact of Research

Ron Messer's essays on supply chain management and logistics describe the impact of e-commerce on aviation globally. In the area of organizational strategy, Ron has proposed a way in which university business programs can distinguish themselves and become world-class institutions.

Overall, Ron's research is helping to develop strategies so that governments can deliver public services more effectively, including airports operating in deregulated environments. His work is influencing the way private and public institutions operate by proposing efficient methods that are globally relevant.

What's Next?

Ron recently published a business case that was used as part of a competition for management accounting students across the United States, along with teaching notes. He has also completed a paper that discusses enhanced teaching methods for management accounting. His most ambitious project to date is examining decision making in speculative markets to understand the underlying mechanisms that govern participant behaviors. This involves analyzing large data sets and developing several heuristic models.

Check out Ron online at:

LinkedIn: https://www.linkedin.com/in/ron-messer-464878b6/?ppe=1

and

Google Scholar: https://scholar.google.ca/citations?user=K95HjQMAAAAJ&hl=en

Brief Summary

This book was written with two objectives in mind:

(1) *To be useful for making business decisions.*
(2) *To show how MS-Excel can be applied to making these decisions.*

It is the type of publication that I wish I had when I was learning how to use this popular spreadsheet package. For the most part, the training I received was disjointed, lacked focus, and did not establish a context for using MS-Excel; for example, how to develop a financial model to decide whether to pursue a business opportunity. For this reason, the starting point for each chapter is a business decision that needs to be made. Each decision is supported by the relevant accounting/finance theory, and then (and only then) is Excel introduced as a tool for addressing a management problem. This process reverses the method commonly used for teaching Excel, where the functionality is demonstrated and then applied to a disparate set of case facts – an approach that incorrectly attempts to find a problem for a solution.

This book provides accounting students in post-secondary institutions with an advanced level understanding of how to use MS-Excel. It reflects real-life applications of this important analytical tool, which has become the industry standard for spreadsheet software. The text focuses on using MS-Excel in situations encountered by accounting and finance students and professionals; these are contextualized in terms of the past, present, and future and reflect a typical operating cycle, which includes initial planning, followed by exercising control, and is completed when feedback is received.

The book also addresses the growing need for data analytic skills (i.e., "big data") and the recent innovations by MS-Excel in this regard, including Power Query (data cleaning and management), Power Pivot (advanced pivot tables using databases), and Power BI (creating executive KPI dashboards). However, while data analytics is important in financial management, it must be remembered that it forms only part of the larger picture that is captured by financial modeling.

The Excel 'shell' files that are used in conjunction with the financial modeling exercises shown in this book are available through the Emerald Publishing website. The completed solutions for the financial models can also be found there.

The Excel files are located at URL: https://bit.ly/finmod2020

Preface

All companies use some type of spreadsheet application in the day-to-day operation of their Accounting and Finance departments. This can be as a stand-alone tool (e.g., mortgage calculator; amortization schedule), or – particularly for smaller companies – a significant part of their financial systems (e.g., payroll application; inventory subledger). For this reason, acquiring competencies in MS-Excel will be extremely valuable for students when they are applying for jobs and will help them tremendously during their employment interviews. Robert Half, the finance and accounting recruiting specialists, have noted in their most recent employer survey that advanced level knowledge of MS-Excel if one of the most sought-after skills by prospective hiring managers.

So, why do we need another textbook on using MS-Excel for business? Unlike previous publications that have focused primarily on management science applications, this text is specifically geared to business decisions that require financial modeling techniques used in Accounting and Finance departments. The applications discussed and models presented are based on the working experience of the author over his more than 25 years of employment in various areas of financial management. In addition, the text structures the practical usage of MS-Excel for decision making in the context of time: past, present, and future. In contrast, many books on this subject are relatively unstructured and dominated by esoteric and infrequently used applications of MS-Excel, primarily for academic audiences.

This text is ideally suited to a one-semester, senior undergraduate course of 14 weeks and addresses the competencies required by professional accounting associations, such as those offering the CPA and CMA designations. It covers the use of MS-Excel in:

- Break-even analysis, for new venture decisions
- Time series forecasting, for sales demand decisions
- Capital budgeting, for major investment decisions
- Regression analysis, for predictive analytics decisions
- Linear programming, for product mix and scheduling decisions
- Corporate valuations, for equity financing decisions
- Data analytics, for customer buying decisions
- KPIs using dashboards, for strategic decisions
- Budget development, for performance management decisions
- Amortization tables, for debt and asset management decisions

Each chapter can be covered in one weekly computer lab, with chapters one and two combined in the first session. This allows for 10 weeks of instruction, two mid-term tests, and one final exam. Chapter 12 integrates materials from the prior chapters and can be used as a stand-alone capstone project for students to complete.

Unique Aspects of this Book

This book is different from similar publications in several respects.

Focus on Accounting and Finance: Most texts that cover using MS-Excel for business address management science applications and do not deal specifically with accounting and finance situations. This book will be valuable to both accounting students as well as financial management professionals for making business decisions.

Practical applications: The content of this book will be immediately relevant to students and practitioners who are, or will be, dealing with similar situations in their professional work. For example, using capital budgeting models to make billion-dollar investment decisions, or developing corporate valuation models to price shares for an IPO.

Real-life examples: The Excel functionality used in decision making is based on the author's more than 25 years of financial management experience. The text will address common business decisions made by financial management professionals.

Decision-making emphasis: Employers want their newly hired employees to assist them in guiding the company. The focus of the book is on making sound business decisions that provide value for the enterprise.

Employer demand: Based on feedback received from our university's alumni and those who hire our graduates, companies increasingly want their employees to have advanced level MS-Excel skills. This book addresses that need. Feedback from our degree holders tells us that the organizations that employ them are impressed with their knowledge of MS-Excel.

The book addresses the day-to-day work done by Accounting and Finance staff in a company. This is illustrated in the table below, which shows how everyday business decisions relate to the accounting and finance concepts addressed in the topical coverage in the text (Table 1).

The book is also different from competing publications because it addresses real-life business situations that the author has encountered during his more than 25 years of work experience. This is summarized in the table below, along with references to the related MS-Excel functionality that is used in the demonstration exercises in the book (Table 2).

Organization of this Book

The book is organized around three dimensions relating to the decisions made by accounting and finance students and professionals, including: (1) time frame, (2) accounting cycle, and (3) financial analytics.

(1) The decision context based on time frame includes the future, present, and past. Note that the normal chronological sequence has been reversed in this book to better align with the accounting cycle.

Table 1. Everyday Business Decisions Covered in this Book.

Business Decisions	Accounting/Finance Concepts	Book Topics (and Chapters)
New business venture	Cost-Volume-Profit analysis	Break-even models (Chapter 2)
Long-term planning	Financial forecasts	Time series forecasting (Chapter 3)
Major investment	NPV, IRR, payback period	Capital budgeting models (Chapter 4)
Predicting the future	Data analytics	Regression analysis (Chapter 5)
Product pricing	Cost-Volume-Profit analysis	Linear programming (Chapter 6)
Financial reporting	Income Statement, Balance Sheet, Cash Flow	Corporate valuations (Chapter 7)
Equity financing	Business valuations	Corporate valuations (Chapter 7)
Interpreting financial information	Descriptive analytics Diagnostic analytics	Data analytics (Chapter 8)
Performance measurement	Key performance indicators	KPIs and Dashboards (Chapter 9)
Corporate strategy	Pro-forma financial statements	KPIs and dashboards (Chapter 9)
Cash management	Cash budgeting	Budget management (Chapter 10)
Budget management	Responsibility accounting and variance analysis	Operating budgets (Chapter 10)
Debt financing	Bond/loan pricing and amortization	Amortization tables (Chapter 11)

(2) The accounting cycle includes distinct phases for planning (future orientation), control (thinking about the present), and feedback (using what has been learned from the past).

(3) Decisions based on the future allow businesses to make plans – using predictive analytics. Decisions made in the present emphasize control, since they guide day-to-day actions – using descriptive analytics. Decisions using past information are reflective and give feedback about the effectiveness of plans in relation to actual results – using diagnostic analytics.

This schema is shown below and reflected in the chapter sequence of the table of contents. The dimension columns are organized according to the time frame in which the decisions are made. They include the applicable part of the accounting cycle and the related financial analytic techniques. The financial models discussed in the book are also listed, based on the applicable time frame and stage of the accounting cycle to which they relate (Table 3).

Table 2. Everyday Business Decisions and Real-life Examples.

Business Decisions	Real Life Examples Using MS-Excel	MS-Excel Functionality (UPPERCASE Lettering)
New business ventures	I have developed financial models to assess the profitability of new business opportunities.	Cost-volume-profit models using GOAL SEEK, DATA TABLES, and SCENARIOS
Long-term planning	I have used forecasting techniques to estimate corporate revenues.	Forecasting techniques in the ANALYSIS TOOLPACK MOVING AVERAGE EXPONENTIAL SMOOTHING
Major investments	I have created capital budgeting models for multimillion-dollar land development projects in both domestic and foreign locations.	NPV, IRR
Predicting the future	I have developed a predictive model, using linear regression techniques, for an organization's program spending.	ANALYSIS TOOLPACK: REGRESSION
Product pricing	I developed a process for pricing the use of airport facilities by using linear programming techniques.	Using SOLVER to optimize product/service pricing
Financial reporting	I have created a monthly management reporting system that monitored corporate performance in relation to an organization's budget.	Variance analysis and FORECAST functions were used
Equity financing	I have published an essay that deals with the use of equity financing for private airports.	Using PIVOT TABLES to analyze various financial datasets
Interpreting financial information	I have prepared analytical reports, based on information obtained from a large data warehouse, using advanced data analysis tools (i.e., Hyperion and Essbase software that interfaced with MS-Excel)	PIVOT TABLES and BI (Business Intelligence) tools were used
Performance measurement	I have identified key performance indicators (KPIs) for monthly reporting to senior management.	Creating executive dashboards, using PIVOT TABLES, SLICER and SPARKLINES functions
Corporate strategy	I was involved in developing a strategic plan for a subsidiary of a large business. I have also authored essays on corporate strategy.	Employed ANALYSIS TOOLPACK forecasting using MOVING AVERAGE and EXPONENTIAL SMOOTHING techniques
Cash management	I have been responsible for managing multi-million-dollar cash portfolios, through purchases of $R1$ and $R2$ rated short-term commercial paper.	Created a financial model (using Excel GRAPHICS) to match risk with return on a portfolio of investments
Budget management	I have developed and managed multi-million-dollar operating and capital budgets for several organizations.	Amalgamated cost center budgets using the CONSOLIDATION function along with PIVOT TABLES tools
Debt financing	I have published an essay dealing with the use of debt financing in relation to residual and compensatory airport pricing models.	Various financial functions: NPV, IRR, PV, FV, RATE along with SOLVER

Table 3. Aligning Financial Modeling Dimensions with the Decision-making Context.

Modeling Dimensions	Decision-making Context		
Time frame	Future ⬇	Present ⬇	Past ⬇
Accounting Cycle	Planning ⬇	Control ⬇	Feedback ⬇
Financial Analytics	Predictive analytics ⬇	Descriptive analytics ⬇	Diagnostic analytics ⬇
Financial Models	Break-even Time-series forecasts Capital budgeting Regression analysis	Linear programming Business valuation Pivot tables	Financial dashboards Budget management Amortization tables

This book is designed for advanced Excel applications and therefore students require an intermediate level knowledge of the software, focused primarily on the functional aspects of using Excel. This will include coverage of the following topics.[1]

Working with Excel Tables, Pivot Tables, and Pivot Charts:

- Explore a structured range of data
- Freezing rows and columns
- Creating an Excel table
- Plan and create an Excel table
- Rename and format an Excel table
- Add, edit, and delete records in an Excel table
- Sort/Filter data
- Insert a Total row to summarize an Excel table
- Split a worksheet into two panes
- Insert subtotals into a range of data
- Use the Outline buttons to show and hide details
- Create and modify a Pivot Table
- Apply Pivot Tables styles and formatting
- Filter and sort a Pivot Table
- Insert a slicer to filter a Pivot Table
- Group Pivot Table items (Home Group/Group Field)
- Create a Pivot Chart

---

[1]The list of topics covered for an intermediate-level knowledge of Excel was supplied to me by my colleague, Richard Wong, who is a faculty member in the School of Business at Kwantlen Polytechnic University.

Managing Multiple Worksheets and Workbooks:

- Create a worksheet group
- Format and edit multiple worksheets at once
- Create cell references to other worksheets
- Consolidate information from multiple worksheets using 3-D references
- Create and print a worksheet group
- Create a link to data in another workbook
- Create and print a worksheet group
- Create a link to data in another workbook
- How to edit links
- Create and use an Excel workspace
- Insert a hyperlink in a cell

Developing an Excel Application:

- Create, edit, and delete defined names for cells and ranges
- Paste a list of defined names as documentation
- Use defined names in formulas
- Add defined names to existing formulas
- Create valid rules for data entry
- Protect the contents of worksheets and workbooks
- Add, edit, and delete comments
- Macros (create, save)

Working with Advanced Functions:

- Working with Logical functions (IF, AND, and OR)
- Working with comparison operators such as $<$, $<=$, $= <>$, $>$, or $>=$ to compare two values
- Inserting calculated columns in an Excel Table
- Using structured references in formulas (Fully qualified and Unqualified)
- Nest the IF function
- Using the VLOOKUP and HLOOKUP functions (to find approximate and exact match)
- Use the IFERROR function
- Use conditional formatting to highlight values
- COUNTIF, SUMIF, AVERAGEIF

Exploring Financial Tools and Functions:

- Work with financial functions such as FV, PV, RATE, NPER, and PMT
- Interpolate and extrapolate a series of values (Home Editing Fill Series)
- Determine a payback period
- Calculate a net present value (NPV) and an internal rate of return (IRR)

Performing What-If Analysis (Data, Data Tools, What-If Analysis):

- Perform what-if analysis with Goal Seek, Data Table, Scenario Manager, and Solver.
- Use Goal Seek to calculate a solution (Goal Seek)
- Create a one-variable data table (Data Table)
- Create a two-variable data table (Data Table)
- Create and apply different Excel scenarios (Scenario Manager)
- Generate a scenario summary report
- Generate a scenario PivotTable report
- Run Solver to calculate optimal solutions (Data Table)
- Create and apply constraints to a Solver model
- Save and load a Solver model

Connecting to External Data:

- Import data from a text file (Data, Get External Data, From Text)
- Working with connections and external data ranges (Data, Connections group)
- Define a trusted location

Collaborating on a Shared Workbook:

- Integrating Excel with Other Office Applications
- Understanding copying and pasting, linking, and embedding objects into Word document
- Linking Excel and Word Files
- Updating a linked object
- Embedding an object
- Modifying an Embedded Object

With these topics as a foundation, the text incorporates more advanced functionality into decision making for accounting and finance students and professionals.

Introduction

Chapter 1

Better Learning Decisions

So, what is this book about?

This book is about financial modeling. It deals with the types of business decisions made by accounting and finance students and professionals. The book's purpose is to teach advanced Excel techniques. All employers value these skills in their staff, and it is expected that the material covered will enhance students' employment prospects and the career advancement of professionals.

Works of this genre are typically part of a management science curriculum and consequently are focused on some topics that Accounting and Finance practitioners do not consider relevant in their day-to-day routine—such as Monte Carlo simulations, using real options and integer programming. Different from many books that explain how Excel is used for decision-making, this text focuses specifically on Accounting and Finance department applications. Each of the decision contexts explored is based on the personal experience of the author, whose employment history includes the following areas of financial management:

- Budget development and management
- Product and service costing and pricing
- Cash management
- Financial reporting
- External and internal auditing
- Evaluating information systems risk and controls
- Enterprise risk management
- Personal and corporate taxation
- Corporate finance
- Capital budgeting
- Financial systems development and implementation
- Developing financial policies and procedures

By using this book, students and professionals will develop an *expert*-level proficiency with Excel and apply these skills to problems in cost accounting, capital

1

budgeting and linear programming. Statistical techniques, such as single- and multivariable regression analysis and forecasting, will also be discussed. Students will learn to work with pivot tables applied to data mining and analysis situations. They will also develop pro forma financial statements and build a discounted cash flow model for purposes of valuing a company. In addition, Excel will be used to create a budget, perform variance analysis, and develop key performance indicators (KPIs), along with executive dashboards. Also addressed will be several common amortization tables used for decision-making.

How to Learn (and Teach) Financial Modeling
Learning Financial Modeling
A common lament heard from those taking Excel training courses is that they thought that they had learned some important techniques but, because they did not put them into practice, the knowledge acquired was soon forgotten. It is not surprising therefore that many people learning how to use the software repeat the same—or similar courses—year after year, which is both expensive and inefficient. This occurs because Excel courses usually focus on either (1) functionality or (2) application, but seldom both. Functional courses address the technical aspects of the software, such as how to create pivot tables. Application courses address the use of Excel for specific problems; for example, preparing a capital budgeting model. Uniquely, this text combines both of these aspects, integrating functionality and application; it explains Excel functions as well as their application to common business problems.

The book is purposefully structured to address common weaknesses in how MS-Excel is taught—to this end it emphasizes being useful to those operating a business. When I worked as a financial systems analyst, one of the most important things I learned was that software should never drive an organization's operations; business operations are primary and must always dictate computerized functionality. This means that the starting point for learning how to use Excel should not be the application itself, but rather the decisions made within the business—such as whether to invest in capital assets. It is for this reason that the text *first* addresses common business decisions, then explains the underlying management theory used in making these decisions and finally proceeds to show how Excel can be employed to decide on a course of action. By taking this approach it turns the traditional "how to teach Excel" approach on its head and hopefully puts end users (and not techies) in charge of the learning process.[1]

For each decision-making context (future, present, and past), a topic is explored in terms of its primary subject area and the types of decisions made. Real-life business situations are described, which are then explored in terms of the underlying theory and financial management techniques used. To facilitate decision-making, the requisite Excel functionality is demonstrated through a detailed exercise.

The chapters follow a consistent format, with examples of real-life Excel applications and include these parts:

---

[1]The obsession with the technical aspects of the software is evidenced by the many Excel course instructors who have advanced degrees in applied mathematics, operations management, and computer science who are fascinated by the arcane minutiae of the application, but seldom clearly explain its practical usage (think: "ivory tower" mentality).

- *Snapshot*: A chapter overview for each decision context, outlining the (1) topic, (2) subject area, (3) decisions made, (4) author's experience, and (5) relevant Excel functionality for building the financial model.
- *Background theory*: As this book addresses both Excel functionality and its application to decision-making, an overview of the relevant accounting and finance theory will be provided—for example, a discussion of discounted cash flows and using the weighted average cost of capital (WACC) when making capital budgeting decisions.
- *Financial management techniques*: The section will address the formulas used in decision–making—for example, the calculation of the break-even point in unit sales is: Fixed costs ÷ unit contribution margin.
- *Using Excel functionality*: The key Excel functions, including formulas, for each decision-making context are discussed.
- *Demonstration Exercise*: A detailed, guided exercise on using Excel to develop a financial model for decision-making is shown.
- *Afterthought*: The author provides some—hopefully, thought-provoking—commentary on the chapter topic as food for thought.

Teaching Financial Modeling

Teaching computer applications is very different from the instruction that takes place during a standard lecture session. It is challenging because a happy medium needs to be achieved between speaking and hands-on practice. As a heuristic, I use a 50/50 ratio—i.e., I spend about half of the class time explaining and demonstrating the application of Excel to decision-making and the other half having students practice their skills. Rather than using a follow-along (i.e., Simon says) approach—where students mimic the keystrokes shown on a screen at the front of the classroom— I provide a context for the decision being made (e.g., determining the valuation for a company), demonstrate how Excel can be used to make the decision and then have them work through a demonstration exercise (using a preformatted Excel "shell" file) at their own pace. As students progress through the exercise, I walk around and troubleshoot, giving assistance when it is needed. I also provide a thorough debriefing on the financial model and post it to a course website for students to review. This process allows both slower as well as more advanced students to have a sense of achievement in working toward a solution, without the frustration of having to catch up to the instructor. My experience as both a teacher and a student has convinced me that this is the most effective way to teach (and learn) these skills.[2]

This book is based on Excel 2016 (although it also applies to Excel versions 2010 to 2013 or Excel 365, which is available free of charge to academic users). Each chapter builds on content developed in prior chapters. The starting point for a section is the decision context, whereby upfront planning (covered in Chapters 2–5) leads to management control (covered in Chapters 6–8) which leads to feedback being received (covered in Chapters 9–11). This is articulated through the management theory relating to the decision (for example, a discussion of the calculation and significance of break-even points when deciding whether to start a new business).

---

[2]I estimate that I have completed several hundred hours in Excel training and in the process been subjected to a number of pedagogies. Based on this experience, I have taken what I believe to be the most effective teaching strategies and incorporated them into my courses, as well as this book.

Only after the groundwork for the business decision has been laid is Excel functionality introduced through a detailed demonstration exercise, providing step-by-step instructions for its completion.

Steps in Developing a Financial Model

The process for creating a financial model includes these considerations[3]:

(1) *Define the problem:* This can be "trickier" than you think and involves careful consideration of the underlying dynamics of the phenomenon being investigated. Here, it is important to take the time necessary to clearly understand the real (as opposed to surface) issues that need to be addressed. (For example, should we invest in an infrastructure development project in Central America and on what basis do we determine our risk-adjusted discount rate for this capital budgeting decision?)

(2) *Gather the data:* This includes identifying the source of the data (internal or external) and whether they exist or need to be collected. (For example, determining net cash flows by identifying the sources of cash inflows and outflows over the project time horizon.)

(3) *Develop the model:* This involves selecting the type of financial model required, which will be determined by the nature of the Excel application being created. (For example, a capital budgeting model is used to make decisions about large investments in the future, whereas a budget variance analysis addresses financial planning decisions made in the past.)

(4) *Optimize the model:* This means making the model efficient by reducing the number of processing steps or using better processes. Excel has several ways of performing the same task (known as, functional redundancy) and some methods will be better than others, depending on the application. (For example, when processing large quantities of data, it is sometimes better to obtain this information from another source, such as an Access database, and then import only those portions of the data—field and/or records—required for specific purposes.)

(5) *Test the model:* The importance of quality assurance (QA) testing cannot be overstated. This involves performing calculations manually and then comparing the results with those generated by the application. (For example, comparing the internal rate of return (IRR) calculated by a capital budgeting model with the company's hurdle rate for investments to determine its reasonableness.)

(6) *Communicate the model:* This is your opportunity to shine by helping the company reduce uncertainty associated with important business decisions. (For example, convincing a room full of nervous investors that your multibillion-dollar infrastructure project in a foreign country is justified based on its net value present (NPV) and IRR.)

The financial models discussed in this text are listed in the table below (**Table 1.1**).

---

[3]This schema is partially based on that provided in Winston, W. L., & Albright, S. C. (2009). *Practical management science* (pp. 8–9). Mason, OH: Cengage Learning. More importantly, it reflects the author's real-life experience in developing financial models used to make decisions in the workplace.

Table 1.1. Summary of Financial Models.

Chapter	Financial Model	Key Excel Functionality
2	Break-even	Goal Seek; Data tables
3	Time-series Forecasting	Analysis Tool pack
4	Capital budgeting	NPV, IRR formulas
5	Regression Analysis	Analysis Tool pack
6	Linear Programming	Solver
7	Business Valuation	NPV, IRR formulas
8	Financial Analytics	Pivot Tables
9	KPIs & Dashboards	Charts, Slicers, Timelines
10	Budget management	Pivot tables, Consolidate
11	Financial Amortizations	PV, PMT formulas

The financial models will be illustrated using demonstration exercises that address important business decisions (which are shown below) (**Table 1.2**).

Some Common Excel Terminology

The table below describes the terminology used in this book to refer to various parts of the Excel application, starting with an overview and then proceeding from the top of the spreadsheet screen to the bottom (**Table 1.3**).

Note that when Excel functionality is discussed, it will be shown in capitalized text—for example, to create a data table, left click on the following: DATA, WHAT-IF ANALYSIS, DATA TABLE. To make the description of navigation within Excel consistent, the starting point in this text's explanations will always be the main menu screen.

Good Financial Modeling Practices[4]

Most companies that develop financial models have standardized procedures for doing so. This is to ensure that those who review or use the models can understand how they work—perhaps, more importantly—so that those who must update the models can understand them too. This book recommends these practices, for the reasons noted below (**Table 1.4**).

Demonstration Exercise

The following workbook application shows the evolution of a financial model, as it progresses from a somewhat idiosyncratic decision-making tool—probably only useful to its creator—to something more robust and comprehensible. A blank Excel "shell" file is available for students to build their own version of this model (file name:

---

[4]This list of modeling practices is similar to that provided in Winston, W. L., & Albright, S. C. (2009). *Practical management science* (pp. 24–25). Mason, OH: Cengage Learning; however, **Table 1.4** is more succinct and is based on the author's personal experience in creating and maintaining financial models.

Table 1.2. Summary of Demonstration Exercises.

Chapter	Company Name	Business Type	Decision(s) to Be Made
1	Alpha Corp.	Junior Achievement company, which is an NPO for high school entrepreneurs	Profitability of a business
2	Park & Wash	Car washing and detailing service	Viability of a new corporate opportunity
3	BWNR	Health supplement retailer	Estimating long-term sales volumes of a new product
4	WTF Builders	Construction company	Expected return on a major infrastructure project
5	Patrick Enterprises	Mechanical engineering firm	Determining product cost for purposes of pricing
6	Screw-it	Screw driver manufacturer	Controlling product mix
	Shoot-it	Hockey stick manufacturer	Controlling product scheduling
7	HAAK	Marijuana cultivation and retail sales	Share price for an Initial Public Offering
8	Food-*stuff*	Meal kit maker and retailer	Understanding customers and product choice
9	GIT-me Entertainment	On-site services for movie productions	KPIs and metrics for implementing company strategy
10	Chill-Dude	Snowboard manufacturer	Budget development and management
11	Geezer Ltd.	Mining Industry	Bond amortization Loan amortization Asset amortization
12	Omega Corp.	High-tech pencil holders	Everything, from soup (starting a business) to nuts (tracking performance)

Alpha Corp(shell).xls) by following the steps outlined below. (The case is based on the author's youthful experience as a budding high school entrepreneur and future accountant.)

Case Facts[5]

Bob (not his real name) is a high school student who has joined an organization known as Junior Achievement (JA), which is a nonprofit group whose purpose is to encourage young people to become entrepreneurs. Members are guided by a

---

[5]This exercise is based on one shown in Winston, W. L., & Albright, S. C. (2009). *Practical management science* (pp. 25–28). Mason, OH: Cengage Learning.

Table 1.3. Excel Terms.

Term	Meaning
Main menu	This is the Excel functionality that appears when the application is opened on your computer. It is the part at the very top of the screen and shows, from left to right: FILE, HOME, INSERT, etc.
Ribbon	The ribbon appears below the main menu when the application is activated and shows formatting functions, from left to right: CLIPBOARD, FONT, ALIGNMENT, etc.
Drop down box	This appears within a ribbon when Excel provides several functional options for a feature, such as what if analysis, which includes SCENARIOS, GOAL SEEK and DATA TABLES.
Check box	A check box allows you select and deselect certain features within an application—for example, which Excel add-ins to include in your main menu (like Solver).
Dialog box	A dialog box (sometimes referred to as a wizard") is a gray icon that appears on the spreadsheet screen and is used to input parameters when using Excel functionality—for example, the Solver application.
Formula bar	The formula box appears below the main menu ribbon and shows the formulas in the cells within a worksheet. (Formulas can also be seen by pressing the F2 function key or by double left clicking on the mouse.)
Name box	This appears to the left of the formula bar, below the main menu ribbon and can be used for creating named ranges (which is discussed below, as part of good modeling practice).
Column/row headings	Columns are shown as letters of the alphabet across the top of the worksheet, while rows are numbered along the side. An Excel worksheet can have more than 1 million rows in a single worksheet.
Worksheet	Sometimes called a tab." It is part of a workbook and appears at the bottom of the spreadsheet.
Workbook	A workbook is comprised of one or more worksheets.
Left-click/right-click	This refers to using the mouse to activate Excel functionality. Sometimes it is easier to use the mouse than working through the main menu. Note that there are typically several ways to perform functions in Excel (referred to as functional redundancy).
Linking files	This can mean either using cell references in other worksheets or workbooks as part of your calculations or creating a hyperlink to external workbooks or other data sources.
File option settings	This allows users to add or remove functionality from Excel, such as Solver (for liner programming), Analysis tool pack (for regression analysis and time series forecasting), and Developer (for creating custom applications).

Table 1.4. Good Modeling Practices.

Recommended Practice	For this Reason ...
Color coding cells that identify specific parts of the financial model: Light gray background cells are for *input* data; these values are hard-coded directly into a cell or by using the formula bar Medium gray background cells are for *decision* variables. Dark gray background cells are for *objective* functions, which are the values we are trying to determine.	Standardized color coding allows users to more easily understand how the application works and the types of data presented in the financial models.
Comment indicators (ensure that these are turned on" by using: FILE, OPTIONS, ADVANCED, DISPLAY, then select the checkbox for INDICATORS ONLY).	Providing comments in a cell within an Excel worksheet allows users to understand important information about the data, such as its source or the units being used.
Named ranges: Creating named ranges and listing named ranges.	Creating named ranges makes it much easier to understand the logic of the financial model, particularly when they are included in formulas.
Keep a separate worksheet for Data" in every workbook. (By convention I always use the left-most worksheet as my data tab.)	To ensure that data is not accidently overwritten, it should be kept separate from other functions in the financial model.
Do not cross-link workbooks.	Linkages within workbooks are extremely useful and often necessary for financial modeling. However, linking across workbooks can cause significant problems when links become corrupted, when files are moved across directories.

mentor from within the business community. A JA operations manual has several prepackaged business plans that can be used, or students can develop their own. To this end, Bob's firm (known as Alpha Corp.) has decided to manufacture pencil holders, which it intends to sell for a profit (probably, mostly to family members). The business will be in operation for one school term (September to December) and any merchandise remaining on December 25 will be sold at a fire sale price. There are 10 other students in the company, and Bob has been elected as the corporate controller because he likes using Excel.

The relevant financial information is as follows:

- Regular selling priece per pencil holder = $15 (from September to December 25)
- Fire sale price of pencil holders = $6 (after December 25)
- Fixed cost of production = $200 (covers a 4-month lease on equipment, including table saws and tube cutters)
- Variable costs per pencil holder = $8 (materials include aluminum tubes and wood for the base; utility costs for the production facility are borne by the non-profit organization JA)
- Expected sales = 200 (assuming every team member's extended family—estimated at 20 people each—purchases one pencil holder)
- Planned production = 150

Bob's dilemma is that he wants to maximize profits but at the same time avoid selling pencil holders at a fire sale price (representing a loss of $2 per item). Bob has developed an Excel financial model that has progressed through four iterations (models 1–4), based on advice and feedback received from his company's business mentor. These models, along with the mentor's comments, are shown on the following pages.

The mentor comments that while Bob's model works (**Fig. 1.1**), it is difficult to understand his calculation of profitability because it uses formulas that reference cell locations, making its logic challenging to comprehend. The advisor recommends incorporating more detailed information into the model to show the fixed and variable costs separately. This is shown in model 2 (**Fig. 1.2**).

The mentor comments that model 2 is an improvement over the first attempt, but it is still difficult to interpret the logic of the calculations used to determine the company's profit. The mentor suggests creating named ranges to refer to cell locations. Named Ranges can be created in three different ways:

(1) They can be created by positioning the cursor in the cell (or group of cells) that you want to name and then left-clicking: FORMULAS, DEFINE NAME. The dialog box shown in **Fig. 1.3** appears and allows you to provide a name for the range; then click OK. (If more than one word is used as a descriptor for a named range, the words can either be concatenated, or joined by an underscore; note that no other textual connectors are allowed when creating a multiword named range.)

(2) Named ranges can be created for a group of contiguous cells that are already named in the worksheet, by giving them the same names. This is done by selecting the group of cells along with their descriptions (as shown in **Fig. 1.4**). Left click on: FORMULAS, CREATE FROM SELECTION. In this case, check the box for "LEFT COLUMN" and then click OK. The names appearing on the electronic worksheet have now been assigned as the named range for the variables in cells B3 to B6.

(3) Finally, named ranges can be created by selecting a cell, a group of contiguous cells, or even noncontiguous cells and positioning the cursor in the "name box" (located in the top left corner, below the main menu ribbon) and typing the name for the cell reference or range; then press ENTER. This is shown in **Fig. 1.5**. (The name box descriptor for the named range "Fixed_cost" is highlighted.)

Bob has listed the named ranges he has created in a blank area of the worksheet (beginning in cell D2) by using: FORMULAS, USE IN FORMULAS, PASTE NAMES. This lists all the named ranges created as well as their location on a worksheet and their cell position within a worksheet. These enhancements are shown in model 3 (**Fig. 1.6**).

By using named ranges, the logic of the calculations is much easier to understand, which is the intent of this modeling exercise.

Model 3 is a vast improvement over the first attempt, but the mentor observes that it can be further enhanced by adding color coding to designate the input, decision and objective cells. Comment indicators can also give additional information about the units used, or the source of the information. This is shown in **Fig. 1.7**.

Fig. 1.1. Model 1, The First Attempt.

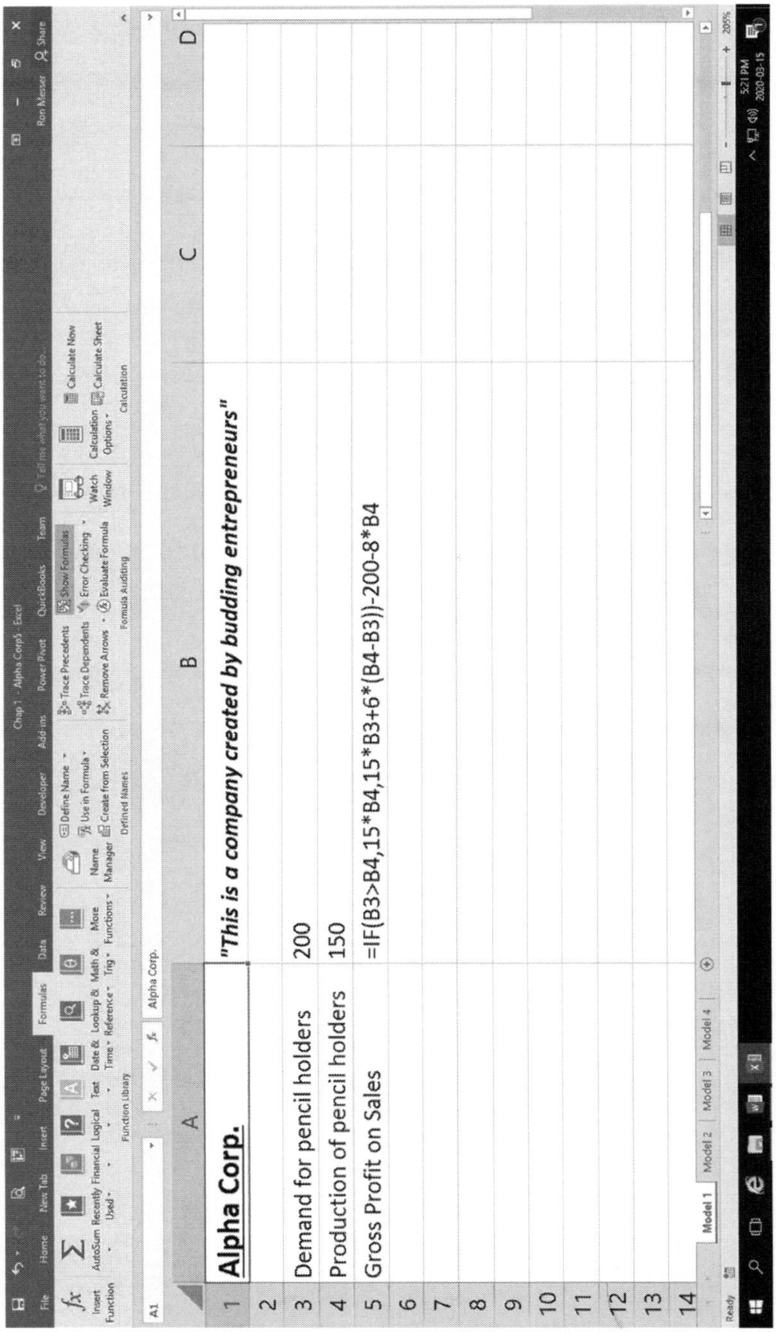

	A	B
1	**Alpha Corp.**	*"This is a company created by budding entrepreneurs"*
2		
3	Demand for pencil holders	200
4	Production of pencil holders	150
5	Gross Profit on Sales	=IF(B3>B4,15*B4,15*B3+6*(B4-B3))-200-8*B4

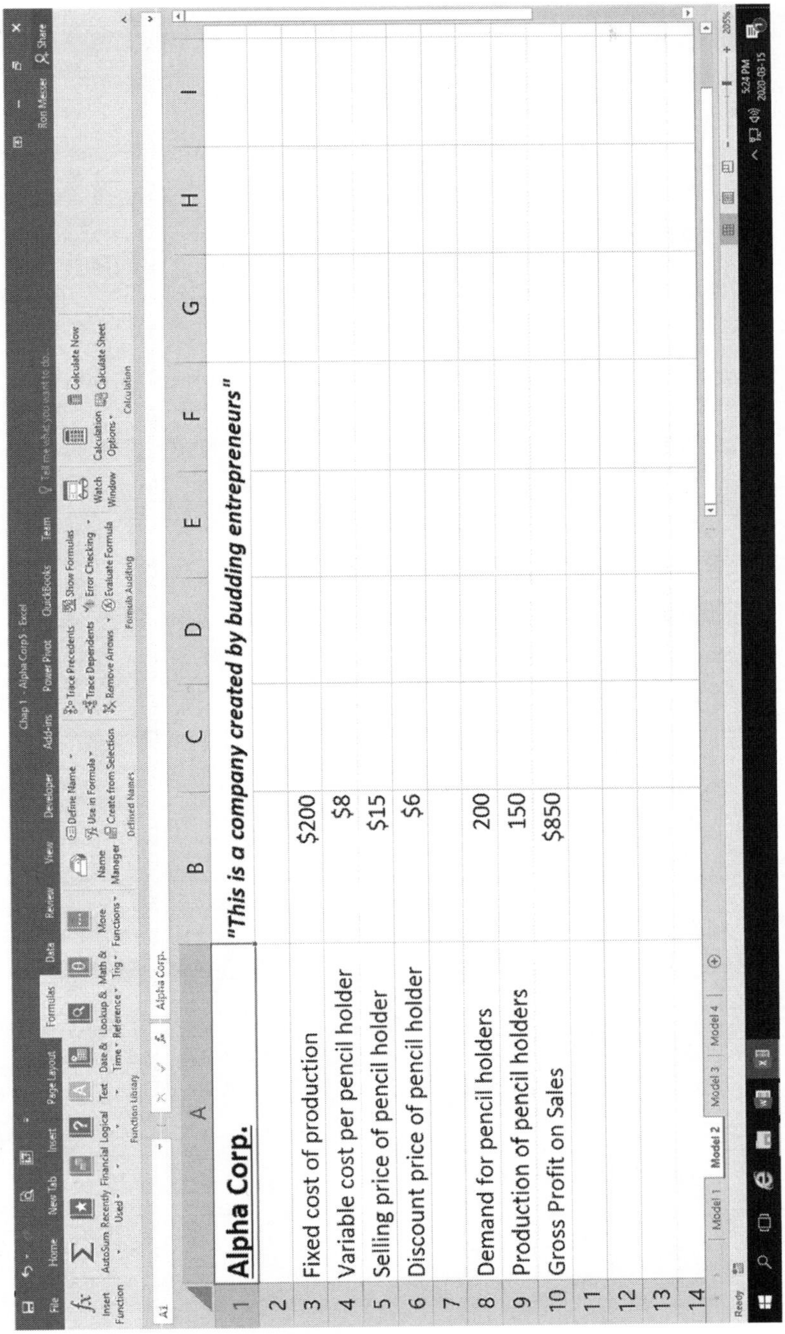
Alpha Corp.
"This is a company created by budding entrepreneurs"
Fixed cost of production
$200
Variable cost per pencil holder
$8
Selling price of pencil holder
$15
Discount price of pencil holder
$6
Demand for pencil holders
200
Production of pencil holders
150
Gross Profit on Sales
$850
Model 1
Model 2
Model 3
Model 4

Fig. 1.2. Model 2, More Detailed Information.

Fig. 1.3. Model 2, Creating Named Ranges (Option 1).

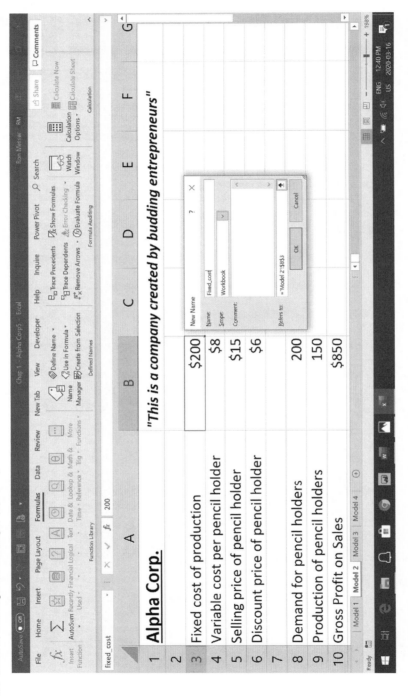

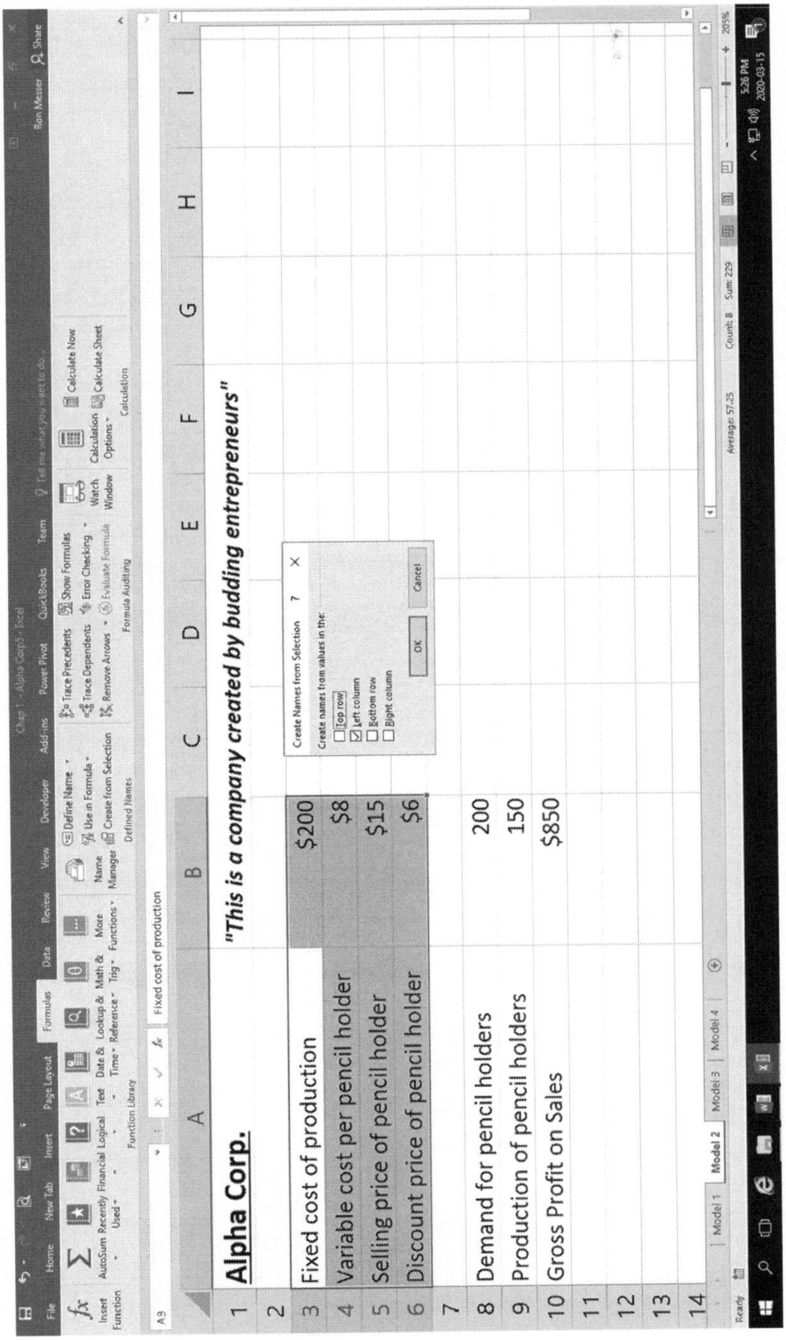

Fig. 1.4. Model 2, Creating Named Ranges (Option 2).

	A	B
1	**Alpha Corp.**	*"This is a company created by budding entrepreneurs"*
2		
3	Fixed cost of production	$200
4	Variable cost per pencil holder	$8
5	Selling price of pencil holder	$15
6	Discount price of pencil holder	$6
7		
8	Demand for pencil holders	200
9	Production of pencil holders	150
10	Gross Profit on Sales	$850
11		
12		
13		
14		

Fig. 1.5. Model 2, Creating Named Ranges (Option 3).

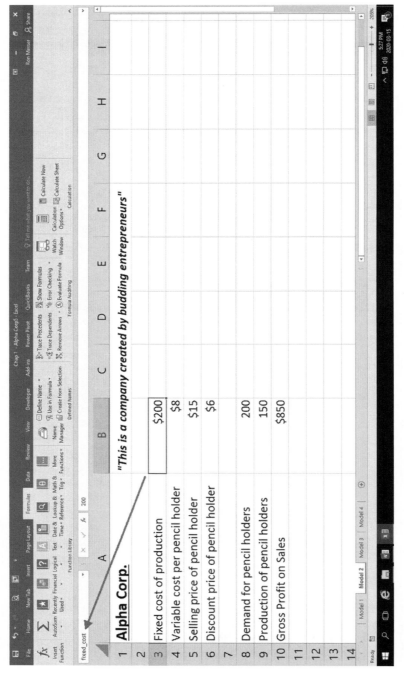

Fig. 1.6. Model 3, Using Named Ranges.

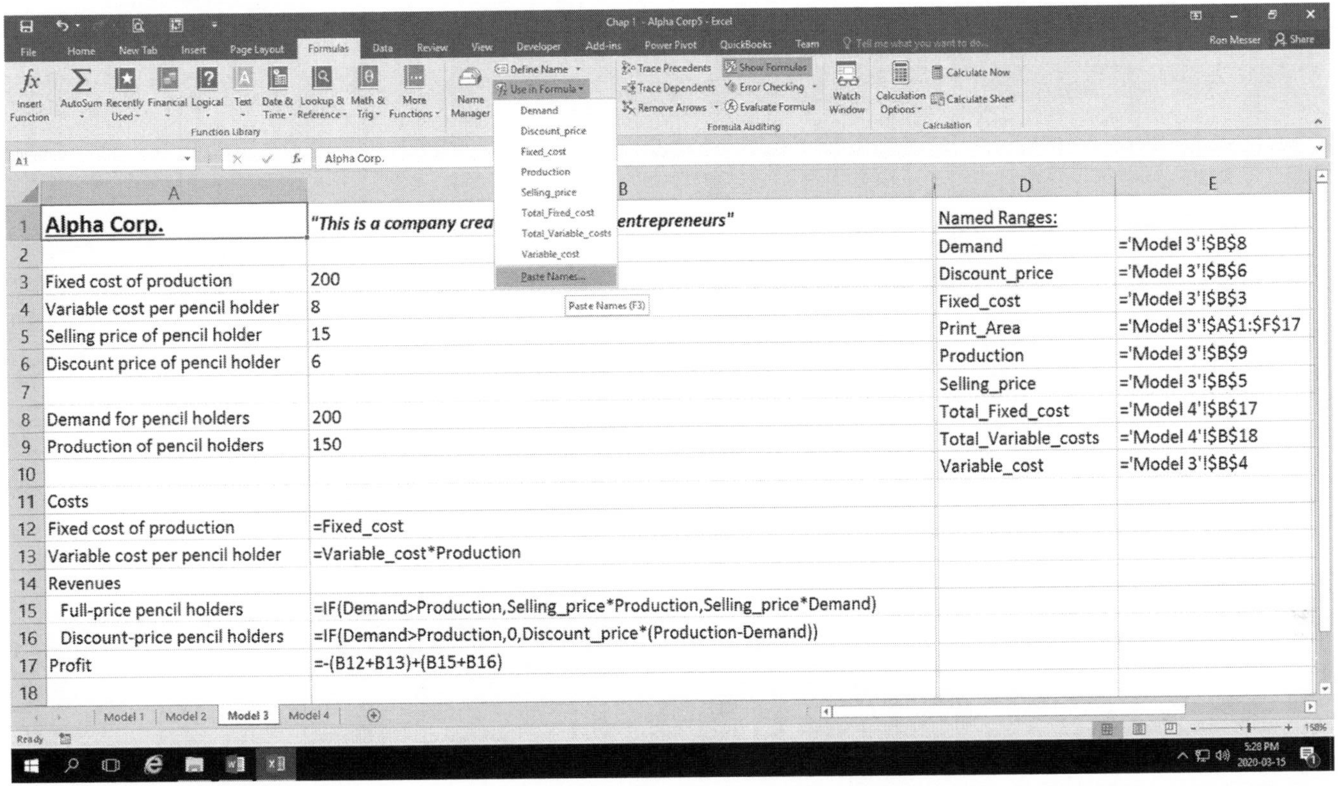

	A	B		D	E
1	**Alpha Corp.**	*"This is a company crea... entrepreneurs"*		Named Ranges:	
2				Demand	='Model 3'!$B$8
3	Fixed cost of production	200		Discount_price	='Model 3'!$B$6
4	Variable cost per pencil holder	8		Fixed_cost	='Model 3'!$B$3
5	Selling price of pencil holder	15		Print_Area	='Model 3'!$A$1:$F$17
6	Discount price of pencil holder	6		Production	='Model 3'!$B$9
7				Selling_price	='Model 3'!$B$5
8	Demand for pencil holders	200		Total_Fixed_cost	='Model 4'!$B$17
9	Production of pencil holders	150		Total_Variable_costs	='Model 4'!$B$18
10				Variable_cost	='Model 3'!$B$4
11	Costs				
12	Fixed cost of production	=Fixed_cost			
13	Variable cost per pencil holder	=Variable_cost*Production			
14	Revenues				
15	Full-price pencil holders	=IF(Demand>Production,Selling_price*Production,Selling_price*Demand)			
16	Discount-price pencil holders	=IF(Demand>Production,0,Discount_price*(Production-Demand))			
17	Profit	=-(B12+B13)+(B15+B16)			
18					

Fig. 1.7. Model 4, Color Coding and Comments.

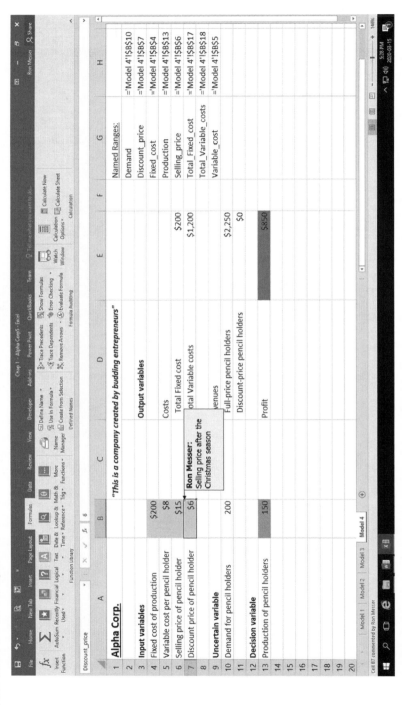

Model 4 clearly shows the cells for input (light gray), decisions (medium gray), and objectives (dark gray). Comment indicators provide information about the discount price. A listing of the named ranges created is also shown.

Now Bob can make more confident decisions about how many pencil holders to produce and guide his JA enterprise to profitability. (In reality, the author's first business venture narrowly broke even, as many of the employees' relatives balked at the $15 price tag.)

Afterthought → *giving thanks for model citizens*

Models are only approximations of real life. They are intended to guide decision-making. In business this means finding the best way to generate profits by operating both efficiently and effectively. Fundamental to this process is an appreciation of a complex matrix of social relationships, whereby each of us seeks our own best interests by—somewhat paradoxically—providing benefits to others. This is, of course, the "invisible hand" that Adam Smith's economic model espoused and that underlies all market activity ... and for this we should give thanks!

Thanking Juan and John

(Take good care of each other)

This morning as I drove to work at YVR drinking my coffee; I finally broke down and did it...I thanked Juan and John. I was grateful to Juan for the wonderful cup of coffee he gave me. John helped with my car. Now, let's be clear about this. I've never actually met Juan or John, but I know that Juan works on a coffee plantation in Guatemala and John at a car assembly plant in Oshawa. I read about them on their company websites on the Internet. Juan harvests the beans for my morning cup of Starbucks. John put the wheels on my Toyota. But Juan and John owe me some gratitude, too. I helped their families fly to Vancouver. Together, we've enriched each other's lives without ever having met.

Anthropologists have observed that there are two things that distinguish humans from other species, these being our division of labor and our penchant for altruism. If we did not divide up the millions of tasks required by modern living, we would not enjoy such an enviable lifestyle. Imagine having to plow the earth, plant the beans, and then wait for a coffee crop to ripen before having that first cup of Joe in the morning—unthinkable! But if we assign numerous, minutely detailed tasks to many individuals who voluntarily agree to share what they produce, we all benefit infinitely more than if we each decided to "go it alone".

Over time, this division of labor has become more finely tuned. For example, think about the Oshawa auto assembly plant where John has spent his entire life tightening wheel lug nuts on Toyota Corollas. If the time needed to perform this task for each car is 10 minutes and assuming an 8-hour working day, by the time he retires John will have tightened the nuts on almost half a million vehicles. As his reward for doing this, he can enjoy a cup of coffee, thanks to Juan, and fly to beautiful Vancouver—partly, thanks to me.

Most of us take for granted the elaborate interconnections in our society. The wired world shows us that it really is a "small world," which is how I found out about Juan and John. So, as I drive to work, I raise my coffee cup to them and say thanks...and ask that they remember me, too, the next time they visit Vancouver.

Part 1
Decisions Made about the Future

PLANNING

Chapter 2

Break Even Decisions

Should I start a new business?

Snapshot

Topic
Cost-Volume-Profit (CVP) Analysis

Subject Area
Management Accounting: cost behavior (distinguishing between fixed and variable costs)

Decisions Made
CVP analysis can be used to determine important business metrics concerning the viability of new ventures, such as:

- Break-even points
- Product mix decisions
- Production allocation decisions

Personal Experience
At a diversified business where I worked as a financial analyst, we were assessing a new opportunity related to our current vehicle parking operations. The head of the division was considering whether to introduce additional value-added services for customers, such as car washing and detailing. This would involve an up-front investment in buildings, equipment and salaried staff. My role was to determine the volume of sales needed to break-even—i.e., to cover the initial fixed costs (in other words, to address the risk associated with this venture). Excel was especially useful in making this decision, not only for creating the financial model, but more importantly for assessing the sensitivities of the decision to changes in the key underlying variables. This was done by using the goal-seek function to calculate the break-even point and data tables to assess the sensitivities.

Excel Funtionality
Goal Seek
Data tables
VLOOKUP

Background Theory
Cost-Volume-Profit Analysis

Cost-volume-profit analysis uses cost behaviors as the basis for making some important decisions about starting and operating a business. These include break-even points, which are the sales volumes in units or dollars that must be achieved before the "downside" risk is covered. The risk of beginning a new venture usually involves significant investments in capital assets—as an example, consider the cost of building an auto assembly line. These costs are considered "fixed" inasmuch as they have the following characteristics:

- They must be incurred prior to earning sales revenues
- They are typically quite substantial and require significant funding
- There is uncertainty about recovering the cost of the investment
- Total fixed costs remain the same, regardless of production quantity
- Unit fixed costs decline, as production quantities increase

Determining Cost Functions

An idealized fixed cost function can be represented as a horizontal line on an x–y graph, showing that the relationships between costs (y-axis) and quantity (x-axis) is the same in total, regardless of the level of activity. But note that the unit fixed costs changes as the quantity changes (i.e., FC ÷ units). Conversely, a purely variable cost function can be seen as a diagonal line originating at the x–y intercept. This means that as the quantity measure increases, so too does the total variable cost; however, the unit variable cost (measured as the slope of the line) remains unchanged. The figure below illustrates these idealized cost functions (**Fig. 2.1**).

Break-even Volumes

Break-even volumes occur when the downside risk of a venture (represented by an investment in fixed costs associated with productive assets) has been covered. At this point profits (more correctly referred to as contribution margin) can be earned. Much like the notion of project break-even (see Chapter 4 on capital budgeting), CVP break-even provides a guide for assessing the viability of a business opportunity.

Financial Management Techniques

The break-even *equation* is:

$$\text{Revenues} - \text{TVC} - \text{FC} = \text{OI}$$

where:

- Revenues = unit selling price × quantity sold
- TVC = total variable costs = unit variable cost × quantity sold
- FC = fixed costs
- OI = operating (pre-tax) income
- Revenues − TVC = TCM, or total contribution margin

From the *equation*, we can algebraically derive the following formulae:

$$\text{BE in units} = \text{FC} \div \text{UCM}$$

Fig. 2.1. Fixed and Variable Cost Functions.

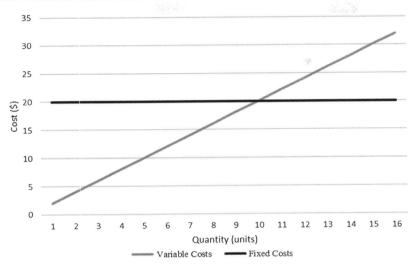

and

$$BE \text{ in sales} = FC \div CM\%$$

where:

- UCM = unit contribution margin, which is the difference between the unit selling price (USP) and the unit variable cost (UVC): UCM = USP − UVC
- CM% = contribution margin percentage, which is the relationship between the unit contribution margin (UCM) and the unit sales price (USP): CM% = UCM ÷ USP

The break-even point informs decision-makers about the volume of sales in units or dollars that will cover their initial investment (or risk). This number becomes the starting point for a discussion about the viability of achieving the calculated volume. Decision-makers may also want to know about the break-even points that, in addition to addressing their upfront risk, incorporate some notion of the opportunity cost of the investment—i.e., what else could be done with the invested capital if it were not used for this project. This additional cost recovery typically includes—at a minimum—the riskless rate of return (such as the rate of return associated with a long-term government bond). The revised break-even point is calculated by including this amount (referred to as the target operating income, or TOI) in the numerator, in addition to the fixed costs:

$$BE \text{ in units} = (FC + TOI) \div UCM.$$

Relevant MS-Excel Functionality

CVP models are driven by both formulas and functions. The formulas require knowledge of the underlying theory of management accounting, as well as some simple mathematical operators that are included in the formulas that are input through the Excel formula bar. The key functions for this type of decision-making model are GOAL SEEK and DATA TABLES.

Demonstration Exercise

New business opportunities emerge all the time and entrepreneurs are quick to spot them. But how can they effectively "run the numbers" to get a sense of the viability of the venture? Cost accounting provides us with the conceptual framework for making this type of decision through break-even analysis, which addresses the fundamental concern about downside risk; this involves the initial investment in productive assets used to run the business, otherwise known as fixed costs (Excel file: Park & Wash (shell).xls).

Case Facts

"Park & Wash" is a subsidiary of a company that manages vehicle parking facilities (both surface and parkade locations) and is considering offering car wash and detailing services to its customers. The owner of the parking business thinks that because cars will be stationed for a period of time anyway, it would make sense for their owners to save time and have the vehicles cleaned while they are doing other things. The initial cost of this venture would include installing an automated car washing machine, purchasing cleaning equipment and hiring an operations manager (i.e., expenditures on fixed costs). Costs that will vary by car wash include cleaning supplies (rags, dusters, wipes, solvents), city water usage, and hourly wages for workers, who will prepare and dry the vehicles before and after they use the car washing equipment. Three service packages are being considered.

The decision-making context of this exercise is to determine the following:

- The break-even volume based on the number of car washes and sales dollars
- The sensitives of the break-even volumes to changes in one of the decision variables
- The sensitives of the break-even volumes to changes in two of the decision variables

The data below consider operating the business at one of the company's current parking locations, which accommodates about 200 vehicles daily. The input variables use base case assumptions and include information about assumed costs, prices, and sales mix.

The expected fixed costs every year are as follows:

- Car washing machine: $10,000; 5-year life, no salvage value; $2,000 straight-line depreciation
- Car wash cleaning equipment: $2,000 for replacement parts for hoses, sprayers, and brushes
- Operations manager salary: $30,000, including all employee benefits
- TOTAL ANNUAL FIXED COST = $34,000

The variable costs, per car wash, include the following:

- Cleaning supplies: $1.00 for cleaning solvents, disposable rags, etc.
- Municipal water use: $1.00, based on the annual water bill divided by 6,000 cars washed

- Hourly wage rate: $10.00 per hour, or $2.50 per wash, where for 1 worker requires 15 minutes to complete a car wash
  (Note that the labor cost per wash for the Economy package is $2.50; this cost increases based on the time required to provide additional detailing services, such as those for the basic and deluxe offerings.)
- UNIT VARIABLE COSTS: Economy = $4.50; Basic = $9.00; Deluxe = $13.50

The sales price per car wash will depend on the level of service desired. Park & Wash is thinking about offering three "packages" for customers:

- Economy wash at $15.00 per car
- Basic wash at $25.00 per car
- Deluxe wash at $40.00 per car

It is expected that 50% of all sales will be for the economy package; 40% for the basic package and 10% for the deluxe treatment. The decision variable in the financial model will be the number of annual car washes, which is shown below (**Fig. 2.2**).

The formulas used to calculate profit are shown in the next figure (**Fig. 2.3**). Hard-coded data appears in the light gray–shaded cells in the worksheet. (Note how using named ranges in the formulas allows users to quickly understand the logic of the calculation.)

Using these base case assumptions, we can expect to make a profit of $51,800 per year operating the new business (see **Fig. 2.4**). But what is the break-even point based on the number of car washes? To find this quantity, we can use the Excel Goal Seek function. At break-even, the total revenues will cover the total costs; in other words, profits will be zero. To activate the Excel functionality, select the following menu items: DATA, WHAT-IF ANALYSIS, GOAL SEEK. A dialog box appears, as shown in **Fig. 2.4**. To find the break-even point in annual car washes, we need to set the profit cell (E16) to a value of zero, by changing the decision variable, which is the annual car washes (cell B16); then click OK.

The break-even point is shown below. We will need to sell 2,378 car washes (or generate $51,119 in sales dollars) per year to break-even, which means covering all of our costs. In other words, our downside risk—which is the fixed cost of the investment—will be covered at this level of sales (**Fig. 2.5**).

The break-even point uses the base case assumptions, which appear in the light gray input cells. To test the sensitivity of the base case model to changes in these variables, we can use the DATA TABLE functionality in Excel. In this model, an important assumption concerns the sales mix between the three service packages offered. Therefore, it would be insightful to examine the impact on profits if the sales mix changes.

To create a one-way data table, we do the following. Using the formula bar, input in cell B19 the formula: =E16 (this is the cell range named "profit"). In the column immediately to the left, hardcode values that are both greater than and less than the base case assumption for the basic wash package, which is 40%. (Note that when testing sensitivities, it is important to test *both* sides of the base case parameter). This is shown in **Fig. 2.6**.

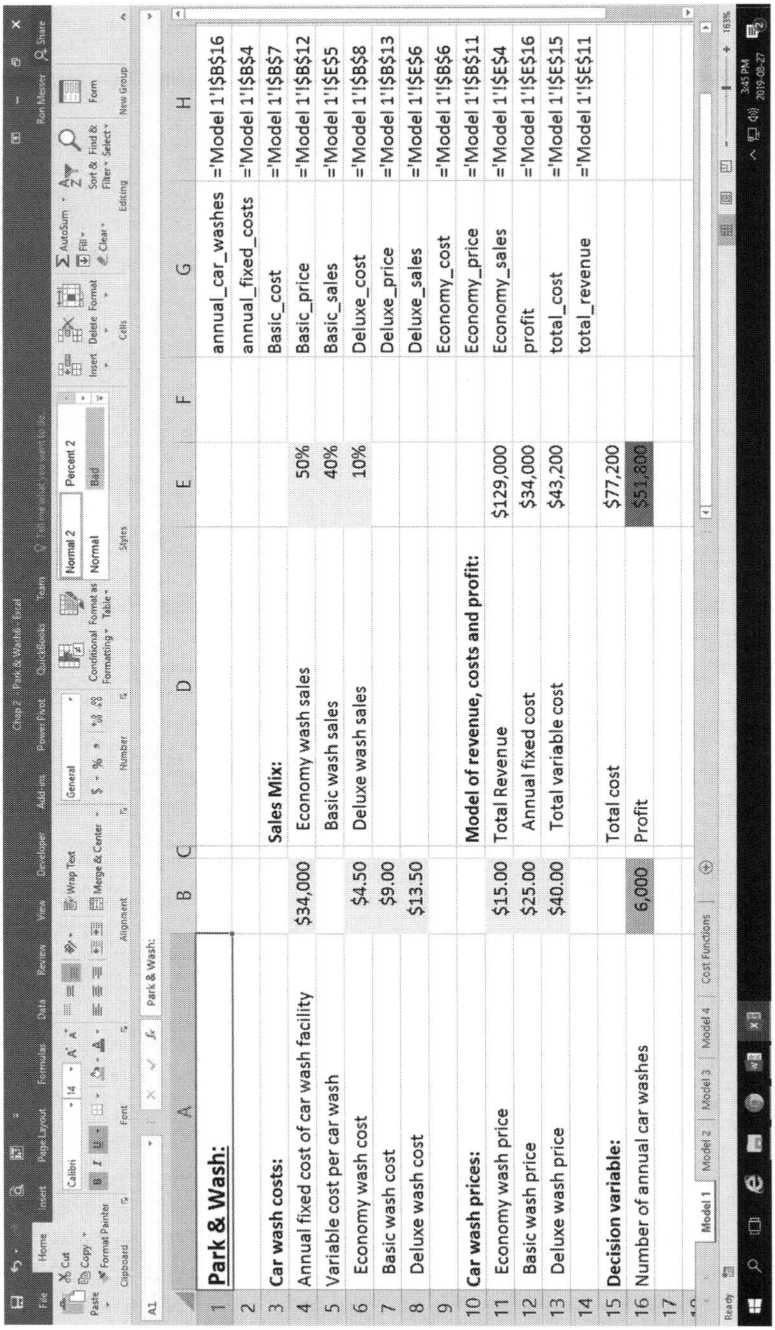

Fig. 2.2. Park & Wash Break-even Model.

	A	B	C	D	E		G	H
1	**Park & Wash:**						annual_car_washes	='Model 1'!$B$16
2							annual_fixed_costs	='Model 1'!$B$4
3	Car wash costs:		Sales Mix:				Basic_cost	='Model 1'!$B$7
4	Annual fixed cost of car wash facility	$34,000		Economy wash sales	50%		Basic_price	='Model 1'!$B$12
5	Variable cost per car wash	$4.50		Basic wash sales	40%		Basic_sales	='Model 1'!$E$5
6	Economy wash cost	$9.00		Deluxe wash sales	10%		Deluxe_cost	='Model 1'!$B$8
7	Basic wash cost	$9.00					Deluxe_price	='Model 1'!$B$13
8	Deluxe wash cost	$13.50					Deluxe_sales	='Model 1'!$E$6
9							Economy_cost	='Model 1'!$B$6
10	Car wash prices:			Model of revenue, costs and profit:			Economy_price	='Model 1'!$B$11
11	Economy wash price	$15.00		Total Revenue	$129,000		Economy_sales	='Model 1'!$E$4
12	Basic wash price	$25.00		Annual fixed cost	$34,000		profit	='Model 1'!$E$16
13	Deluxe wash price	$40.00		Total variable cost	$43,200		total_cost	='Model 1'!$E$15
14							total_revenue	='Model 1'!$E$11
15	Decision variable:			Total cost	$77,200			
16	Number of annual car washes	6,000		Profit	$51,800			
17								

Model 1 | Model 2 | Model 3 | Model 4 | Cost Functions

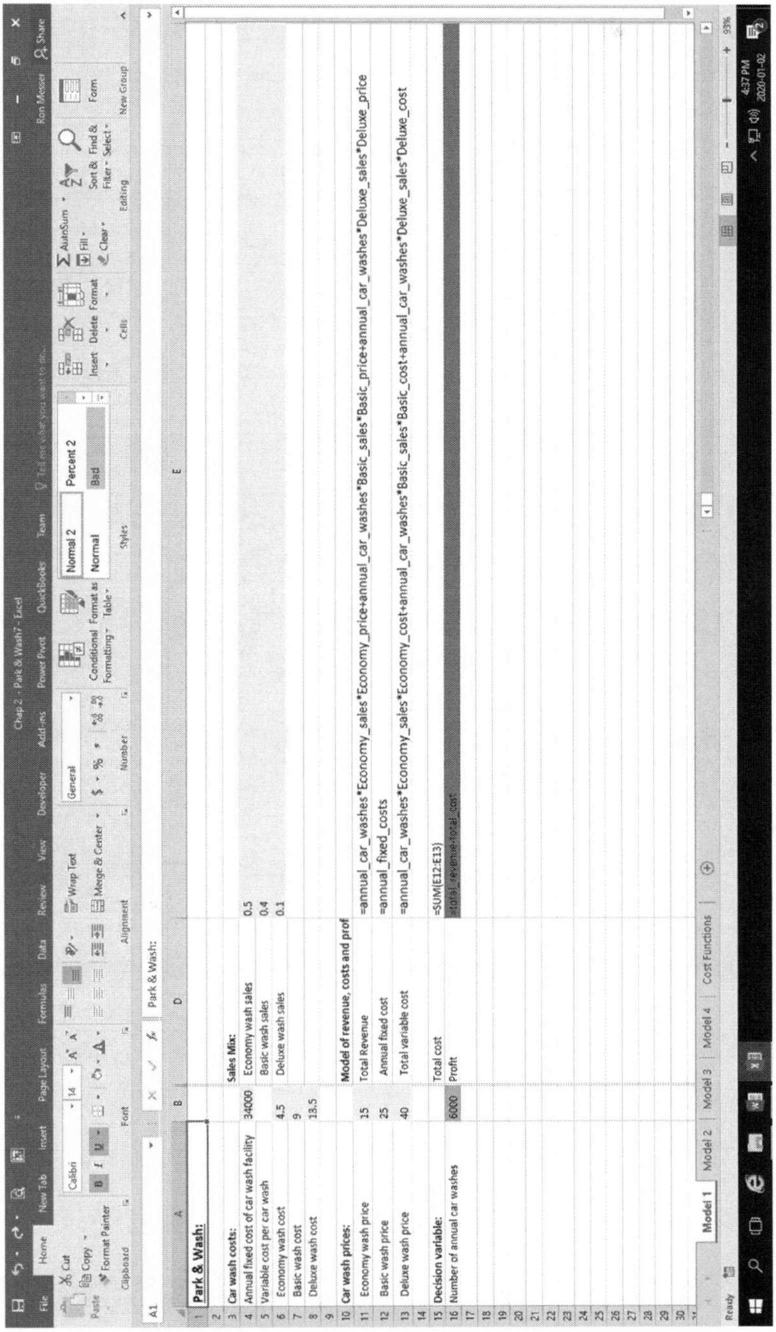

Fig. 2.3. Park & Wash CVP Model Formulas.

Fig. 2.4. Park & Wash CVP Model Goal Seek.

	A	B	C	D	E	F	G	H
1	**Park & Wash:**						annual_car_washes	='Model 1'!$B$16
2							annual_fixed_costs	='Model 1'!$B$4
3	Car wash costs:			Sales Mix:			Basic_cost	='Model 1'!$B$7
4	Annual fixed cost of car wash facility	$34,000		Economy wash	50%		Basic_price	='Model 1'!$B$12
5	Variable cost per car wash			Basic wash sales	40%		Basic_sales	='Model 1'!$E$5
6	Economy wash cost	$4.50		Deluxe wash sales	10%		Deluxe_cost	='Model 1'!$B$8
7	Basic wash cost	$9.00					Deluxe_price	='Model 1'!$B$13
8	Deluxe wash cost	$13.50					Deluxe_sales	='Model 1'!$E$6
9							Economy_cost	='Model 1'!$B$6
10	Car wash prices:			**Model of revenue, costs and profit:**			Economy_price	='Model 1'!$B$11
11	Economy wash price	$15.00		Total Revenue	$129,000		Economy_sales	='Model 1'!$E$4
12	Basic wash price	$25.00		Annual fixed cost	$34,000		profit	='Model 1'!$E$16
13	Deluxe wash price	$40.00		Total variable cost	$43,200		total_cost	='Model 1'!$E$15
14							total_revenue	='Model 1'!$E$11
15	Decision variable:			Total cost	$77,200			
16	Number of annual car washes	6,000		Profit	$51,800			
17								
18								

Fig. 2.5. Park & Wash CVP Model Break-even Units and Sales.

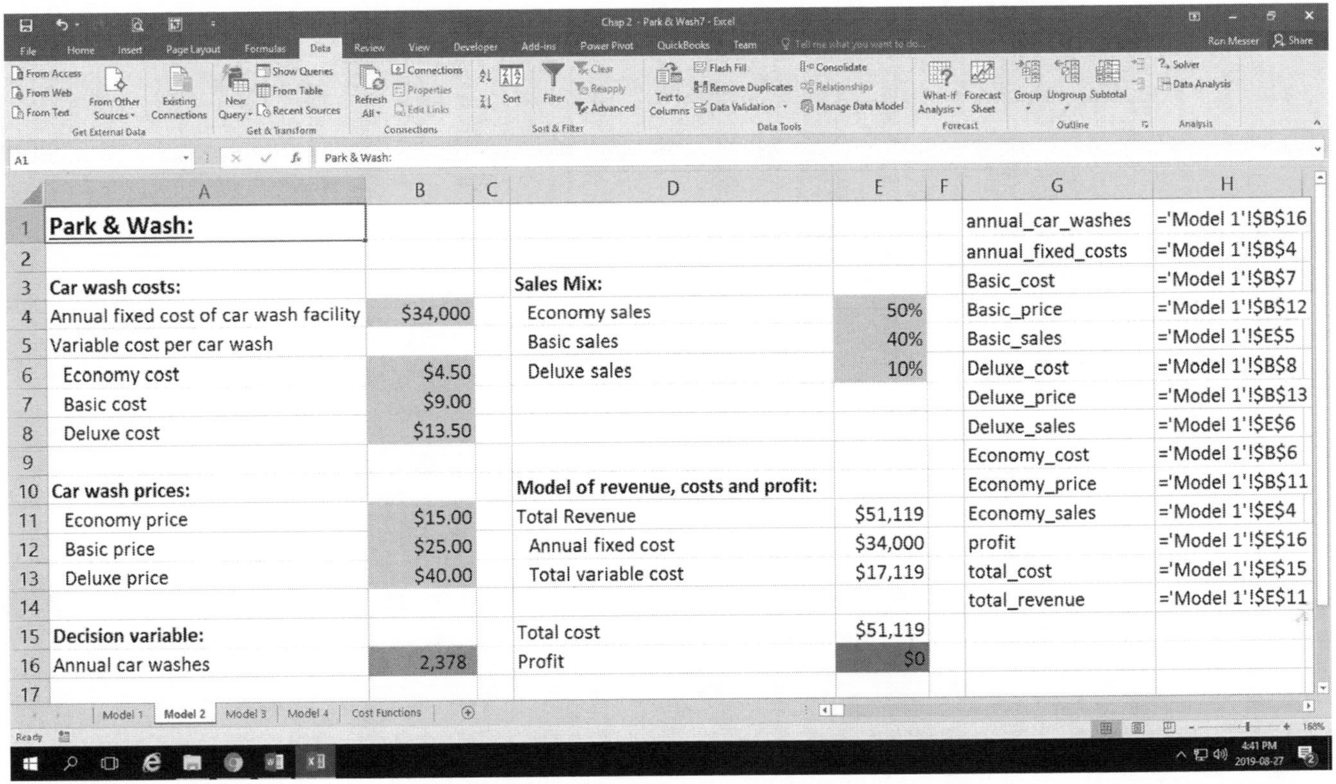

Fig. 2.6. Park & Wash CVP Model One-way Data Table (Step 1).

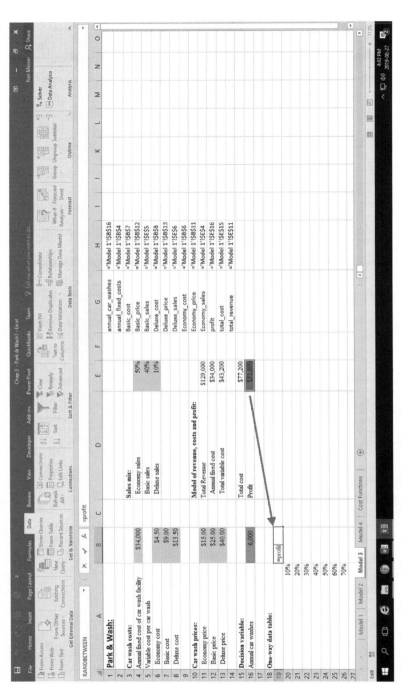

To create a one-way data able, highlight cells A19 to B26 and then use the following functions (as shown in **Fig. 2.7**): DATA, WHAT-IF ANALYSIS, DATA TABLE.

Because the input data that relates to the changing assumptions about the basic sales mix is located in a column (cells B20 to B26), we select the "Column input cell" option, (i.e., cell E5). The results of the data table are shown in **Fig. 2.8**.

The one-way data table shows that as the percentage of economy sales increase, profits increase. (Note that the other sales mix percentages automatically adjust so that they sum to 100%.)

We can also test the model's sensitivity to changes in the base case assumptions for two parameters at the same time, such as changes to the variable cost and the selling price for the economy car wash. This is shown in **Fig. 2.9** below.

To create a two-way data table, position the cursor in an empty cell location in the same worksheet as the financial model and reference, by using the formula bar, the variable of interest—which in this case will be the calculation of profit (cell E16). In row 18, for columns F through M, hard code economy car wash prices that are both less than and greater than the base case amount of $15.00. Do the same for the economy car wash cost, by showing values on both sides of the base case (i.e., $4.50) in cells E19 to E25 (see below).

To create the two-way data table, highlight the entire area from cells E18 to M25, inclusive and then left-click: DATA, WHAT IF ANALYSIS, DATA TABLE; then select the appropriate cell references for the cost (column input: cell B6) and price (row input: cell B11) of an economy car wash, as shown below (**Fig. 2.10**).

Once you select OK, the two-way data table is created (**Fig. 2.11**). (Note that conditional formatting was used in the table to show those combinations of variable costs and selling prices that result in a loss; these situations are highlighted in dark gray in the two-way data table.)

An important point to remember when using both one-way and two-way data tables is that the data table *must* be located in the same worksheet where the metric of interest is being calculated, which in this example is the determination of profit. This means that you cannot place your data tables in another worksheet in the same workbook, or in another workbook.

Note that scenario analysis can also be incorporated into break-even models. This Excel functionality allows users to quickly assess the impacts of changes in the base case, best case and worst-case assumptions. This functionality provides dynamism to financial modeling and is discussed and illustrated in Chapter 4, which deals with capital budgeting.

Afterthought → *is there something else I should consider?*

Models used to calculate break-even points are based on a number of assumptions. Therefore, it is important to clearly understand the foundational premises that support the financial model, as well as the limitation of the technique. Notably, break-even quantities only provide a starting point for a discussion about the viability of a new business opportunity. Sometimes non-quantitative or "gut" measures (intuition?) should also be considered.

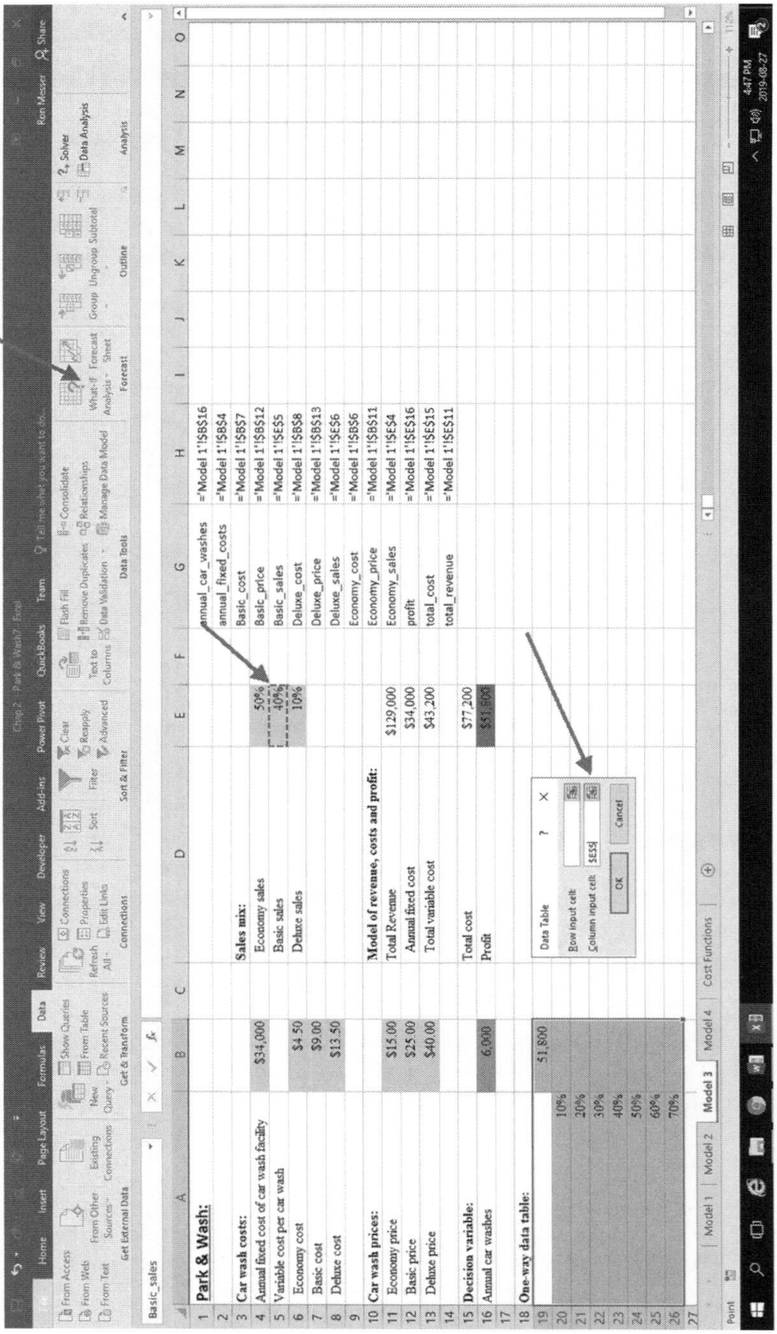

Fig. 2.7. Park & Wash CVP Model One-way Data Table (Step 2).

Fig. 2.8. Park & Wash CVP Model One-way Data Table (Completed).

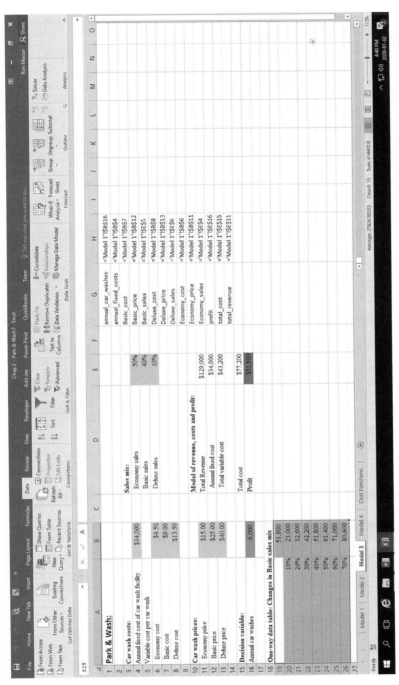

Fig. 2.9. Park & Wash Break-even Model Two-way Data Table (Step 1).

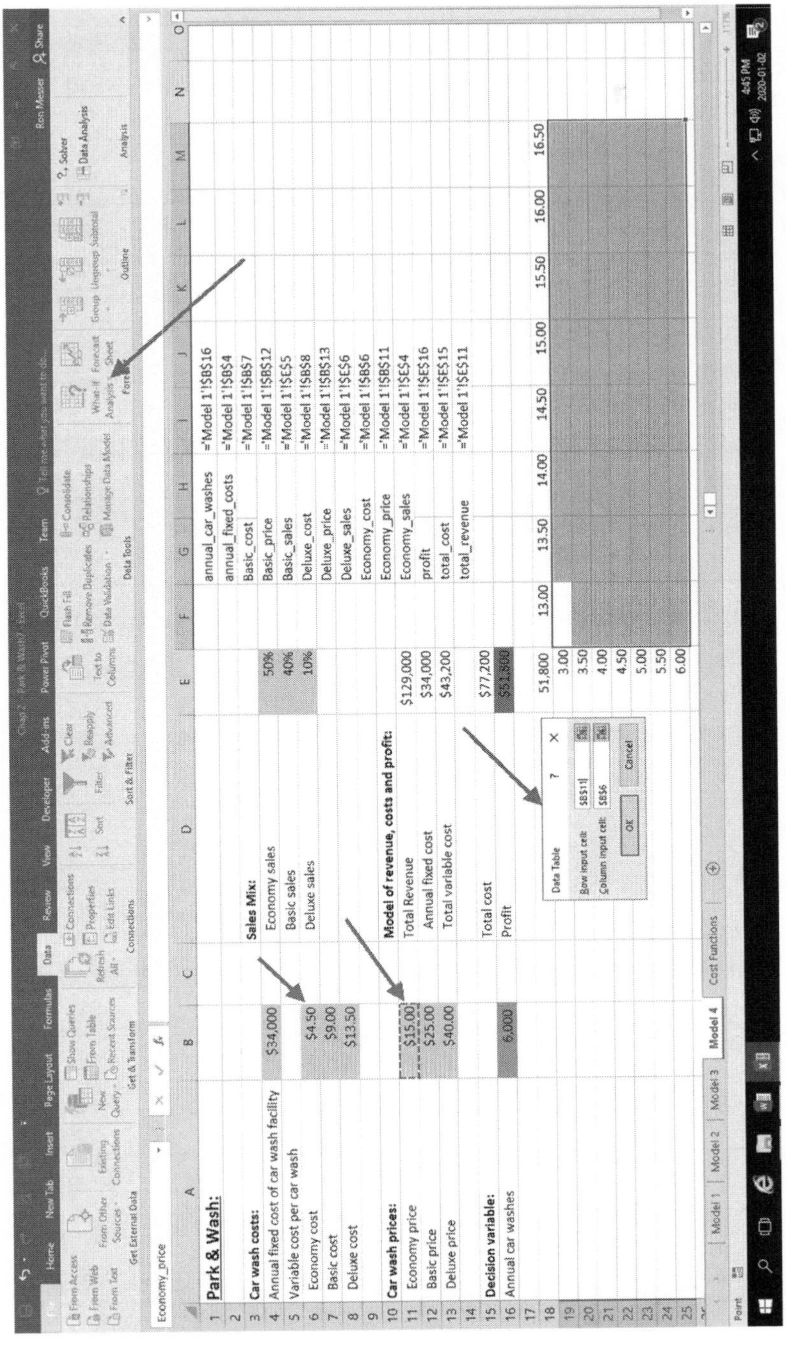

Fig. 2.10. Park & Wash Break-even Model Two-way Data Table (Step 2).

Fig. 2.11. Park & Wash Break-even Model Two-way Data Table (Completed).

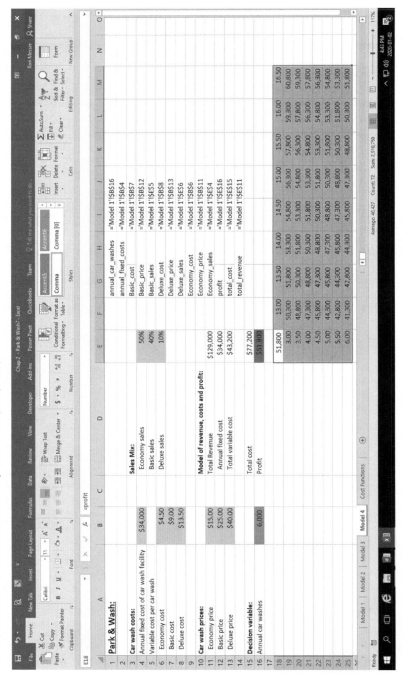

Decisions, Decisions: Guts and Quants

(Should I go with my gut, or leave it to the quants?)

I've always been fascinated by how people make decisions. Some rely on their instincts and, to use a popular phrase, "go with their gut" when making tough calls—like whether to produce a new product or service. Other folks prefer a more rational approach, applying logic and quantitative decision-making techniques to rigorously reach a conclusion. During the past 50 years, each of these different schools of thought—the *guts* versus the *quants*—has had its proponents and, depending on the fashion of the time, been reasonably persuasive in arguing the merits of their approach.

I must admit that I often vacillate between being a gut and a quant. Being a gut means having a sixth sense, or some intuitive ability that others lack. Naturally, this is a desirable quality, as it suggests some prescient skill. Yet (quite conveniently) when my gut decisions have been less than spectacular, I've returned to quantitative methods when making decisions. Numbers don't lie and therefore must be right. Break even volumes, trend analysis, regression equations (single and multiple variable types—take your pick) and hypothesis-testing techniques all have the indisputable benefit of being scientific and consequently unassailable—although not always correct! So, what's a poor decision-maker to do?

While in business school, I read an interesting essay that showed that when gut decisions were compared with quant decisions, the gut call was frequently wrong. This is simply because the human brain cannot possibly handle the numerous facts that must be considered when making a decision. Recently, I read another article that compared the ability of farmers and professional meteorologists at predicting weather patterns. As it turns out, folk wisdom was more reliable than the complex computer algorithms used to forecast tomorrow's weather. SCORE: QUANTS: 1, GUTS: 1.

Many years ago, a university professor told me something that I have found useful when making decisions. He said, "*You can never make the right decision, you can only make the best decision with the information available at the time.*" This means that it is incumbent on each of us to thoroughly research any decision before taking action. It also means that we should use the tools most appropriate to the situation—which may be quantitative or judgmental. Finally, the professor's nostrum warns against being a *gutless quant* (analysis paralysis), or a *quantifiable gut* (voodoo economist). In the end, we all need to work the numbers, take a deep breath, and then act...who knows, we may even turn out to be right!

Chapter 3

Times Series Forecasting Decisions

What will happen in the future?

Snapshot

TOPIC
Forecasting

SUBJECT AREA
Business statistics

DECISIONS MADE
Sales and revenue growth
Changes in business spending

PERSONAL EXPERIENCE
As a junior financial analyst, I successfully predicted—by examining time series data sets—future spending for a large division within a decentralized organization. I observed that there was a noticeable trend, as well as seasonal pattern in expenditures, and therefore, having a wealth of historical data available, I was able to forecast—within 1% of the final amounts—the spending for the fiscal year. The forecasting model that I developed reduced uncertainty about divisional disbursements, thereby making financial planning much easier for the company.

EXCEL FUNTIONALITY

ANALYSIS TOOLPACK
Moving average method
Exponential smoothing method

Background Theory
Types of Forecasting Models
Predicting the future is a popular pursuit among forecasters of all stripes, regardless of whether they are economic, political or social prognosticators. To make a prediction, three main techniques are used. Judgmental forecasts rely on individual (or group) expertise within a field of study, which is obtained through education, training and experience; for example, predicting the future price of a barrel of oil (WTI).[1] Econometric models rely of analyses of large datasets to discern causal relationships between variables, such as the demand for international air travel based on changes in world GDP. Time series models use longitudinal studies to uncover systematic patterns in data to make predictions.

Detecting Patterns in Time
Time series data use increments based on duration (such as days, weeks, months, years, etc.) as the causative variable to make predictions; this means that if patterns are found in the data, they can be used to forecast the future. There are three general types of time series patterns that are considered predictive:

(1) Trending
(2) Seasonality
(3) Cyclicity

Trending is indicated by constant increases or decreases, over time, in some measure that is related to a data set; for example, changes in sales volume for a new product over the last several years.

Seasonal patterns emerge during the course of a year and are associated with certain types of behavior; for example, increases in sales of soft drinks in the hotter summer months or increases in purchases of children's toys over the Christmas season.

Cycles relate to the volume of business activity and cover periods of economic expansion (i.e., growth in GDP) or contraction (i.e., recessions) in the economy. The duration of business cycles has varied, but the data from 1945 to the present suggest an average expansion of approximately 58 months (about 5 years) and an average contraction of about 11 months.[2]

Once data have been gathered, it is analyzed to detect these types of patterns. Note that time series patterns can also occur in combinations; for example, an upward trend with observed seasonal patterns that track the business cycle.

Time Series Forecasting Methods
To forecast the future based on time series data, we use methodologies that look to the past to predict the future; after all, we have no other basis than what has already happened to make a prediction. The methods available differ only with respect to how they incorporate the past into their models. The moving average method selects a

---

[1]WTI stands for West Texas Intermediate, which is a standard measure for oil quality.
[2]"What's an average-length boom and bust cycle?" Investopedia. Retrieved from https://www.investopedia.com/ask/answers/071315/what-average-length-boom-and-bust-cycle-us-economy.asp. Accessed on January 19, 2020.

number of prior periods and averages them to estimate what will happen next (note that with this method each period is equally weighted in terms of significance). Exponential smoothing allows for unequal weighting of past results, emphasizing either recent or older events as being more significant.

Financial Management Techniques

To develop a financial model using time series forecasting techniques, data are first collected in a data table (or a series of tables, called a database). The variable in the data table linked to time is plotted on the y-axis and the variable related to the passage of time appears on the x-axis. The observations are then charted as a scatterplot and examined to discern any of the three patterns noted. Examples of each of these are shown in the charts below.

Note how the volume of sales increases as we move from left to right along the horizontal (time) axis in the chart and how the data points are fairly closely clustered (**Fig. 3.1**).

In the next illustration, there are periodic spikes in the volume of sales, which are associated with recurring monthly (seasonal) patterns (**Fig. 3.2**).

In a cyclic pattern, peaks and valleys are observed over time, which are related to periods of economic expansion or contraction; for example, the 1982–1983 recession, which appears as a "dip" in the scatterplot (**Fig. 3.3**).

Once the data set has been charted, a visual review of the scatterplot should indicate whether a noticeable pattern exists. If there is a pattern, then both time series forecasting methodologies are used together (moving average and exponential smoothing), and the best predictor is selected based on a measure known as the MAPE, which is the Mean Absolute Percentage Error. The MAPE compares each of the forecast values with the related observed (actual) values and calculates the percentage difference between the two amounts in absolute terms (this means that there are no negative values).

Fig. 3.1. Trending Sales Pattern.

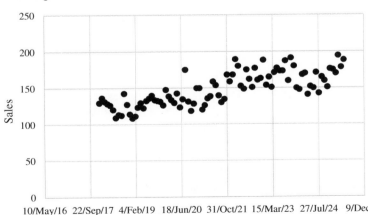

Fig. 3.2. Seasonal Sales Pattern.

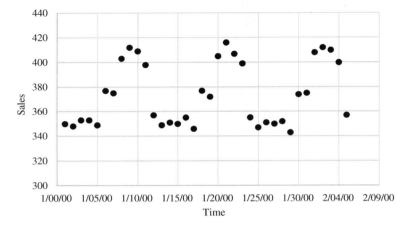

Fig. 3.3. Cyclical Sales Pattern. *Source:* UK Cumulative GDP (https://www.theguardian.com/news/datablog/2009/nov/25/gdp-uk-1948-growth-economy).

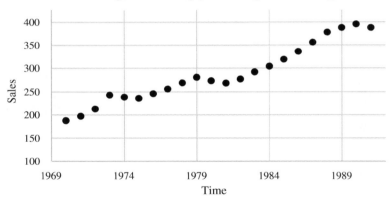

In summary, the steps required to develop a time series forecasting model include the following:

(1) Create a scatterplot to assess whether a pattern exists.
(2) Perform a moving average forecast for at least three time intervals (shown below).
(3) Perform an exponential smoothing forecast for at least two dampening factors (shown below).
(4) Optimize the exponential smoothing dampening coefficient.
(5) Calculate and evaluate the MAPE for all forecasts.

Relevant Excel Functionality

Statistical tools are available as an Excel add-in and are part of the ANAYSIS TOOLPACK; these can be used to forecast time series data and are accessed as follows: from the main menu screen,

(1) Left-click on FILE in the upper left corner of the main menu
(2) Left-click to select OPTIONS
(3) Left-click to select ADD-INS
(4) Left-click to select MANAGE EXCEL ADD-INS
(5) Left-click to select GO
(6) Select the ANALYSIS TOOLPACK ADD-IN from the check box (but, not the VBA version)
(7) Left-click to select OK

The ANALYSIS TOOLPACK add-in will appear under the DATA tab in the main menu and will be located on the far-right side of the main menu ribbon.

Demonstration Exercise

Long-term planning is crucial for all enterprises. This entails making reasonable guesses, based on past experience, about future events. This typically includes sales forecasts as well as estimates of other volumes of business activity (Excel file: BWNR(shell).xls).

Case Facts

As the population of North America ages, it is becoming increasingly concerned about its health prospects and longevity. The postwar "baby boomer" generation seemingly wants to continue working forever, and therefore, your company, Live-Long-and-Prosper, or LL&P (borrowing its name from a well-known adage by Dr Spock on the television series *Star Trek*), has developed a line of vitamin supplements based on ginseng, known as "BWNR" (which stands for: Boomers Will Never Retire). Long popular in Asia as a stimulant and purporting to possess aphrodisiac properties, the pill form of the herb has been touted for its health-related benefits. Your company wants to forecast future sales of its ginseng product in conjunction with a planned bond issue that will help finance expansion of the company's production capacity.

Step 1: Create a Scatterplot to Assess whether a Pattern Exists

As the financial analyst for LL&P, you are trying to predict future levels of sales. This information will be included as part of the securities offering document and hopefully attract potential investors. You first assemble the current sales data in a table, which shows sales by month and year and generate a scatterplot, as shown below (**Figs. 3.4 and 3.5**). (Excel steps: select the cell range in the dataset [A3 to B92] and then left-click: INSERT, CHARTS, choosing the drop-down box for SCATTER.)

Step 2: Perform a Moving Average Forecast for at Least Three Time Intervals

A review of the chart strongly suggests that the product sales have been trending upward over the past months. Based on this knowledge, you now activate the ANALYSIS TOOLPACK and select MOVING AVERAGE as the forecasting technique, as shown in the next figure (**Fig. 3.6**).

Fig. 3.4. Scatterplot of Sales Volume (Input).

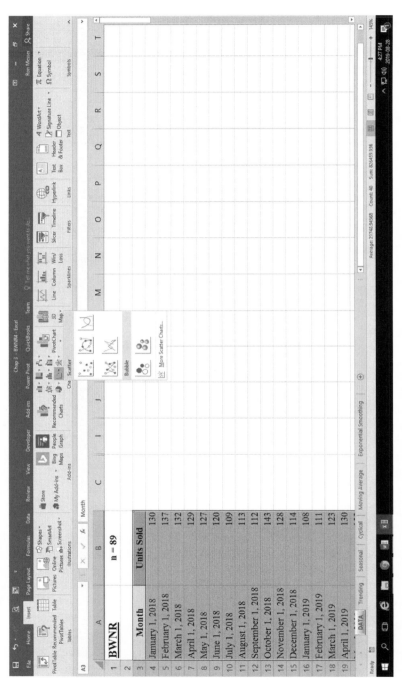

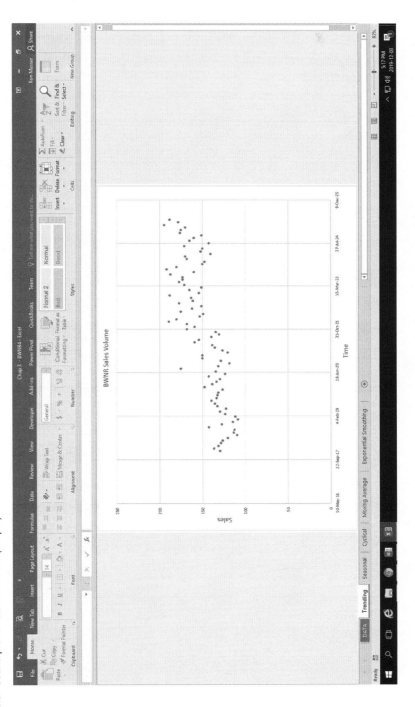

Fig. 3.5. Scatterplot of Sales Volume (Output).

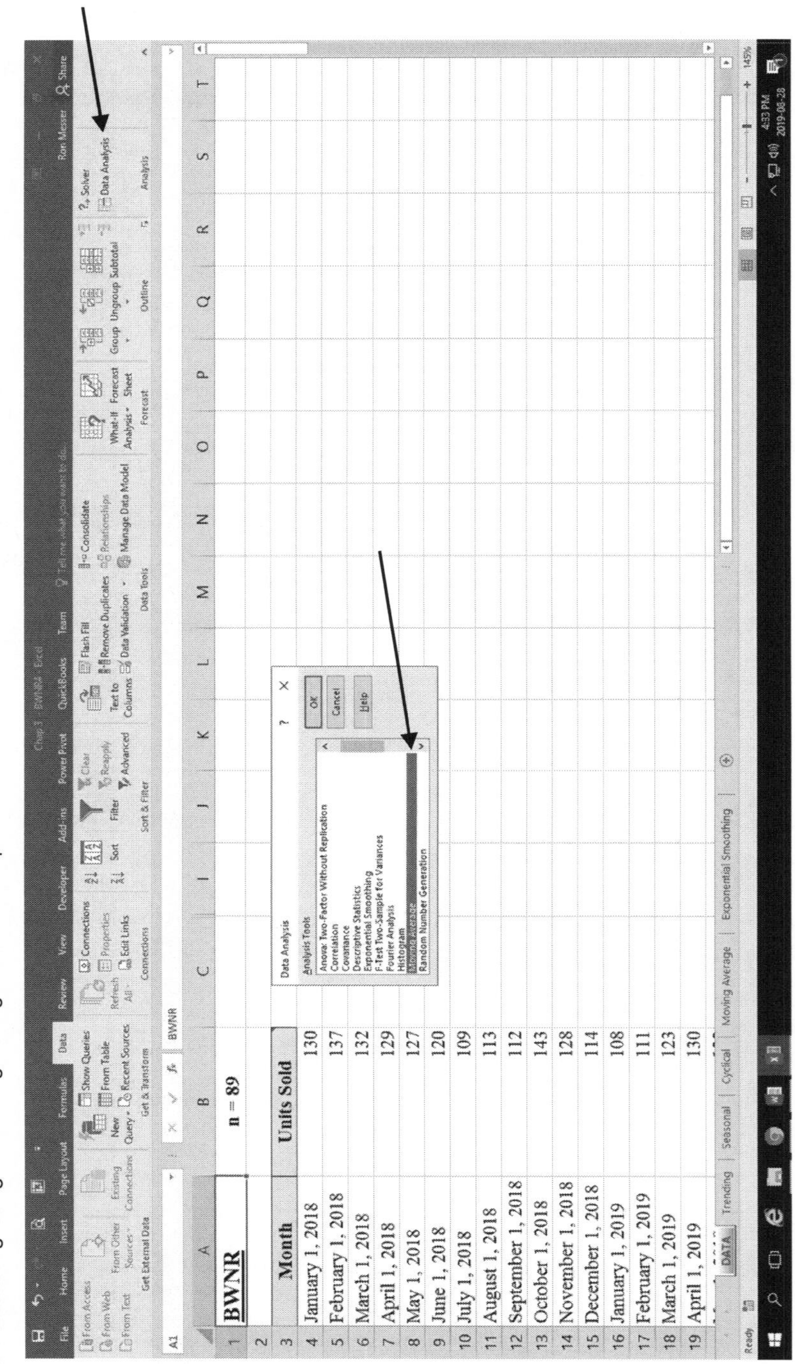

Fig. 3.6. Forecasting Using the Moving Average Method—Step 1.

You then complete the dialog box, indicating the input range (cells B3 to B92), which shows the unit sales volume by month. Note that the value in cell B3 is the variable name (label) for the "Units Sold" and by selecting it, the name will appear in the output. Also, remember to choose an output location on the worksheet that does not overwrite the data table. The item called "interval" refers to the number of months to include in the moving average calculation—select a 3-month interval (see **Fig. 3.7**).

You should position your output field in a cell that is one row greater than the interval selected; for example, for a 3-month moving average, locate the starting point of your forecast 4 rows after the start of the input range. In **Fig. 3.7**, the input values begin in row 4 and therefore the output should start in row 7 (i.e., row 4 + 3 period interval = row 7). The starting point for the forecast will be positioned in cell D7. After you left click OK, the forecast results will appear. The worksheet below shows three iterations of the moving average calculation, for intervals of 3, 6 and 12 months. Using three intervals for the moving average allows a more comprehensive evaluation of the forecast results, based on the MAPE (see **Fig. 3.8**).

Step 3: Perform an Exponential Smoothing Forecast Using at Least Two Dampening Factors

Next we will activate the exponential smoothing forecast, again by using the ANALYSIS TOOLPACK and selecting EXPONENTIAL SMOOTHING, as shown below (select OK) (**Fig. 3.9**).

Fig. 3.10 shows the parameters required for the exponential smoothing technique, including:

- The input data (cells B3 to B92).
- The dampening factor, which is the co-efficient that weights the significance of the current and previous forecast periods when generating a forecast.
- The output location.

The results of this forecast appear in the figure below. Note that the output is positioned one row below the starting row for the input range (i.e., in row 5 of column D). The initial forecast value will always be the previous period's actual result (in this case, showing a value of 130 for the period of January 1, 2018). The exponential smoothing methodology uses this amount as the starting point for the forecast.

Two iterations of the exponential smoothing method are produced in **Fig. 3.11**, using different dampening factors (as shown in cells D1 and E1).

The figure below illustrates the formulas used to determine the forecast results and how it is affected by the dampening factor (**Fig. 3.12**). (The named range "alpha" refers to the value in cell D1, which is set at 0.2 or 20%. This means that 20% of the previous forecast is included in the current forecast.)

The forecast for March 2018 weights the most recent observation of unit sales more heavily (at 80%—or 1 minus alpha, which is 1–0.2—of the predicted value) than the previous month's forecast, shown in cell D3 (i.e., 130 units sold in January 2018). The forecast results in column E use a dampening factor of 10%, which means that this forecast makes the most recent observation even more significant (at 90% of the previously observed value) than the previous period's forecast shown in column D.

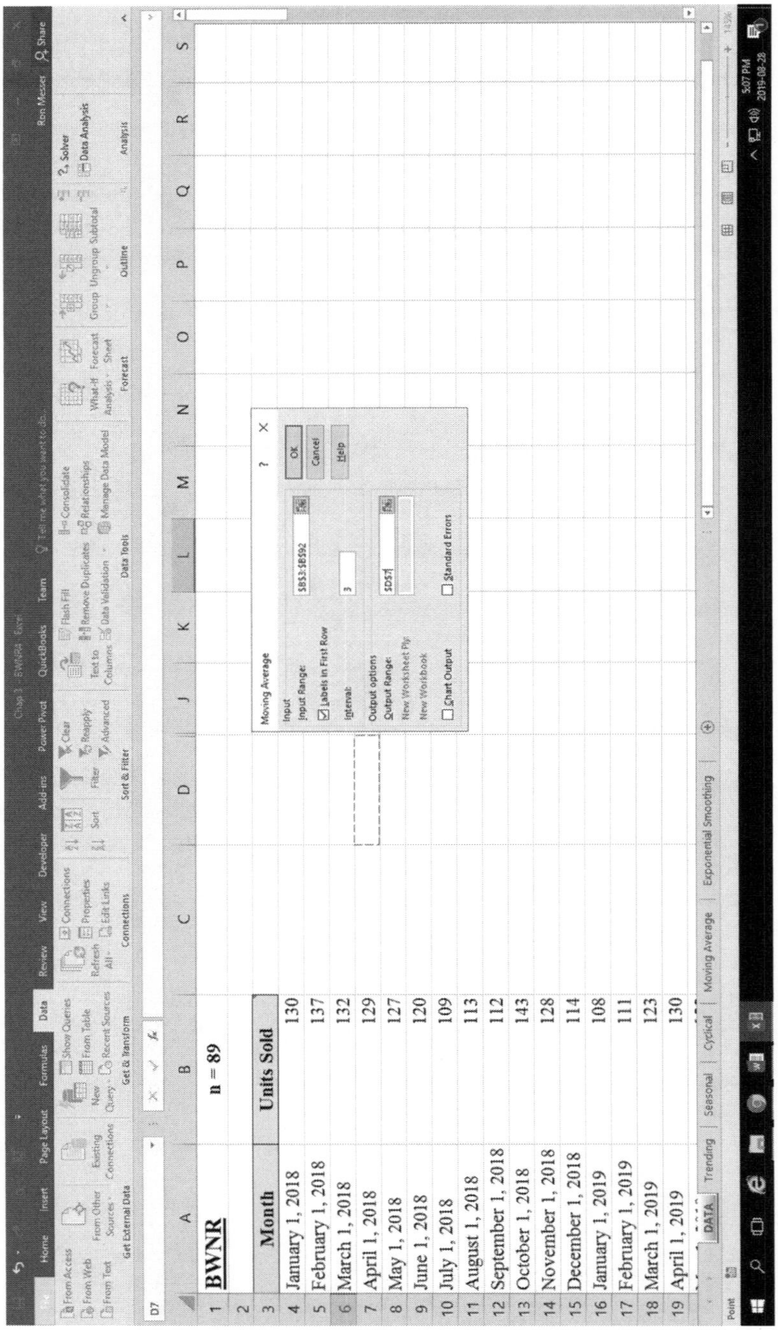

Fig. 3.7. Forecasting Using the Moving Average Method—Step 2.

Fig. 3.8. Forecasting Using the Moving Average Method—Step 3.

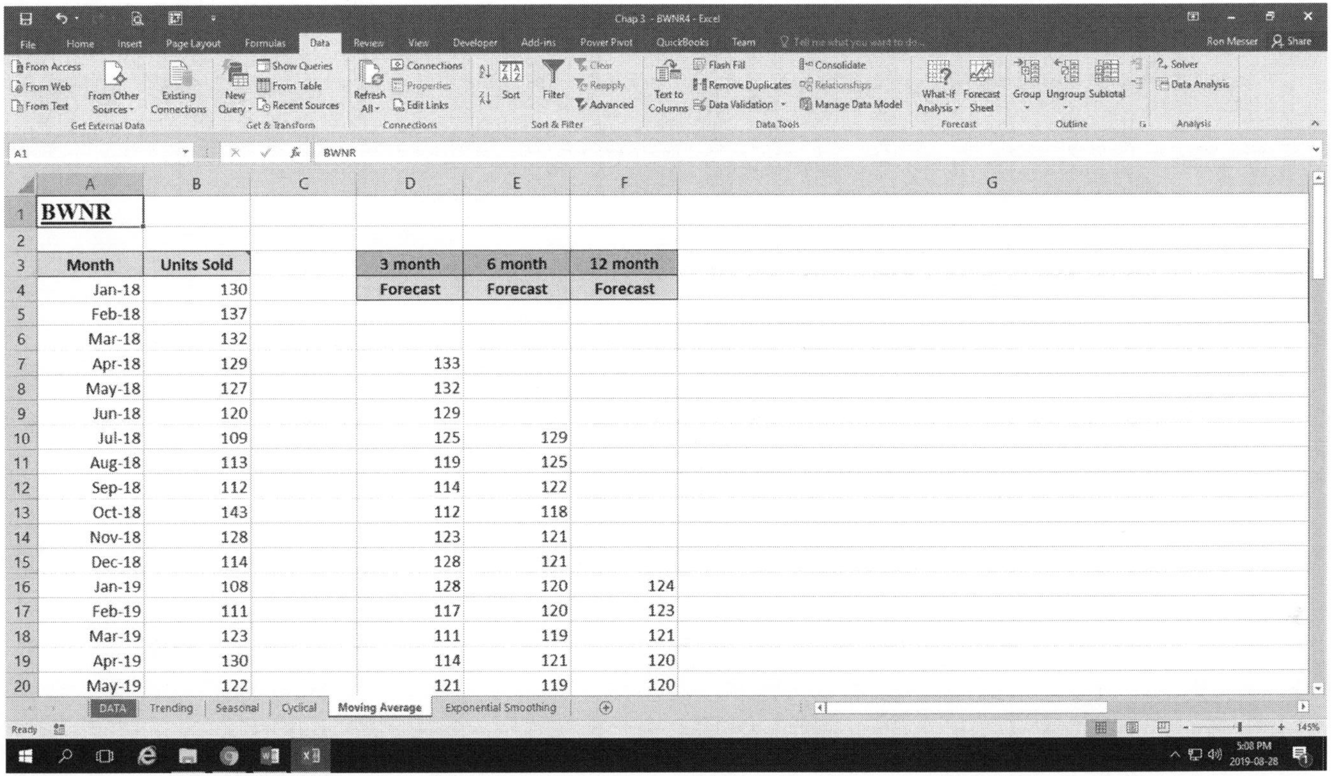

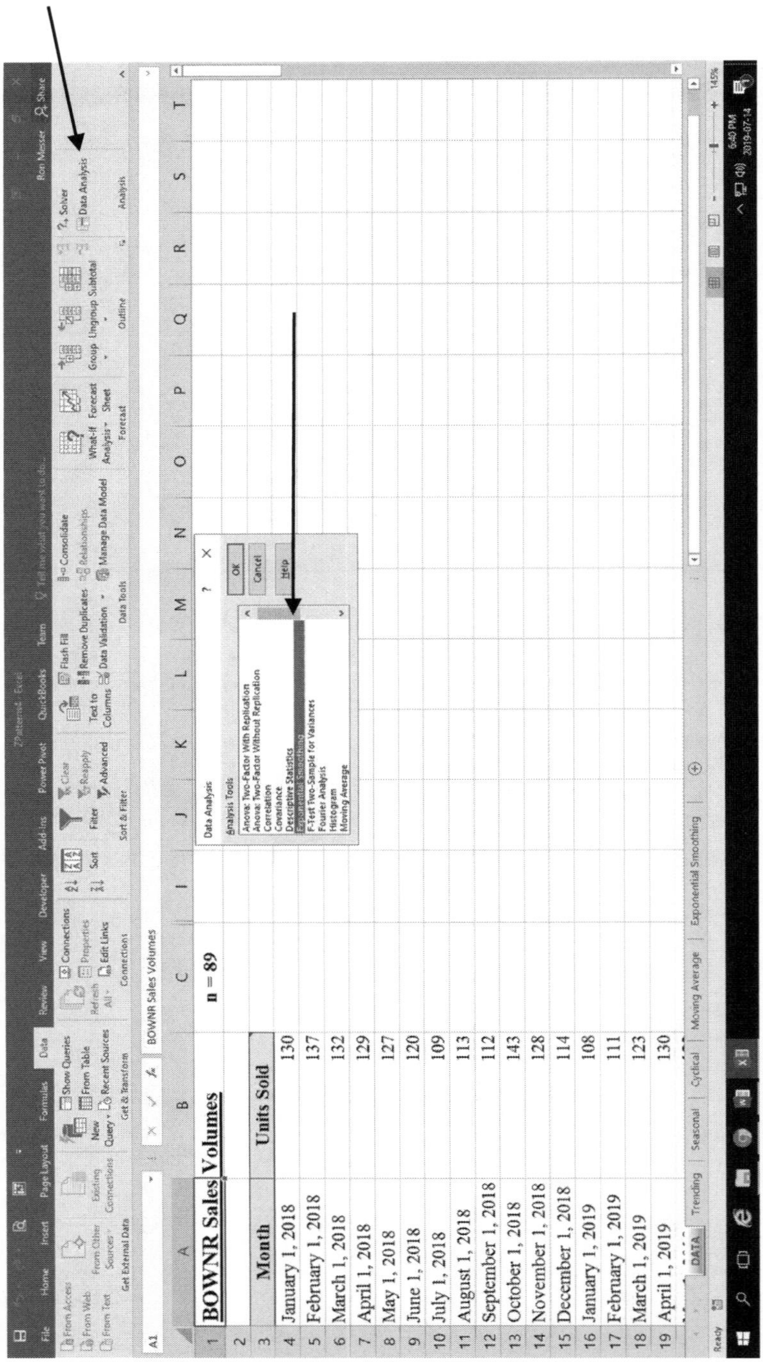

Fig. 3.9. Forecasting Using the Exponential Smoothing Method—Step 1.

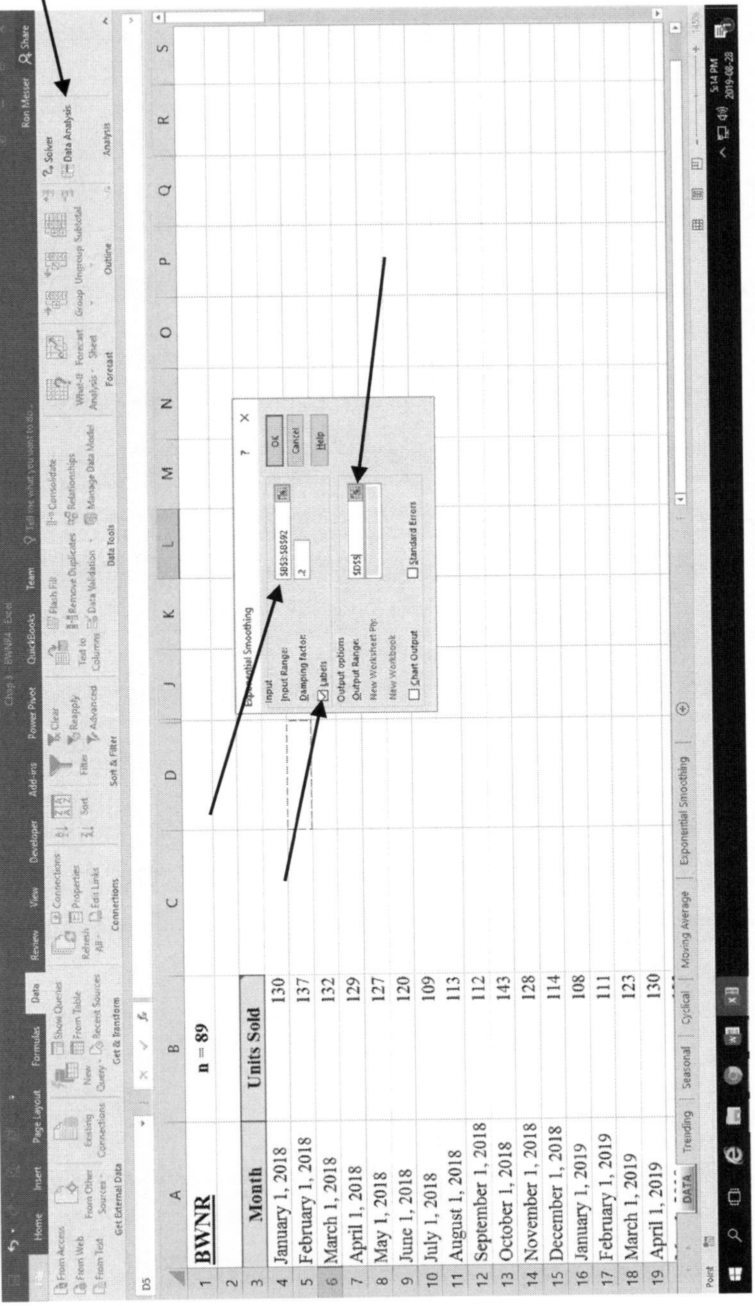

Fig. 3.10. Forecasting Using the Exponential Smoothing Method—Step 2.

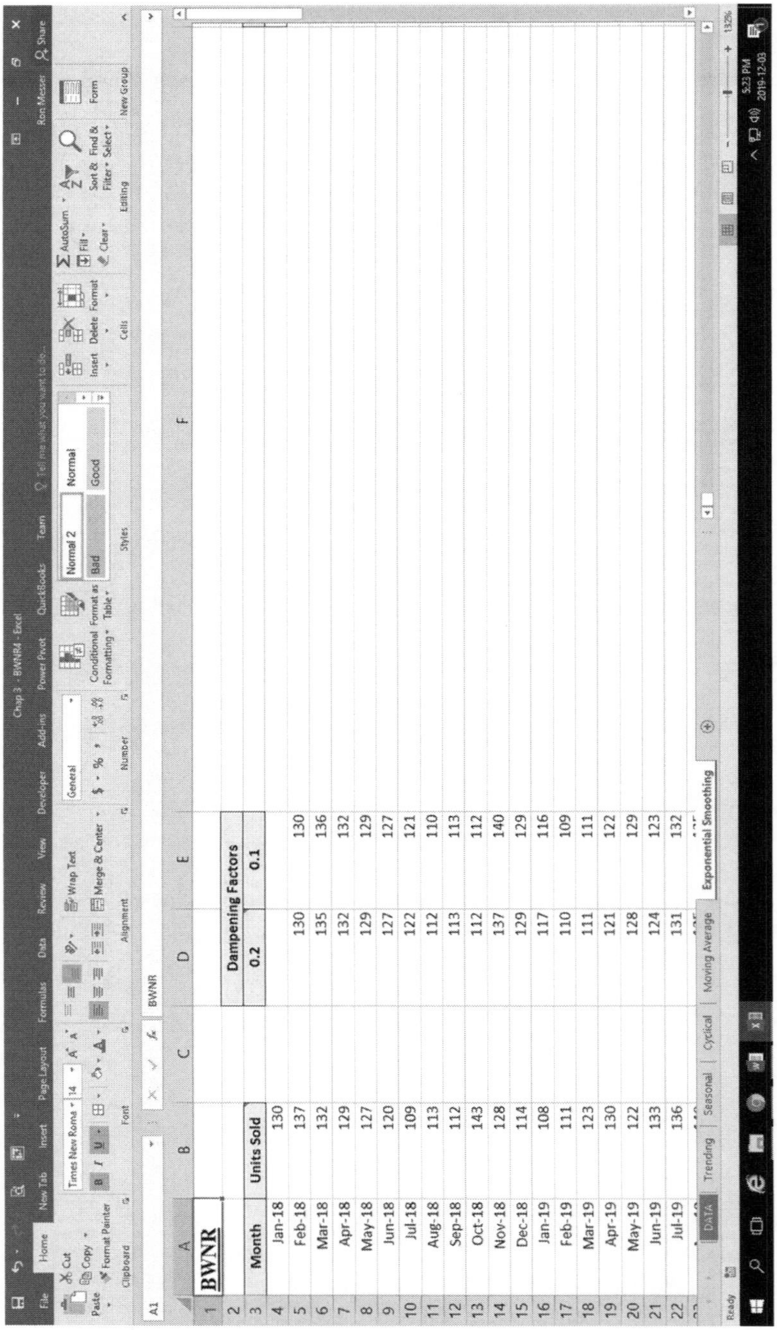
BWNR
Month | Units Sold | Dampening Factors 0.2 | 0.1
Jan-18 130
Feb-18 137 130 130
Mar-18 132 135 136
Apr-18 129 132 132
May-18 127 129 129
Jun-18 120 127 127
Jul-18 109 122 121
Aug-18 113 112 110
Sep-18 112 113 113
Oct-18 143 112 112
Nov-18 128 137 140
Dec-18 114 129 129
Jan-19 108 117 116
Feb-19 111 110 109
Mar-19 123 111 111
Apr-19 130 121 122
May-19 122 128 129
Jun-19 133 124 123
Jul-19 136 131 132
DATA
Trending
Seasonal
Cyclical
Moving Average
Exponential Smoothing

Fig. 3.11. Forecasting Using the Exponential Smoothing Method—Step 3.

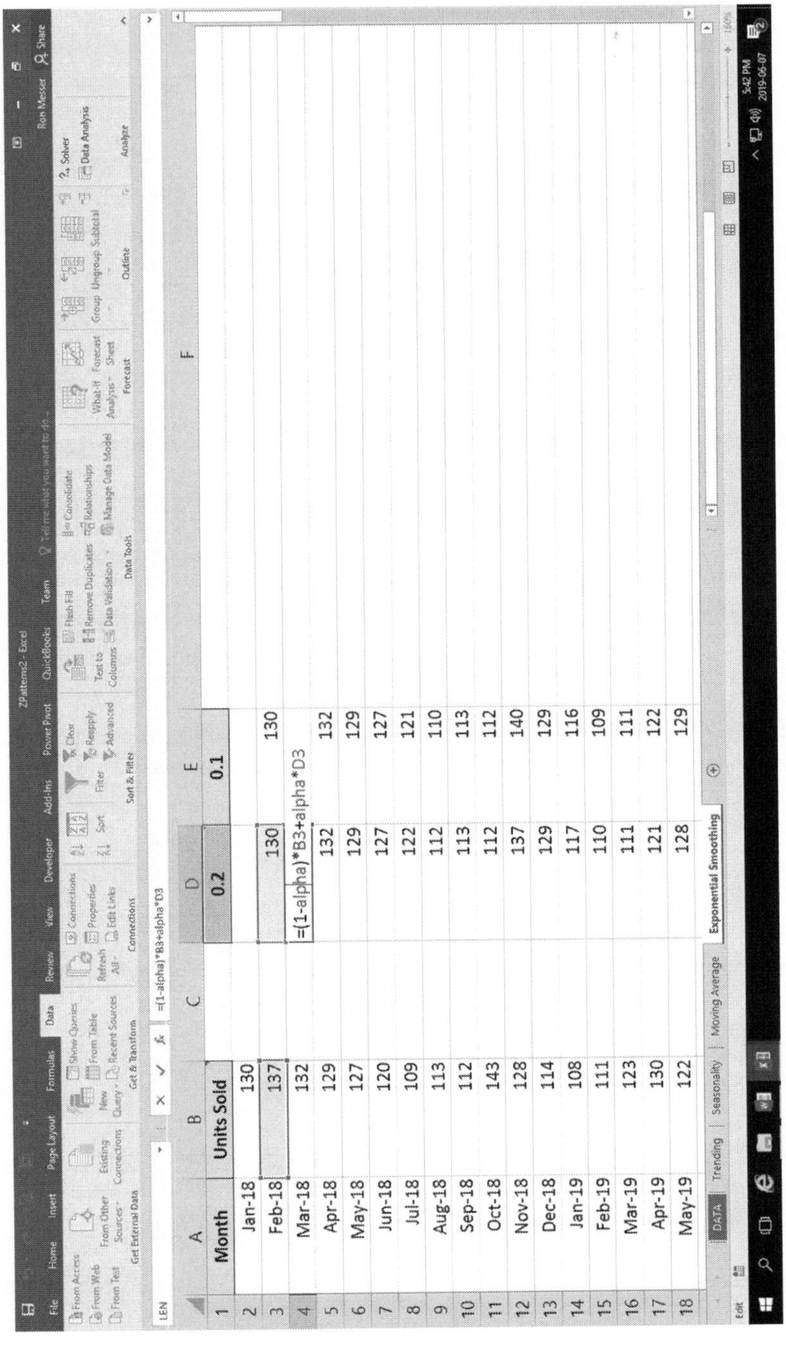

Fig. 3.12. Forecasting Using the Exponential Smoothing Method—Step 4.

	A	B	C	D	E	F
1	Month	Units Sold		0.2	0.1	
2	Jan-18	130				
3	Feb-18	137		130	130	
4	Mar-18	132		=(1-alpha)*B3+alpha*D3		
5	Apr-18	129		132	132	
6	May-18	127		129	129	
7	Jun-18	120		127	127	
8	Jul-18	109		122	121	
9	Aug-18	113		112	110	
10	Sep-18	112		113	113	
11	Oct-18	143		112	112	
12	Nov-18	128		137	140	
13	Dec-18	114		129	129	
14	Jan-19	108		117	116	
15	Feb-19	111		110	109	
16	Mar-19	123		111	111	
17	Apr-19	130		121	122	
18	May-19	122		128	129	

=(1-alpha)*B3+alpha*D3

Step 4: Optimize the Exponential Smoothing Dampening Coefficient
The dampening factor used in exponential smoothing can be optimized using the Solver tool (which is discussed in detail, in Chapter 6, on linear programming). This allows us to calculate the coefficient that will minimize the MAPE. The completed Solver dialog box to accomplish this is shown in the figure below (**Fig. 3.13**). (Excel function: DATA, SOLVER. Note that SOLVER is an Excel add-in, just like the ANALYSIS TOOLPACK.)

Using the Solver tool, we pick cell G4 as our objective (which calculates the average MAPE) and then select the check box to minimize it (shown as "Min"). We do this by changing the named range "alpha" (located in cell D3). When we click the SOLVE bottom at the bottom of the dialog box, the dampening factor changes to 0.61871426 (or, approximately 62%) and the MAPE becomes 7.6%, as shown in **Fig. 3.14**.

Step 5: Calculate and Evaluate the MAPE for all Forecasts
To determine which method and which parameters provide the best forecasting methodology, the MAPE is calculated for each of the six forecasts (i.e., the three predictions using the moving average method and the three based on exponential smoothing, including the optimized version). This is shown in the figures that follow (**Figs. 3.15 and 3.16**).

The calculation for the MAPE appears in cells H5 to J5 and is the average of the differences calculated in cells H7 to H92. (Note the use of the ABS function, to calculate only absolute amounts for the error percentages.)

A summary of the five MAPE calculations is presented in the table below (**Table 3.1**).

Based on these results, we can conclude that the exponential smoothing method, using the optimized dampening factor, provides the best forecast because it has the least amount of error when compared to the observed results. We can use this methodology to predict future sales volumes for the product.

Table 1.1. Summary of Financial Models.

Chapter	Financial Model	Key Excel Functionality
2	Break-even	Goal Seek; Data tables
3	Time-series Forecasting	Analysis Tool pack
4	Capital budgeting	NPV, IRR formulas
5	Regression Analysis	Analysis Tool pack
6	Linear Programming	Solver
7	Business Valuation	NPV, IRR formulas
8	Financial Analytics	Pivot Tables
9	KPIs & Dashboards	Charts, Slicers, Timelines
10	Budget management	Pivot tables, Consolidate
11	Financial Amortizations	PV, PMT formulas

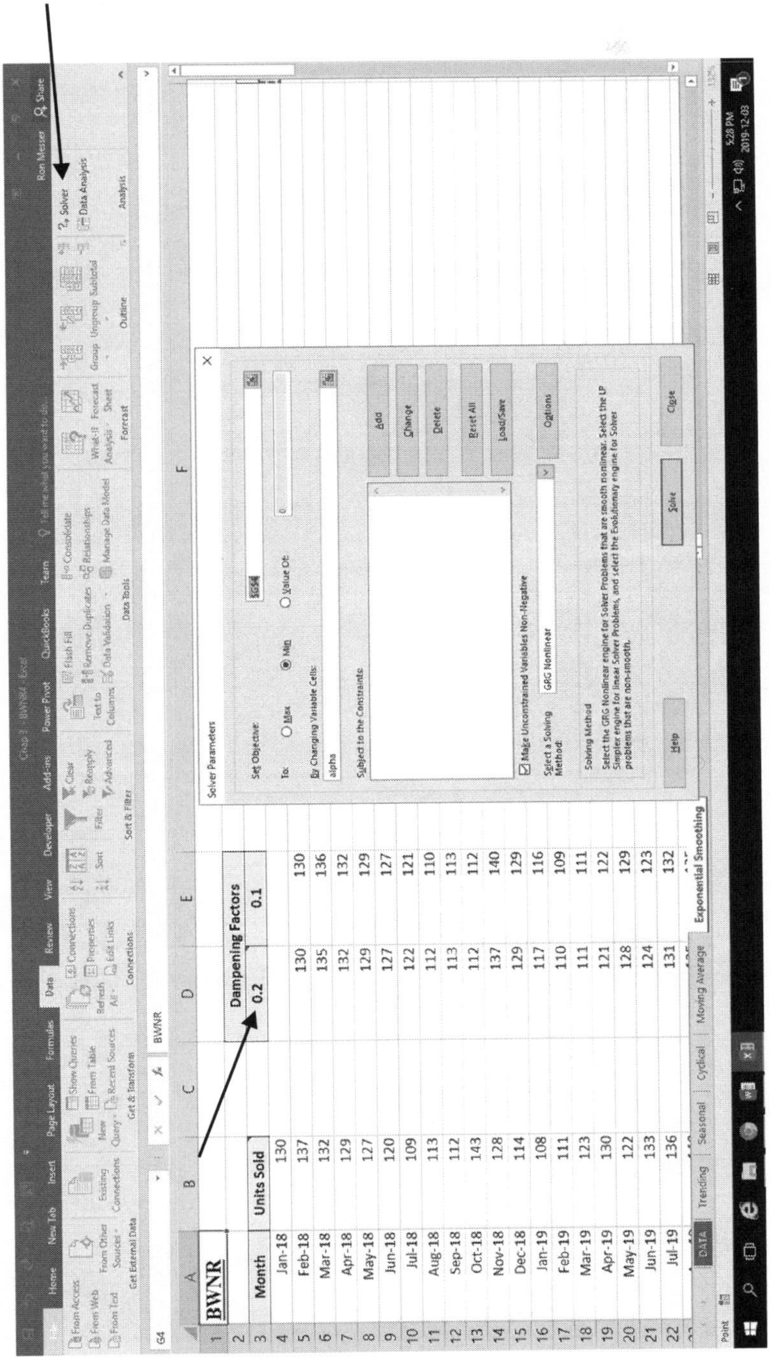

Fig. 3.13. Forecasting Using the Exponential Smoothing Method (Optimized)—Step 1.

Fig. 3.14. Forecasting Using the Exponential Smoothing Method (Optimized)—Step 2.

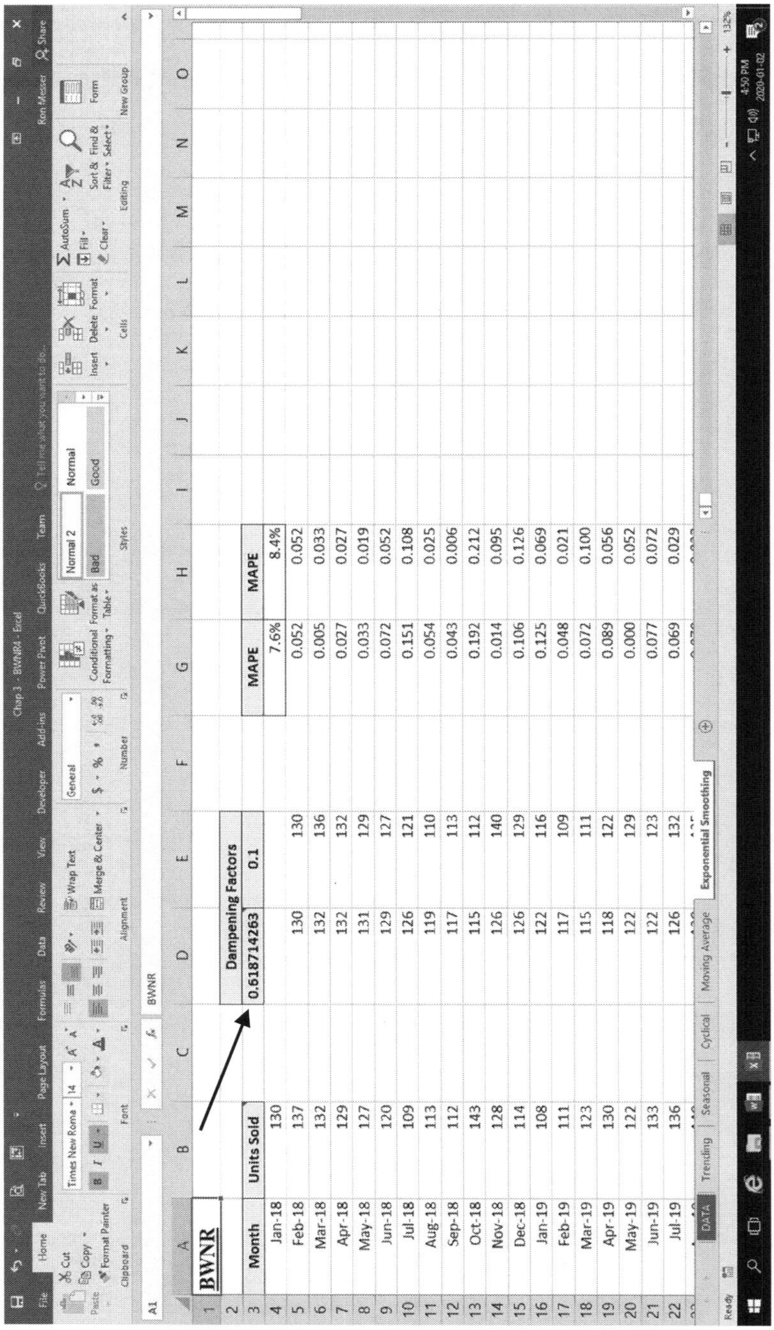

Fig. 3.15. Calculating the MAPE for the Moving Average Forecast.

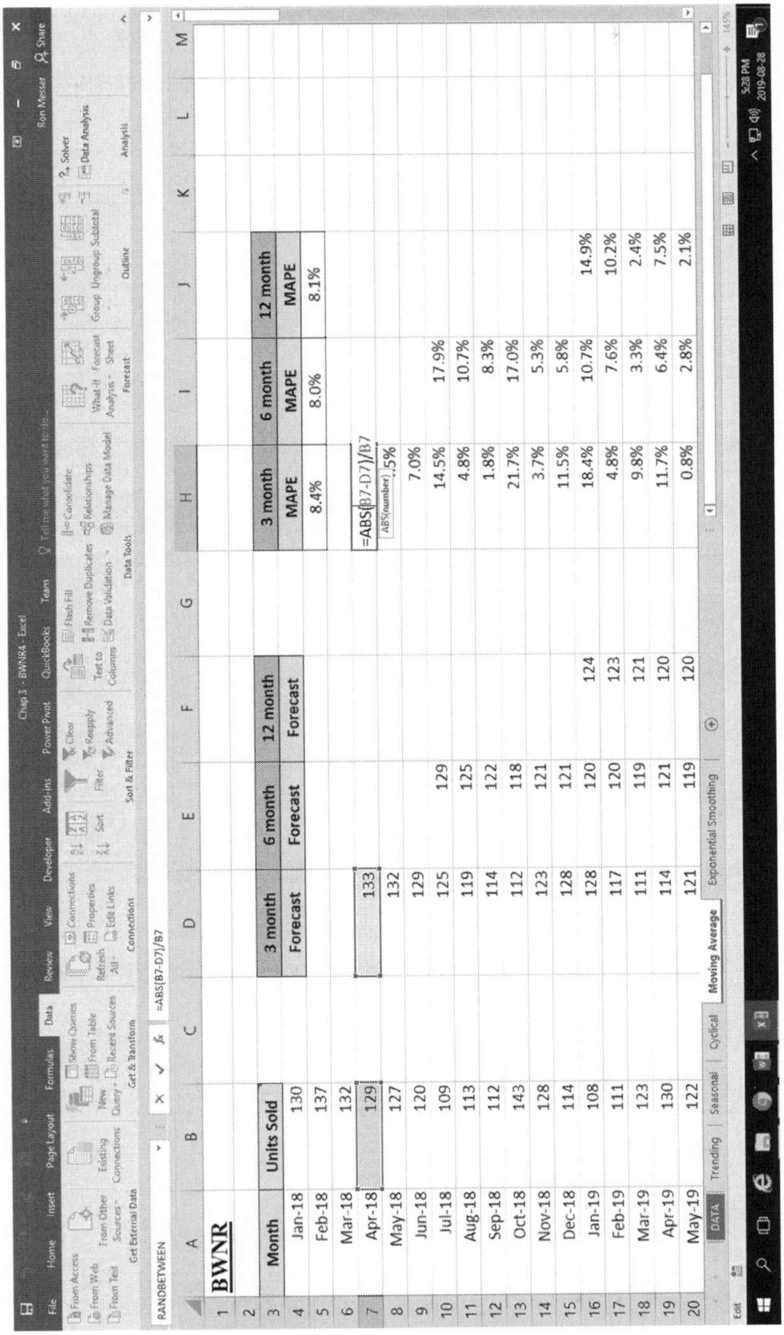

Month	Units Sold	3 month Forecast	6 month Forecast	12 month Forecast	3 month MAPE	6 month MAPE	12 month MAPE
					8.4%	8.0%	8.1%
Jan-18	130						
Feb-18	137						
Mar-18	132				=ABS(B7-D7)/B7		
Apr-18	129	133			ABS(number1,-5%		
May-18	127	132					
Jun-18	120	129			7.0%		
Jul-18	109	125	129		14.5%	17.9%	
Aug-18	113	119	125		4.8%	10.7%	
Sep-18	112	114	122		1.8%	8.3%	
Oct-18	143	112	118		21.7%	17.0%	
Nov-18	128	123	121		3.7%	5.3%	
Dec-18	114	128	121		11.5%	5.8%	
Jan-19	108	128	120	124	18.4%	10.7%	14.9%
Feb-19	111	117	120	123	4.8%	7.6%	10.2%
Mar-19	123	111	119	121	9.8%	3.3%	2.4%
Apr-19	130	114	121	120	11.7%	6.4%	7.5%
May-19	122	121	119	120	0.8%	2.8%	2.1%

Fig. 3.16. Calculating the MAPE for the Exponential Smoothing Forecast.

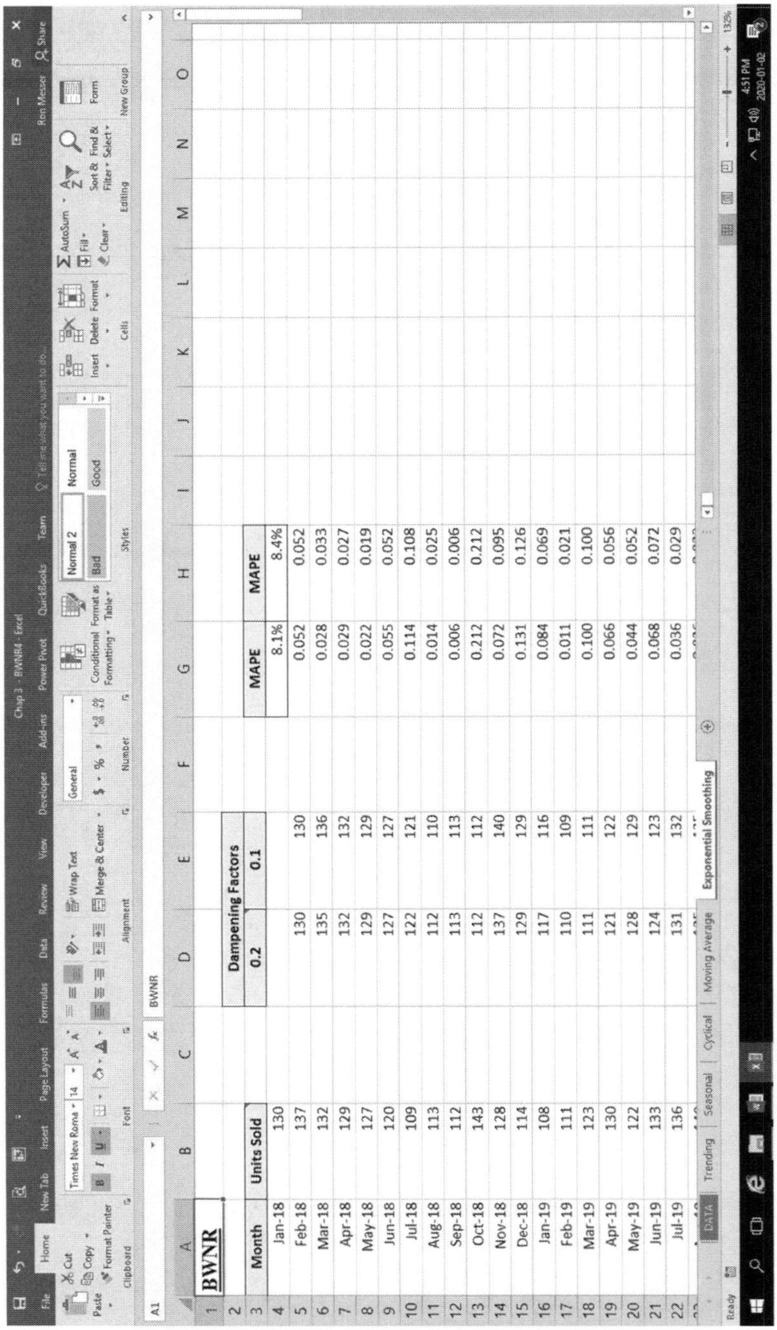

Month	Units Sold		Dampening Factors			MAPE	MAPE
			0.2	0.1		8.1%	8.4%
Jan-18	130						
Feb-18	137		130	130		0.052	0.052
Mar-18	132		135	136		0.028	0.033
Apr-18	129		132	132		0.029	0.027
May-18	127		129	129		0.022	0.019
Jun-18	120		127	127		0.055	0.052
Jul-18	109		122	121		0.114	0.108
Aug-18	113		112	110		0.014	0.025
Sep-18	112		113	113		0.006	0.006
Oct-18	143		112	112		0.212	0.212
Nov-18	128		137	140		0.072	0.095
Dec-18	114		129	129		0.131	0.126
Jan-19	108		117	116		0.084	0.069
Feb-19	111		110	109		0.011	0.021
Mar-19	123		111	111		0.100	0.100
Apr-19	130		121	122		0.066	0.056
May-19	122		128	129		0.044	0.052
Jun-19	133		124	123		0.068	0.072
Jul-19	136		131	132		0.036	0.029

Afterthought → *back to the future*

What is time? Einstein considered time to be inextricably linked to location and proposed the notion of space-time as a coordinating principle for his general theory of relativity. To some extent, he and others have done away with popular conceptions of time as a measure of duration. Consider this story.

It's about Time

(Teenage angst can guide us)

Is it just me or are there really so few original ideas out there? Much like the trend in Hollywood over the past decade, where a paucity of original scripts has led to the re-emergence of such chestnuts as *Starsky and Hutch* and the (seemingly endless) *Batman* series, the well of management thinking is running dry. Maybe this is why ideas from other disciplines have appeared as "original" business theories, such as the concept of *paradigm shifts* (from Thomas Kuhn's 1962 *The Structure of Scientific Revolutions*) and *business process outsourcing* based on Vilfredo Pareto's 1906 economic theories.

One evening, as I was driving my teenaged son home from his hockey game, we talked about some "deep" stuff. I asked him if he would like to know what was going to happen to him in the future. He thought about this for a moment and then replied: *"Uh...well, like...then, what'd be the purpose? You know...if you always know what's going to happen, then why bother?"*

Although he may not be a brilliant orator, his comments made me think. Notions of time are fundamental to many disciplines, including finance. Consider, for example, the concept of the *time value of money*. The underlying premise is that value changes with time. Yet, think about what would happen to capital markets if we all knew what was going to occur tomorrow. Investors would anticipate the impact of good and bad news and act accordingly, either increasing or decreasing their holdings. But since everyone knows what's going to happen, there would be no change in value, as all gains or losses would be neutralized. Perfect knowledge about the future means no change in wealth, which is a bad thing. If wealth does not change, then economies do not grow and we are left with the status quo—forever! Or, as my teenager said, *"what'd be the purpose?"*

This anecdote of teenaged angst suggests that a good place to look for the *next big business idea* may be your teenager (*...sweet!*). While their music may be dreadful and choice of clothing questionable, their insights can, at times, be quite surprising. As they move from childhood to adulthood and confront the ambiguities of adolescence, they can offer a unique perspective. So, the next time my nascent adult proudly announces that he's finally gotten around to doing what I asked him to do, I'll say: *"It's about time!"*

Chapter 4

Capital Budgeting Decisions

Should I make an investment?

Snapshot

TOPIC
Capital budgeting

SUBJECT AREA
Management accounting; corporate finance

DECISIONS MADE
Go or no-go decisions about what are, typically, large dollar investments in capital projects where there is uncertainty about future outcomes.

PERSONAL EXPERIENCE
I was the Finance department representative on a large capital expansion project that required an upfront investment of about $100 million. It was my job to determine the base, best, and worst case scenarios for this decision by calculating the net incremental annual cash flows for our planning horizon which covered 20 years. Using an appropriate discount rate, I then had to find the net present value (NPV), internal rate of return (IRR), and payback period for the investment (which are all standard metrics used with this technique). My analysis formed part of the project submission that was presented to the Board of Directors for their review and approval.

I am happy to say that they used my financial model as the basis for making this important spending decision and also that—in hindsight—many of the modeling assumptions proved correct. I also learned about some important things to consider when developing capital budgeting models, which I highlight in the demonstration exercise for this chapter.

EXCEL FUNTIONALITY
NPV
IRR
SCENARIOS
DATA TABLES

Background Theory

The Importance of Cash Flows

Capital budgeting should not be confused with budgeting for capital; the latter is part of an enterprise's planned spending on capital assets after they have first been approved through the capital budgeting exercise. Capital budgeting makes certain assumptions about incremental cash flows—such as sales growth and cost inflation—to build a financial model that generates the following metrics: NPV, IRR, and payback period. Of these measures, NPV and IRR use discounted cash flows (DCF), while the payback period is not discounted. The payback measure is provided primarily for those who are not comfortable with the concept of the time value of money (i.e., DCF), which typically include non–financially trained decision-makers (such as those with backgrounds in Operations Management or Human Resources, for example).

Incremental cash flows relate to the net inflows compared to outflows of cash that result directly from an investment. Note that these types of models use cash flows and not generally accepted accounting principles (GAAP) accrual based concepts to forecast the expected incremental returns from the project. If net income amounts are used in the model, they must be converted into cash flow measures, usually by making adjustments such as adding back noncash items, like depreciation and including the entire amount of capital expenditures (capex) when they occur. (Under GAAP capex is recognized in income through the annual depreciation charge.) In this regard, it is particularly important to add back the after tax interest expense when arriving at cash flows. This is because this amount will be incorporated in the discounted cash flows using the risk adjusted WACC (in other words, we want to avoid double counting this expenditure).

NPV, IRR, and Payback Period

A positive NPV calculation indicates that the project should be accepted because it recovers its risk-adjusted cost of capital. The IRR will also be equal to, or greater than, the discount rate when the NPV is positive. Typically, if the capital budgeting model is going to be challenged it will be because of either a low—but positive—value calculated for the NPV (which can be explained in terms of the cost of capital and time value of money) or the discount rate being used. For the latter concern, a sensitivity analysis is both useful and instructive.

The Discount Rate

The IRR is the discount rate that makes NPV equal to zero. It is sometimes referred to as the "hurdle rate" and represents the rate of return on a project. The discount rate used in the NPV calculation is generally based on the company's weighted average cost of capital (WACC), adjusted for the risk associated with the project. Riskier investments will have their WACC adjusted upwards; for example, capital projects in a foreign jurisdiction where there is political instability, and/or the local currency fluctuates significantly in relation to the home-country exchange rate. Risk can be modeled by examining the volatility of these factors over time.[1]

The cost of capital is based on the market valuation of a company's debt and equity financing. These amounts can be obtained from any current financial record of stock

---

[1] An excellent source of information that can be used to assess the risk of investments in foreign jurisdictions is the CIA World Fact Book, which is available free of charge at: https://www.cia.gov/library/publications/the-world-factbook/. By determining the volatility of the key risk factors (based on standard deviation), these uncertainties can be measured and incorporated into the risk adjusted discount rate.

and bond prices (like the *Wall Street Journal*). However, because these are market-based measures, they require periodic rebalancing, as the cost of capital is a relative measure that changes as securities prices change and consequently will affect the average cost of financing for the enterprise.

The cost of debt is a function of the coupon, or stated, annual amounts payable under the terms of the bond indenture, adjusted for any bond discounts or premiums. Discounts or premiums occur when the bond's coupon rate is less than the prevailing market rate of interest at the time of sale (discount), or more than what the market rate is currently paying (premium). Bond discounts will increase the cost of debt, while premiums reduce the interest expense. (Note that the effective interest method will be used to amortize bond discounts or premiums—see Chapter 11 in this regard.)

The cost of equity for corporations can be determined by using the capital asset pricing model (CAPM), which is based on a combination of factors, including the (1) riskless rate of return, (2) equity risk premium, and (3) company's beta coefficient. The riskless return is provided by the interest rate on government long-term bonds (typically of 10, or more years' duration). The equity premium is the historical difference between the riskless rate of return and the average return on investments in common shares (usually about 5%–6%). The beta is the co-efficient that applies to the equity risk premium; it represents the value of an individual stock in relation to the entire stock market and measures the stock's volatility when compared to the market as a whole.

Financial Management Techniques
In capital budgeting, it is common practice to provide at least three scenarios for project evaluation, including base case, best case, and worst case options. Each of these options presents decision-makers with possible outcomes relating to the viability of major capital investments.

Creating financial models for capital budgeting decisions involves the following steps:

(1) Determining the *discount rate* using a risk adjusted cost of capital
(2) Determining the incremental *net cash flows* for the project
(3) Developing a *base case* scenario for the key decision variables
(4) Determining the *NPV, IRR, and payback period* for the three scenarios

Relevant Excel Functionality
Capital budgeting models are primarily driven by formulas (in contrast to more functionally driven applications, such as linear programming models that deal with optimization decisions, using the Solver tool). The key Excel functions used for these models include NPV and IRR. Both of these financial formulas use irregular periodic cash flows (as opposed to the annuities required for the PV and FV financial functions), which typically occur at the end of the period. (Note that the timing of cash flows can be modified to include payments made or received at midyear intervals.) The syntax of the Excel financial formulas for NPV and IRR includes the parameters for the: (1) discount rate and (2) net cash flows.

Demonstration Exercise
Making large capital investments can be truly scary. For construction companies these projects represent multimillion (or, billion) dollar outlays that represent huge risks for investors. Consequently, developing an intelligent and useful model for this decision is

crucial and should be part of every financial manager's toolkit (Excel file: WTF Builders(shell).xls).

Case Facts[2]

WTF Builders (WTF) is an infrastructure design and engineering services company that constructs bridges, highways, and other large capital projects on behalf of governments. They have expanded their operations globally and recently been approached by a rapidly growing Central American republic (population of about 30 million inhabitants) concerning constructing a toll bridge over a major river that flows through the country. The river separates the rural areas—where most of the workers live—from its industrialized core. Currently, rural drivers must navigate country roads around the water body, which requires about 2 hours of travel time. Using the bridge is expected to save time and money (including gas and vehicle wear and tear) for workers commuting to their places of employment.

John Canuck, an analyst in the WTF corporate finance group, has been tasked by his company to build a financial model that will help assess the viability of the bridge project. WTF will be compensated by receiving a percentage of annual revenues as part of a concession agreement for running the toll bridge, which is expected to have a useful life of 20 years. After talking with his supervisor and various contact personnel in the design and engineering departments of the company, John gathered the following information.

- Cost of bridge: $40,000,000 CAD (including contingency and escalation amounts)[3]
- Number of drivers using bridge in year 1: 3,000,000 (about 10% of the population)
- One-way toll price: $2.50 CAD (a round trip is therefore $5.00 CAD)
- Incremental cash flow percentage: 33% (one-third of all toll revenues)
- Annual incremental cash flows: $5,000,000 CAD (one-third of 3 million users at $5.00 each)
- Taxes will not be assessed in the country, under the terms of the concession agreement
- Annual growth rate in bridge users: 5% (based on similar experience in other countries)
- Years of increasing number of bridge users: 15 (based on similar experience)
- After 15 years, usage rates will remain constant at year 15 levels.
- WTF's WACC: 10% (based on a combination of the company's debt and equity financing)
- Risk adjustment: 2% (because of the relative instability of the local currency)

Step 1: Determining the Discount Rate Using a Risk-adjusted Cost of Capital

The risk-adjusted cost of capital will be made up of the company's WACC, which is 10% based on its existing capital structure, plus the risk adjustment relating to

---

[2]This exercise is loosely based on one provided in Winston, W. L., & Albright, S. C. (2009). *Practical management science* (pp. 58–61). Mason, OH: Cengage Learning. The exercise follows a fairly standard template used for capital budgeting models by identifying net incremental cash flows over a period of years and then discounting these to the present time.

[3]Contingencies relate to unexpected future spending and are usually set at 10%–15% of the base budget, while escalation clauses relate to inflationary price increases associated with the cost of construction materials and labor.

operating in a foreign jurisdiction, which has been determined to be 2%—i.e., 10% + 2% = 12%.

Step 2: Determining the Incremental Net Cash Flows for the Project
As the concession agreement gives one-third (33%) of all revenues to WTF, the annual amount of cash received is expected to be $5,000,000.

Step 3: Developing a Base Case Scenario for to the Key Decision Variables
The financial model for the base case decision (i.e., using the most likely set of assumptions) is shown in **Fig. 4.1** below.

The formula used to calculate the net incremental cash flows for each year is included in cells D18 to V18. For the end of year 2 (cell D18), the calculation uses the following IF formula:

$$= \textbf{IF(C15}< = \textbf{Years\_of\_increasing\_cash\_flows},$$
$$\textbf{B16}^*\textbf{(1+Annual\_increase\_in\_cash\_flows)},$$
$$\textbf{B16}^*\textbf{(1−Rate\_of\_decrease\_after\_increase))}$$

This IF statement evaluates, by year, whether the predetermined period of increase (years of increasing cash flows) has been reached. Note that the year 0 development cost is shown as a negative amount (i.e., cash outflow) and is not discounted because it is assumed to occur at the beginning of the investment period.

The NPV calculation in cell B20 is as follows:

$$= −\textbf{Construction\_cost+NPV(Discount\_rate, C18 : V18)}$$

The resulting NPV is positive and therefore suggests that we should proceed with the project. The IRR is 15.3% and the payback period is a little more than 5 years. The formula for the IRR calculation in cell B21 is as follows:

$$= \textbf{IRR(B18 : V18)}$$

The payback period calculation in cell B22 is as follows:

$$= \textbf{Construction\_cost/AVERAGE(C18 : V18)}$$

Using these base case assumptions, we can test the sensitivities of the key variables in the financial model. The most important assumption made is with regard to the *discount rate* (cell B12) and a one-way data table provides information about changes in the NPV, IRR and payback period when this variable changes. (Creating data tables—both one-way and two-way—was discussed in Chapter 2.) This is shown in **Fig. 4.2**. Note that as the discount rate increases, the NPV declines and the project becomes nonviable at a 16% cost of capital. This is an important inflection point, as it addresses the risk profile associated with nondomestic investments such as this one. In other words, it evaluates the outer limits of the risk of the currency depreciating, which means that it can decline as much as 6% before this investment opportunity is rejected. (The IRR and payback are unaffected by the change in the discount rate because these metrics rely only on the incremental cash flows, which remain unchanged.)

Fig. 4.1. WTF builders investment.

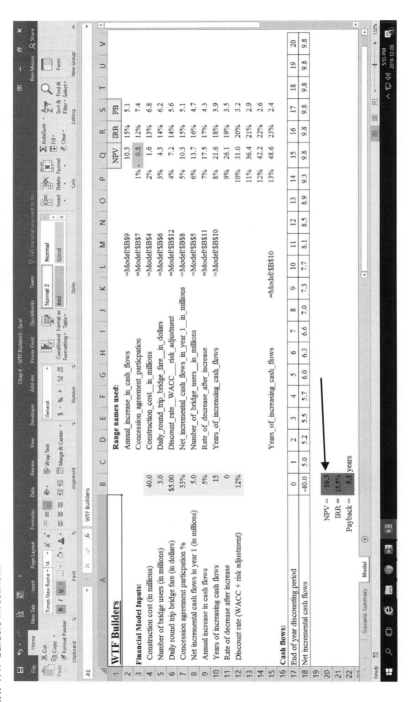

Fig. 4.2. WTF Investment and Discount Rate Sensitivity Analysis.

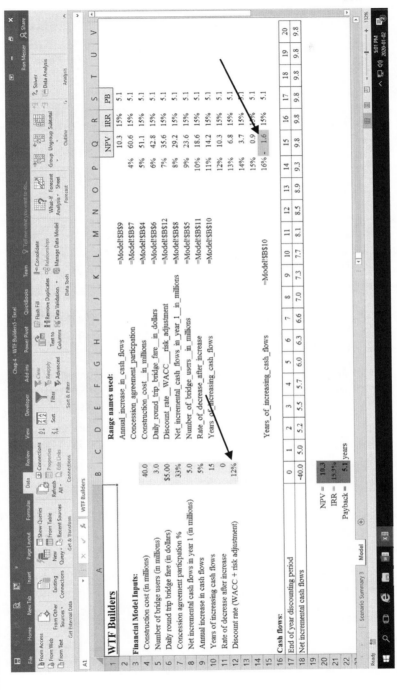

Note that when completing the one-way data table, all three of the metrics (NPV, IRR, and payback) can be calculated at once. This is accomplished by selecting all of the measures in the model (referenced in cells Q2 to S2, which are linked to the values for NPV [cell B20], IRR [cell B21], and payback [cell C22]) and changing the variable of interest, the discount rate, which is shown in column format (cells P3 to P15).

The sensitivity analysis for changes to the *annual increase in cash flows* (cell B9) in shown **Fig. 4.3**.

This analysis shows that if the cash flows grow by less than 2% annually (with all other base case assumptions unchanged), the NPV becomes negative, making the project unviable. It also demonstrates that as sales increase, so too does the IRR, while the payback period decreases.

Step 4: Determining the NPV, IRR and Payback Period for Each Scenario

To develop scenarios for base, best, and worst case outcomes, we can use the Excel scenario manager, which is accessed by left clicking: DATA, WHAT-IF ANALYSIS, SCENARIO MANAGER. The scenario manager allows users to create alternative business cases and determine their impact on the key decision measures for NPV, IRR, and payback. **Table 4.1** below shows the parameters used for each of these scenarios.

To create these scenarios in the worksheet that contains the capital budgeting financial model, use the scenario manager functionality to add a new business case. This is done by providing a scenario name (e.g., Base Case) and then selecting the cell range from B4 to B6 as the changing cells and including the parameters noted in **Table 4.1** above. Click OK to select a scenario and then repeat the steps to add the best case and worst case situations. This is shown in **Figs. 4.4 and 4.5**.

Fig. 4.6 (below) shows the base case using the appropriate assumptions for the capital cost, number of users and round trip fare (select DATA, WHAT-IF ANALYSIS, SCENARIOS and then left-click in the scenario manager: SHOW).

The following two figures (**Figs. 4.7 and 4.8**) show the best case and worst case outcomes using the scenario manager.

The financial model shows that the NPV goes from a high of $63.9 million (best case) to a loss of $23.2 million (worst case), with a base case of $10.3 million. A scenario summary can be produced by selecting this option in the scenario manager screen (blue arrow), as shown in the dialogue box in **Fig. 4.8**. The output from selecting this option is shown below (**Fig. 4.9**).

Afterthought → q*ue sera, sera*

Uncertainty is a fact of life. How we deal with it is not. While the future is, by definition, unknowable, it is not unpredictable. Consider the following prognostication.

Table 4.1. Parameters for Project Base Case, Best Case, and Worst Case Scenarios.

Parameter	Base Case	Best Case	Worst Case
Capital cost	$40 million CAD	$30 million CAD	$50 million CAD
Number of users	3 million	4 million	2 million
Round trip fare	$5 per round trip	$7 per round trip	$4 per round trip

Fig. 4.3. WTF Investment and Annual Cash Flow Increase Sensitivity Analysis.

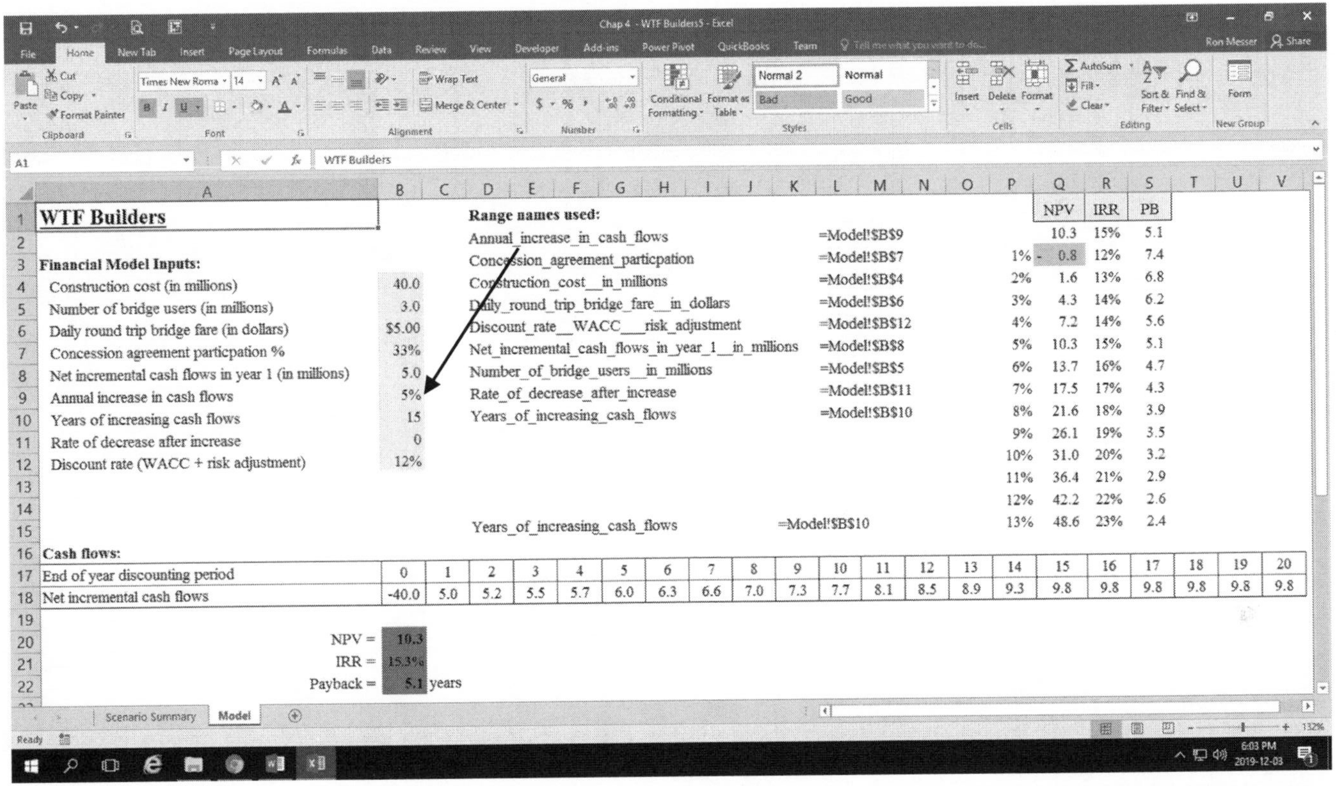

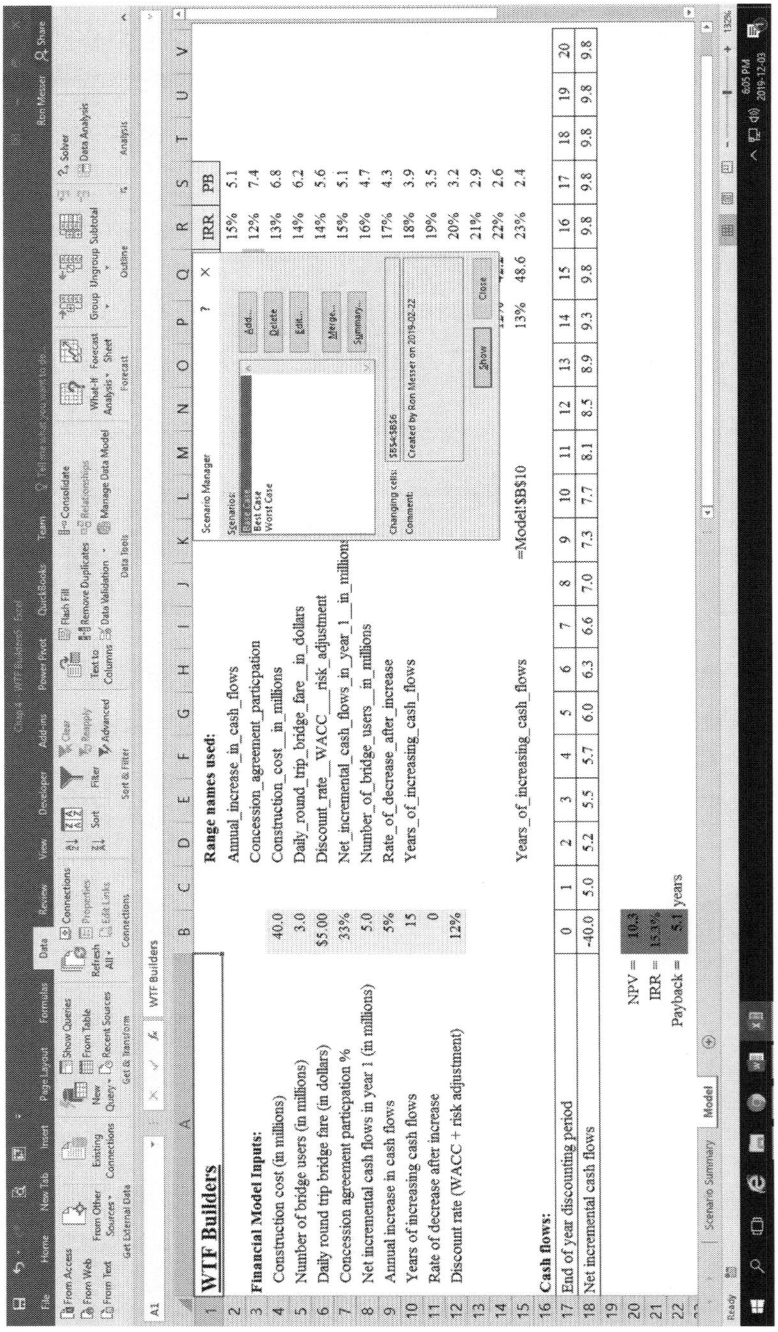

Fig. 4.4. Creating a Series of Scenarios (Step 1).

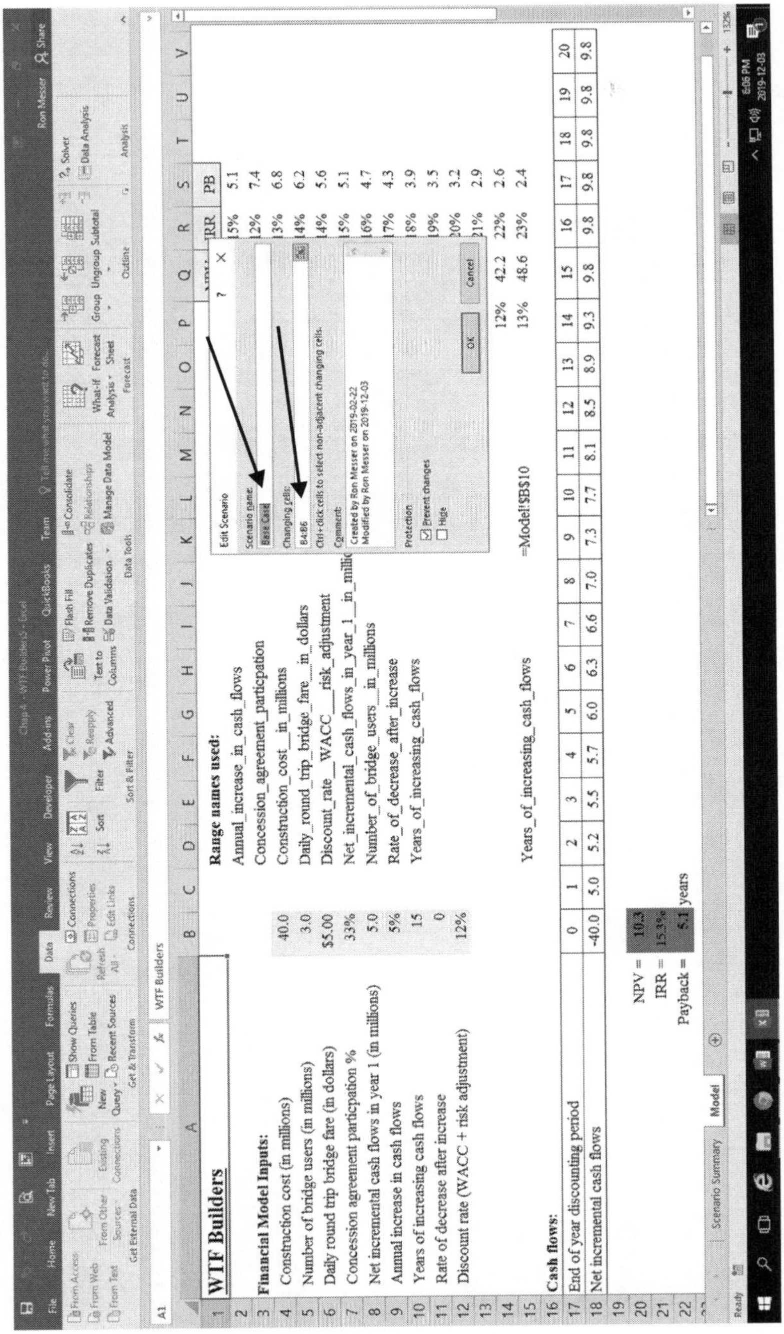

Fig. 4.5. Creating a Series of Scenarios (Step 2).

Fig. 4.6. WTF Investment Base Case Outcome.

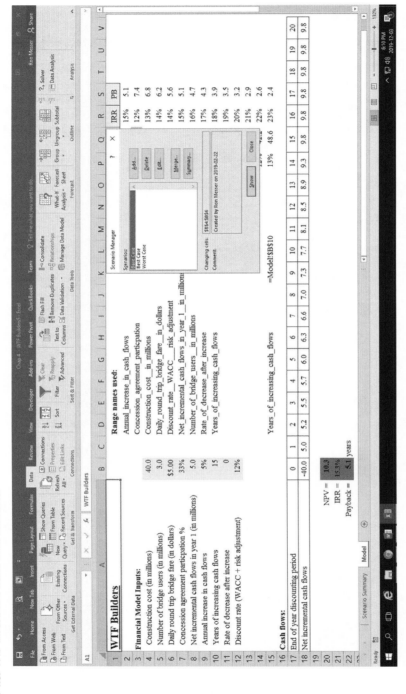

Fig. 4.7. WTF Investment Best Case Outcome.

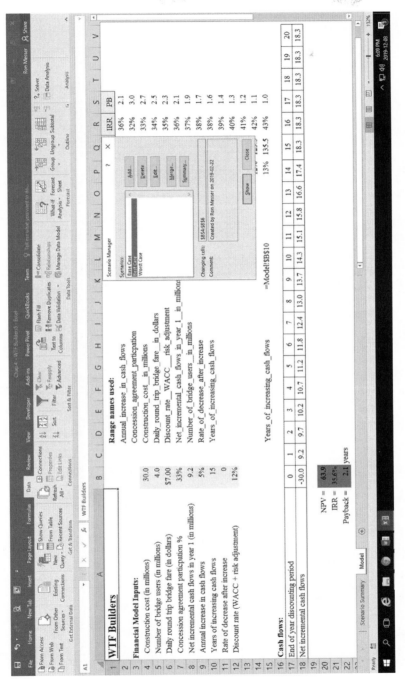

Fig. 4.8. WTF Investment Worst Case Outcome.

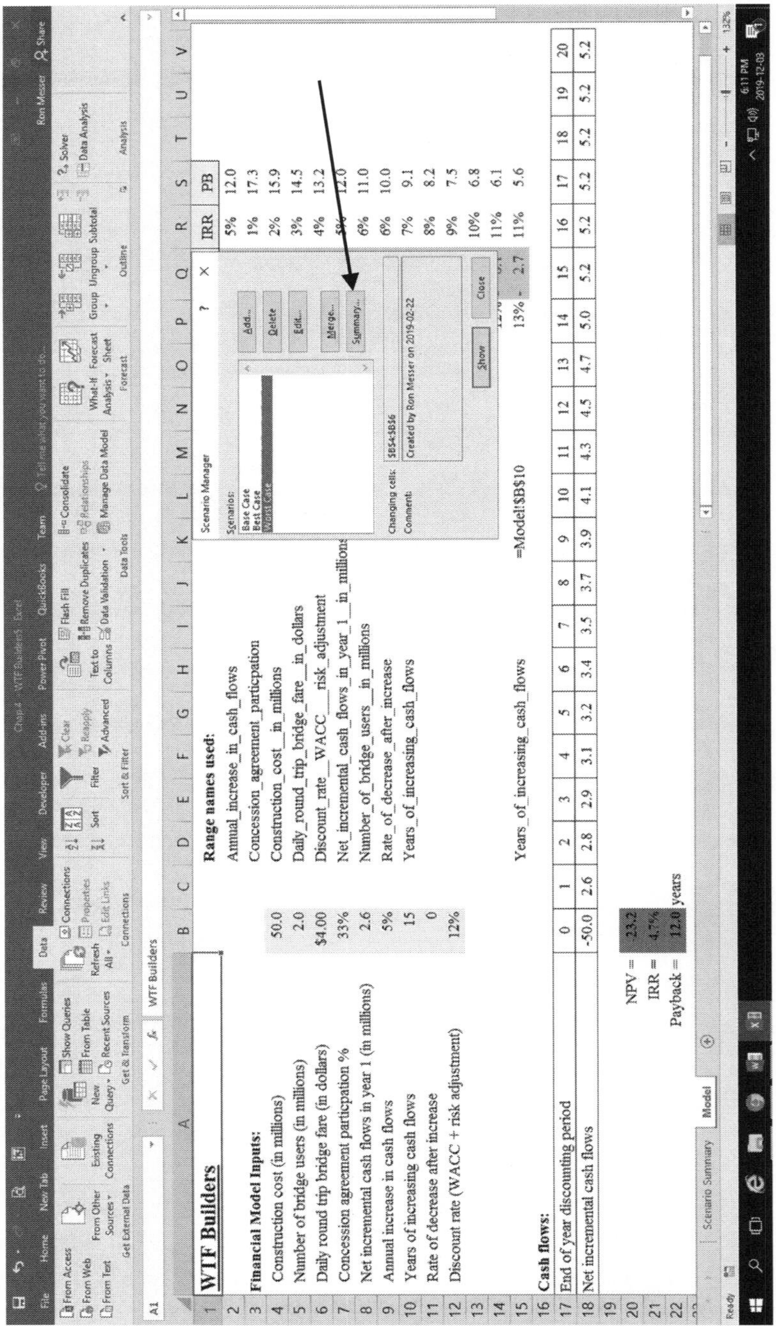

Fig. 4.9. WTF Investment Scenario Summary.

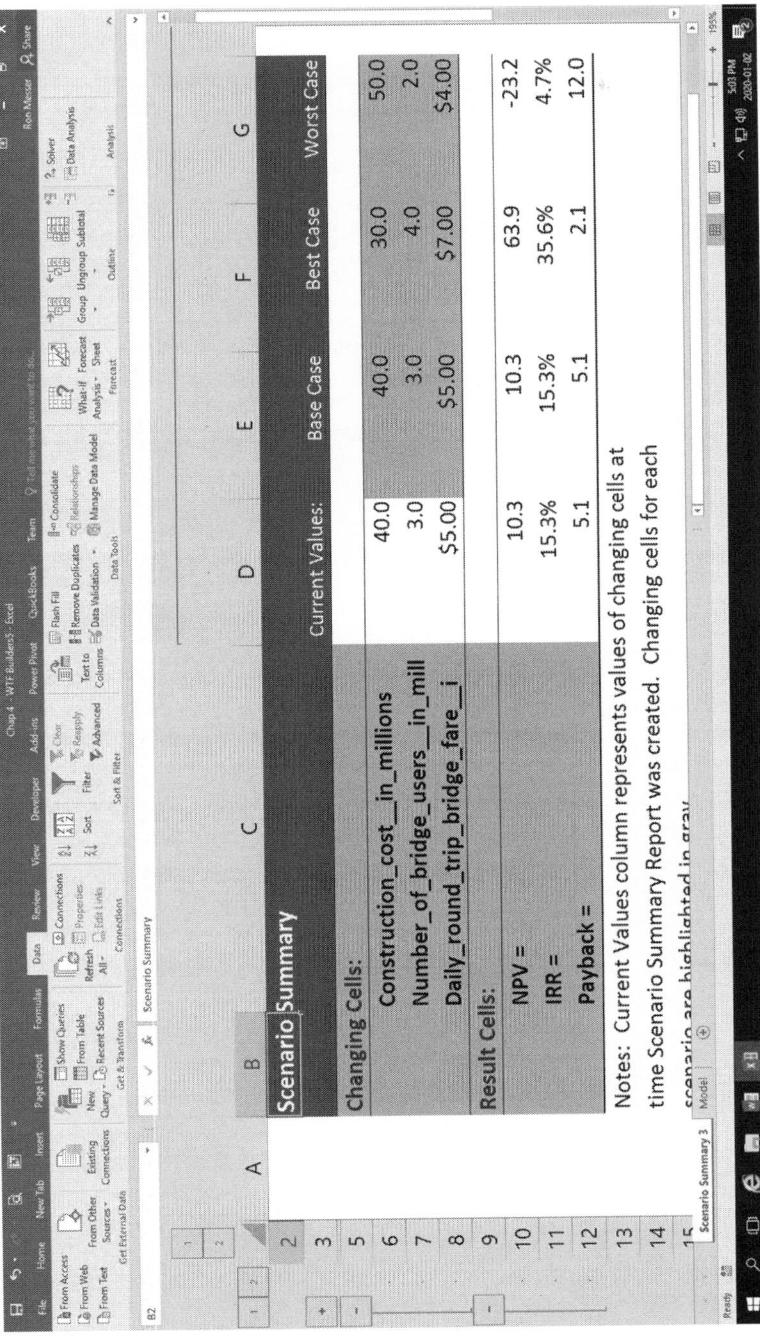

Scenario Summary

	Current Values:	Base Case	Best Case	Worst Case
Changing Cells:				
Construction_cost__in_millions	40.0	40.0	30.0	50.0
Number_of_bridge_users__in_mill	3.0	3.0	4.0	2.0
Daily_round_trip_bridge_fare__i	$5.00	$5.00	$7.00	$4.00
Result Cells:				
NPV =	10.3	10.3	63.9	-23.2
IRR =	15.3%	15.3%	35.6%	4.7%
Payback =	5.1	5.1	2.1	12.0

Notes: Current Values column represents values of changing cells at
time Scenario Summary Report was created. Changing cells for each
scenario are highlighted in gray

Tealeaves, Entrails, and Other Unpleasantness

(*Vegas pros vs Oxford dons*)

Uncertainty is a fact of life. Everyone deals with the unknown in a different way. In ancient times the responsibility for deciphering the future was delegated to shamans, priests and other visionaries. Like modern-day prognostications, predictions of next year's harvest (or DOW index) were closely followed events. Predicting the future was then—and certainly is now—big business (consider the success of futurists such as John Naismith and Faith Popcorn). To do well at this game one must either be right, or at least be convincing.

For example, scientists at Oxford University have developed a computer model that predicts changes in the stock market based on how people play games. Similarly, in Las Vegas, researchers claim that an economic slowdown can be predicted based on the amount of business solicited by those involved in the world's oldest profession (prostitution).

Deciphering random patterns in tealeaves or animal viscera is not unlike trying to predict the future by watching random patterns in stock markets. One does not have to be a genius to talk about, or attempt to predict, the future. In fact, your chances of being right are about as good as mine. Consider this lesson from history.

After developing a theory about how really large objects move, like planets in the universe, Albert Einstein attempted to predict the location of subatomic particles such as the electron by using the same deterministic models, but without success. His contemporary, the Danish physicist Niels Bohr thought about this problem differently and used statistical principles of probability to suggest that there was no specific place to find the electron, but rather a "likely" path to track its movement. Bohr's theory caused Einstein some consternation and reputedly led to his famous remark that "God does not play dice with the universe." Bohr was subsequently proven correct and awarded the Nobel prize.[4]

The lesson we can learn from this story is that you don't have to be an Einstein to make good predictions—just play the odds. Uncertainty is unpleasant, and the future is best understood in terms of probabilities. For example, how probable was it that stock markets would continue to advance on the strength of unprofitable Internet business models? While Oxford dons may ponder over this question, the good folks in Las Vegas have always known that the future is unpredictable, but nonetheless business prospects will probably improve.

---

[4]Bohr–Einstein debates. Wikipedia. Retrieved from https://en.wikipedia.org/wiki/Bohr%E2%80%93Einstein_debates. Accessed on January 19, 2020.

Chapter 5

Regression Analysis Decisions

How did that happen?

Snapshot

Topic
Regression analysis using single and multiple variables

Subject Area
Management accounting and business statistics

Decisions Made
By examining corporate data, relationships between variables can be identified that may be used to explain causation. For example, to determine the best cost drivers for allocating indirect (overhead) costs to goods being produced in a manufacturing plant.

Personal Experience
When working for a large government organization, our division (Finance) was attempting to model program spending for a specific responsibility under the mandate of the ministry. By analyzing data from prior years, I was able to identify a causal relationship between variables affecting the annual expenditures for the program. Using this information, I developed a regression model that allowed me to predict future spending with a relatively high degree of accuracy; this improved financial planning for the organization by significantly reducing uncertainty about future disbursements.

Excel Funtionality

Analysis Toolpack (Add-in)
Regressions
Correlations

Charts
Scatterplots
Trend lines

Background Theory

Finding Correlations

Pivot table analysis is the starting point for identifying relationships between data elements (which is discussed in Chapter 8). Items of interest can be analyzed by using a one-by-one matrix, showing one variable in the rows of a spreadsheet and the other in the columns. At the intersection of the rows and columns, relationships (correlations) can be identified, which can then be used to create predictive models. Scatterplots are useful for visualizing the degree to which two data elements (also known as fields in a data table) move together.

Data can be analyzed to quantify the degree to which one variable moves in relation to another. This is done by creating correlation tables and determining the coefficient (more correctly, the "Pearson moment correlation coefficient," known as the "r"), or relationship, for a number of variables. This correlation coefficient shows the degree to which variables change in relation to each other – i.e., to what extent does an increase/decrease in one result in an increase/decrease to the other. As a heuristic (i.e., rule of thumb), the strength of the relationship between variables can be interpreted as shown in **Table 5.1**. (Note that when $r = 1.0$, there is a perfect correlation and one variable moves exactly in harmony with the other. Correlations can be positive, when variables move in the same direction, or negative, when they move in opposite directions, in which case $r = -1.0$.)

Determining Causation

The metric known as the r^2, or coefficient of determination (which is simply the r-value raised to the power of 2), has greater significance for making predictions because it posits a relationship of causality, whereby changes in one variable are *responsible* for changes in another. The variable being affected is referred to as the dependent variable (sometimes called the response variable), and the variable affecting it is known as the independent variable (or, explanatory variable). Simply put, the larger the r^2, the better the explanation for what causes what. Causation is at the root of predictive analytics.

Regression Analysis

The r^2 is the key measure resulting from a regression analysis; however, there are other metrics produced in a regression report. Along with the coefficient of determination, the following measures are usually generated.

- p-values: This metric tells us whether we can use the data to infer causation. It measures the probability (or risk) that we will incorrectly posit a relationship of causation between the dependent and independent variables when there is no causality. Generally, we are willing to accept a 5% risk (which means that we want to be 95% confident) of being wrong about the relationship (this is referred to as a type 1 error in inferential statistics).

Table 5.1. Assessing the Strength of Relationships.

r-Value	Strength of Relationship
0.0–0.3	Weak
0.3–0.6	Moderate
0.6–1.0	Strong

- Regression equation: This is the straight line (hence, the more correct term of "linear" regression) that best fits the observed values for the dependent and independent variables. The dependent variable is plotted on the y-axis and the independent variable on the x-axis of a two-dimensional graph. It is also known as the "line of best fit" and identifies the coefficient(s) for the dependent variable(s), as well as an intercept on the y-axis when the independent variable has a value of zero (0).
- Standard error: This is a measure of the magnitude of the difference between the predicted value of the dependent variable calculated by using the regression equation and the observed result (i.e., what actually happened). The lower the standard error, the more accurate the prediction.
- Confidence interval: This shows the range of possible values for the coefficient(s) in the regression equation based on 90%, 95%, and 99% confidence levels. (Note that the reciprocal of confidence is the degree of risk; in other words, a 95% confidence interval means a 5% risk tolerance.) Normally, a 95% confidence level is considered sufficient for drawing inferences about causality from a data set.
- Residuals plot: This graphs the difference between predicted and actual results when using the data set. To check on causality, a random pattern should be observed in the residuals.

Financial Management Techniques

Making predictions based on past data involves identifying the drivers of an enterprise's activity, whether these relate to costs or sales. By knowing the business drivers, expectations about the future can be formed. A classic example for manufacturers is the determination of how to allocate indirect costs, or overhead, to production. By their nature, indirect costs must be assigned through a proxy value because they cannot be traced directly to something being produced. Since the cost driver is only an approximate measure, the stronger the relationship between overhead costs and its driver, the better the allocation and hence the costing of the product. Better cost assignment, in turn, means making more informed decisions about product pricing, which ultimately translates into greater sales success for the company.

In developing a predictive model to allocate indirect costs, the following steps are completed.

(1) *Explore potential relationships between variables of interest:* Identifying these variables will be based on the experience of the analyst, oftentimes relying on intuition, or "gut" instincts to examine particular areas.
(2) *Create two-dimensional scatterplots for the variables:* These graphs will show the degree of dispersion of the dependent and independent variables. Plots of variables that are highly correlated will approximate a straight line. It should appear that the data points are increasing/decreasing on the y-axes (dependent variable) as the observations move from left to right along the x-axis (independent variable), assuming a positive correlation.
(3) *Prepare a correlation table for the variables identified:* This will quantify the strength of the relationships between the variables identified – in a cross tabular format – showing the correlation coefficient (i.e., r-value).
(4) *Determine dependent and independent relationships for the variables:* This is the step where analysts frequently experience difficulty in identifying what causes what. This conundrum can be addressed by mentally phrasing two

statements and then assessing which is more plausible such as, do sales lead to advertising expenditures or does spending on advertising result in sales. As the latter statement is obviously more logical, we conclude that sales must be dependent on the amounts spent for advertising.

(5) *Generate a single-variable regression report for each of the independent variables:* The regression reports will show the r^2, standard error, p-values, confidence interval, and the equation for the regression line. These measures are important in determining whether the predictive model will be useful for decision-making.

(6) *Generate a multivariable regression for all of the independent variables combined:* The measures produced in step 5 will also be generated here, except that they will now relate to a number in explanatory variables. In a multivariable regression model, the r^2 should increase and the standard error decrease, in comparison to the single-variable regressions.

(7) *Optimize the predictive model:* Using the multivariable regression report, examine the p-values for each of the explanatory variables to ensure that they are less than 0.05 (5%), which is the standard risk tolerance when we want to be 95% confident about the validity of the results; this is important for purposes of making predictions about the future. Remove all independent variables which have a p-value greater than 5% (0.05) and rerun the final regression model.[1]

With the optimal regression equation, the key metrics from the report can then be interpreted and explained to decision makers.

Relevant Excel Functionality

With the Excel, "Analysis Tool-pack" add-in, a number of statistical functions are available; these are sorted alphabetically in the dialogue box for this feature, in ascending order (a to z). The correlation and regression functions will be used extensively for developing predictive models. **Table 5.2** shows how Excel functionality applies to each of the steps for developing a predictive analytic model using regression analysis.

Demonstration Exercise

Managing uncertainty is all about being able to predict (model) the future. Statistical techniques allow us to do this by using cause and effect relationships that have worked in the past, to make a reasonable guess about future experience. (Excel file: Patrick Enterprises(shell).xls.)

Case Facts[2]

Patrick Enterprises is a small but well-established mechanical engineering company that manufactures industrial goods. Along with several other companies, it produces

---

[1]This method of optimization is only an approximation of the more rigorous process usually undertaken in statistical analysis, whereby changes to the adjusted r^2 are incrementally assessed to determine their explanatory power. This is done through forward, backward, and stepwise regressions.

[2]This exercise is partially based on one provided in Albright, S. C., Winston, W. L., & Zappe, C. (2009). *Data analysis and decision making with Microsoft Excel* (pp. 577–579). Belmont, CA: Wadsworth Publishing Co. The exercise is also used in an advanced management accounting case–based course that I teach (Suregrip Pliers Company) that addresses the use of activity-based costing to determine product pricing in a highly competitive business environment.

Table 5.2. Steps to Creating a Predictive Analytic Model.

Step	Developing a Regression Model	Excel Function(s)
1	Explore potential relationships	Pivot tables and charts
2	Create two-dimensional scatterplots	Charts: scatterplots
3	Prepare a correlation table	Analysis tool pack: correlation
4	Determine dependent and independent variables	(Based on the analyst's experience)
5	Create a single-variable regression	Analysis tool pack: regression
6	Create a multivariable regression	Analysis tool pack: regression
7	Optimize the predictive model	Based on p-values

specialized replacement parts for short haul commercial aircraft that fly regional routes, servicing point to point destinations. The company incurs both direct and indirect costs when making its parts. Direct costs include materials and labor, which are tracked through the company's job costing system. Indirect manufacturing costs are for depreciation on equipment, various lubricants and ball bearings used to maintain the machinery, outlays for utilities such as electricity, heat and water, insurance for the facility, as well as property taxes. As a highly automated plant, indirect costs make up a large portion of the total costs of production. Therefore, determining the best way to allocate these costs is critical for making effective pricing decisions for replacement parts in this competitive business environment.

Because of the specialized nature of the business, manufacturing occurs in small quantities, or "batches." Each batch is part in a production run that is completed on one of three assembly lines, which all use different equipment. Every week a different assembly line, and production equipment, is used. This is done to allow preventative maintenance on the unused machinery, as required by the manufacturer's warranty. (Note that wear and tear is based on the period of usage – i.e., weeks – and not the number of units produced.)

Jordan, who is the new financial analyst at Patrick Enterprises, has gathered data that he believes may be related to indirect costs. He wants to develop a predictive model to allocate overhead and has collected weekly data for almost 2 years relating to the company's indirect costs and what he believes are the relevant cost drivers, including machine hours, labor hours, and production runs.[3] Jordan then proceeds with the seven steps outlined above to create a predictive data analytic model.

Step 1: Exploring Relationships
In this step, Jordan creates three pivot tables showing how machine hours, labor hours, and production runs are related to overhead costs. These relationships are illustrated in the pivot charts below, which show the average spending on indirect costs in relation to each of the cost drivers. (See Chapter 8 for a discussion on how to create pivot tables.)

---

[3]In "real life," collecting this type of data can be very time consuming. For example, each of the company's accounts in the general ledger must be evaluated to determine whether expenses (costs) are direct or indirect.

Figs. 5.1–5.3 suggest a strong linear (and positive) relationship for overhead and machine hours and overhead and production runs, but a weaker correlation between overhead and labor hours.

Step 2: Creating Scatterplots

The trend lines in the pivot charts for machine hours and production runs suggest a positive relationship with overhead. Labor hours appear to show a weak and negative relationship with overhead costs. Jordan next prepares scatterplots to see if these will provide any additional insights (**Figs. 5.4–5.6**).

He observes that the scatterplot for machine hours appears to be trending upward; as machine hours are increasing, so too are overheard costs. The pattern for labor hours is mostly random,

Fig. 5.1. The Relationship between Overhead and Machine Hours.

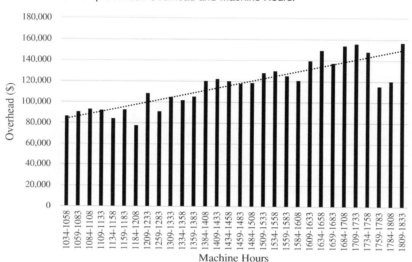

Fig. 5.2. The Relationship between Overhead and Labor Hours.

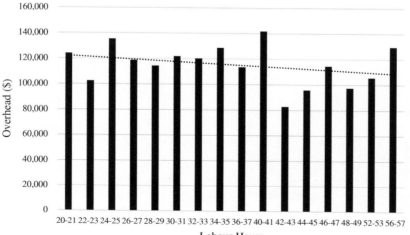

Fig. 5.3. The Relationship between Overhead and Production Runs.

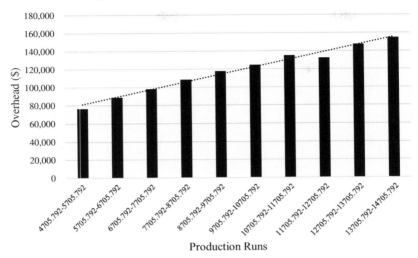

Fig. 5.4. Scatterplot of Overhead and Machine Hours.

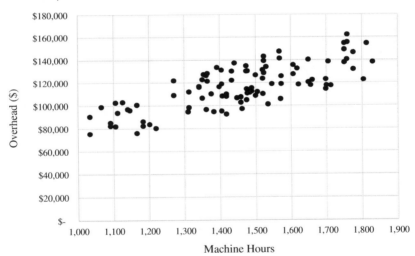

while production runs are trending in a positive direction in relation to indirect costs. Jordan decides to also examine the scatterplot showing the relationship between two of the independent variables: machine hours and production runs (**Fig. 5.7**).

The pattern for these two variables appears to be random, which suggests that they are not correlated; in other words, they are *not* explaining each other. If these variables were correlated, the regression analysis would show a situation of multicollinearity, as indicated by p-values greater than the risk tolerance – which is typically 5%. Multicollinearity is not good for determining causality, as it suggests that the independent variables are explaining each other – and not the dependent variable – and therefore, one of them must be removed from the analysis.

Fig. 5.5. Scatterplot of Overhead and Labor Hours.

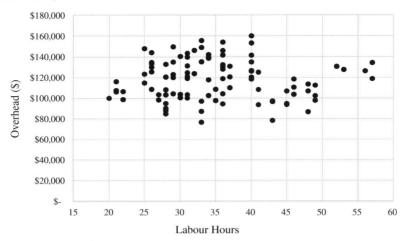

Fig. 5.6. Scatterplot of Overhead and Production Runs.

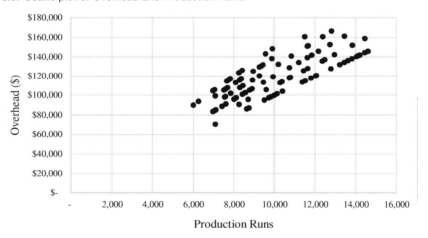

Step 3: Measuring Correlations

Jordan now wants to determine the relative strength of the relationships that he thinks could be potentially significant. To do this, he uses Excel to generate a correlation table. This is done by left clicking DATA, DATA ANALYSIS, CORRELATION, as shown in **Fig. 5.8**.

The selection parameters for this functionality include the data range, along with the header row for the table, as seen in **Fig. 5.9**.

The check box showing "Labels in First Row" should be selected. This will ensure that the output report provides the names of the variables in the correlation table. The default setting for the output is in a new worksheet. This is done to protect the data in the workbook and prevent it from being accidently overwritten. The correlation table for the data set is shown in **Fig. 5.10**. (The areas highlighted in yellow have been provided by the author to better illustrate the correlations.)

Jordan observes from the correlation table that the r-value for overhead and machine hours (0.770) and overhead and production runs (0.779) suggest strong relationships

Fig. 5.7. Scatterplot of Machine Hours and Production Runs.

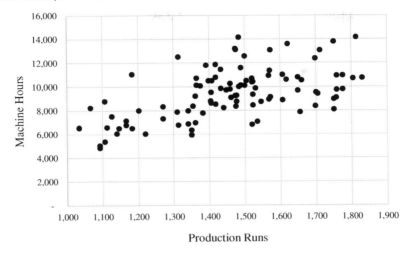

between the variables. However, the relationship between overhead and labor hours (−0.170) is both weak and negative. (Refer to **Table 5.1** on how to assess the relative strength of the relationships between variables.)

Step 4: Determine Dependent and Independent Variables

Jordan observes that because he is trying to predict future overhead costs, based on a single or multiple cost driver(s), indirect costs will be dependent on machine hours and/or production runs, as these variables have the strongest correlations with overhead (as shown in the correlation table). He then uses Excel functionality to create three regression reports, with overhead as the dependent variable and the following independent variables: machine hours, labor hours, and production runs.

Step 5: Create a Single-variable Regression

To complete this step, Jordan left clicks: DATA, DATA ANALYSIS, REGRESSION, as shown in **Fig. 5.11**.

He left clicks OK, and the regression analysis dialogue box appears (**Fig. 5.12**).

In the dialogue box he enters the cell range for the dependent (y) variable for overhead (located in cells E3 to E103), as well as the cell range for the independent (x) variable for machine hours (located in cells B3 to B103). By including the header rows (row 3) and selecting "Labels," the variable names will appear in the output. He also selects, by checking the appropriate box, the 95% confidence interval as well as "Residuals" and "Residual Plots" as part of his report. (This is shown in **Fig. 5.12**.) When he left clicks on OK, the following report is produced. (Note that the highlighted cells have been created by the author to more clearly illustrate the explanations (**Figs. 5.13–5.15**).)

Table 5.3 summarizes the key output metrics from the three regression reports.

Step 6: Create a Multivariable Regression

Based on his analysis of the single-variable regression reports, Jordan concludes that the best explanation for what causes overhead costs are machine hours and production runs. Labor hours are not considered a good explanatory variable because the p-value is in

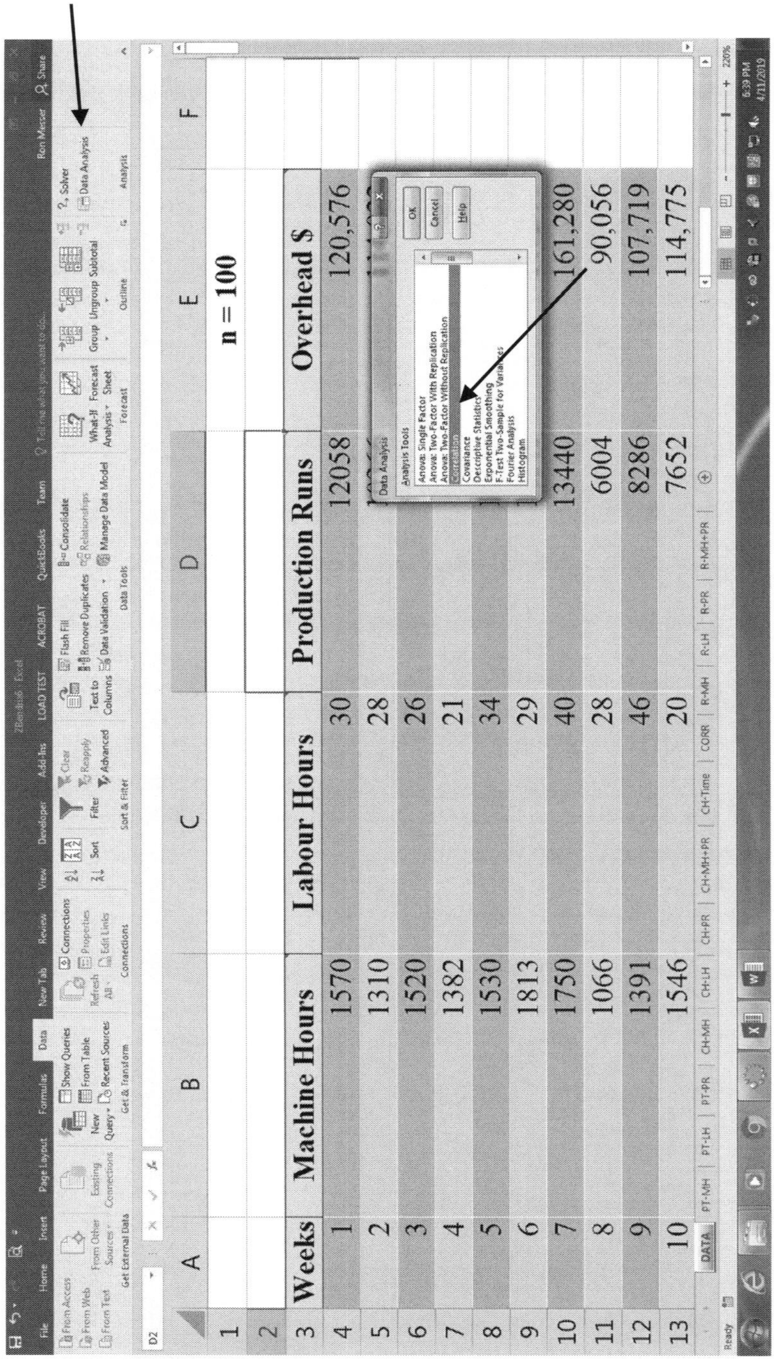

Fig. 5.8. Creating a Correlation Table.

A	B	C	D	E	F
				n = 100	
Weeks	**Machine Hours**	**Labour Hours**	**Production Runs**	**Overhead $**	
1	1570	30	12058	120,576	
2	1310	28			
3	1520	26			
4	1382	21			
5	1530	34			
6	1813	29			
7	1750	40	13440	161,280	
8	1066	28	6004	90,056	
9	1391	46	8286	107,719	
10	1546	20	7652	114,775	

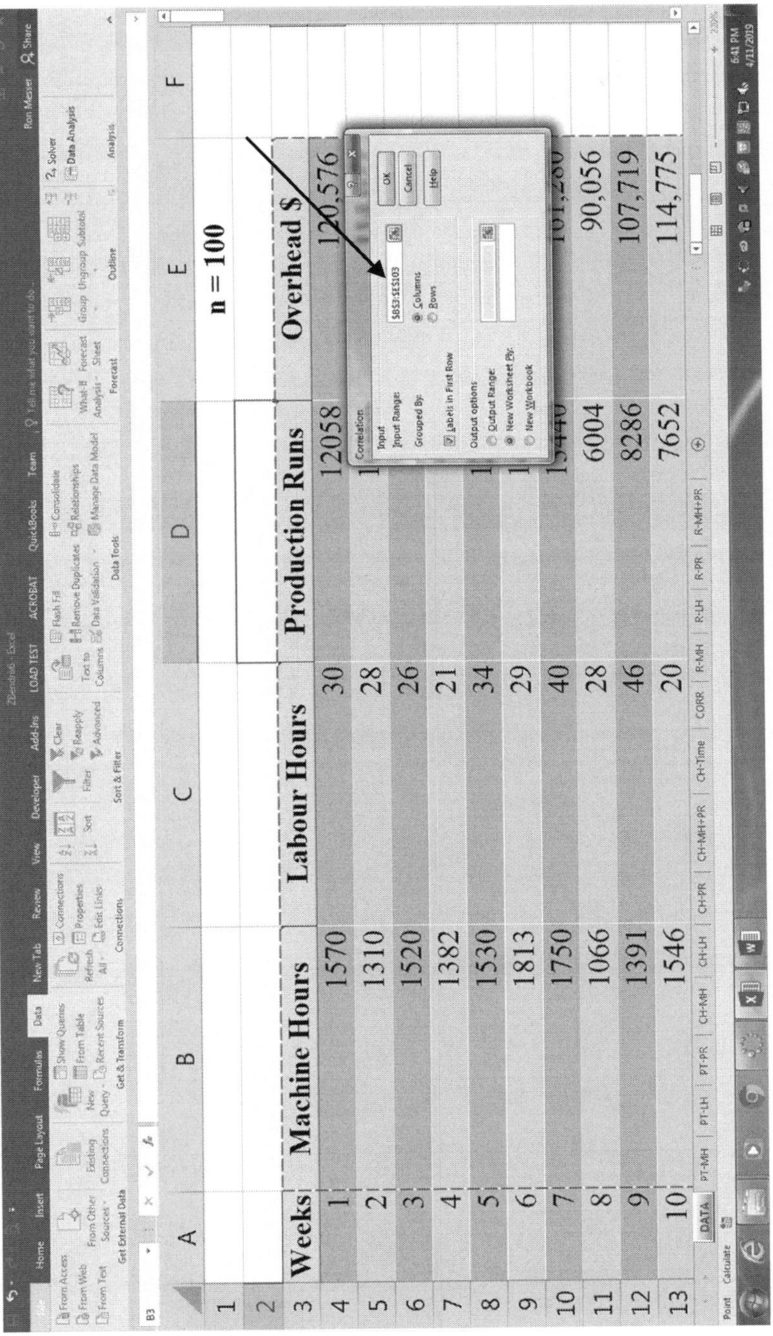

Fig. 5.9. Creating a Correlation Table (Continued).

Fig. 5.10. Creating a Correlation Table.

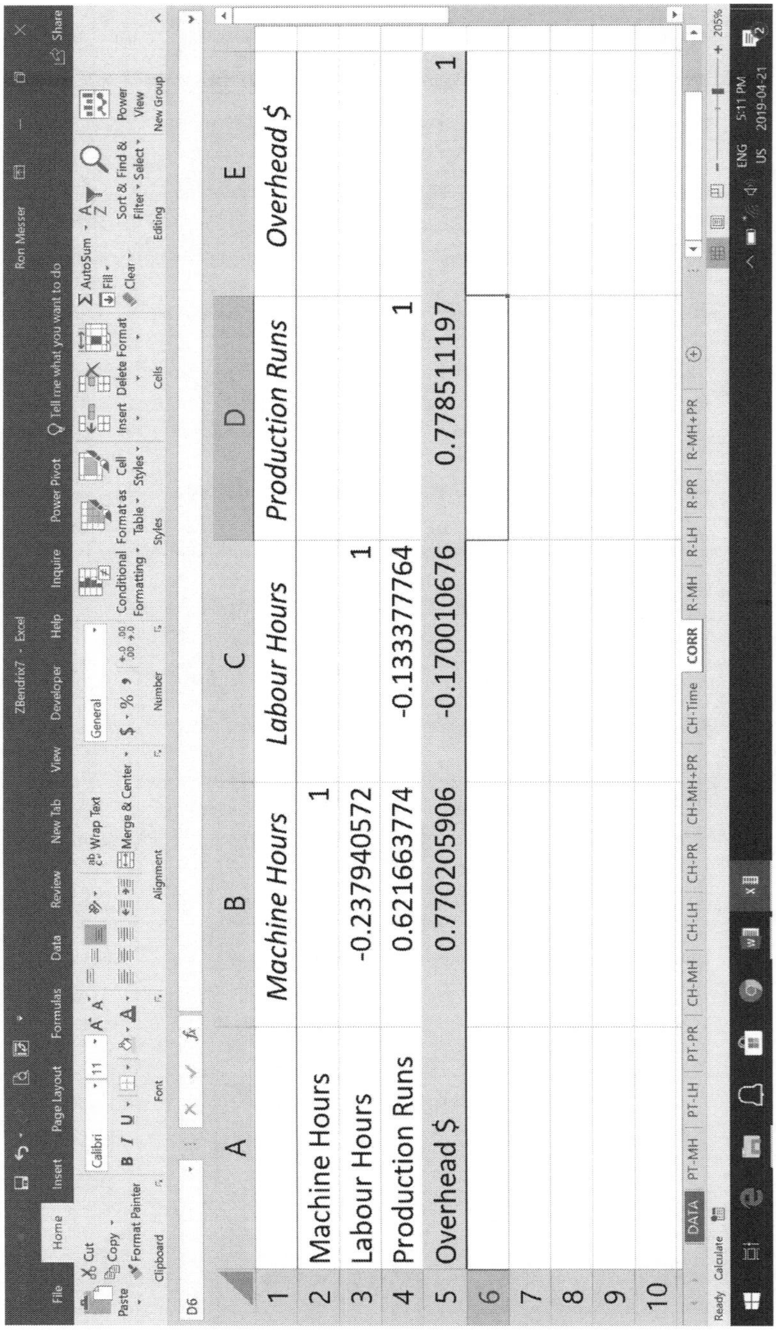

	Machine Hours	Labour Hours	Production Runs	Overhead $
Machine Hours	1			
Labour Hours	-0.237940572	1		
Production Runs	0.621663774	-0.133377764	1	
Overhead $	0.770205906	-0.170010676	0.778511197	1

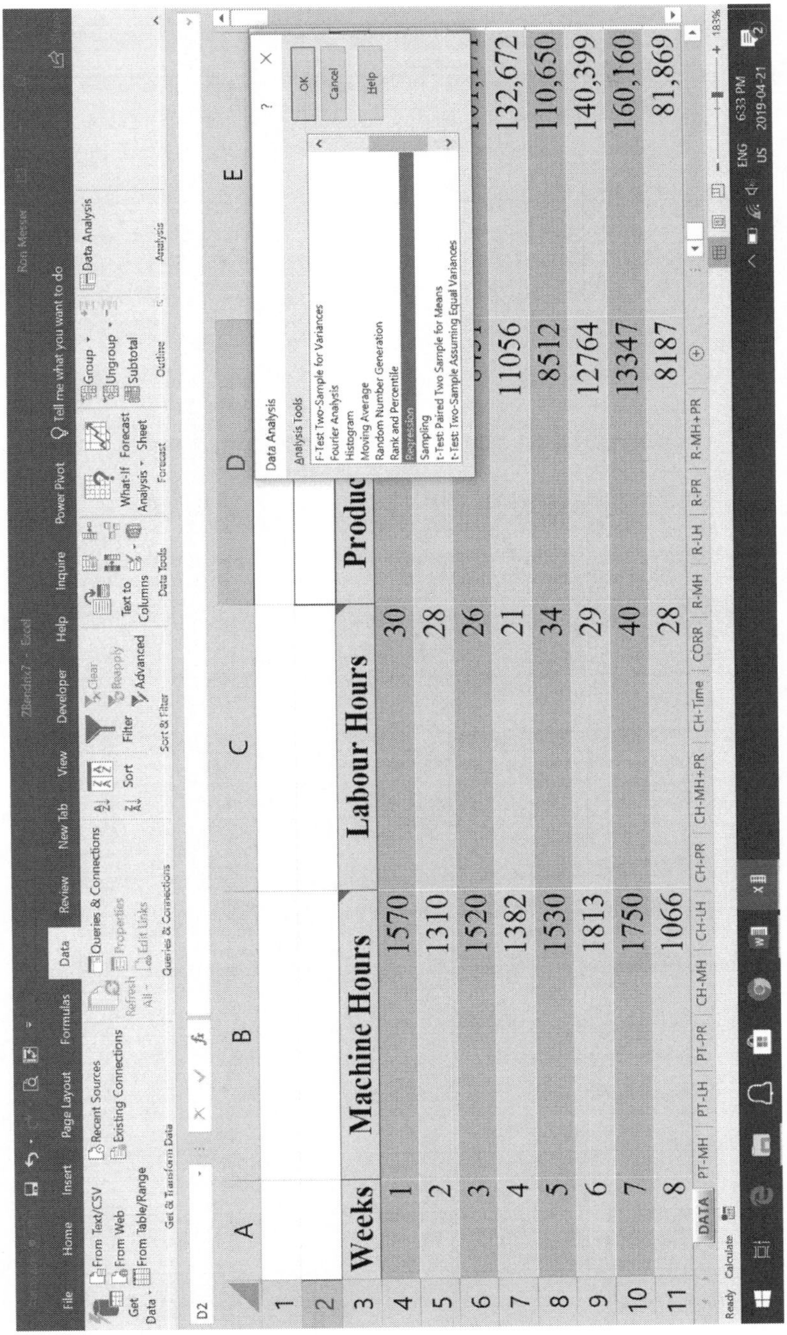

Fig. 5.11. Regression Report for Overhead and Machine Hours.

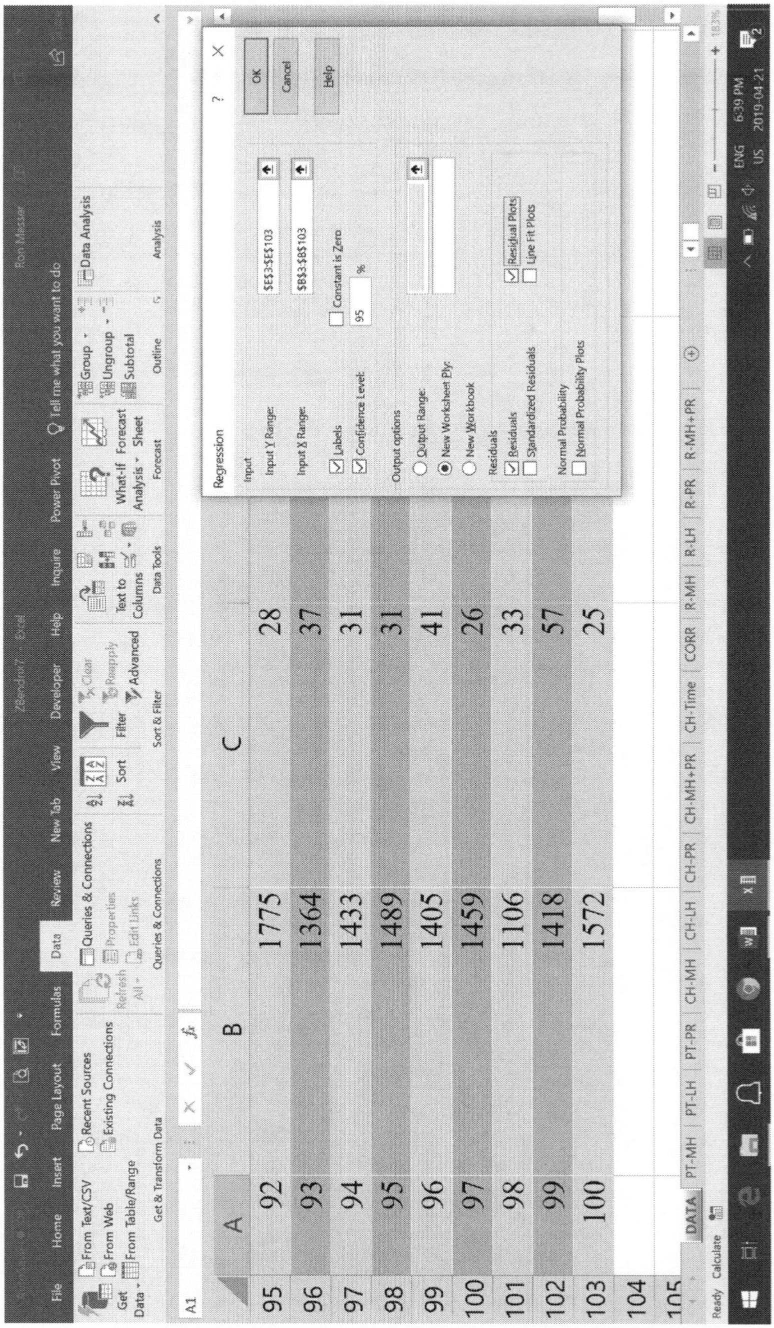

Fig. 5.12. Regression Report for Overhead and Machine Hours (Continued).

Fig. 5.13. *R1* – Regression Report for Overhead and Machine Hours.

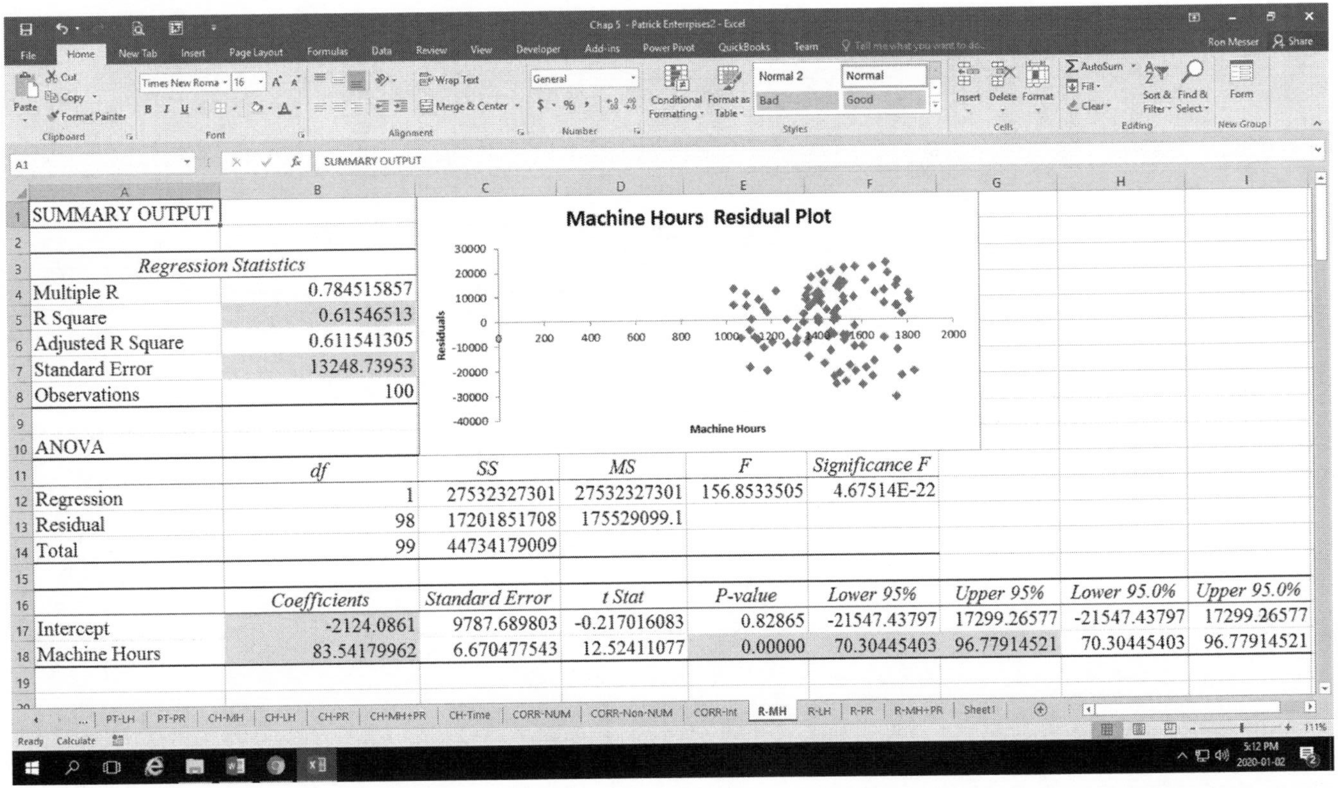

Fig. 5.14. *R2* – Regression Report for Overhead and Labor Hours.

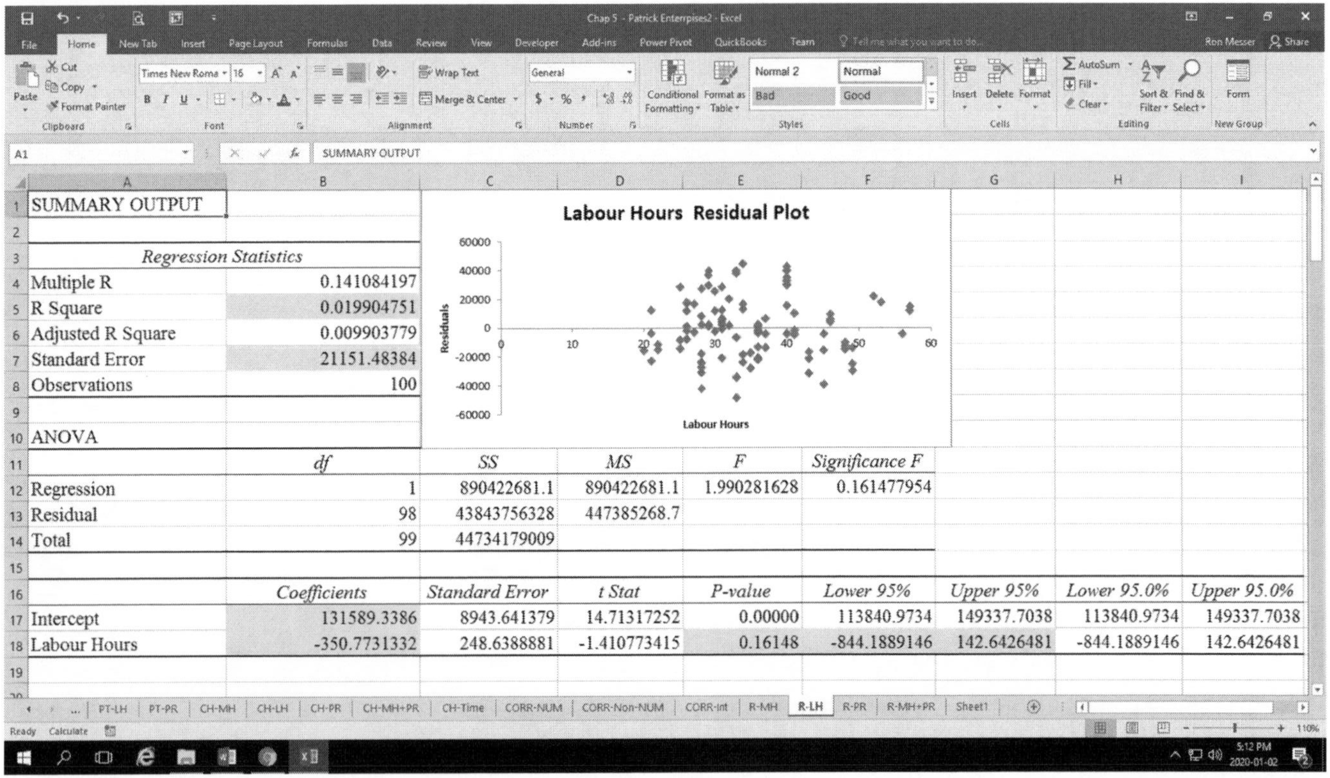

SUMMARY OUTPUT

Regression Statistics	
Multiple R	0.141084197
R Square	0.019904751
Adjusted R Square	0.009903779
Standard Error	21151.48384
Observations	100

ANOVA

	df	*SS*	*MS*	*F*	*Significance F*
Regression	1	890422681.1	890422681.1	1.99028163	0.161477954
Residual	98	43843756328	447385268.7		
Total	99	44734179009			

	Coefficients	*Standard Error*	*t Stat*	*P-value*	*Lower 95%*	*Upper 95%*	*Lower 95.0%*	*Upper 95.0%*
Intercept	131589.3386	8943.641379	14.71317252	0.00000	113840.9734	149337.7038	113840.9734	149337.7038
Labour Hours	-350.7731332	248.6388881	-1.410773415	0.16148	-844.1889146	142.6426481	-844.1889146	142.6426481

Fig. 5.15. *R3* – Regression Report for Overhead and Production Runs.

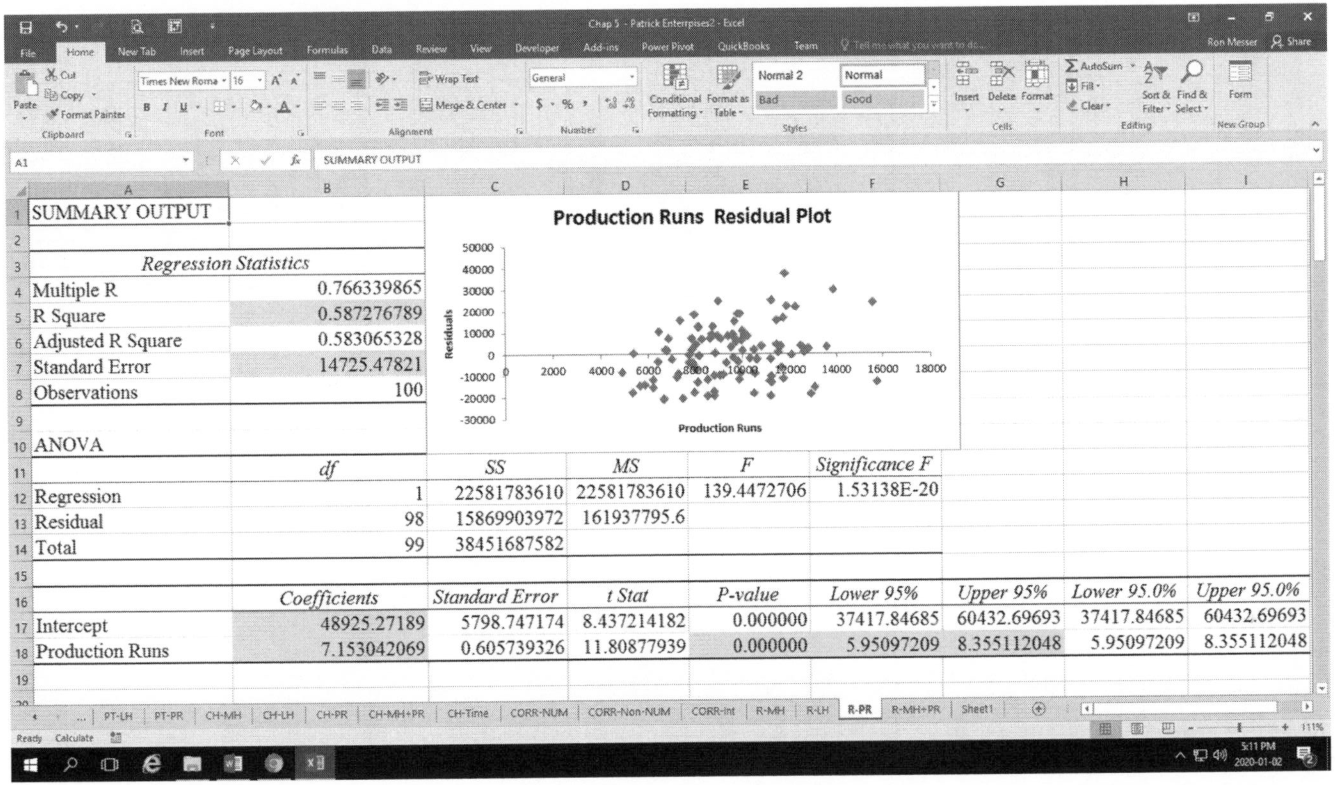
Chap 5 - Patrick Enterprises2 - Excel
SUMMARY OUTPUT
Regression Statistics
Multiple R 0.766339865
R Square 0.587276789
Adjusted R Square 0.583065328
Standard Error 14725.47821
Observations 100
Production Runs Residual Plot
Residuals
Production Runs
ANOVA
df SS MS F Significance F
Regression 1 22581783610 22581783610 139.4472706 1.53138E-20
Residual 98 15869903972 161937795.6
Total 99 38451687582
Coefficients Standard Error t Stat P-value Lower 95% Upper 95% Lower 95.0% Upper 95.0%
Intercept 48925.27189 5798.747174 8.437214182 0.000000 37417.84685 60432.69693 37417.84685 60432.69693
Production Runs 7.153042069 0.605739326 11.80877939 0.000000 5.95097209 8.355112048 5.95097209 8.355112048

Table 5.3. Regression Report Output.

Metric	Value (Rounded)	Explanation
R^2 (Cell B5)	$R1 = 0.62$ $R2 = 0.02$ $R3 = 0.59$	The r^2 shows the percentage of the variation in the dependent variable (overhead) explained by the independent variable(s), where $R1$ = machine hours; $R2$ = labor hours; $R3$ = production runs. For example, for $R1$, 62% of the variation in overhead is explained by machine hours.
p-value (Cell E18)	$R1 = 0.00000$ $R2 = 0.16148$ $R3 = 0.00000$	If the p-value is less than 0.05 (5%), then we can be reasonably sure that there is a relationship between the dependent and independent variables. For $R2$ (labor hours), there is a 16% risk that there is no relationship, which exceeds our 5% risk tolerance and for this reason we reject this independent variable as a possible explanation for indirect costs. (More correctly, the p-value tells us the probability of incorrectly rejecting the null hypothesis – which is a type 1 error. The null hypothesis states that there is no relationship between the dependent and independent variables.)
Regression equation (Cell B17 to B18)	$R1$: O/H = $83.54 \times$ MH $- 2,124$ $R2$: O/H = $-350 \times$ LH $+ 131,589$ $R3$: O/H = $7.15 \times$ PR $+ 48,925$ MH = machine hours LH = labor hours PR = production runs	The regression coefficients for MH, LH, and PR represent dollar amounts relating to indirect costs. For example, $R1$ indicates that for every machine hour used in production, overhead costs will increase by $83.54. The constant in $R1$ ($-2,124$) is the point at which the linear regression equation intercepts the y-axis when MH are 0. It could mean that when no machine hours are being used, overhead costs decrease by $2,124.
Standard error (Cell B7)	$R1 = 13,248$ $R2 = 21,151$ $R3 = 12,725$	The standard error for $R1$ means that if the linear regression equation of OH = $83.54 \times$ MH $- 2,124$ were used to predict indirect costs, the actual result would differ from the calculated amount by about $13,248. Note that for each of the regression equations ($R1$, $R2$, $R3$) as the R^2 increases the standard error decreases. $R1$: $r^2 = 0.62$; $s_e = 13,248$ $R3$: $r^2 = 0.59$; $s_e = 14,725$ $R2$: $r^2 = 0.02$; $s_e = 21,151$

Table 5.3. (*Continued*)

Metric	Value (Rounded)	Explanation
Confidence interval (Cell F18 to G18)	$R1 = 70$ to 96 $R2 = -842$ to 142 $R3 = 5.9$ to 8.3	The confidence interval shows the range of possible values for the coefficients for MH, LH, and PR. What is noteworthy is that the range of values should not include the value of zero (0). A value of 0 suggests that there is no relationship between the dependent and independent variables. Note that the confidence interval for labor hours is -842 to $+142$, which includes the value 0, therefore indicating a lack of causality.
Residuals (Graph)	$R1 = $ machine hours $R2 = $ labor hours $R3 = $ production runs	The scatterplot of the residuals represents the differences between the predicted overhead amounts, calculated by using the regression equation, and the actual results shown in the data table. The plot should appear random; otherwise if it is not — for example, by showing some type of pattern — it suggests that the dependent and independent variables are not closely related. All three residuals plots appear to be random.

excess of 5% (i.e., the risk tolerance). In addition, (1) the r^2 is extremely low, accounting for virtually none of the changes in the dependent variable (overhead) and (2) the standard error is quite large. For these reasons, only machine hours and production runs will be used to generate a multivariable regression report, as shown in the next step.

Step 7: Optimize the Model

When we re-run the regression report to include only machine hours and production runs, the following output is produced (**Fig. 5.16**).

This will be Jordan's optimal regression model predicting future overhead costs, based on anticipated activity levels for machine hours and production runs. In his report to the manager, Jordan notes that the r^2 has been maximized and now explains about 71% of the variation in overhead costs, based on the explanatory variables. The p-values are well below the 5% risk tolerance. The regression equation also tells us that Patrick Enterprises is expected to incur $55.10 of indirect costs for each machine hour used and $4.65 for every production run. On average, by using this equation, our predicted results will differ from actual overhead spending by about $11,787.

Nonnumeric Variables

The variables analyzed in this data set were all numeric, which means they have both ordinal and cardinal properties. Having ordinal characteristics means that the values can be arranged in a hierarchical sequence – i.e., 3 is greater than 2 which is greater than 1; so the numeric – ascending – order is 1, 2, 3. Another numeric characteristic is that of cardinality, or quantum, which means that the numbers represent size, where 3 has greater value than 1. Sometimes data can be nonnumeric and we want to incorporate it into our regression models. For example, Jordan may want to determine how

Fig. 5.16. Optimal Regression Model.

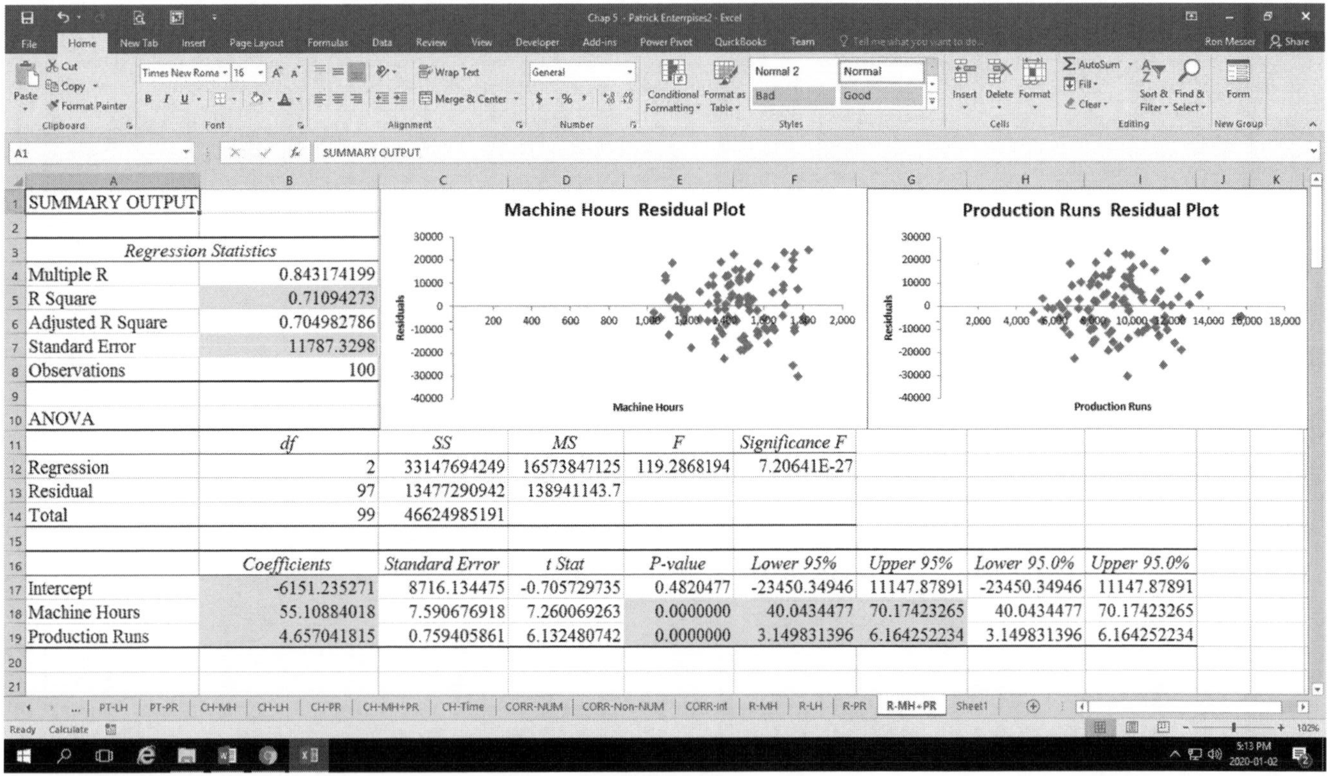

SUMMARY OUTPUT

Regression Statistics	
Multiple R	0.843174199
R Square	0.71094273
Adjusted R Square	0.704982786
Standard Error	11787.3298
Observations	100

ANOVA

	df	SS	MS	F	Significance F
Regression	2	33147694249	16573847125	119.2868194	7.20641E-27
Residual	97	13477290942	138941143.7		
Total	99	46624985191			

	Coefficients	Standard Error	t Stat	P-value	Lower 95%	Upper 95%	Lower 95.0%	Upper 95.0%
Intercept	-6151.235271	8716.134475	-0.705729735	0.4820477	-23450.34946	11147.87891	-23450.34946	11147.87891
Machine Hours	55.10884018	7.590676918	7.260069263	0.0000000	40.0434477	70.17423265	40.0434477	70.17423265
Production Runs	4.657041815	0.759405861	6.132480742	0.0000000	3.149831396	6.164252234	3.149831396	6.164252234

machinery acquired from different suppliers used in the production process affects overhead costs. This is of interest because he already knows that there is a strong correlation between indirect costs and machine hours ($r = 0.77$). So, to what extent are overhead costs related to the type of machinery acquired from different suppliers?

To include nonnumeric variables in a regression model, they must first be transformed into category variables. A category variable has only two possible values: 1 or 0. A value of 1 means that the variable is part of that category and 0 means it is not (i.e., it is a simple binary system for inclusion or exclusion). Jordan gathers additional data for the suppliers of the machinery used in each week's production runs. These are shown in **Table 5.4**.

By using a simple IF statement, values of 1 or 0 can be assigned to the three suppliers. The following formulas are coded into the appropriate cells to accomplish this.

$$\text{In cell G4:} \quad \text{IF(F4} = \text{``Parker} - \text{Hannifin''}, 1, 0)$$
$$\text{In cell H4:} \quad \text{IF(F4} = \text{``Mitsubishi''}, 1, 0)$$
$$\text{In cell I4:} \quad \text{IF(F4} = \text{``Siemens''}, 1, 0)$$

The resulting category variables are shown in **Fig. 5.17**. (The data in column J are a copy of the overhead dollars originally shown in column E. The data were copied because the input for the correlations table must be located in contiguous columns.)

Fig. 5.18 shows the correlation between suppliers and overhead costs.

Based on this analysis, Jordan observes that all of the relationships are weak (i.e., the r-value is less than 0.3) and therefore will not warrant further investigation to determine whether any of the equipment is costlier to operate, for example, because it requires more electricity or additional outlays for maintenance.

Interaction Variables
Interaction effects can also be useful and involve analyzing the impacts of combinations of the following variables:

- A numeric variable and another numeric variable
- A nonnumeric variable and a numeric variable
- A nonnumeric variable and another nonnumeric variable

This is accomplished by creating new fields in the data table that multiply the results of other – two, or theoretically, more – fields together. For example, it may be informative to analyze how overhead spending is affected by the number of hours that particular types of equipment are in operation. **Fig. 5.19** shows how to create interaction variables, by multiplying a numeric variable – number of machine hours (in column B) – with a nonnumeric variable, Parker-Hannifin (in column G).

The results of the correlations for the interaction variables are shown in **Fig. 5.20**.

Table 5.4. Suppliers of Manufacturing Equipment.

Equipment Supplier	Country of Manufacture
Parker-Hannifin	United States
Mitsubishi	Japan
Siemens	Germany

Fig. 5.17. Creating Category Variables.

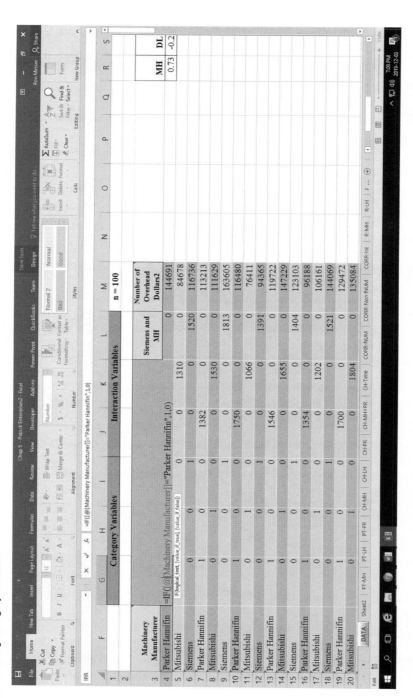

Fig. 5.18. Correlation of Overhead and Nonnumeric Variables (Equipment Suppliers).

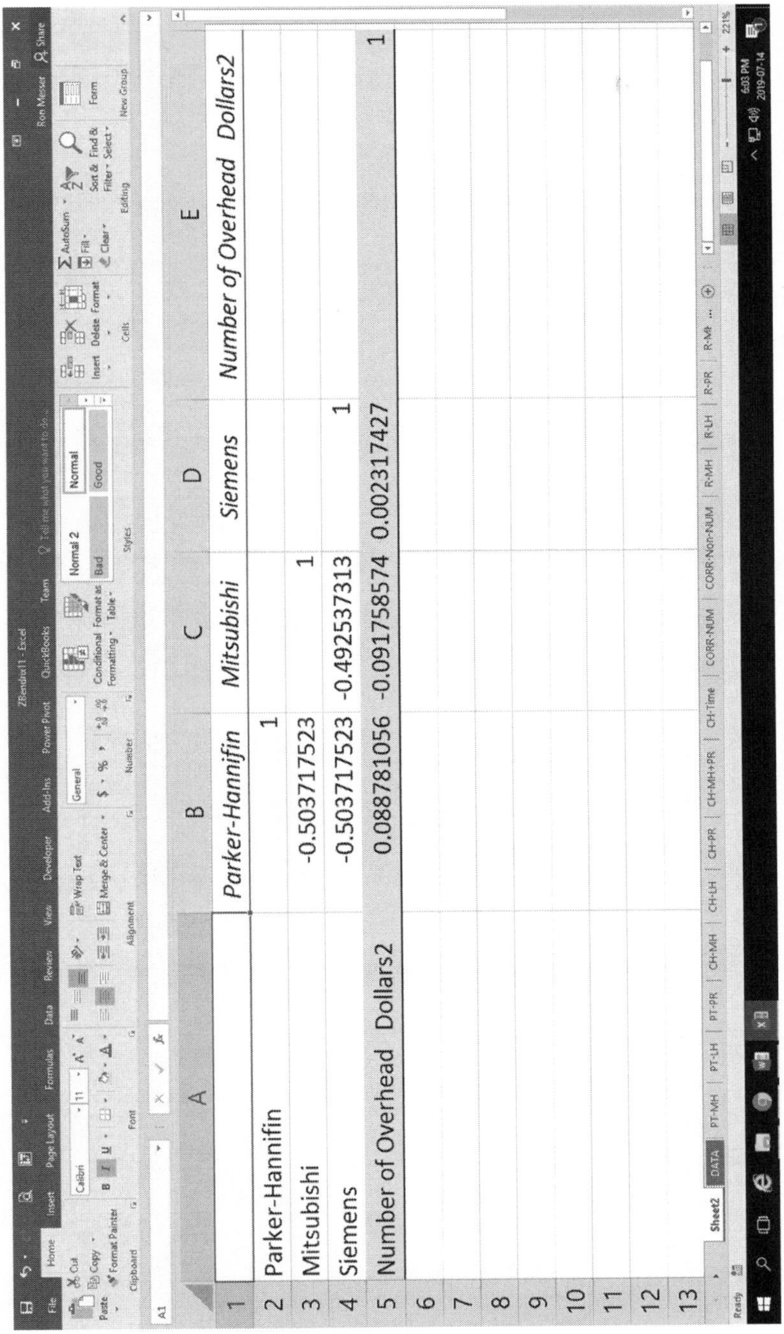

	Parker-Hannifin	Mitsubishi	Siemens	Number of Overhead Dollars2
Parker-Hannifin	1			
Mitsubishi	-0.503717523	1		
Siemens	-0.503717523	-0.492537313	1	
Number of Overhead Dollars2	0.08878105	-0.091758574	0.002317427	1

Fig. 5.19. Creating Interaction Variables.

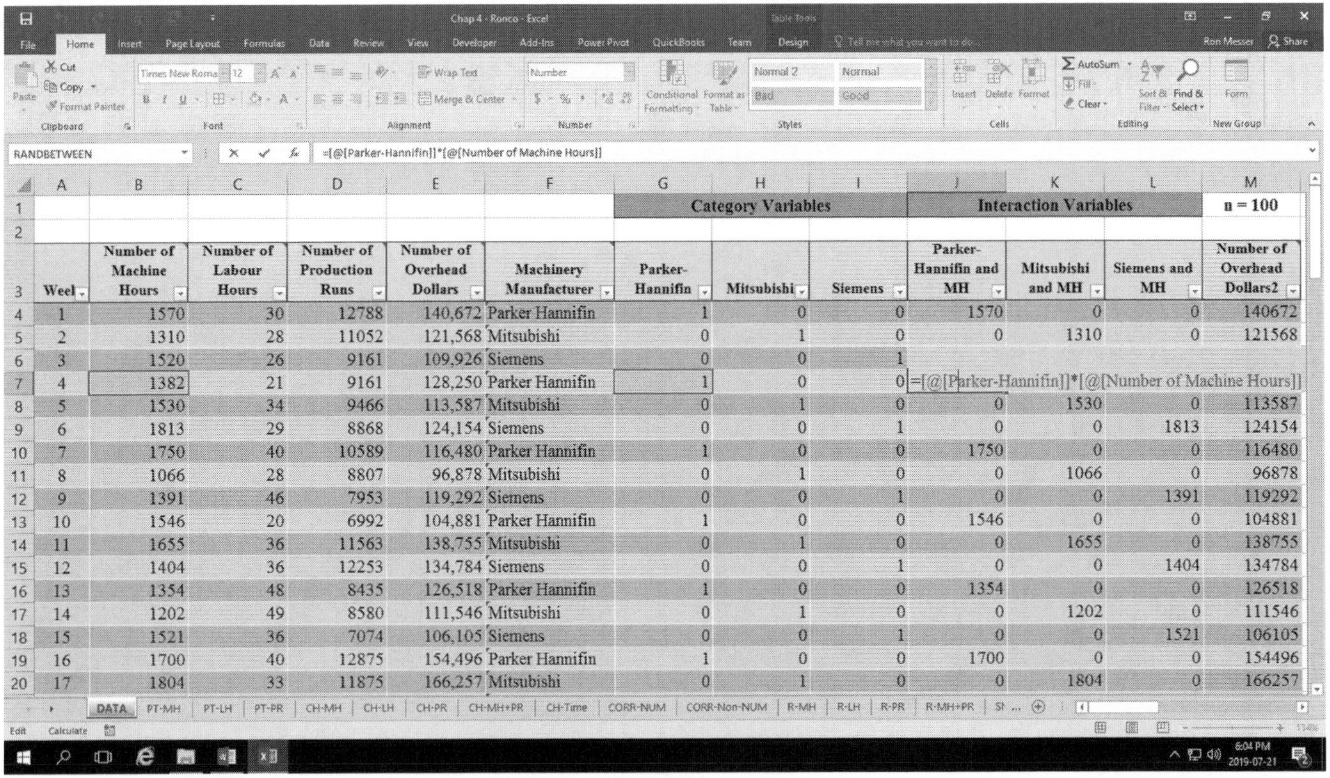
Chap4 - Ronco - Excel
RANDBETWEEN
=[@[Parker-Hannifin]]*[@[Number of Machine Hours]]
Category Variables
Interaction Variables
n = 100
Week | Number of Machine Hours | Number of Labour Hours | Number of Production Runs | Number of Overhead Dollars | Machinery Manufacturer | Parker-Hannifin | Mitsubishi | Siemens | Parker-Hannifin and MH | Mitsubishi and MH | Siemens and MH | Number of Overhead Dollars2
1 | 1570 | 30 | 12788 | 140,672 | Parker Hannifin | 1 | 0 | 0 | 1570 | 0 | 0 | 140672
2 | 1310 | 28 | 11052 | 121,568 | Mitsubishi | 0 | 1 | 0 | 0 | 1310 | 0 | 121568
3 | 1520 | 26 | 9161 | 109,926 | Siemens | 0 | 0 | 1
4 | 1382 | 21 | 9161 | 128,250 | Parker Hannifin | 1 | 0 | 0 | =[@[Parker-Hannifin]]*[@[Number of Machine Hours]]
5 | 1530 | 34 | 9466 | 113,587 | Mitsubishi | 0 | 1 | 0 | 0 | 1530 | 0 | 113587
6 | 1813 | 29 | 8868 | 124,154 | Siemens | 0 | 0 | 1 | 0 | 0 | 1813 | 124154
7 | 1750 | 40 | 10589 | 116,480 | Parker Hannifin | 1 | 0 | 0 | 1750 | 0 | 0 | 116480
8 | 1066 | 28 | 8807 | 96,878 | Mitsubishi | 0 | 1 | 0 | 0 | 1066 | 0 | 96878
9 | 1391 | 46 | 7953 | 119,292 | Siemens | 0 | 0 | 1 | 0 | 0 | 1391 | 119292
10 | 1546 | 20 | 6992 | 104,881 | Parker Hannifin | 1 | 0 | 0 | 1546 | 0 | 0 | 104881
11 | 1655 | 36 | 11563 | 138,755 | Mitsubishi | 0 | 1 | 0 | 0 | 1655 | 0 | 138755
12 | 1404 | 36 | 12253 | 134,784 | Siemens | 0 | 0 | 1 | 0 | 0 | 1404 | 134784
13 | 1354 | 48 | 8435 | 126,518 | Parker Hannifin | 1 | 0 | 0 | 1354 | 0 | 0 | 126518
14 | 1202 | 49 | 8580 | 111,546 | Mitsubishi | 0 | 1 | 0 | 0 | 1202 | 0 | 111546
15 | 1521 | 36 | 7074 | 106,105 | Siemens | 0 | 0 | 1 | 0 | 0 | 1521 | 106105
16 | 1700 | 40 | 12875 | 154,496 | Parker Hannifin | 1 | 0 | 0 | 1700 | 0 | 0 | 154496
17 | 1804 | 33 | 11875 | 166,257 | Mitsubishi | 0 | 1 | 0 | 0 | 1804 | 0 | 166257
DATA PT-MH PT-LH PT-PR CH-MH CH-LH CH-PR CH-MH+PR CH-Time CORR-NUM CORR-Non-NUM R-MH R-LH R-PR R-MH+PR

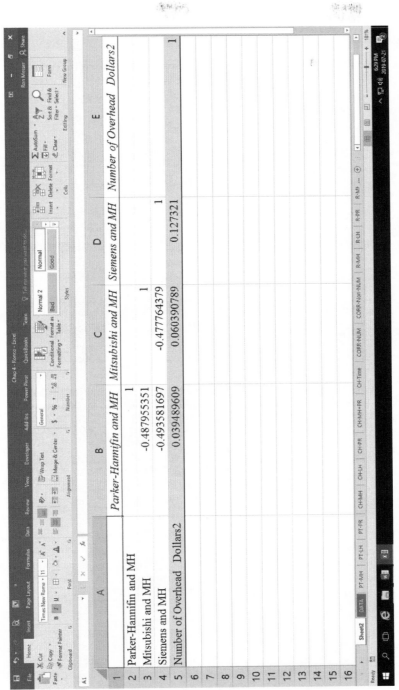

Fig. 5.20. Creating Interaction Variables.

Jordan determines that none of the interaction effects are significant, as they all indicate weak correlations (because the r-values are less than 0.3) and therefore will not be further investigated.

Afterthought → *that's probably normal*

Statistics is a subject dreaded by most students because it involves working with "numbers." While I am hardly a mathematics savant, I have always found that analyzing data to find potentially causative relationships to be quite exciting. Underlying all statistical thinking is the concept of the norm (think: Bell curve) and what it means to be normal. Consider a famous museum ...

What about Norm?

(*Approaching Normal*)

In the foyer to Chicago's Field Museum of Natural History there is a statue of a man called "Norm." The interesting thing about *Norm* is that he is the quintessential average guy – average height, weight, age, income, and so on. Norm is a statistical composite of the American population and is interesting to you and me because he serves as a point of reference. Is your family size larger or smaller than Norm's 2.3 children? Are your shoes bigger than his size nines? Let's face it, we all like to compare.

You may have noticed an interesting phenomenon that has been taking place on the Internet: polling buttons. These are the questions to which readers of online publications respond to see where they stand relative to the "norm." For example, *The Globe and Mail* recently asked whether their readers thought that the US had made progress in Iraq since the end of the war. Of 15,980 readers who answered this question, 78% (including me) indicated that they did not think that the US had made any progress. You can find similar types of questions and responses in just about every online newspaper or magazine.

So, why is this worth mentioning? Well...having a point of reference is important when making decisions. Given the public sentiment expressed in the Globe and Mail poll, the Canadian government may now feel vindicated in its decision not to support the US in its invasion of Iraq. In many business undertakings, knowing where you stand relative to the norm can provide important cues about what you *should* be doing with your products or services. Approaching normal can guide business decisions by framing personal perspectives in terms of those of your customers – such as the traveling public, in the case of airports. Do they feel safe traveling with commercial air carriers? Do they think that airports are more, or less, secure in a post 9/11 environment?

Providing a framework for what is normal means matching your perceptions with those of others. These people can be your customers, your employees, your suppliers or your competitors. As you approach normal you come to a better understanding of their attitudes and beliefs. But more importantly, once you know these, you can begin to predict their behavior, which is a huge strategic advantage for any business. Understanding others means understanding yourself...just think about Norm.

Part 2
Decisions Made about the <u>Present</u>

CONTROL

Chapter 6

Linear Programming Decisions

How can I improve my business?

Snapshot

TOPIC
Linear programming

SUBJECT AREA
Management accounting

DECISIONS MADE
Linear programming is used by businesses to determine how to maximize profits or minimize costs, subject to constraining factors such as resource limitations for materials and labor. It is used in the following decision contexts:

- Product or service mix
- Production scheduling

PERSONAL EXPERIENCE
At a diversified company in the transportation and distribution sector where I worked as an analyst in the corporate finance group, we were trying to determine a pricing policy for using our facilities. Our infrastructure had capacity constraints as well as scheduling issues associated with peak load times. We used Excel's linear programming tool—the Solver add-in—to identify a pricing mechanism that addressed the capacity issues as well as optimized the schedule of activities to provide our organization with maximum revenues.

EXCEL FUNTIONALITY
SOLVER
SUMPRODUCT

Background Theory

Some History

Linear programming was originally developed by the American mathematician and Stanford University professor George Dantzig. It revolutionized the way in which organizations planned their operations. During the postwar period linear programming techniques were deployed to many industries, allowing them to make important decisions about product mix and production scheduling.[1] The original mathematical models used the linear simplex algorithm, which allowed optimal decision-making when constraints were present.

In business, the most common applications of linear programming include determining how to (1) maximize profits and revenues or (2) minimize costs. These decisions will be subject to constraints associated with resources, such as materials (input quantities), labor (time and manpower), capacity (production output), and demand (minimum or maximum sales). By determining an objective function—for example, to maximize the profits for a product line—and incorporating production constraints, an optimal solution can be found.

Product Mix

Many businesses face the uncomfortable decision about allocating capacity among a number of product offerings when they have limited factory scale. Management accounting teaches that, in this situation, we should maximize total contribution margin by optimizing unit margins, subject to constraining factors. While this is a relatively simple calculation when there are only one or two constraints, it becomes more daunting with there are numerous factors to consider, such as restrictions on materials and labor, as well as meeting specific levels of demand.

Production Scheduling

Producing something involves careful consideration of both revenues and expenses. As costs change over time, scheduling becomes an important decision for managers. With an objective of minimizing costs when prices change, and subject to constraints relating to a company's ability to store inventory as well as make products, the decision context becomes complicated by excess inventories carried from one period to the next.

Financial Management Techniques

In management accounting, production allocation decisions must often be made. In this context the objective is to maximize profits, based on total contribution margin. When resources are unconstrained, this can be achieved by producing as much as possible of the product with the highest unit contribution margin. However, when resources are constrained, the decision becomes progressively more complex, depending on the number of constraints. With one constraining factor, the allocation of production is determined based on the unit contribution margin (UCM) of a product (which is the difference between its selling price and the variable costs of production) in relation to a

---

[1]Linear Programming. Wikipedia. Retrieved from https://www.google.com/search?q=who+developed+linear+programming&rlz=1C1GCEB_enCA830CA830&oq=who+developed+linear+programming&aqs=chrome..69i57.6726j0j8&sourceid=chrome&ie=UTF-8. Accessed on January 19, 2020.

constraint, such as available machine hours (MH)—i.e., UCM ÷ MH. When two constraints exist, the optimal solution can be determined mathematically by solving simultaneous equations. When there are more than two constraints, a linear programming application is required.

Relevant Excel Functionality

SOLVER is an add-in to Excel, which is accessed as follows: from the main menu screen,

(1) Left-click on FILE in the upper left corner of the main menu,
(2) Left-click to select OPTIONS,
(3) Left-click to select ADD-INS,
(4) Left-click to select MANAGE EXCEL ADD-INS,
(5) Left-click to select GO,
(6) Select the SOLVER ADD-IN from the check box, and
(7) Left-click to select OK

The SOLVER add-in will appear under the DATA tab in the main menu and will be located on the far-right side of the main menu ribbon. **Fig. 6.1** shows the dialog box when Solver is activated.

Demonstration Exercise 1

Determining the product mix that maximizes profits (Excel file: Screw-it(shell).xls).

Case Facts[2]

Screw-It is a company that manufactures four different types of custom screw drivers (referred to as "custom 1, 2, 3, and 4," respectively) that are used primarily by the precision trades (such as electricians and equipment service technicians). These premium quality tools are made from high-grade materials and assembled largely by hand. A steel rod is superheated and then molded into a custom shape by a stamping machine. After the tool shape has been created, it moves through various cooling and grinding processes, which are mostly performed by individual workers. A hard-coated specialty plastic composite handle is then added to create a secure grip for the tool. Information about producing each of the screwdrivers, along with the maximum anticipated sales volume for the 4 types, is shown below (**Tables 6.1 and 6.2**).

Production is constrained by having only 5,000 hours of labor, 6,500 kilograms of steel, and 11,000 ounces of plastic available to meet demand.

When developing a financial model for linear programming applications, the following steps should be performed, in sequence:

(1) Create the Excel worksheet model
(2) Complete the Excel Solver dialog box
(3) Activate Solver and generate the sensitivity report

---

[2]This exercise is based on one shown in Winston, W. L., & Albright, S. C. (2009). *Practical management science* (pp. 101–107). Mason, OH: Cengage Learning. The exercise is also part of a case discussion (Suregrip Pliers Company) used in my advanced management accounting course.

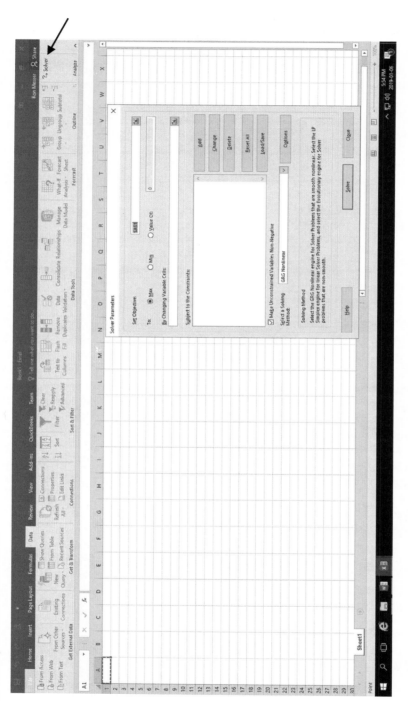

Fig. 6.1. Loading the Excel Solver Add-in.

Table 6.1. Screw-It Case Facts—Unit Input Quantities and Costs.

Screwdriver	Labor (hrs)	Labor ($8/hr)	Steel (kg)	Steel ($0.50/kg)	Plastic (oz)	Plastic ($0.75/oz)
Custom 1	2.0	$16.00	3.0	$1.50	4.0	$3.00
Custom 2	1.0	$8.00	1.0	$0.50	1.0	$0.75
Custom 3	2.5	$20.00	4.0	$2.00	5.0	$3.75
Custom 4	2.0	$16.00	2.0	$1.00	3.0	$2.25

Table 6.2. Screw-It Case Facts—Unit Selling Prices and Sales Volumes.

Screwdriver	Unit Price ($)	Total Sales (Units)
Custom 1	$26.00	1,000
Custom 2	$12.50	2,000
Custom 3	$31.50	500
Custom 4	$21.50	1,000

Note that *each* of the three modeling steps must be completed *entirely* before proceeding to the next. Many students will be tempted to partially complete step 1 (the Excel worksheet) and then move onto step 2. However, they soon realize that this cannot be done until the financial model in step 1 has been finished. This important point needs to be emphasized when completing the demonstration exercise.

Step 1: Create the Excel Worksheet Model
The first step in this process, which incorporates the case facts for Screw-It (from **Table 6.1**) appears in **Fig. 6.2**.

The formulas used to build this model are shown in the next worksheet (**Fig.. 6.3**).

Note the following:

- Use the SUMPRODUCT function (cells B21, B22, and B23) to determine the quantity of the constrained resources used.
- Use appropriate relative and absolute references when copying the formulas to determine the costs of inputs for labor, steel and plastic (cells B29 to E31).
- For the decision variable, screwdrivers produced (cells B16, C16, D16, and E16 in **Fig. 6.2**), use trial values such as 100, 200, 300, and 400 (note that **Fig. 6.2** already shows the optimal production plan).

Step 2: Complete the Excel Solver Dialog Box
In this step, the Solver dialog box is activated, as shown in **Fig. 6.4**. The following is done to complete the dialog box.

(1) In "Set Objective," reference the objective function (which is contained in the dark gray shaded cell F32), which is the calculation of profit, measured as total contribution margin.

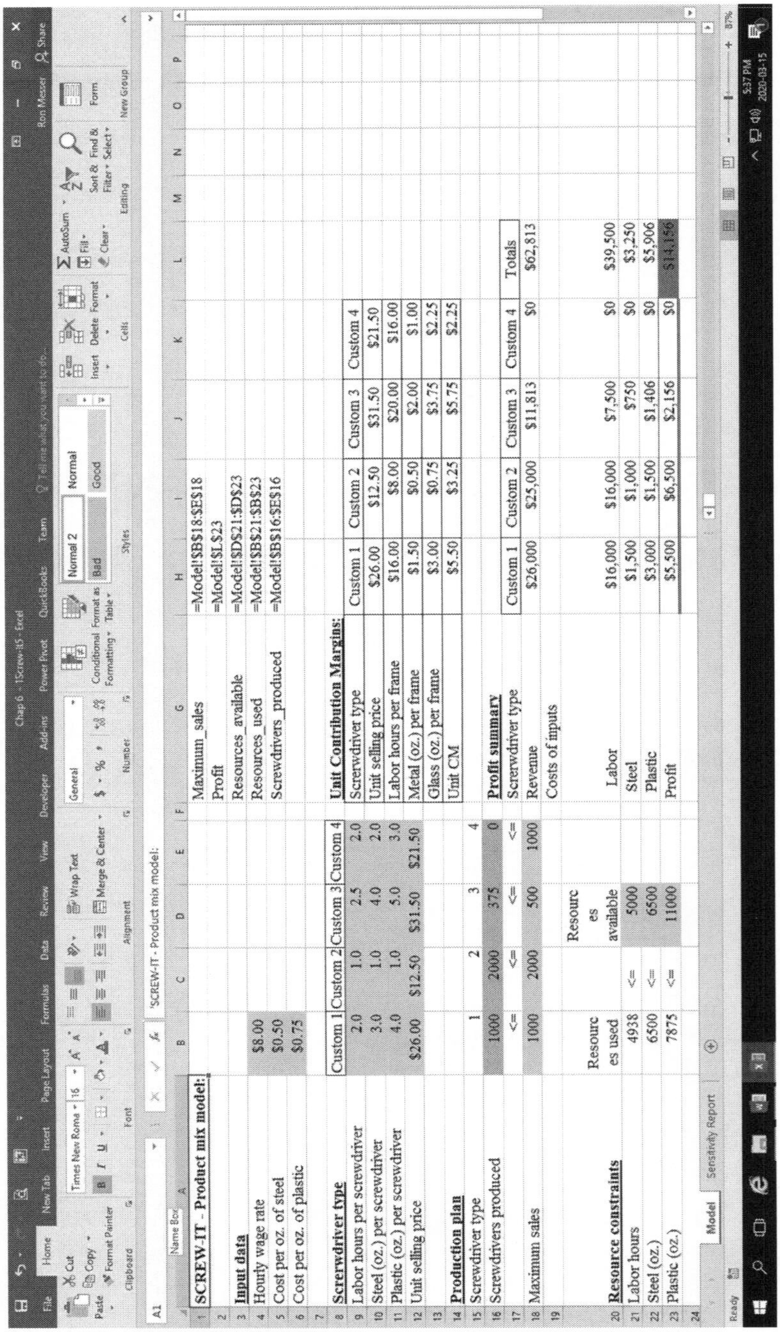

Fig. 6.2. Step 1—Creating the Excel Worksheet.

SCREW-IT - Product mix model:

Input data

Hourly wage rate	$8.00
Cost per oz. of steel	$0.50
Cost per oz. of plastic	$0.75

Screwdriver type

	Custom 1	Custom 2	Custom 3	Custom 4
Labor hours per screwdriver	2.0	1.0	2.5	2.0
Steel (oz.) per screwdriver	3.0	4.0	4.0	2.0
Plastic (oz.) per screwdriver	4.0	1.0	5.0	3.0
Unit selling price	$26.00	$12.50	$31.50	$21.50

Production plan

	1	2	3	4
Screwdriver type				
Screwdrivers produced	1000	2000	375	0
	<=	<=	<=	<=
Maximum sales	1000	2000	500	1000

Resource constraints

	Resources used		Resources available
Labor hours	4938	<=	5000
Steel (oz.)	6500	<=	6500
Plastic (oz.)	7875	<=	11000

Maximum_sales	=Model!$B$18:$E$18
Profit	=Model!$L$23
Resources available	=Model!$D$21:$D$23
Resources used	=Model!$B$21:$B$23
Screwdrivers produced	=Model!$B$16:$E$16

Unit Contribution Margins:

Screwdriver type	Custom 1	Custom 2	Custom 3	Custom 4
Unit selling price	$26.00	$12.50	$31.50	$21.50
Labor hours per frame	$16.00	$8.00	$20.00	$16.00
Metal (oz.) per frame	$1.50	$0.50	$2.00	$1.00
Glass (oz.) per frame	$3.00	$0.75	$3.75	$2.25
Unit CM	$5.50	$3.25	$5.75	$2.25

Profit summary

Screwdriver type	Custom 1	Custom 2	Custom 3	Custom 4	Totals
Revenue	$26,000	$25,000	$11,813	$0	$62,813
Costs of inputs					
Labor	$16,000	$16,000	$7,500	$0	$39,500
Steel	$1,500	$1,000	$750	$0	$3,250
Plastic	$3,000	$1,500	$1,406	$0	$5,906
Profit	$5,500	$6,500	$2,156	$0	$14,156

Fig. 6.3. Step 1—Formulas for Creating the Excel Worksheet.

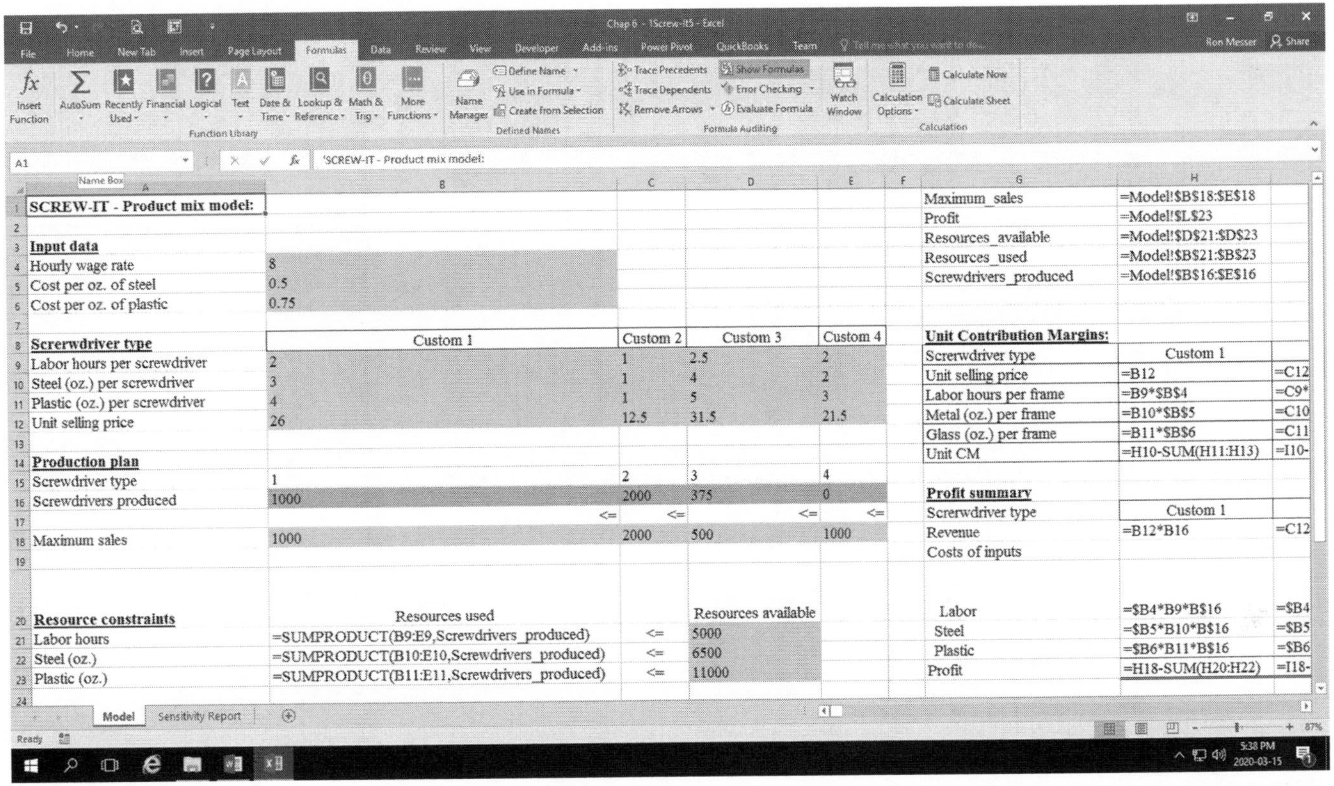
Chap 6 - 1Screw-It5 - Excel
File Home New Tab Insert Page Layout Formulas Data Review View Developer Add-ins Power Pivot QuickBooks Team
Ron Messer Share
Insert Function AutoSum Recently Used Financial Logical Text Date & Time Lookup & Reference Math & Trig More Functions
Function Library
Name Manager Define Name Use in Formula Create from Selection
Defined Names
Trace Precedents Trace Dependents Remove Arrows Show Formulas Error Checking Evaluate Formula
Formula Auditing
Watch Window Calculation Options Calculate Now Calculate Sheet
Calculation
A1
'SCREW-IT - Product mix model:
SCREW-IT - Product mix model:
Input data
Hourly wage rate 8
Cost per oz. of steel 0.5
Cost per oz. of plastic 0.75
Screrwdriver type Custom 1 Custom 2 Custom 3 Custom 4
Labor hours per screwdriver 2 1 2.5 2
Steel (oz.) per screwdriver 3 1 4 2
Plastic (oz.) per screwdriver 4 1 5 3
Unit selling price 26 12.5 31.5 21.5
Production plan
Screwdriver type 1 2 3 4
Screwdrivers produced 1000 2000 375 0
<= <= <= <=
Maximum sales 1000 2000 500 1000
Resource constraints
Resources used
Resources available
Labor hours =SUMPRODUCT(B9:E9,Screwdrivers_produced) <= 5000
Steel (oz.) =SUMPRODUCT(B10:E10,Screwdrivers_produced) <= 6500
Plastic (oz.) =SUMPRODUCT(B11:E11,Screwdrivers_produced) <= 11000
Maximum_sales =Model!$B$18:$E$18
Profit =Model!$L$23
Resources_available =Model!$D$21:$D$23
Resources_used =Model!$B$21:$B$23
Screwdrivers_produced =Model!$B$16:$E$16
Unit Contribution Margins:
Screrwdriver type Custom 1
Unit selling price =B12 =C12
Labor hours per frame =B9*$B$4 =C9*
Metal (oz.) per frame =B10*$B$5 =C10
Glass (oz.) per frame =B11*$B$6 =C11
Unit CM =H10-SUM(H11:H13) =I10-
Profit summary
Screrwdriver type Custom 1
Revenue =B12*B16 =C12
Costs of inputs
Labor =$B4*B9*B$16 =$B4
Steel =$B5*B10*B$16 =$B5
Plastic =$B6*B11*B$16 =$B6
Profit =H18-SUM(H20:H22) =I18-
Model Sensitivity Report
Ready
5:38 PM 2020-03-15

Fig. 6.4. Step 2—Complete the Excel Solver Dialog Box (Objective).

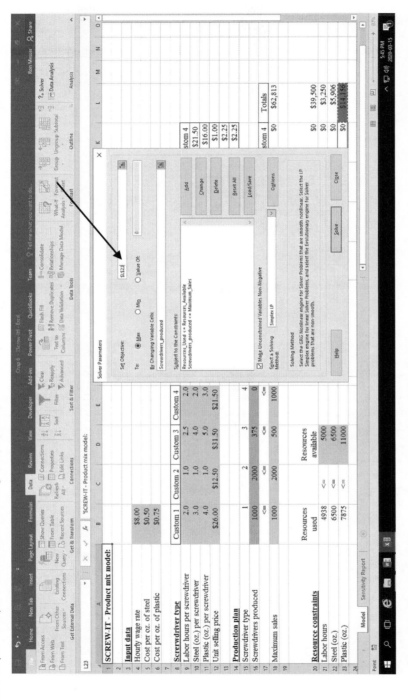

(2) The default setting is to maximize ("Max") the objective function, which is also the purpose for the financial model. (Note that it is critically important to be sure of the intended objective of your modeling exercise, as in some situations the purpose may be to minimize, i.e., "Min," costs, or to achieve a specific value, i.e., "Value Of.")

(3) Indicate the named range for the decision variable (described as "by changing variable cells" in the dialog box). In this model, the medium gray colored cells (B16 to E16) represent the decision concerning the allocation of production for each of the four types of screwdrivers (named range = "screwdrivers_produced").

(4) Outline the constraints in the model. In this case, they relate to labor hours, materials (steel and plastic) and (maximum) demand (sales constraint). This can be done by left-clicking on the "ADD" button and the screen shown in **Fig. 6.5** will appear. This portion of the dialog box allows the user to outline the constraining factors, which is done by providing the (1) cell references, (2) direction of the equality/inequality, and (3) values associated with the constraint (as shown in **Fig. 6.5**, under "Subject to the Constraints").

Named ranges have been created for the constraints associated with labor, materials, and sales demand. Once steps 1 and 2 have been completed, left-click on the "Solve" button at the bottom of the Solver dialog box, and the screen in **Fig. 6.6** will appear.

Under "Reports," select "Sensitivity" and then left click OK. The optimal solution appears in **Fig. 6.7** and the sensitivity report is shown in **Fig. 6.8**.

The optimal production plan results in a total profit of $14,156, where the custom 1 and 2 products meet the market demand, the custom 3 screwdriver—at 375 units produced—is less than the expected market requirement and custom 4 is not produced.

Step 3: Activate Solver and Generate the Sensitivity Report
Two important metrics appear in the sensitivity report:

(1) The shadow price.
(2) The reduced cost.

The shadow price indicates how the objective function will change when one more unit of the constraining resource is made available. For example, the report shows that of the 6,500 kg of steel that can be used for production (noted as the "Constraint R.H. Side"), all of the material was employed in the optimal production plan. The shadow price of 1.4375 (rounded to 1.44) tell us that if we were to acquire one more kg of steel, our profits would increase by $1.44. Also, if we had one less unit of steel available, our profit would decrease by $1.44. This holds true for each kg of steel, up to an additional 100 kg and for a reduction of up to 1,500 kg of the material. (It is a good idea to test this interpretation of the sensitivity report by making the appropriate changes to the worksheet model—for example, increasing the steel constraint from 6,500 kg to 6,501 kg—and then rerunning Solver to see if the profit increases by exactly $1.44, as we would expect.)

Note that resources for both labor hours and plastic have not been fully utilized in the optimal solution. For this reason, the shadow price appears as zero (0) and the allowable decease for both, when deducted from the "Constraint R.H. Side," will be

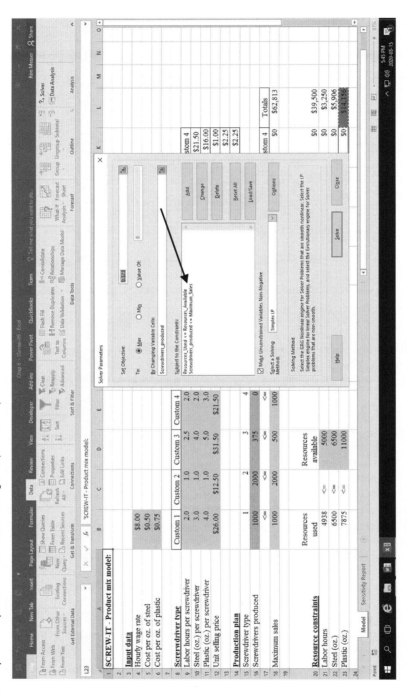

Fig. 6.5. Step 2—Complete the Excel Solver Dialog Box (Constraints).

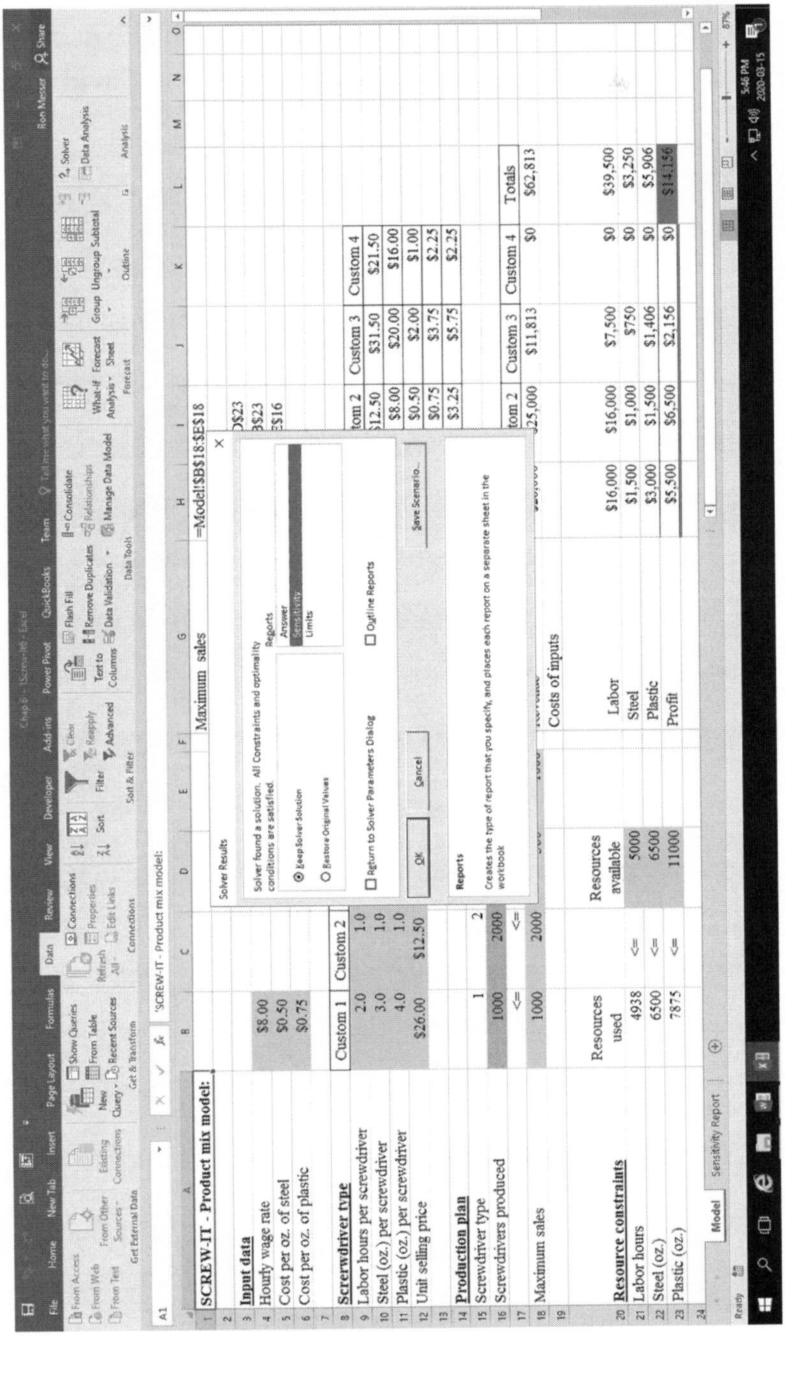

Fig. 6.6. Step 3—Activate Solver.

SCREW-IT - Product mix model:

Input data
Hourly wage rate	$8.00
Cost per oz. of steel	$0.50
Cost per oz. of plastic	$0.75

Screwdriver type
	Custom 1	Custom 2	Custom 3	Custom 4
Labor hours per screwdriver	2.0	1.0		
Steel (oz.) per screwdriver	3.0	1.0		
Plastic (oz.) per screwdriver	4.0	1.0		
Unit selling price	$26.00	$12.50		

		Custom 2	Custom 3	Custom 4
		$12.50	$31.50	$21.50
		$8.00	$20.00	$16.00
		$0.50	$2.00	$1.00
		$0.75	$3.75	$2.25
		$3.25	$5.75	$2.25

Production plan
	Custom 1	Custom 2			
Screwdriver type	1	2			
Screwdrivers produced	1000	2000			
	<=	<=			
Maximum sales	1000	2000			

	tom 2	Custom 3	Custom 4	Totals
	25,000	$11,813	$0	$62,813

Resource constraints
	Resources used		Resources available
Labor hours	4938	<=	5000
Steel (oz.)	6500	<=	6500
Plastic (oz.)	7875	<=	11000

Costs of inputs
		Custom 2	Custom 3	Custom 4	Totals
Labor		$16,000	$7,500	$0	$39,500
Steel		$1,500	$750	$0	$3,250
Plastic		$3,000	$1,500? $1,406	$0	$5,906
Profit		$5,500	$6,500 $2,156	$0	$14,156

Maximum sales

=Model!$B$18:$E$18

Solver Results

Solver found a solution. All Constraints and optimality conditions are satisfied.

Reports
Answer
Sensitivity
Limits

◉ Keep Solver Solution
○ Restore Original Values

☐ Return to Solver Parameters Dialog   ☐ Outline Reports

OK   Cancel   Save Scenario...

Reports
Creates the type of report that you specify, and places each report on a separate sheet in the workbook

Model | Sensitivity Report

Fig. 6.7. Step 3—Activate Solver (Optimal Solution).

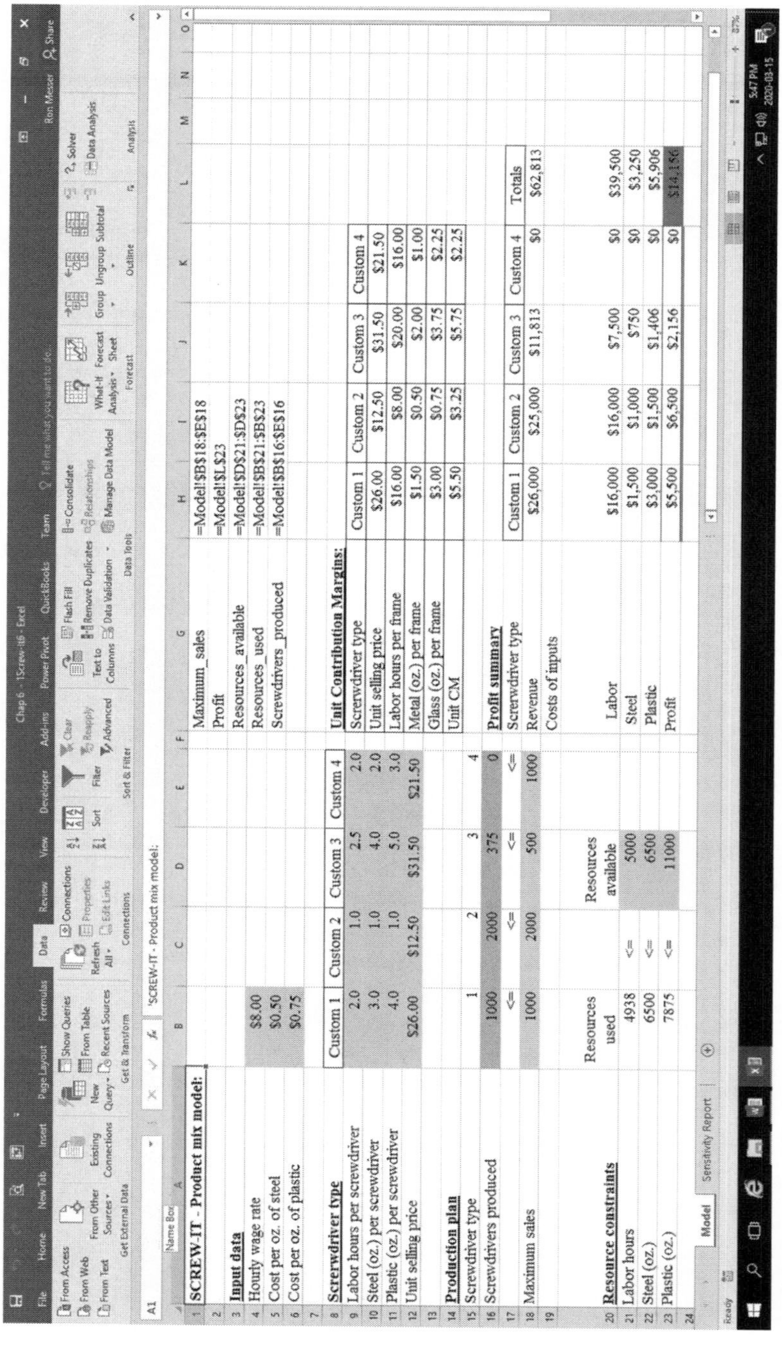

Fig. 6.8. Step 3—Generate the Sensitivity Report.

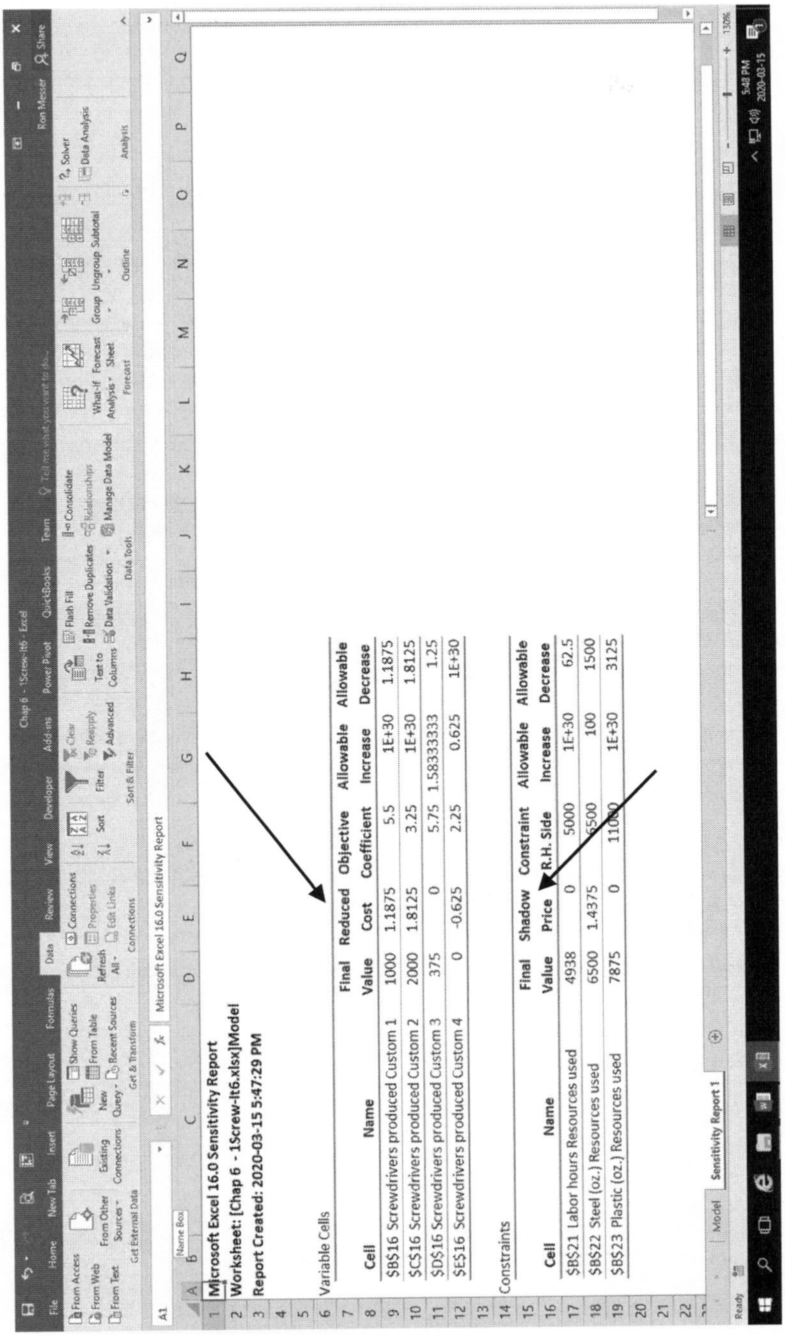

Microsoft Excel 16.0 Sensitivity Report
Worksheet: [Chap 6 - 1Screw-lt6.xlsx]Model
Report Created: 2020-03-15 5:47:29 PM

Variable Cells

Cell	Name	Final Value	Reduced Cost	Objective Coefficient	Allowable Increase	Allowable Decrease
$B$16	Screwdrivers produced Custom 1	1000	1.1875	5.5	1E+30	1.1875
$C$16	Screwdrivers produced Custom 2	2000	1.8125	3.25	1E+30	1.8125
$D$16	Screwdrivers produced Custom 3	375	0	5.75	1.58333333	1.25
$E$16	Screwdrivers produced Custom 4	0	-0.625	2.25	0.625	1E+30

Constraints

Cell	Name	Final Value	Shadow Price	Constraint R.H. Side	Allowable Increase	Allowable Decrease
$B$21	Labor hours Resources used	4938	0	5000	1E+30	62.5
$B$22	Steel (oz.) Resources used	6500	1.4375	6500	100	1500
$B$23	Plastic (oz.) Resources used	7875	0	11000	1E+30	3125

equal to the current usage shown (i.e., the "final value"). It can be seen that the allowable increase is a very large number, which means that regardless of how much additional labor or steel is available, their usage will remain unchanged in the optimal solution. The shadow price provides useful information for decision-making concerning whether additional costs should be incurred in acquiring resources, such as hiring more workers or buying raw materials.

The "reduced cost" tells us about the "indifference point" relating to the company's objective, which is to maximize total contribution margin (this is a proxy measure for profitability). The reduced cost amounts relate to the "objective coefficients"; these are the unit contribution margins for each of the four products (custom 1, 2, 3, and 4). For custom 1 and 2, the plan is to produce the maximum quantity demanded for each of the products (i.e., 1,000 and 2,000 units, respectively). Therefore, the allowable increase to the coefficients is infinite (because you can't produce more than the sales demand), but the allowable decrease tells us how much the unit contribution margin must be reduced before the production plan changes. For example, if the unit contribution margin for custom 1 drops by at least $1.19, then the optimal production will change, and a quantity between 0 to 999 units will be produced. This is also true for custom 2, with the proviso that between 0 and 1,999 units will be produced if we decrease the unit contribution margin by at least $1.81.

For the custom 3 product, the sensitivity report tells us the amount of the increase and decrease to the unit contribution margin before a change occurs to the production plan. If the unit contribution margin increases by at least $1.59, then the revised production will be between 375 units and the maximum demand of 500 units. If the unit contribution margin decreases by a minimum of $1.25, then the number of custom 3 products produced will decrease to between 0 and 375 units. Because no custom 4 screwdrivers are being produced, if the unit contribution margin increases by at least $0.63, the sensitivity report tells us that production will be somewhere between 0 and 1,000 units.

The reduced cost provides information that assists managers in deciding whether to change prices for their products and/or modify their cost structure in order to maximize profits by selling a different combination of products. This may be desirable for strategic reasons, such as being able to offer a complete product line similar to those of competitors.

Demonstration Exercise 2

Determining the production schedule that minimizes costs (Excel file: Shoot-it(shell). xls).

Case Facts[3]

Shoot-It! is a manufacturer of inexpensive ice hockey sticks that it sells in bulk, online through an e-commerce website. Its primary customers are the numerous junior

---

[3]These types of production scheduling models follow a common pattern, including (1) calculating the difference between the quantity available and sold in a period and (2) identifying the unsold inventory in one period that is carried forward to the next period. The objective is always to minimize production costs over time.

hockey teams that are scattered throughout North America and form part of the feeder system for players into the professional teams that comprise the National Hockey League (NHL). Nowadays, hockey sticks are very light and flexible, but at the same time can break easily. Consequently, teams use a significant number of them in a season.

Because of the huge influx of cheap sporting goods from Southeast Asia, particularly mainland China, cost control has become critical to running a profitable business. Production costs include a variety of materials, such as wood, fiberglass, graphite, Kevlar and titanium. Unlike the old days, when hockey sticks consisted of a wood shaft attached to a straight blade, today the equipment is manufactured as a single piece that is custom molded to specifications for the length of the shaft, the angle of the lie (where the shaft meets the blade) and curvature of the blade. The costs for many of these inputs can vary dramatically from month to month and therefore scheduling production to keep expenditures to a minimum is important. (Note that because of its small size, entering into a forward agreement or buying commodity futures is not an option for hedging the company's exposure to fluctuating input prices for materials.)

The company expects the following production-related costs and sales demand over the next 4 months (**Table 6.3**). (Holding costs include inventory insurance and warehouse related expenditures for storing excess production. There is no beginning inventory for January.)

The Excel worksheet for this financial model appears below (**Fig. 6.9**).

The formulas used to build this model appear in the worksheet below (**Fig. 6.10**).

Note the following:

- One period's ending inventory is the following period's beginning inventory (e.g., February's beginning inventory is January's ending inventory).
- The number of sticks available is determined by production for the period and the beginning inventory.

In **Fig. 6.11**, the value in cell B21 is our objective function, which is to *minimize* costs by changing the decision variables located in cells B10 to E10 (which have been given the named range, "production"). Once Solver is activated, the optimal production schedule that minimizes total production costs is shown. The sensitivity report for this model is shown in **Fig. 6.12**.

Total costs are minimized at $102,800 by producing the expected sales demand for January through April (as shown in cells B10 to E10).

The shadow price shows that there are binding constraints for stick production in every month. This means that the sales demand for those months have been met.

Table 6.3. Shoot-It Unit Production Costs and Sales Volume.

Measure	January	February	March	April
Cost to produce a hockey stick ($)	$40.00	$42.00	$39.00	$41.00
Holding costs per hockey stick ($)	$4.00	$4.00	$4.00	$4.00
Anticipated hockey stick sales (#)	450	500	900	700

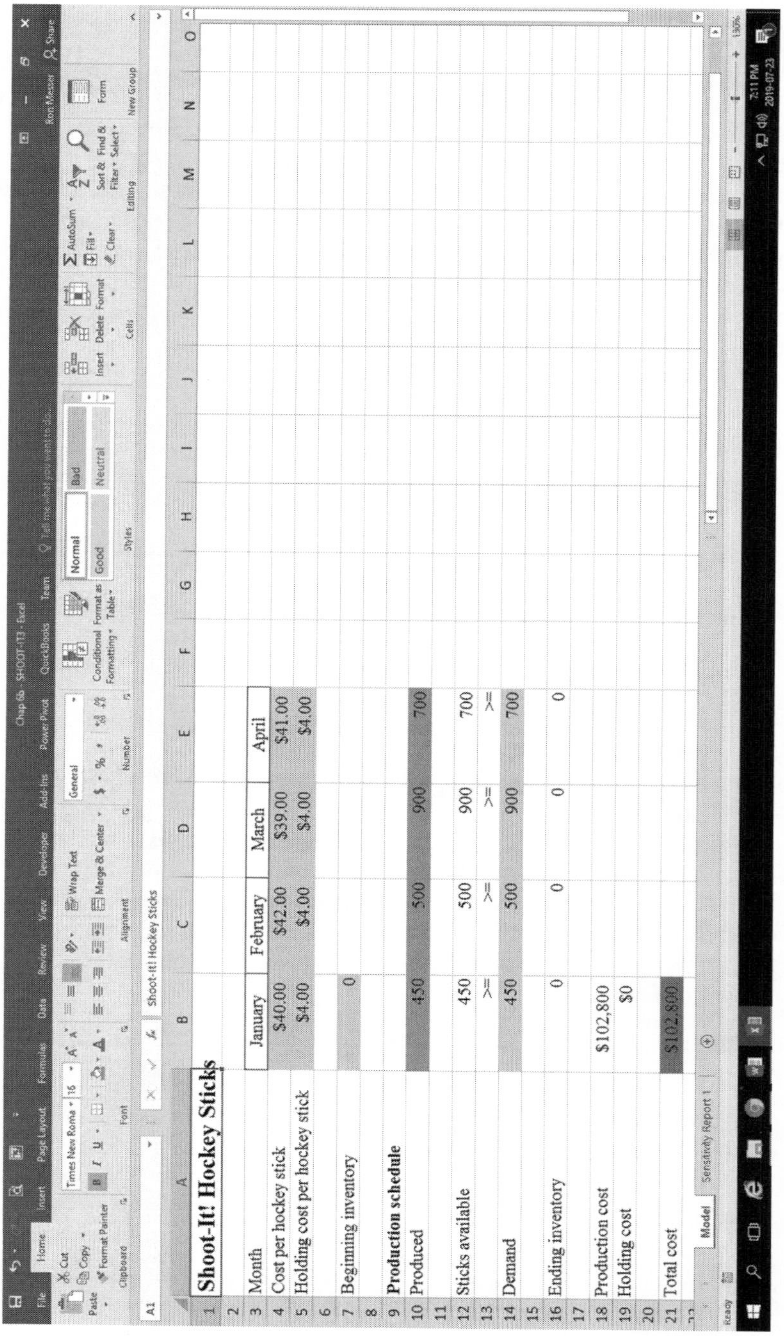

Fig. 6.9. Step 1—Creating the Excel Worksheet.

Shoot-It! Hockey Sticks

	January	February	March	April
Month				
Cost per hockey stick	$40.00	$42.00	$39.00	$41.00
Holding cost per hockey stick	$4.00	$4.00	$4.00	$4.00
Beginning inventory	0			
Production schedule				
Produced	450	500	900	700
Sticks available	450	500	900	700
	>=	>=	>=	>=
Demand	450	500	900	700
Ending inventory	0	0	0	0
Production cost	$102,800			
Holding cost	$0			
Total cost	$102,800			

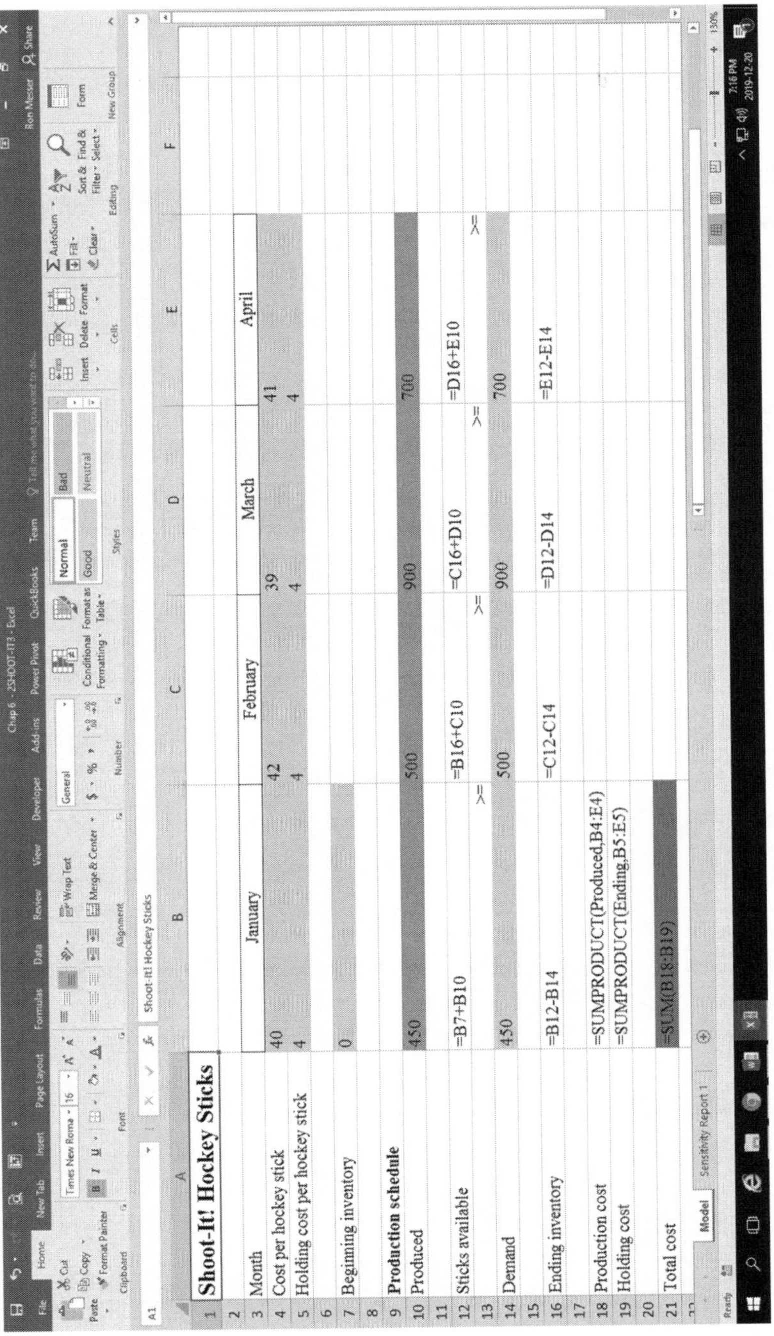

Fig. 6.10. Step 1—Formulas for Creating the Excel Worksheet.

Shoot-It! Hockey Sticks

	January	February	March	April
Month				
Cost per hockey stick	40	42	39	41
Holding cost per hockey stick	4	4	4	4
Beginning inventory	0			
Production schedule				
Produced	450	500	900	700
Sticks available	=B7+B10	=B16+C10	=C16+D10	=D16+E10
	>=	>=	>=	>=
Demand	450	500	900	700
Ending inventory	=B12-B14	=C12-C14	=D12-D14	=E12-E14
Production cost	=SUMPRODUCT(Produced,B4:E4)			
Holding cost	=SUMPRODUCT(Ending,B5:E5)			
Total cost	=SUM(B18:B19)			

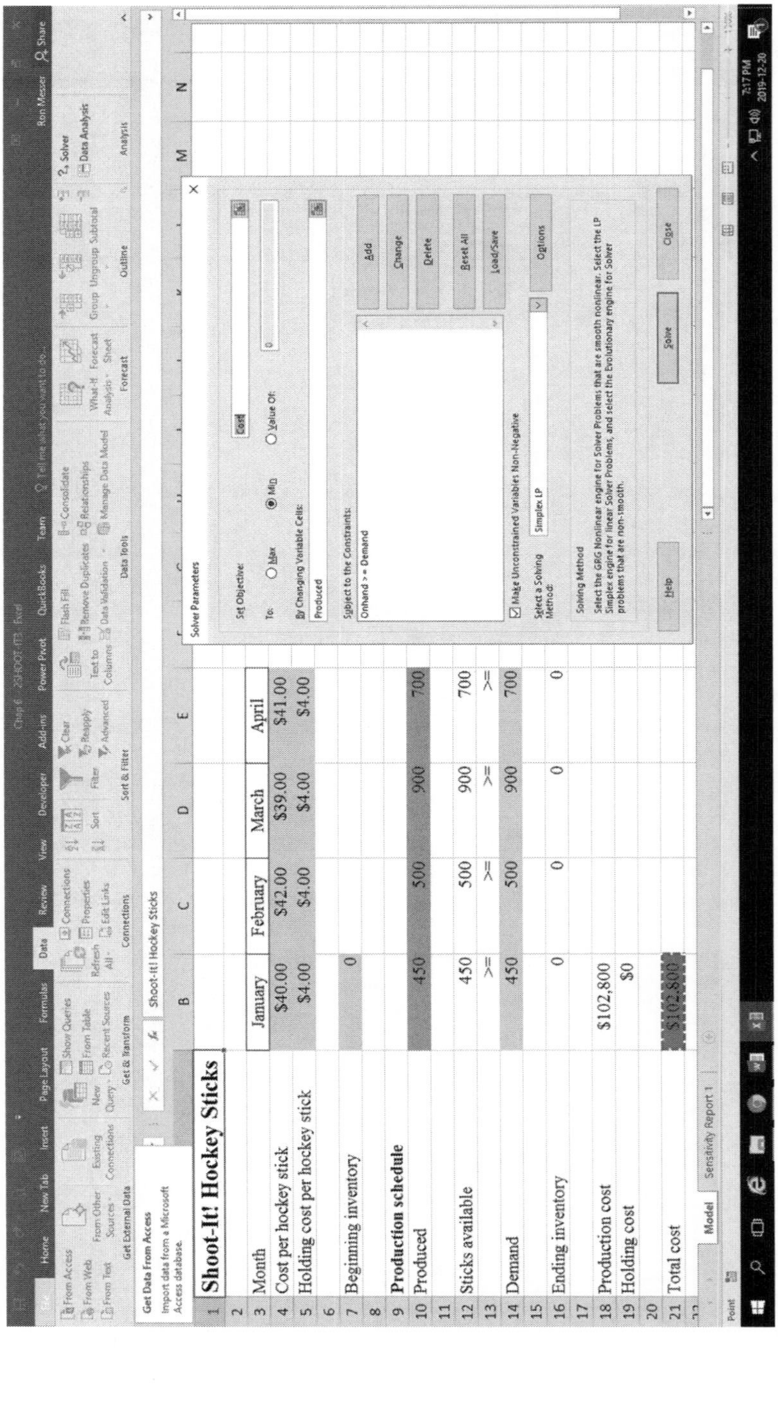

Fig. 6.11. Step 2 — Complete the Excel Solver Dialog Box.

Fig. 6.12. Step 3—Generate the Sensitivity Report.

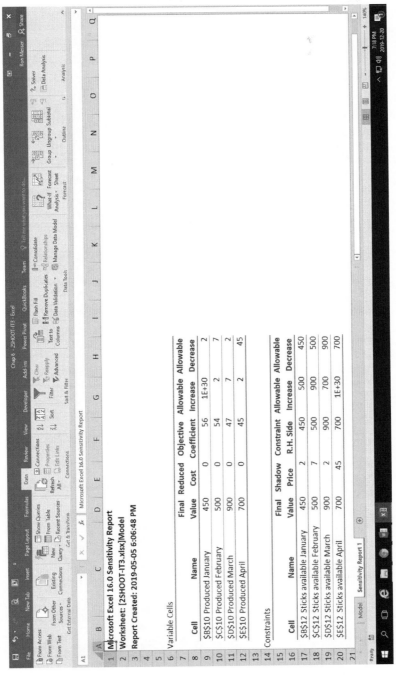

(Note that these are *minimum* sales demands; in other words, we need to produce *at least* this amount of output.) The shadow price of 2.00 for January tells us that the costs will increase by $2.00 for every additional hockey stick demanded in that month. This will be true for increases up to 500 units; also, costs will decline by $2.00 for up to 450 fewer hockey sticks manufactured. The infinite allowable increase in the minimum demand for April means that for every additional stick produced, costs will increase by exactly $45.00 (which is the sum of the unit production and holding costs for that month—i.e., $41 in production costs and $4 in holding costs).

The reduced cost provides information about the changes to unit costs that will alter the production plan. For example, in January, the number of sticks made is equal to the demand. To produce more than the planned amount would require a decrease of $2.00 in costs, per unit (February cost decrease would be $7.00; March, $2.00; and April, $45.) The allowable increase indicates how many fewer sticks will be produced each month, based on cost increases of an infinite amount, $2.00, $7.00, and $2.00 per unit (for the months of January to April, respectively). In January, the increase is infinite because no amount will change the plan.

Afterthought → *your fate is a matter of luck*

Mathematical modeling has provided many important insights for making business decisions. As discussed in this chapter, it can be used to maximize profits when there are resource limitations. At its heart, a financial model helps us deal with uncertainty when making decisions. Think about this powerful illustration of dealing with an unknown future ...

Risky Business

(*Finding meaning in random events*)

There is a scene from the movie *Saving Private Ryan* that is difficult to forget. It is in the opening 20 minutes when the D-day troops are landing on the beaches of Normandy. As the front-end of their amphibious vehicles are lowered, the soldiers charge the German battlements. Some never make it out of the landing craft. Others are gunned down as they reach the beach, either shot dead or mortally wounded. For each soldier, there is tremendous meaning attached to who lives and who dies. But the truth is that what separates those who "*made it*" from those who didn't is nothing more than a random event—some call it luck.

Statistical theory was developed in the 1700s by French mathematician Blaise Pascal. The purpose of the discipline was to predict unknown outcomes by using recognized patterns in observed events. In its time statistics was considered heretical because it deviated from the deterministic models used by science, where observed phenomena were ascribed meaning based on clearly defined cause and effect relationships—such as Newton's laws of physics. In contrast, statistics was not deterministic, but rather suggested that we could deal with random events based on predictable patterns of outcomes.

While business leaders think that they can manage their environment, research has shown that as many as 65% of the critical events affecting a company are completely out of the control of those running it. These events include the things that *"we don't know we don't know"* —like 9/11, SARs, and the Asian tsunami—who could have known about that! Much like the troops rushing into battle at Normandy, outcomes are not always certain and what separates those who make it from those who don't is ultimately—and we can say this only in hindsight—a matter of chance. Soldiers and corporations do survive uncertain events, but these outcomes are based on probabilities and not bold—but meaningless—declarations of victory, or corporate success.

But, if this is the case, then what purpose does management serve? How do leaders provide meaning to corporate activity? How can they better control their good fortune? Managing uncertain events, or risk, is a popular notion in business. It entails identifying a company's critical exposures and then estimating the likelihood of an unfortunate event. While there is no certainty to these occurrences, probabilities can help better manage those risks that are identified.

Statistics has shown that we are the masters of our own fate only within limits. To a larger extent, we are only observers to events that are uncontrollable. While we cannot be certain of the future, we can nevertheless give a context to the unknown by understanding that risk, uncertainty and randomness are not so much matters of luck—which is meaningless—as they are about probabilities, which provide a better way of managing the unknown. And in that, there is something meaningful.

Chapter 7

Business Valuation Decisions

How much is my company worth?

Snapshot

TOPIC
Business Valuations

SUBJECT AREA
Corporate finance

DECISIONS MADE
Determining the price of common shares for an initial public offering (IPO) or providing additional financing for an existing business.

PERSONAL EXPERIENCE
A subsidiary of a company for which I worked as a corporate finance analyst wanted to enter into a consortium agreement with two other business partners who would provide investment capital and engineering services for a large infrastructure project. My department in the parent company was tasked with valuing our portion of the contribution to the consortium. By using discounted cash flow models and a calculated cost of capital we were able to place a value on our "share" of the project. This became important information when we later sold (at a considerable profit) our interest in the subsidiary to an outside investor.

EXCEL FUNCTIONALITY
FILE, OPTIONS (settings)
NPV
IRR

Background Theory
The valuation of a business is based on its expected future cash flows. It is affected by the financial relationships found in the most recent period of activity, which can be used to extrapolate results into the future (since the best predictor of tomorrow is what happened today). In developing a valuation model, forecast assumptions are made for sales growth and a cost relating to the source of financing – typically for a 5 to 10-year period.

Business valuation models are like capital budgeting exercises in that they use discounted net cash flows to arrive at a present value. However, because it is assumed that an enterprise is a going concern, it is not expected that the forecast assumptions will hold into the future and for this reason a terminal value – which occurs at the end of the forecast period – is required. The terminal value represents the present value of an annuity which is paid forever (i.e., in perpetuity). This annual amount is based on the cash flow in the final year of the forecast period, adjusted for an assumed growth rate.

Analyzing the Cost of Capital
The capital asset pricing model (CAPM) is a tool that can be used to determine the cost of equity financing. It is calculated by using the formula:

$$ER_i = R_f + \beta_i(ER_m - R_f)$$

where:

ER_i = expected return of investment (this is the cost of equity),
R_f = risk-free rate (usually based on government issued 10-year bonds),
β_i = beta of the investment (how share prices move in relation to the market),
ER_m = expected return of market (based on a broad-based index, like the S&P 500),
$(ER_m - R_f)$ = market risk premium (riskless rate less the equity premium).[1]

Pro-forma Financial Statements
A forecast income statement and balance sheet needs to be prepared based on the sales growth assumptions and the relationships extant in the historical financial information – for example, cost of goods sold relative to sales. These financial statements will use GAAP accrual-based accounting methods. Typically, only a 5-year projection is done, as to forecast beyond this period is highly unreliable (and unrealistic).

Forecasting Assumptions
In this type of modeling exercise, the most important forecast assumptions relate to sales growth and the discount rate, which are based on the cost of capital. The starting point for the valuation exercise will be the company's most recent financial information, which is analyzed to identify the relationship between (1) sales and cost of sales and (2) sales and assets and (3) sales and liabilities. The financial model assumes that current equity levels are maintained, and that bank borrowing is repaid with cash on hand as of the last balance sheet date.

The model then "plugs" the amounts relating to cash balances in the forecast period. In other words, it will force the balance sheet to balance. Doing this provides important information about the viability of the enterprise, based on whether positive cash

---

[1]*Source:* https://www.investopedia.com/terms/c/capm.asp.

figures result. If these amounts are negative, it suggests that the venture may not be tenable in the long run.

Financial Management Techniques

In the modeling exercise, it is important to distinguish between accrual-based accounting measures (i.e., GAAP financial statements) and cash flows. The former helps us develop the latter; but it is the cash flows that are critical to the business valuation. In this regard, the concept of the cash cycle, taken from corporate finance is instructive. The cash cycle views all business activity in terms of the flow of cash into and out of the corporate entity. A company begins with a pile of cash that it converts into a bigger pile of cash (if it is profitable) by selling things that it makes – as a manufacturer – or buys, as a retailer, for resale. When customers pay their invoices, cash returns to the enterprise.

Relevant Excel Functionality

When preparing the pro-forma financial statements, it is important to remember that the accounting equation, Assets = Liabilities + Equity, is a tautology; this means that the equality is considered to be true by definition. This truism is also the foundation for double entry bookkeeping (which has been with us for about 600 years). Something that is true only because we say it is, creates a problem for most computer programs. This is the difficulty presented by a continuous loop in the calculation logic, which is referred to as a circular reference in Excel (see **Fig. 7.1**). It is an issue that must be addressed in financial modeling.

To remove the arrow lines in column C (which is a warning that something appears to be wrong), do the following: After left-clicking on File, Options, Formulas, there is a check list in the dialogue box that appears indicating "Enable iterative calculation" (see **Fig. 7.2**). Normally, it is advisable to leave this box unchecked, so that any circular references in a financial model can be identified and addressed. However, in modeling a business valuation, this box should be checked to prevent an error message appearing indicating that a circular reference has occurred, which is inevitable given the premise underlying the accounting equation.[2]

Business valuation models created using Excel are primarily formula driven. The key functions used are NPV, to discount the anticipated cash flows, and one-way data tables to test sensitivities for key variables. The remainder of the modeling exercise relies on simple add, subtract, multiply, and divide type calculations to generate the pro-forma financial statements. The foundation for determining business valuation is an understanding of the fundamentals of financial accounting as well as corporate finance theory.

Demonstration Exercise

Almost every start-up company hopes to one day become a larger enterprise. As these businesses grow and prosper, they eventually realize that in order to achieve significant volume they must expand their operations. This inevitably requires additional financing that often comes by way of selling shares through an initial public offering (IPO). How does a company determine the price of corporate equity? The following exercise illustrates how this is done. (Excel file: HAAK(shell).xls.)

---

[2]Technically, checking this box does not prevent the iterative calculation, it only allows it to occur 100 times and then, basically, "give-up" and accept the problem without complaint.

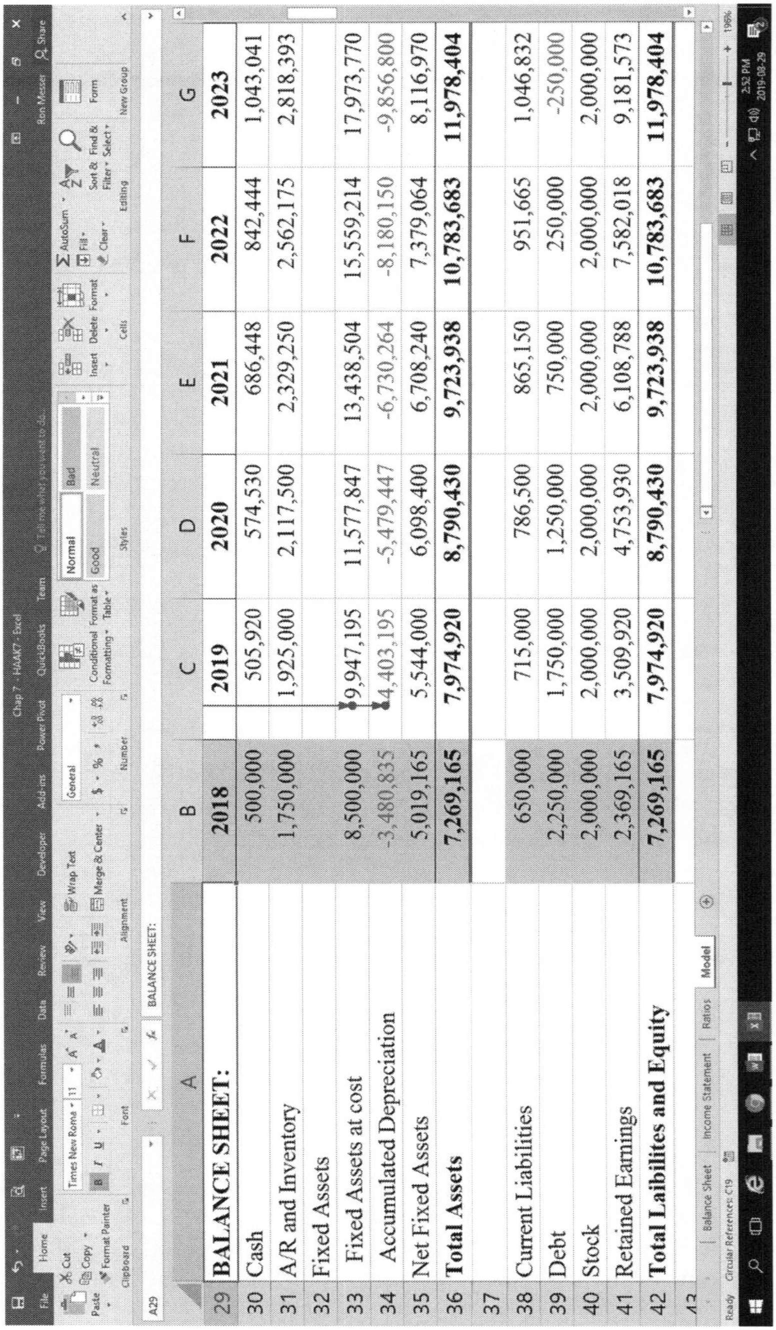

Fig. 7.1. A Circular Reference in Excel.

	A	B	C	D	E	F	G
		2018	2019	2020	2021	2022	2023
29	**BALANCE SHEET:**						
30	Cash	500,000	505,920	574,530	686,448	842,444	1,043,041
31	A/R and Inventory	1,750,000	1,925,000	2,117,500	2,329,250	2,562,175	2,818,393
32	Fixed Assets						
33	Fixed Assets at cost	8,500,000	9,947,195	11,577,847	13,438,504	15,559,214	17,973,770
34	Accumulated Depreciation	-3,480,835	-4,403,195	-5,479,447	-6,730,264	-8,180,150	-9,856,800
35	Net Fixed Assets	5,019,165	5,544,000	6,098,400	6,708,240	7,379,064	8,116,970
36	**Total Assets**	**7,269,165**	**7,974,920**	**8,790,430**	**9,723,938**	**10,783,683**	**11,978,404**
37							
38	Current Liabilities	650,000	715,000	786,500	865,150	951,665	1,046,832
39	Debt	2,250,000	1,750,000	1,250,000	750,000	250,000	-250,000
40	Stock	2,000,000	2,000,000	2,000,000	2,000,000	2,000,000	2,000,000
41	Retained Earnings	2,369,165	3,509,920	4,753,930	6,108,788	7,582,018	9,181,573
42	**Total Laibilites and Equity**	**7,269,165**	**7,974,920**	**8,790,430**	**9,723,938**	**10,783,683**	**11,978,404**

Fig. 7.2. Enabling an Iterative Calculation.

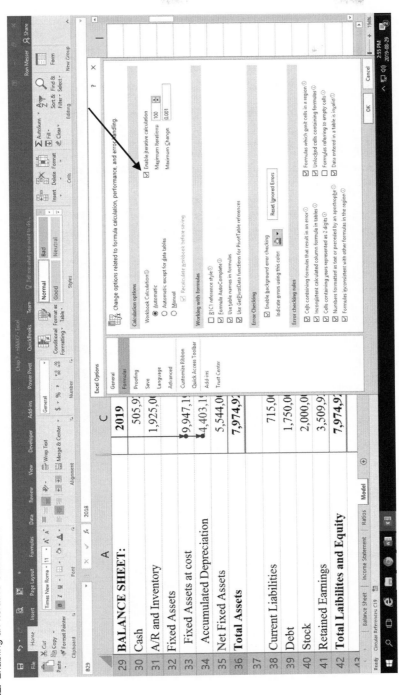

Case Facts[3]

With the legalization of recreational marijuana sales in many parts of the United States – including their northern neighbor Canada – numerous business ventures have entered this new market. One such operator is *High-As-A-Kite* (HAAK), which has been growing and retailing cannabis products for the past 5 years (previously for medicinal use only). With an initial investment of about $200,000, the founding members grew the business because of their expertise in cultivating unique and desirable plant strains. For this reason, expansion of the company's outlets has been rapid. Now the owners want to gain a first mover advantage and obtain public financing for a significant expansion into more locations. To do this, HAAK has incorporated the business and approached an investment bank about an IPO of its shares.

The investment bankers are given the most recent financial statements for the company (see **Figs. 7.3 and 7.4**) and must determine how to price the share offering. This will involve the following steps.

(1) Identify relationships in the historical financial statements, including the balance sheet and income statement that will inform the forecast financial information.
(2) Develop reasonable assumptions – including base-case, best-case, and worst-case scenarios – regarding sales growth. (Note that future sales are the key driver in the financial model.)
(3) Using the modeling assumptions concerning sales growth and the financial statement relationships identified, create a pro-forma income statement and balance sheet for a 5-year period.
(4) Convert the after-tax profit in the pro-forma income statement into cash flows. (This is required because businesses are valued based on their ability to generate cash.)

Fig. 7.3. HAAK Balance Sheet for 2018.

High-As-A-Kite (HAAK)
Balance Sheet
31-Dec-18

Current Assets:		Current Liabilities:	
Cash	500,000	Current Liabilities	650,000
A/R and Inventory	1,750,000	Bank Loans	2,250,000
Subtotal	2,250,000		2,900,000
Non-Current Assets:		*Equity:*	
Property, Plant and Equipment	8,500,000	Owner's Equity	2,000,000
Accumulated Depreciation	-3,480,835	Retained Earnings	2,369,165
Subtotal	5,019,165		4,369,165
Total Assets	**7,269,165**	**Total Liabilities and Equity**	**7,269,165**

---

[3]This exercise is based on one provided in Benninga, S. (2006). *Principles of finance with excel.* Oxford: Oxford University Press. In practice, all valuation models using cash flows follow the same steps in developing a forecast income statement to calculate cash flows, which then forms the basis for determining a company's share price.

Fig. 7.4. HAAK Income Statement for 2018.

High-As-A-Kite (HAAK)
Income Statement
31-Dec-20

Sales	7,000,000
Cost of Good Sold	-3,500,000
Depreciation	-657,714
Interest expense	-320,000
Interest earned on cash	64,000
Profit before tax	2,586,286
Taxes (40%)	-1,034,514
Net Income	1,551,772
Dividends	-512,085
Retained Earnings	1,039,687

(5) Discount the forecast cash flows, including the terminal value – using an appropriate risk-adjusted cost of capital – to the present day.

(6) Determine the per share value of the discounted cash flows and test important sensitives in the model, particularly regarding the sales growth, which is our key valuation assumption.

Step 1: Calculate Financial Ratios for Forecasting
Table 7.1 shows the financial statement relationships in the most recent financial information (December 31, 2018).

Step 2: Develop Reasonable Forecast Assumptions
The key assumptions used in developing the pro-forma financial statements relate to sales growth (in dollars) and the cost of capital. The base case model assumes that

Table 7.1. Financial Statement Relationships and Assumptions for 2020 (Amounts Rounded).

Relationship or Assumption	2020
Sales growth per year	10%
Current assets compared to sales (excludes cash)	25%
Current liabilities compared to sales	9%
Net property, plant, and equipment compared to sales	72%
Cost of goods sold compared to sales	50%
Depreciation rate (declining balance)	10%
Interest expense (cost of bank borrowing)	5%
Interest earned on cash (short-term surpluses)	2%
Tax rate (on corporate income)	40%
Dividend payout (one-third of profits)	33%
Number of common shares to be issued	500,000

sales will grow at 10% annually and that debt financing will be replaced by equity sources through the sale of common shares. Generalizing from the CAPM, with a riskless rate of 2% (based on long-term sovereign debt rates) and an equity premium of 6%, with a beta coefficient of 1 (i.e., an exact correlation with the market, such as the S&P 500 index), the cost of capital will be $2\% + (1 \times 6\%) = 8\%$. (It is also assumed that the risk profile of this project is similar to that of other businesses selling over-the-counter medicinal or healthy living products, like vitamin and health-supplement stores.) Future sales growth after the forecast period are assumed to show an excess of 2% over anticipated long-term government inflation targets, which have historically been about 2%.

Step 3: Create the Forecast Income Statement and Balance Sheet

Figs. 7.5–7.9 show the pro-forma financial statements, as well as the key assumptions and financial ratios used.

Note the following with respect to the pro-forma Income Statement calculations:

- Sales = prior year sales $\times$ (1 + 10%)
- Cost of goods sold = 50% of current year sales
- Depreciation = average of fixed assets at cost $\times$ 10%
- Interest on debt = average of debt $\times$ 5%
- Interest on cash = average of cash $\times$ 2%

The model predicts a positive cash balance throughout the forecast period (cells C30 to G30), which indicates that the business is viable. Note the following with respect to the Balance Sheet calculations:

- Cash = a "plug" number that forces the equality: Assets = Liabilities + Equity
- A/R and inventory = current year sales $\times$ 25%
- Fixed assets at cost = net fixed assets + accumulated depreciation
- Accumulated depreciation = prior year accumulated depreciation + current year depreciation
- Net fixed assets = current year sales $\times$ 72%
- Debt = prior year amount less 500,000 per year until fully paid
- Owners' equity = assumed constant at $2,000,000
- Retained earnings = prior year retained earnings + net income − dividends

When calculating the depreciation expense, as well as the interest on debt and cash balances, an average for the balance sheet amounts for fixed assets at cost, debt and cash balances (respectively) is used; this consists of the beginning of the year amounts and the closing balances averaged over the two periods. This method is employed as it better approximates the balance in these accounts throughout the year, rather than assuming that the closing numbers remain constant over the entire period.

Step 4: Convert Net Income into Cash Flows

To change the GAAP accrual-based income measure into cash flows, the following adjustments (additions and deductions) must be made, as shown in **Tables 7.2 and 7.3**.

---

[4]Cell references can be traced to previous figures shown in the worksheet labeled "Model."

Fig. 7.5. Pro-forma Financial Statement Assumptions for HAAK.

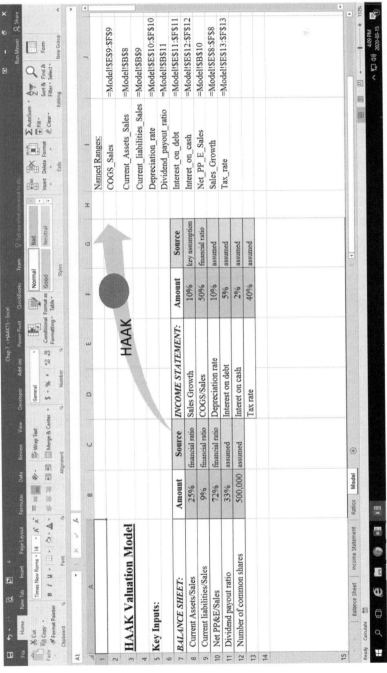

Fig. 7.6. Pro-forma Income Statement for HAAK.

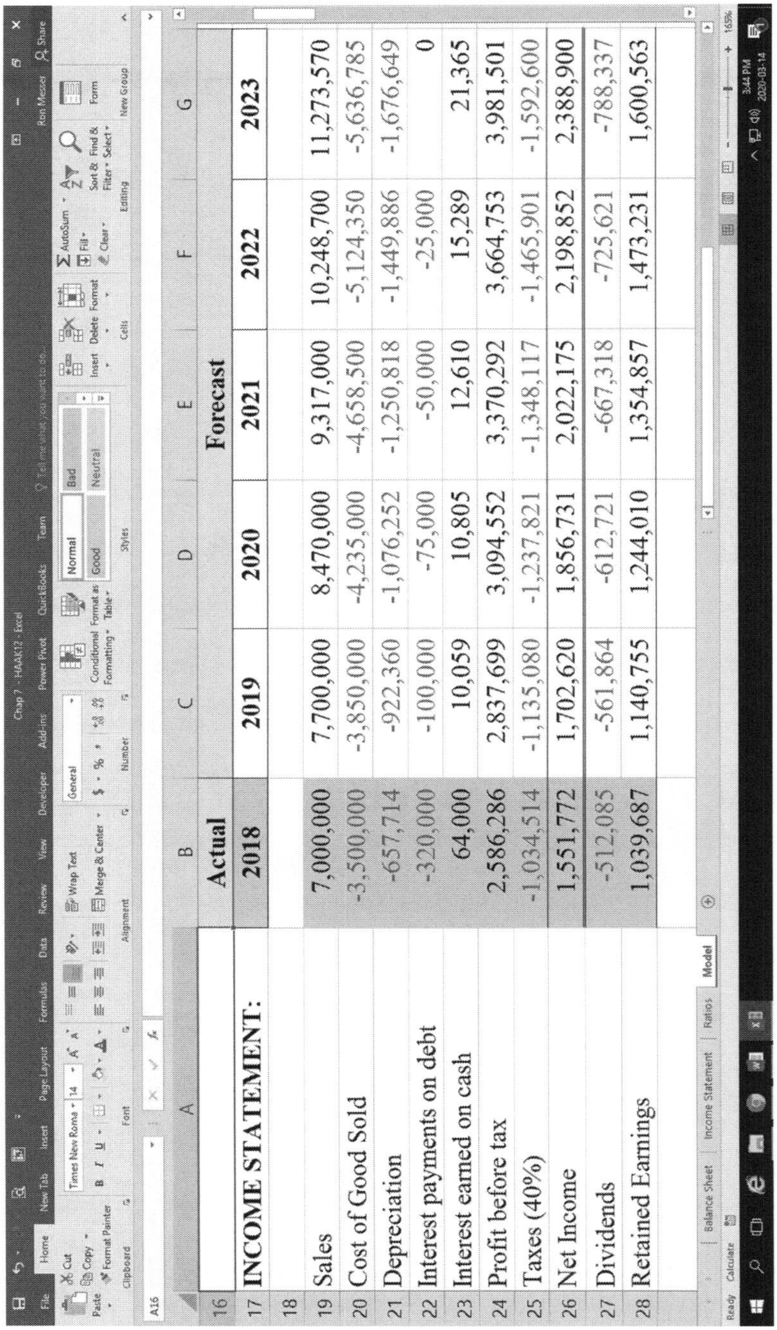

	A	B	C	D	E	F	G
16		Actual			Forecast		
17	INCOME STATEMENT:	2018	2019	2020	2021	2022	2023
18							
19	Sales	7,000,000	7,700,000	8,470,000	9,317,000	10,248,700	11,273,570
20	Cost of Good Sold	-3,500,000	-3,850,000	-4,235,000	-4,658,500	-5,124,350	-5,636,785
21	Depreciation	-657,714	-922,360	-1,076,252	-1,250,818	-1,449,886	-1,676,649
22	Interest payments on debt	-320,000	-100,000	-75,000	-50,000	-25,000	0
23	Interest earned on cash	64,000	10,059	10,805	12,610	15,289	21,365
24	Profit before tax	2,586,286	2,837,699	3,094,552	3,370,292	3,664,753	3,981,501
25	Taxes (40%)	-1,034,514	-1,135,080	-1,237,821	-1,348,117	-1,465,901	-1,592,600
26	Net Income	1,551,772	1,702,620	1,856,731	2,022,175	2,198,852	2,388,900
27	Dividends	-512,085	-561,864	-612,721	-667,318	-725,621	-788,337
28	Retained Earnings	1,039,687	1,140,755	1,244,010	1,354,857	1,473,231	1,600,563

Fig. 7.7. Pro-forma Income Statement for HAAK (Formulas).

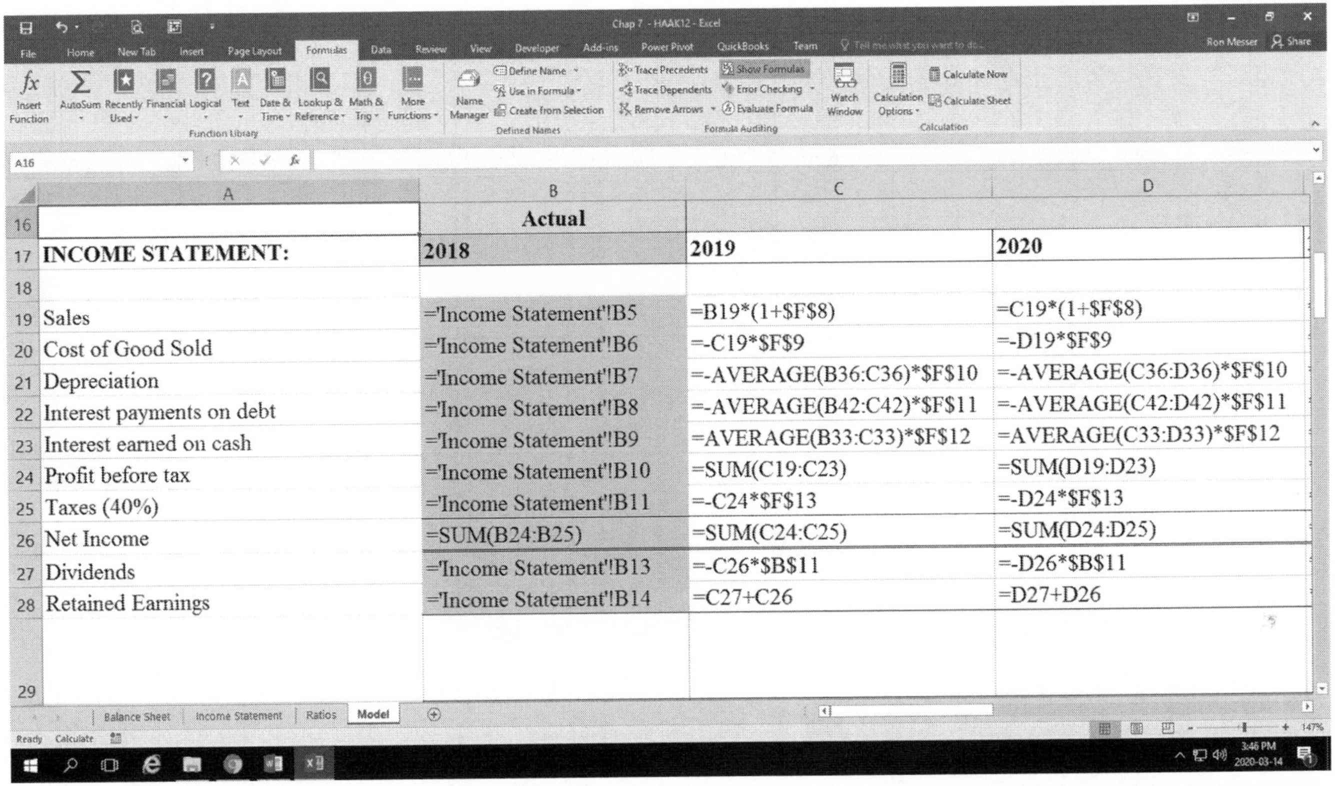

	A	B	C	D
16				
17	**INCOME STATEMENT:**	**Actual**		
18		2018	2019	2020
19	Sales	='Income Statement'!B5	=B19*(1+$F$8)	=C19*(1+$F$8)
20	Cost of Good Sold	='Income Statement'!B6	=C19*$F$9	=D19*$F$9
21	Depreciation	='Income Statement'!B7	=-AVERAGE(B36:C36)*$F$10	=-AVERAGE(C36:D36)*$F$10
22	Interest payments on debt	='Income Statement'!B8	=-AVERAGE(B42:C42)*$F$11	=-AVERAGE(C42:D42)*$F$11
23	Interest earned on cash	='Income Statement'!B9	=AVERAGE(B33:C33)*$F$12	=AVERAGE(C33:D33)*$F$12
24	Profit before tax	='Income Statement'!B10	=SUM(C19:C23)	=SUM(D19:D23)
25	Taxes (40%)	='Income Statement'!B11	=-C24*$F$13	=-D24*$F$13
26	Net Income	=SUM(B24:B25)	=SUM(C24:C25)	=SUM(D24:D25)
27	Dividends	='Income Statement'!B13	=-C26*$B$11	=-D26*$B$11
28	Retained Earnings	='Income Statement'!B14	=C27+C26	=D27+D26
29				

Fig. 7.8. Pro-forma Balance Sheet for HAAK.

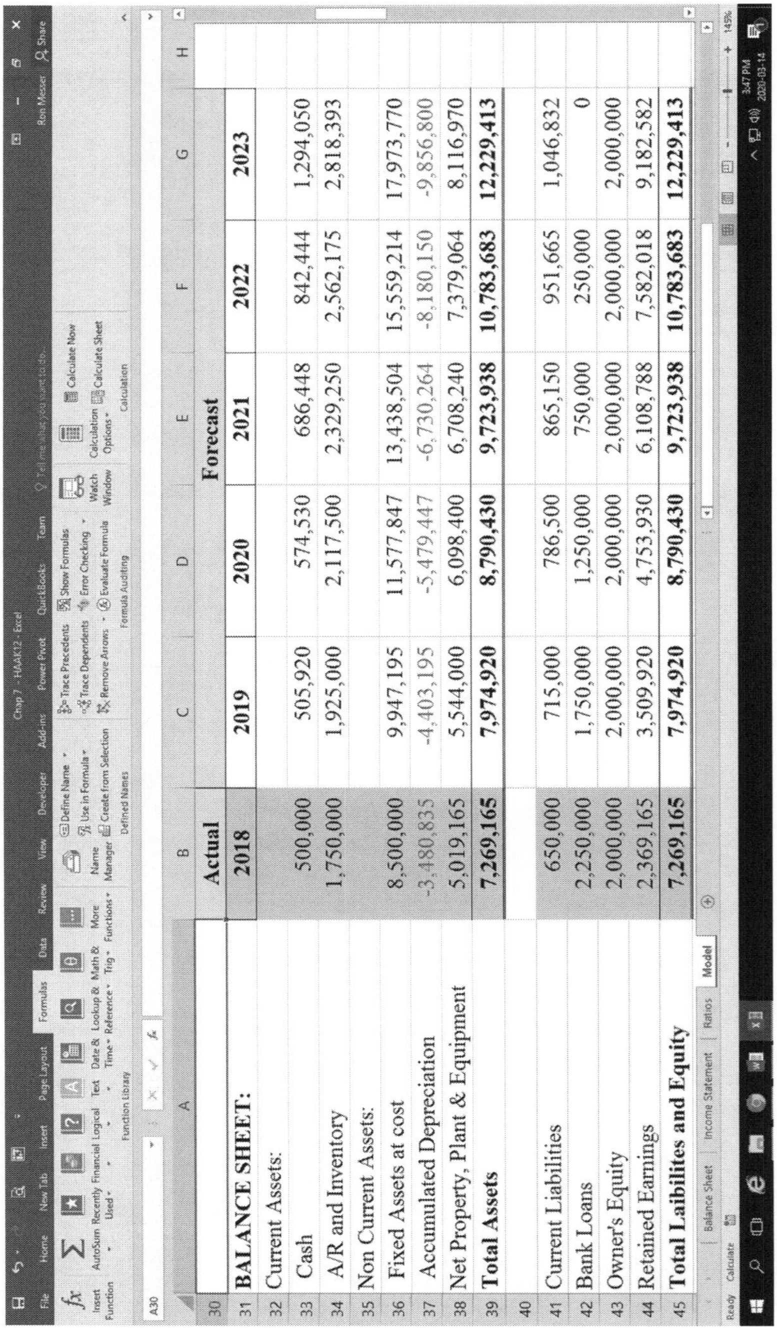

	Actual		Forecast			
	2018	**2019**	**2020**	**2021**	**2022**	**2023**
BALANCE SHEET:						
Current Assets:						
Cash	500,000	505,920	574,530	686,448	842,444	1,294,050
A/R and Inventory	1,750,000	1,925,000	2,117,500	2,329,250	2,562,175	2,818,393
Non Current Assets:						
Fixed Assets at cost	8,500,000	9,947,195	11,577,847	13,438,504	15,559,214	17,973,770
Accumulated Depreciation	-3,480,835	-4,403,195	-5,479,447	-6,730,264	-8,180,150	-9,856,800
Net Property, Plant & Equipment	5,019,165	5,544,000	6,098,400	6,708,240	7,379,064	8,116,970
Total Assets	**7,269,165**	**7,974,920**	**8,790,430**	**9,723,938**	**10,783,683**	**12,229,413**
Current Liabilities	650,000	715,000	786,500	865,150	951,665	1,046,832
Bank Loans	2,250,000	1,750,000	1,250,000	750,000	250,000	0
Owner's Equity	2,000,000	2,000,000	2,000,000	2,000,000	2,000,000	2,000,000
Retained Earnings	2,369,165	3,509,920	4,753,930	6,108,788	7,582,018	9,182,582
Total Laibilities and Equity	**7,269,165**	**7,974,920**	**8,790,430**	**9,723,938**	**10,783,683**	**12,229,413**

Fig. 7.9. Pro-forma Balance Sheet for HAAK (Formulas).[4]

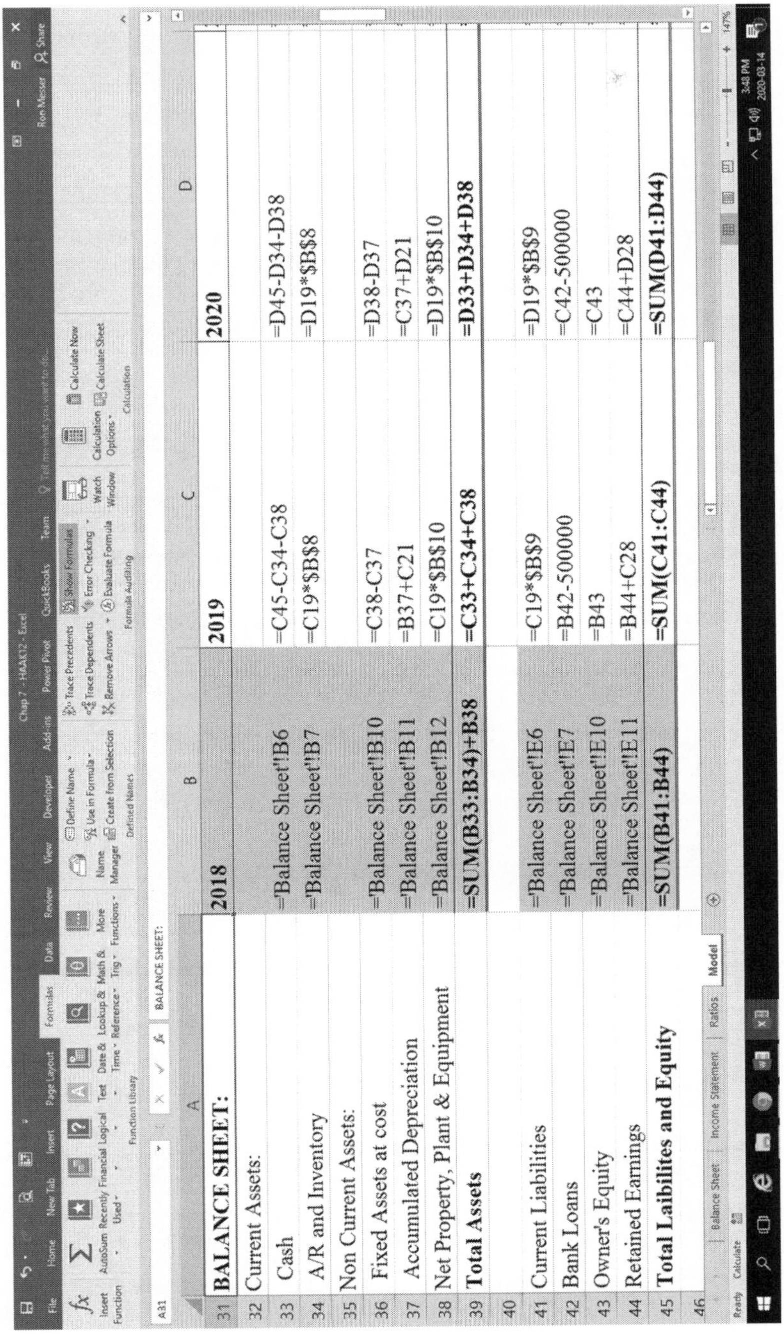

	A	B	C	D
31	**BALANCE SHEET:**	2018	2019	2020
32	Current Assets:			
33	Cash	='Balance Sheet'!B6	=C45-C34-C38	=D45-D34-D38
34	A/R and Inventory	='Balance Sheet'!B7	=C19*$B$8	=D19*$B$8
35	Non Current Assets:			
36	Fixed Assets at cost	='Balance Sheet'!B10	=C38-C37	=D38-D37
37	Accumulated Depreciation	='Balance Sheet'!B11	=B37+C21	=C37+D21
38	Net Property, Plant & Equipment	='Balance Sheet'!B12	=C19*$B$10	=D19*$B$10
39	**Total Assets**	**=SUM(B33:B34)+B38**	**=C33+C34+C38**	**=D33+D34+D38**
40				
41	Current Liabilities	='Balance Sheet'!E6	=C19*$B$9	=D19*$B$9
42	Bank Loans	='Balance Sheet'!E7	=B42-500000	=C42-500000
43	Owner's Equity	='Balance Sheet'!E10	=B43	=C43
44	Retained Earnings	='Balance Sheet'!E11	=B44+C28	=C44+D28
45	**Total Laibilites and Equity**	**=SUM(B41:B44)**	**=SUM(C41:C44)**	**=SUM(D41:D44)**
46				

Table 7.2. Additions to Net Income.

Financial Statement Item	Reason for Adjustment
Depreciation expense	This is an accounting (GAAP) calculated amount and does not impact cash flows.
Increase in current liabilities	By not paying debts (for example, trade payables), cash is conserved.
After tax interest expense	Interest expense is a financing charge that will be included in the cost of capital that is used to discount the cash flows. If it is not excluded, we would be double counting this amount. (The after-tax amount is used because of the deductibility of interest charges in determining taxable income, which eectively reduces the cost of the financing.)

Table 7.3. Deductions from Net Income.

Financial Statement Item	Reason for Adjustment
Capital expenditures (CAPEX)	Unlike GAAP, which allocates the cost of capital assets to accounting periods based on estimated usage (through depreciation charges), the cash flows associated with purchases of PP&E are recognized when they occur.
Increase in current assets	As cash is invested in inventories and A/R, prior to payments being received, it represents a usage of cash. (This is the cash cycle of cash → inventory → A/P →A/R → cash.)

The results of the adjustments made to determine the expected cash flows for each year in the 5-year forecast period are shown in **Figs. 7.10 and 7.11**.

Step 5: Calculate the Present Value of the Cash Flows

This is done by using the NPV function in Excel, as follows (refer to the cell references in **Fig. 7.12**).

$$= \text{NPV}(\text{discount rate}, \text{future cash flows})$$
$$= \text{NPV}(\text{B55}, \text{C64: G64})$$

The formulas for the NPV calculation are shown in **Fig. 7.13**.

Step 6: Determine the Share Value and Test Sensitivities

If 500,000 shares are issued, the price of equity is about $41.33 per share. Using a one-way data table (see Chapter 2), we can test the key variables in the model relating to sales growth and the discount rate. This is shown in **Fig. 7.14**.

Fig. 7.14 shows that as sales continue to grow the share price will gradually level off. This occurs because of the company's aggressive capital expansion program, where 72% of sales revenues are reinvested in capital assets. Thereby, the company may want to revisit this decision. As the discount rate increases, the share price decreases exponentially (i.e., it is a power function), which is also normal, given that higher

Fig. 7.10. Calculating Cash Flows.

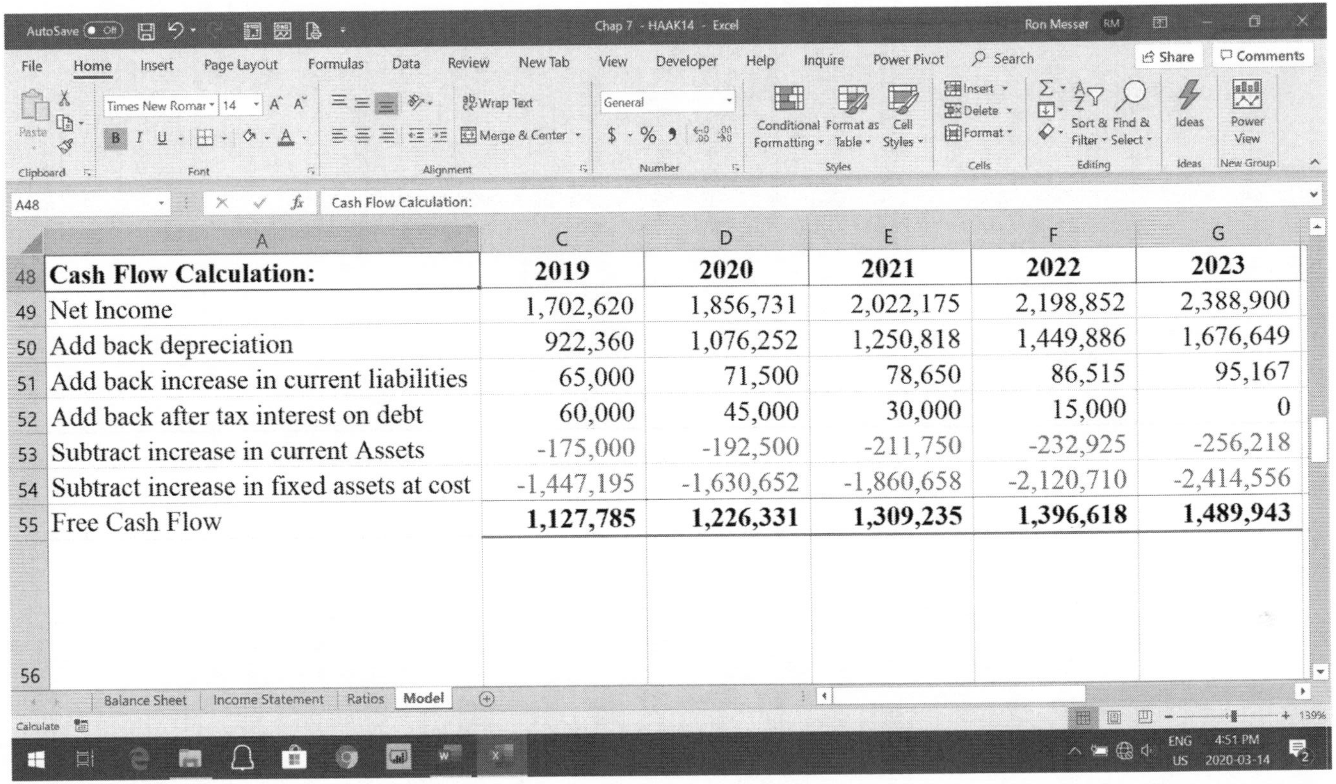

Cash Flow Calculation:	2019	2020	2021	2022	2023
Net Income	1,702,620	1,856,731	2,022,175	2,198,852	2,388,900
Add back depreciation	922,360	1,076,252	1,250,818	1,449,886	1,676,649
Add back increase in current liabilities	65,000	71,500	78,650	86,515	95,167
Add back after tax interest on debt	60,000	45,000	30,000	15,000	0
Subtract increase in current Assets	-175,000	-192,500	-211,750	-232,925	-256,218
Subtract increase in fixed assets at cost	-1,447,195	-1,630,652	-1,860,658	-2,120,710	-2,414,556
Free Cash Flow	1,127,785	1,226,331	1,309,235	1,396,618	1,489,943

Fig. 7.11. Calculating Cash Flows (Formulas).

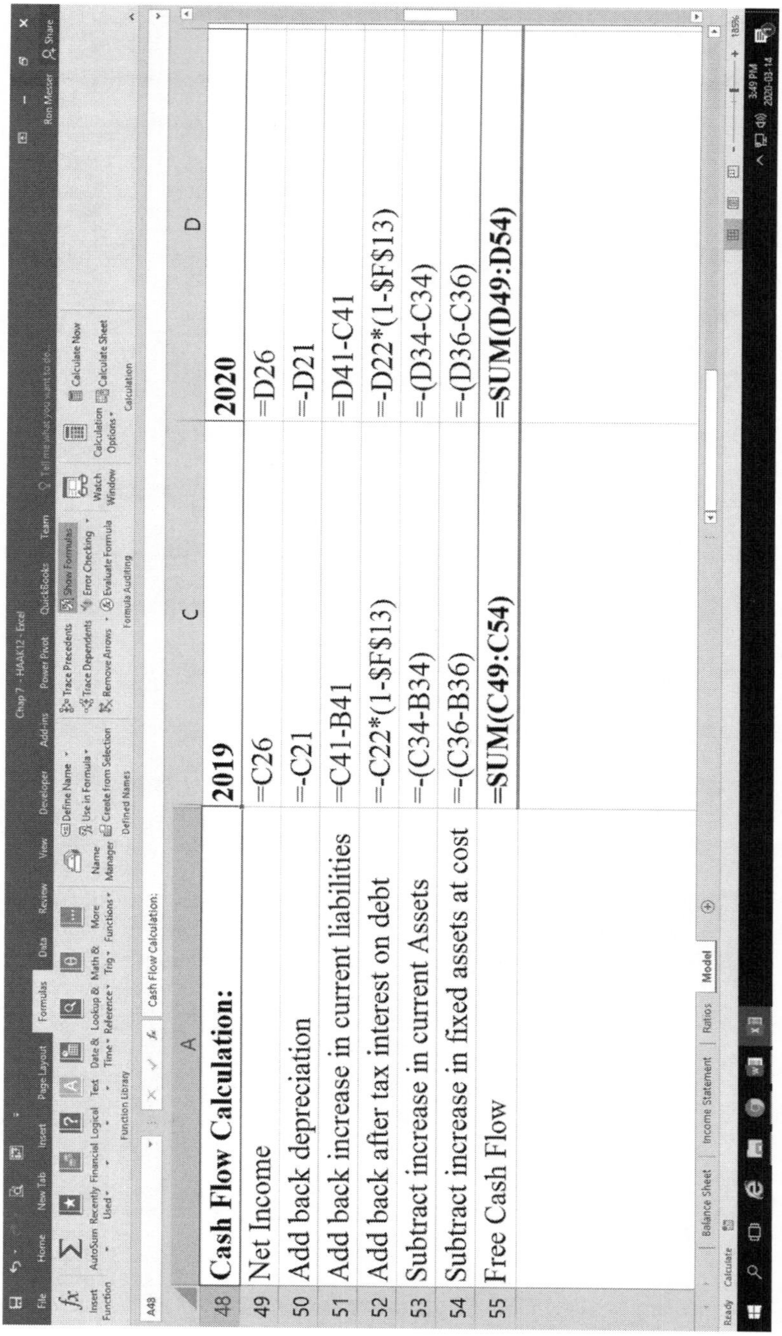

	A	C	D
48	**Cash Flow Calculation:**	**2019**	**2020**
49	Net Income	=C26	=D26
50	Add back depreciation	=-C21	=-D21
51	Add back increase in current liabilities	=C41-B41	=D41-C41
52	Add back after tax interest on debt	=-C22*(1-$F$13)	=-D22*(1-$F$13)
53	Subtract increase in current Assets	=-(C34-B34)	=-(D34-C34)
54	Subtract increase in fixed assets at cost	=-(C36-B36)	=-(D36-C36)
55	Free Cash Flow	=SUM(C49:C54)	=SUM(D49:D54)

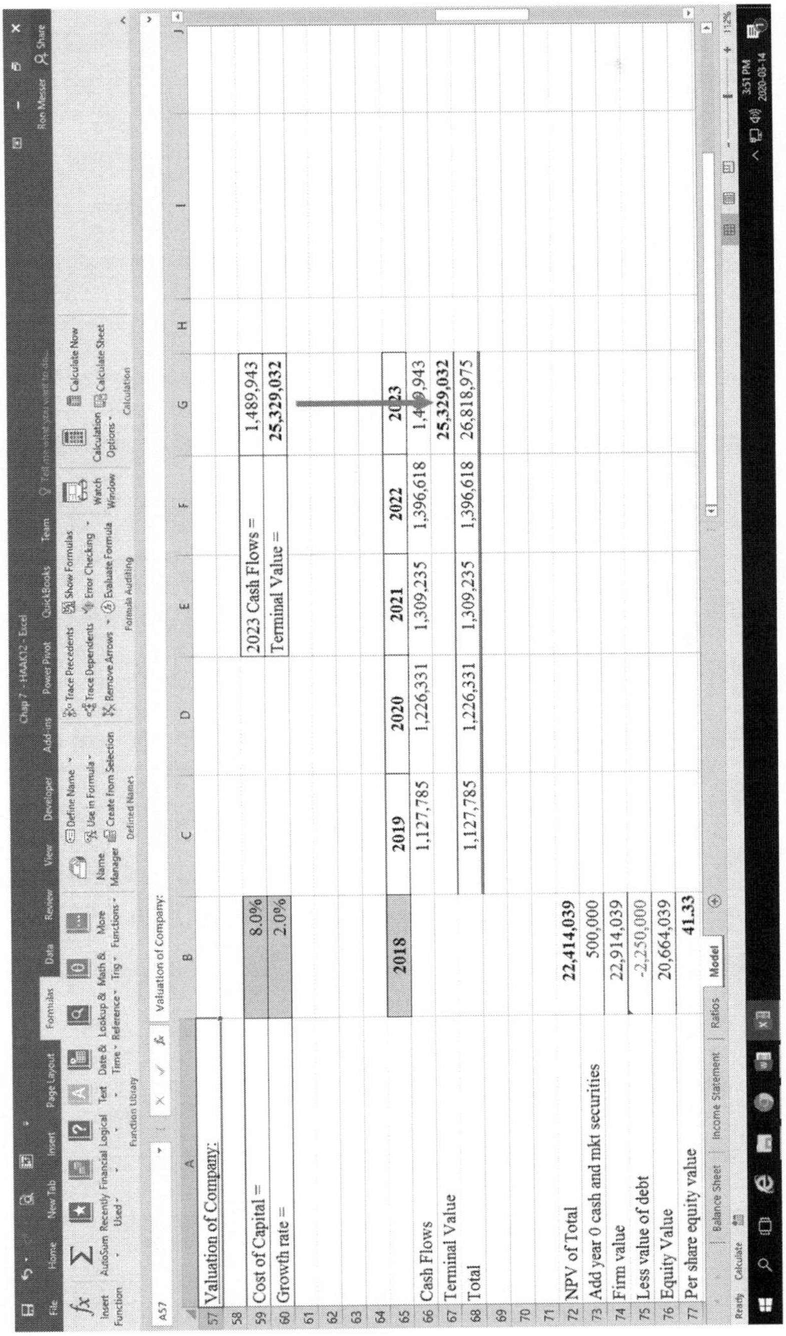

Fig. 7.12. Discounting the Cash Flows.

Fig. 7.13. Discounting the Cash Flows (Formulas).

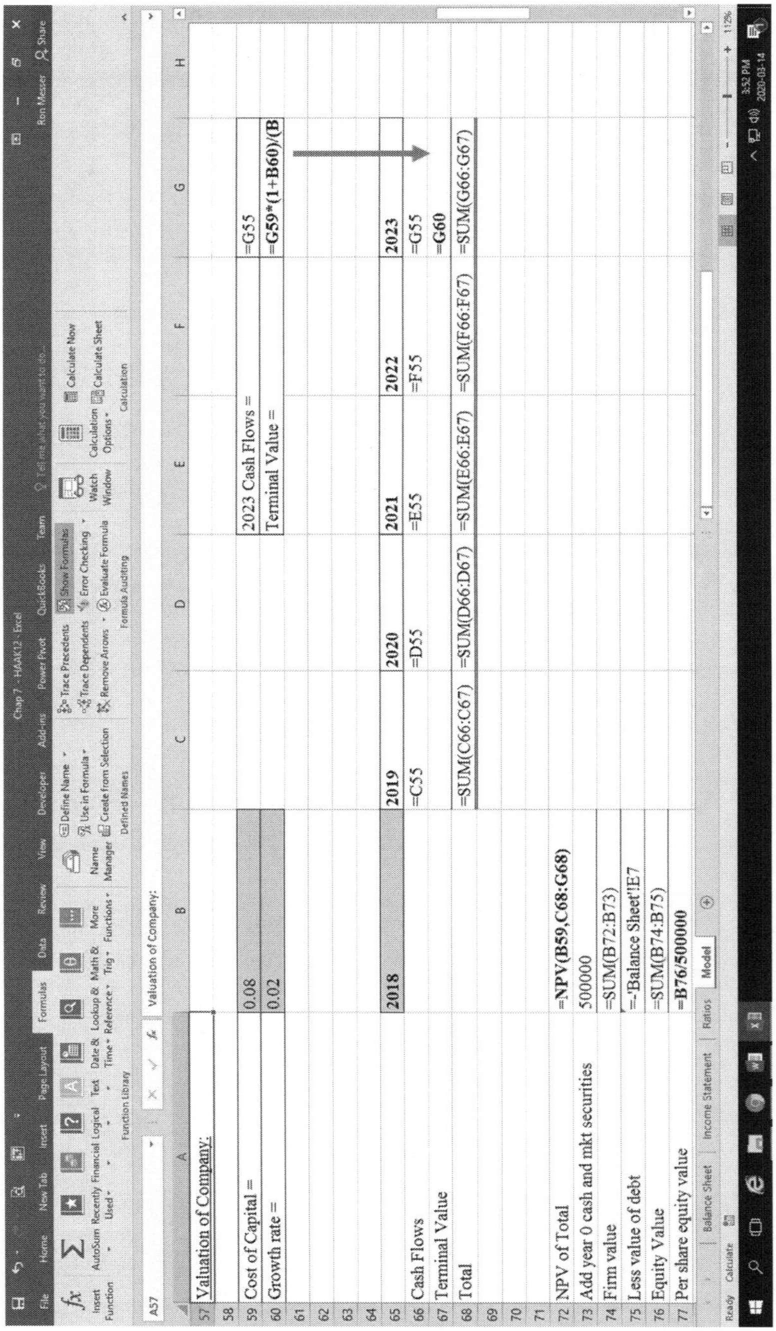

Cell: A57 — *fx* Valuation of Company:

	A	B	C	D	E	F	G	H
57	Valuation of Company:							
58								
59	Cost of Capital =	0.08			2023 Cash Flows =		=G55	
60	Growth rate =	0.02			Terminal Value =		=G59*(1+B60)/(B	
61								
62								
63								
64								
65		2018	2019	2020	2021	2022	2023	
66	Cash Flows		=C55	=D55	=E55	=F55	=G55	
67	Terminal Value						=G60	
68	Total		=SUM(C66:C67)	=SUM(D66:D67)	=SUM(E66:E67)	=SUM(F66:F67)	=SUM(G66:G67)	
69								
70								
71								
72	NPV of Total	=NPV(B59,C68:G68)						
73	Add year 0 cash and mkt securities	500000						
74	Firm value	=SUM(B72:B73)						
75	Less value of debt	=-'Balance Sheet'!E7						
76	Equity Value	=SUM(B74:B75)						
77	Per share equity value	=B76/500000						

Sheet tabs: Balance Sheet | Income Statement | Ratios | Model

Fig. 7.14. Sensitivity of Share Price to Sales Growth and Discount Rate.

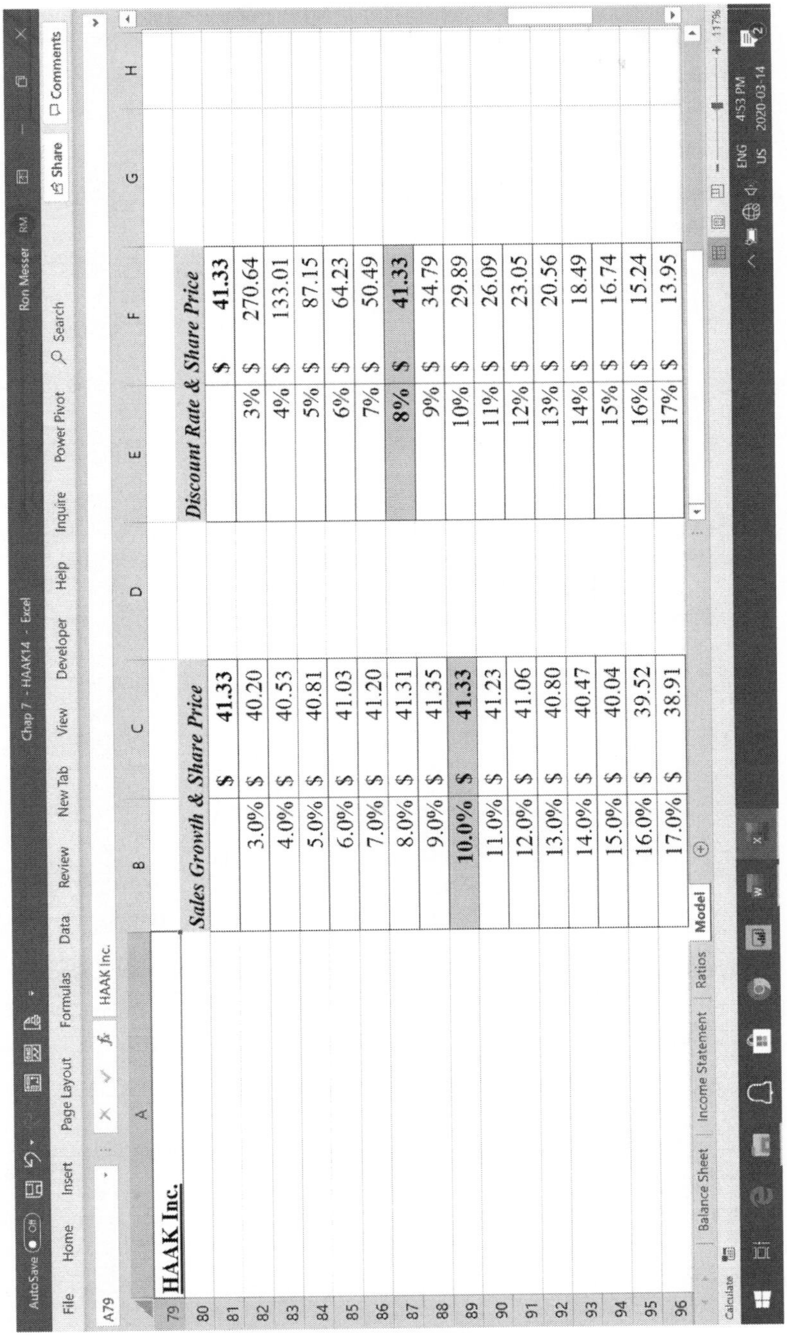

HAAK Inc.

Sales Growth & Share Price

	$	41.33
3.0%	$	40.20
4.0%	$	40.53
5.0%	$	40.81
6.0%	$	41.03
7.0%	$	41.20
8.0%	$	41.31
9.0%	$	41.35
10.0%	$	41.33
11.0%	$	41.23
12.0%	$	41.06
13.0%	$	40.80
14.0%	$	40.47
15.0%	$	40.04
16.0%	$	39.52
17.0%	$	38.91

Discount Rate & Share Price

	$	41.33
3%	$	270.64
4%	$	133.01
5%	$	87.15
6%	$	64.23
7%	$	50.49
8%	$	41.33
9%	$	34.79
10%	$	29.89
11%	$	26.09
12%	$	23.05
13%	$	20.56
14%	$	18.49
15%	$	16.74
16%	$	15.24
17%	$	13.95

costs of capital will dramatically affect the discounting of cash flows, which are compounding annually.

Based on this financial model, the investment bankers can prepare their "dog and pony" show to sell the 500,000 HAAK shares to potential investors at an IPO price of $41.33 per share. This should not be difficult given HAAK's ability to attract customers to their product.

Afterthought → *just monkeying around*

Valuing a company is an imprecise exercise, at best. While models exist for determining the worth of corporate shares, they are always subject to the whims of the marketplace, which involves numerous players with varying levels of sophistication and knowledge. So, aside from simply guessing, is there a better way of determining how much to pay for a business? Can anyone provide some guidance?

The Tao of the Chimp

(Won't you please show me the way)

There have been many theories advanced about how stock markets work. Some are scientific while others are more behavioral. Scientific interpretations about the markets focus on long-term trends, such as changes in GDP, market volatility, and the money supply. The quantitative approach assumes that what happened in the past is the best predictor about what will happen in the future. In contrast, behavioral models are less rigorous, but a lot more fun. You may have heard about some of the more fanciful notions put forward by this school of thought about when to invest, such as based on the coming years' fashion trends (short skirts indicate optimism, which is good for investors.), or based on the success of the New York Mets baseball team.

The basic premise underlying behavioral models is that investors do not behave rationally, but instead are guided by emotions when they make their investment decisions. The behaviorists' insights do not so much suggest that the scientific school is incorrect, but rather that it is probably incomplete. While the behavioral proponents have come up with some interesting observations, they do not present a unified theory about how markets actually work. In contrast, the scientific school has developed the well-known capital assets pricing model ("CAP-M," for short).

Finally, as a way of understanding the dynamics of the stock market, there is the Tao of the Chimp. Some of you may have read about the chimpanzee that was blindfolded by some (probably bored) Yale University professors and then given darts to throw at a page of stocks listed in the *Wall Street Journal*. Apparently, in a comparison with professional financial advisors, the chimp's stock picks provided the best returns.

So, what should you do with your investments? Economic forecasts for Canada and the United States are largely optimistic; however, there is still considerable uncertainty because of ongoing political instability in the world. Fashion trends are unclear, pointing to a conservative, yet sensual "look" for the coming year. The New York Mets are at the bottom of the Eastern conference, but then again, the team *could* come back. Personally, I'd follow the Chimp. While the scientists calculate and the behaviorists fret, the Chimp simply "is." Without suggesting that there is any "monkey business" involved, if you realize that stock markets are truly random, then the Tao – "the way" – becomes abundantly clear.

Chapter 8
Pivot Tables Decisions

What is the data telling me?

Snapshot

Topic
Analysis of financial (BIG) data

Subject Area
Multidisciplinary, including cost and financial accounting, as well as corporate finance

Decisions Made
Financial analytics can be used to answer specific questions about data (for example, how many American Airlines Boeing 737 aircraft landed in Vancouver in July 2018, whose flight originated in New York City?). This is referred to as descriptive analytics. Diagnostic analytics seeks to answer more general problems by carefully analyzing and interpreting the data. For example, What is the trend in different types of aircraft – Boeing compared to Airbus airplanes – landing in Vancouver and how is this impacting runway utilization?

Personal Experience
When working at a privatized airport, I encountered a situation where revenues received from commercial airlines for landing fees had decreased significantly (and unexpectedly) over the prior year. Landing fees represented a significant portion of the airport's revenues and were charged based on the weight of an airplane. Through a careful analysis of the data using Excel pivot tables, I discovered that this was occurring because of a phenomenon known as downgauging. This occurs when commercial air carriers fly smaller aircraft to fill more of the available seats, such as when an airline uses Airbus 340 series airplanes (which carry up to 350 passengers), whereas previously they were flying Boeing 747s (with a capacity of up to 660 passengers). The Airbus aircraft are substantially smaller (with fewer seats) and therefore lighter than the Boeing airplanes and for this reason landing fees declined.

Excel Functionality
Pivot Tables
Power Query
Power Pivot

Background Theory

Everything Old Is New Again

Data analytics may appear to be the "next big thing," but in reality, analyzing data has been something that financial professionals have been doing for a long time. What has changed is that data sets are now larger and more varied. This means that in addition to spreadsheets and documents, a variety of file types can now be accommodated in centralized repositories, referred to as data warehouses (or, data marts); this includes PowerPoint presentations, geographic information system (GIS) files, images (jpeg), pdf formats, flat files (e.g., comma delimited), and audio/video clips. Some of these file formats use large amounts of storage space, which in the past has been quite costly. Nowadays, with cheaper storage media available, capturing data in a variety of forms is relatively easy and inexpensive, and hence the notion of "big data" has become a reality.

Data can be obtained from many sources, both in-house and outside the company. Some are publicly available (through both free and subscription-based services) and some are proprietary to the company, such as its general ledger accounting information. Excel can access and analyze data from several sources. In this regard, however, it is of utmost importance to ensure the integrity of the data being retrieved and, in some situations, may require modifications to the data sets.

There are three separate but interrelated aspects to data analytics:

(1) *Data Access*: This involves deciding on the data sets to analyze, ensuring their integrity, and then downloading the information. For large and complex data sets, such as those found in a data mart, IT professionals should be involved. This is because of the complexity of the storage media and the need to use more sophisticated data retrieval tools, such as SQL scripts (Structured Query Language programs), which select only those data elements needed for the analysis. (This is sometimes referred to as a data "view").[1] For less complex data structures (such as those contained in an Access database), some manipulation may be required before analysis in undertaken – for example, creating separate fields for year, month, and day from a single date field (using the YEAR, MONTH and DAY functions), or making sure that there are no unnecessary blank spaces in data elements (using the TRIM function).

---

[1]The fields in a database are described in a document known as a "data dictionary." This is a detailed description of the database contents; for example, whether data on household income includes (1) income of the primary breadwinner, or (2) income of the primary breadwinner and the other spouse, or (3) income of the primary breadwinner, the spouse, and any working children living at home. The data dictionary also defines data formats (e.g., alpha or numeric), structure (e.g., field size limits), and other parameters (e.g., values that cannot exceed a certain amount).

(2) *Data Analysis*: This text uses pivot tables as the primary tool for analyzing data. It illustrates their application in the demonstration exercises. It also incorporates some general principles concerning good financial modeling practices. What is most important to this part of the process is the skill of the individual analyst, particularly in knowing what to investigate and the appropriate questions to ask relating to the data.

(3) *Data Visualization*: I sometimes – rather cynically – refer to this part of the exercise as making "pretty pictures." The intent here is to present data, as information, in an intuitive way so that decision makers can act. My cynicism revolves around the fact that the real "meat" of the process is found within the analysis; data visualization is like the desert in dinner, which occurs only after first enjoying a fine main course.

Some Data Terminology

Important terms used in data analytics include the following:

- *Fields* are the variables, or descriptors in the header row of a data table. (Data tables use column headings to describe the information that is assembled.)
- *Records* are located below the header row and represent the data that have been collected.
- A group of records is called a *data table*.
- A group of data tables is called a *database*.
- A group of databases is called a *data warehouse* (or data mart).
- Data are dumb, but must have integrity (i.e., they need to be accurate and consistent over time).
- Data become information when they answer questions that are important to us.
- Information become knowledge when we can use them to predict the future (see Chapter 5 on regression analysis and Chapter 3 on time series forecasting).

The analysis of data is an ongoing concern for financial management professionals. I can remember using a software package more than 40 years ago, that is still employed today, called SPSS (Statistical Package for the Social Sciences). It allows users to perform multidimensional analysis of data (referred to as cross-tabular analysis, or cross-tabs); for example, examining the difference in salaries between male and female employees at a company. Excel pivot tables permit users to do the same type of analysis. In addition, Excel Power Pivot incorporates databases, which connect several data tables together and are created through data modeling. Data marts are typically analyzed using more expensive software tools, such as Oracle Essbase, which accesses a data warehouse. (Fortunately, the Essbase data analysis tools look and behave very much like Excel pivot tables and are therefore easy to learn.)

Types of Data Analytics

The current fascination with data analytics is probably best understood in terms of a continuum, rather than a fixed point on the horizon of understanding. That continuum begins with data, which are analyzed to provide information and are subsequently converted into knowledge, when we use the information to predict the future. Broadly speaking there are three types of data analytics.

- *Descriptive analytics* – which answers specific questions about a data set (e.g., what is the number of females living in Toronto, under 30 years of age, with an MBA who are employed in retail banking and earning more than $100,000 annually?)
- *Diagnostic analytics* – which converts data into information through insights gained by addressing specific problems, typically, by identifying relationships between variables (e.g., to what extent do the salaries paid to men and women differ in retail banking?)
- *Predictive analytics* – which uses correlations between variables in a data set to determine causality and generates probabilistic models. (For example, how can we predict the salaries of men and women who are MBA graduates and starting a career in retail banking, based on variables, such as the ranking of the business school they attended, previous work experience, and GPA).

Financial Management Techniques

Data analytics can be used to answer specific questions about large data sets; for example, concerning a company's stock market performance relative to that of its competitors or to explore the relationship between overheard in a manufacturing company and what causes those indirect costs to occur. Financial analytics will typically involve the use of ratios (which are discussed in detail in Chapter 9, in terms of KPIs and dashboards).

When using pivot tables, it is important to be clear about the best way to construct data analytic models. The following points address some good modeling practices.

(1) Limit you pivot tables to one-by-one (1×1) matrices; in other words, include only one field (i.e., variable) in the rows and one in the columns. Creating more complex pivot tables (such as 2×1 or 1×2 matrices) makes the information very difficult to interpret. (Note that the Excel pivot table report filter can be used to add a third variable, in necessary.)

(2) In the values section – i.e., the $\sum$ (summa) symbol, which indicates summation (shown in the lower half, bottom right quadrant of the pivot table dialogue box), you will typically use the following value field summaries: COUNT, SUM, AVERAGE. The COUNT summation records whenever data are contained in a record; SUM adds the data elements, if they are numerical values; AVERAGE gives the arithmetic mean for numerical data. For example, if a field has records containing the numerical values 1, 2, and 3, then: COUNT = 3; SUM = 6; AVERAGE = 3. The salient point here is to be clear about what result you want to obtain, and which summation method allows you to find the answer you desire.

(3) If you are calculating a percentage (i.e., a proportionate amount), be clear about the difference between percentages expressed as rows, columns, or grand totals. A row percentage is proportionate to the variable in the row, while a column percentage relates to the proportion for a column. A grand total percentage addresses the conjoined variables in a 1×1 matrix. For example, consider the following pivot tables which show whether a customer liked or disliked a product offering based on their gender (categorized as male or female). There are three different interpretations of the value relating to females who liked the product (highlighted in the following tables).

Interpretation 1: Expressed as a Percentage of the *Row* Total

Count of Gender	Gender		
Liked Product	Female	Male	Grand Total
Yes	44%	56%	100%
No	50%	50%	100%
Grand Total	46%	54%	100%

Note: This pivot table tells us that of *all the people who **liked** the product*, 44% were female.

Interpretation 2: Expressed as a Percentage of the *Column* Total

Count of Gender	Gender		
Liked Product	Female	Male	Grand Total
Yes	54%	61%	58%
No	46%	39%	42%
Grand Total	100%	100%	100%

Note: This pivot table tells us that of *all the **females** who tried the product*, 54% liked it.

Interpretation 3: Expressed as a Percentage of the *Grand* Total

Count of Gender	Gender		
Liked Product	Female	Male	Grand Total
Yes	25%	33%	58%
No	21%	21%	42%
Grand Total	46%	54%	100%

Note: This pivot table tells us that of *all the people who **tried** and **liked** the product*, 25% were female.

Relevant Excel Functionality

Creating Data Tables

When developing a financial model for data analytics, create a separate worksheet for the data set and label it "DATA." Nothing other than data should be included in this tab. Tables should show the column header row (i.e., field listing) and the records (i.e., data observations) should appear below the fields. It is also a good practice to indicate the number of records in your data table (e.g., $n = 100$). After the data set has been created, place the cursor anywhere inside the data table and left click on the main menu: INSERT and then TABLE. The perimeter of your data table will be outlined and a dialogue box will appear asking "where is the data for your table?" Left click on OK (as shown in **Fig. 8.1**).

The data set will now be recognized as a table and will change to appear, as follows (**Fig. 8.2**).

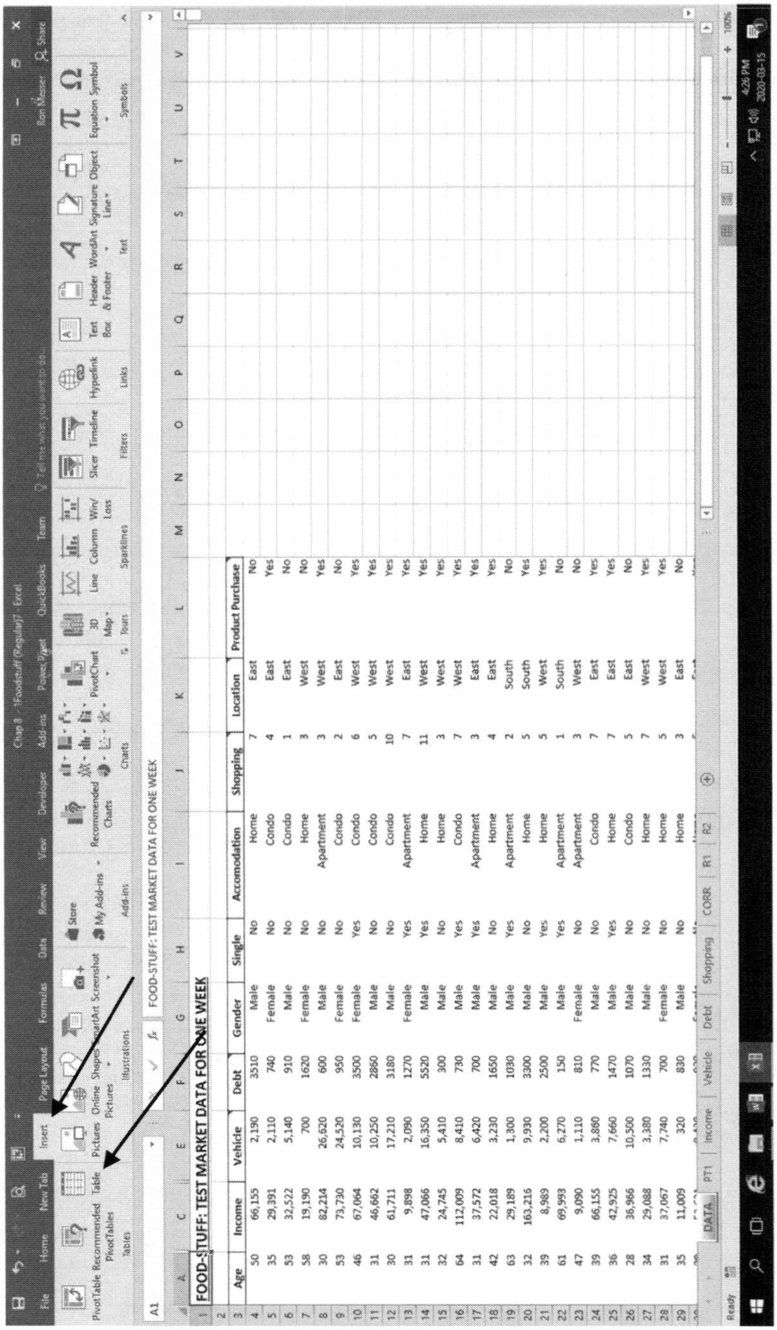

Fig. 8.1. Creating a Data Table.

FOOD-STUFF: TEST MARKET DATA FOR ONE WEEK

Age	Income	Vehicle	Debt	Gender	Single	Accomodation	Shopping	Location	Product Purchase
50	66,155	2,190	3510	Male	No	Home	7	East	No
35	29,391	2,110	740	Female	No	Condo	4	East	Yes
53	32,522	5,140	910	Male	No	Condo	1	East	No
58	19,190	700	1620	Female	No	Home	3	West	No
30	82,214	26,620	600	Female	No	Apartment	3	West	Yes
53	73,730	24,520	950	Female	No	Condo	2	East	No
46	67,064	10,130	3500	Female	Yes	Condo	6	West	Yes
31	46,662	10,250	2860	Male	No	Condo	5	West	Yes
30	61,711	17,210	3180	Male	No	Condo	10	West	Yes
31	9,898	2,090	1270	Female	Yes	Apartment	7	East	Yes
31	47,066	16,350	5520	Male	Yes	Home	11	West	Yes
32	24,745	5,410	300	Male	No	Home	3	West	Yes
64	112,009	8,410	730	Male	Yes	Condo	7	West	Yes
31	37,572	6,420	700	Male	No	Apartment	3	East	Yes
42	22,018	3,230	1650	Male	No	Home	4	East	No
63	29,189	1,300	1030	Male	No	Apartment	2	South	Yes
32	163,216	9,930	3300	Male	No	Home	5	South	Yes
39	8,989	2,200	2500	Male	Yes	Home	5	West	Yes
61	69,993	6,270	150	Male	Yes	Apartment	1	South	No
47	9,090	1,110	810	Female	No	Apartment	3	West	Yes
39	66,155	3,860	770	Male	No	Condo	7	East	Yes
36	42,925	7,660	1470	Male	Yes	Home	7	East	No
28	36,956	10,500	1070	Male	No	Condo	5	East	Yes
34	29,688	3,380	1330	Male	No	Home	7	West	Yes
31	37,067	7,740	700	Female	No	Home	5	West	Yes
35	11,009	320	830	Male	No	Home	3	East	No

Fig. 8.2. Creating a Data Table.

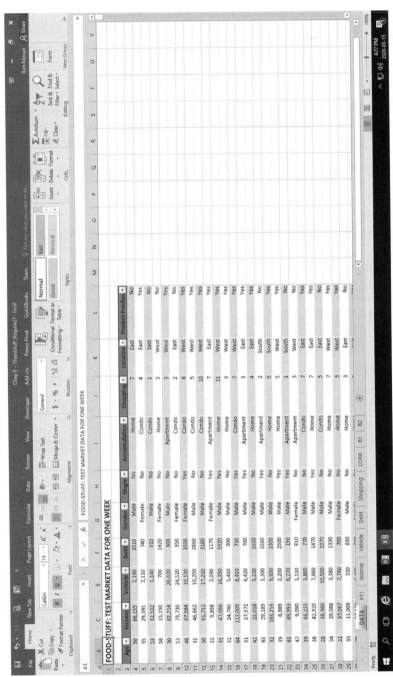

By specifying that your data is in fact in a "table," updating information is easily facilitated, especially when creating and using pivot tables. Doing this allows you to add, delete, and modify the records in your data set and have them automatically updated in your pivot tables. If the table is not created in this way, the changes will not be recognized in your analysis. (Should this occur, a more cumbersome process that involves redefining the parameters of the table will be necessary.)

Cleaning Data

An important step in performing analytics is to review the data to ensure that it is (1) complete and accurate and also (2) that the analyst understands the contents of the data sets. Often, some manipulation is required, for example, to remove unnecessary spaces or to separate data elements, such as someone's first name and last name contained in a single field. Data cleaning can be accomplished using a number of Excel formulas that relate to text, including LEFT, RIGHT, MID, TRIM, FIND, SUBSTITUTE, REPLACE, and CONCATENATE. The function of these text manipulators is described in **Table 8.1**.

These manipulations are useful for fixing data that have known or observed errors, which is often true for many older data sets. The TEXT TO COLUMNS functionality, which appears in the ribbon below the DATA tab in the main menu is also useful for converting data into a number of selected fields in a data table, using either delimiters or predetermined fixed widths. This is shown in the figure below (left click on: DATA, TEXT TO COLUMNS) (**Fig. 8.3**).

In column A (cells A4 to A7) of this data set, we want to separate the first and last names using a delimiter, which in this case is a single space that separates the names. After selecting "Next," the following dialogue box appears (**Fig. 8.4**).

Table 8.1. Formulas for Manipulating Text Data.

Text Formula	What It Does ...
LEFT (text, number-of-characters)	When a cell is selected this function returns only a specified number of characters, starting from the left-most position.
RIGHT (text, number-of-characters)	When a cell is selected this function returns only a specified number of characters, starting from the right-most position.
TRIM (text)	Removes all spaces in a text string except for spaces between words.
FIND (text)	Gives the starting position for a specified text string (specified in quotes) within a larger text.
SUBSTITUTE (text, old-text, new-text)	Replaces text in an existing text string with new text.
REPLACE (old-text, start-number, number-of-characters, new-text)	Replaces old text with new text based on a specified starting position and text length.
CONCATENATE (text1, text2, etc.)	Joins text strings together. (Note that the ampersand symbol, &, can also be used to do this.)

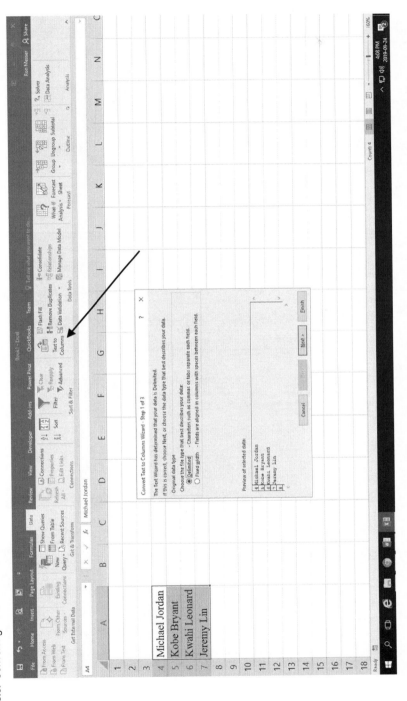

Fig. 8.3. Converting Text to Columns.

Fig. 8.4. Converting Text to Columns.

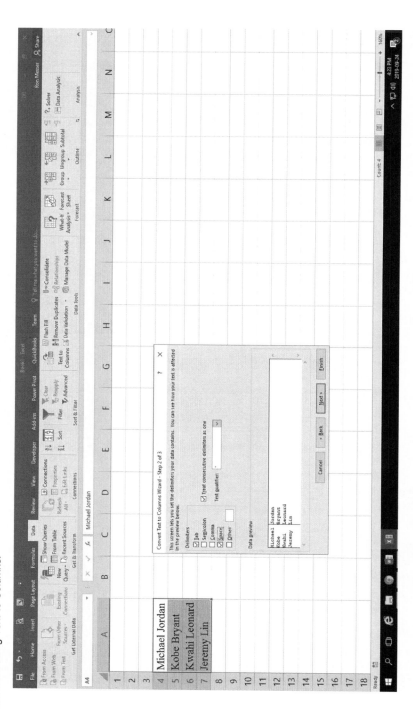

We select the check box for "Space" as the delimiter and the new data table, now containing two fields, is shown in the "data preview" section of the screen. We then select "Next" and choose an area in the worksheet where we want to place the output (beginning in cell C4); then press "Finish." The text has been converted from a single column (field) into two new fields (located in columns C and D), which can be used for further analysis (**Fig. 8.5**).

To activate pivot tables, on the main menu, return to the DATA worksheet and place the cursor anywhere inside the data table and left click on INSERT and then select PIVOT TABLES.

Demonstration Exercise

Data analytics is a popular field of study that has been applied to a variety of decision-making contexts, from sports (think of Michael Lewis's book *Moneyball*) to marketing (the beer and diapers story), to hedge fund algorithms.[2] An analysis of information is common when a business is seeking answers to specific questions or trying to understand the behaviors portrayed in the data collected. (Excel file: Food-stuff(shell).xls.)

Case Facts

In many young families, both parents are employed full time and as a result, preparing a healthy and appetizing meal after work is often a challenge. Due to these changing demographics, there is an unmet need in the marketplace that is being satisfied by food retailers who have started providing "meal kits." These include preassembled ingredients, along with recipe cards, that give step-by-step instructions on how to prepare a delicious, family-made, supper in less than 30 minutes. "Food-stuff" is one such company. It is offering four varieties of prepacked meal kits using the following ingredients: chicken, beef, fish, and a vegan option. Test market studies for their product were conducted in several cities over a period of 1 week (Monday to Sunday) in May 2019. Data have been collected to assess the best way to position their offerings to generate sales.[3] The variables of interest are shown as field headers (row 3) in **Fig. 8.6**.

Descriptive Analytics

As a first step, let's examine the data to better understand product usage. The company's CEO (let's call him Dave) wants to know what proportion of people purchased the product, based on their gender (male or female), as this may affect product presentation. He also wants to know how many people who used the product were high- or low-income earners, because this may affect product pricing. Nathan, a newly hired

---

[2]Although the origins of this story are sometimes considered apocryphal, others contend that it actually occurred. Anyway ... through analysis of its large POS gathered data sets, Wal-Mart discovered that sales of diapers were related to beer purchases, particularly on Friday nights. The company determined that the correlation occurred because working men, who had been asked by their spouse to pick up diapers on their way home from the job, also bought a six pack as a means of stress relief. See: Xiaojuntian, November 25, 2014, "Beer and Nappies." Retrieved from https://bigdatabigworld.wordpress.com/2014/11/25/beer-and-nappies/. Accessed on January 19, 2020.

[3]I often tell my students that much of the time and expense associated with data analytics relates to obtaining the data. The skill involved in doing this requires a knowledge of research methodologies as well as statistical sampling techniques.

Fig. 8.5. Converting Text to Columns.

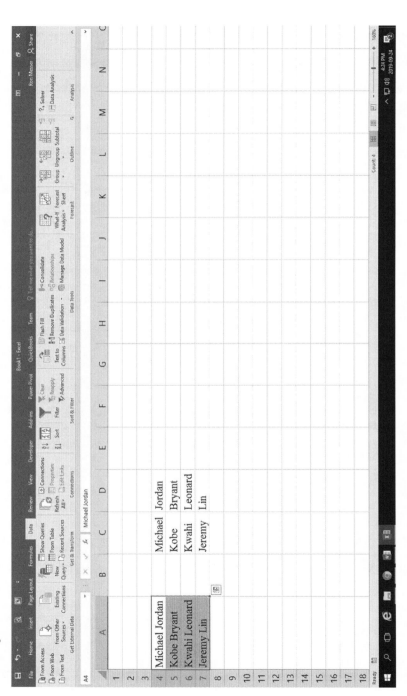

Fig. 8.6. Food-stuff Demographic Data.

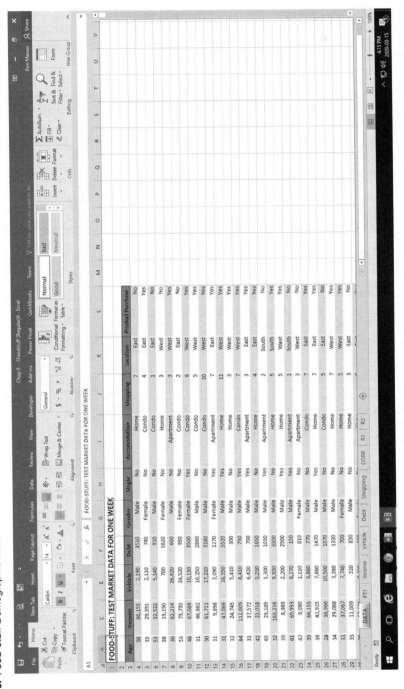

business school graduate who is proficient in Excel, has been tasked with helping Bob analyze the data.

When addressing specific questions such as these about a data set, it is important to first identify the variables of interest. To answer the CEO's initial question, we need to use the following fields: (1) "Product Purchase" and (2) "Gender." Bob also asked that the results be expressed as a percentage (i.e., he wanted a measure of "proportion"). To do this, we use the Excel pivot tables functionality.

As a first step, however, it is important to ensure that our data are recognized as a table by Excel. To do this, position the cursor anywhere in the table and then left click on the following Excel functions: INSERT and then TABLE. A dialogue box will appear, as in **Fig. 8.3**, showing the cell range for the table. Click "OK" to recognize your data set as a table (**Fig. 8.7**).

Next, again position the cursor anywhere inside the data table. From the main menu, left click on the following functions: INSERT and then PIVOT TABLES. A dialogue box will appear on the right side of the worksheet which – in the default view – will show the fields in the data table's header row as variables (arranged vertically) in the upper half. The bottom half of the dialogue box shows four quadrants. The rows and columns will include the variables of interest relating to "Product Purchase" and "Gender." This is shown in **Fig. 8.8**.

(Note that the pivot table will initially show the fields as "row labels" and "column labels." To provide the correct description for these fields, left click to select in PIVOTTABLE TOOLS, DESIGN; then select REPORT LAYOUT and choose any form other than "compact" – which is the default setting.)

To determine the percentage of males and females who liked the product, we need to use the "Values" quadrant (lower right), located in the bottom half of the dialogue box. But first, we need to choose a field to calculate. Select the gender field. Next, we need to determine what type of calculation to perform, which is shown in **Fig. 8.9**. Select "COUNT" because we only want to know whether data exist in a record for the gender field. (Note: COUNT only recognizes whether any data is present in a field for a record.)

Now, from the dialogue box we indicate that we want to express our results as a percentage of a row total. **Fig. 8.10** shows the completed pivot table.

In answer to the CEO's question, 56.36% (Cell C5) of the respondents who purchased the product were males. Also, 43.64% (cell B5) of females bought the product.

To summarize, when addressing a specific question (i.e., descriptive analytics) about a data set, follow these steps:

(1) Identify the fields required to answer the question. This can be determined by isolating the data elements that most closely approximate the information request. Question: What proportion of people *purchased the product*, based on whether they were *male or female*. The wording of this query directs us to consider the relationship between the fields "Product Purchase" and "Gender."

(2) Place these fields in the rows and columns of the dialogue box, respectively. (As a rule of thumb, I always put the field with the fewest categories in the columns; this is because column widths in Excel are wider than row heights and therefore the results can be better viewed on the computer screen.)

Fig. 8.7. Creating a Data Table.

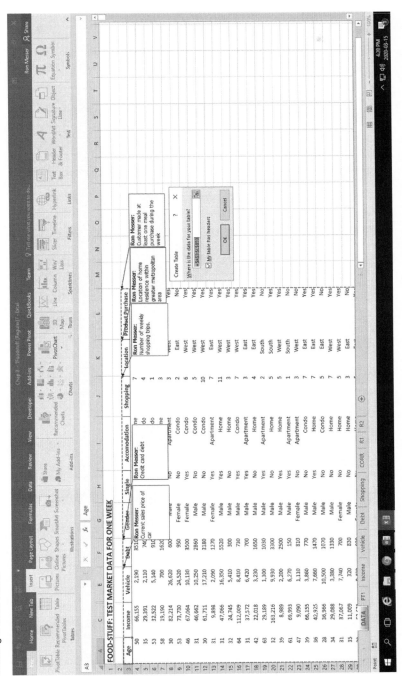

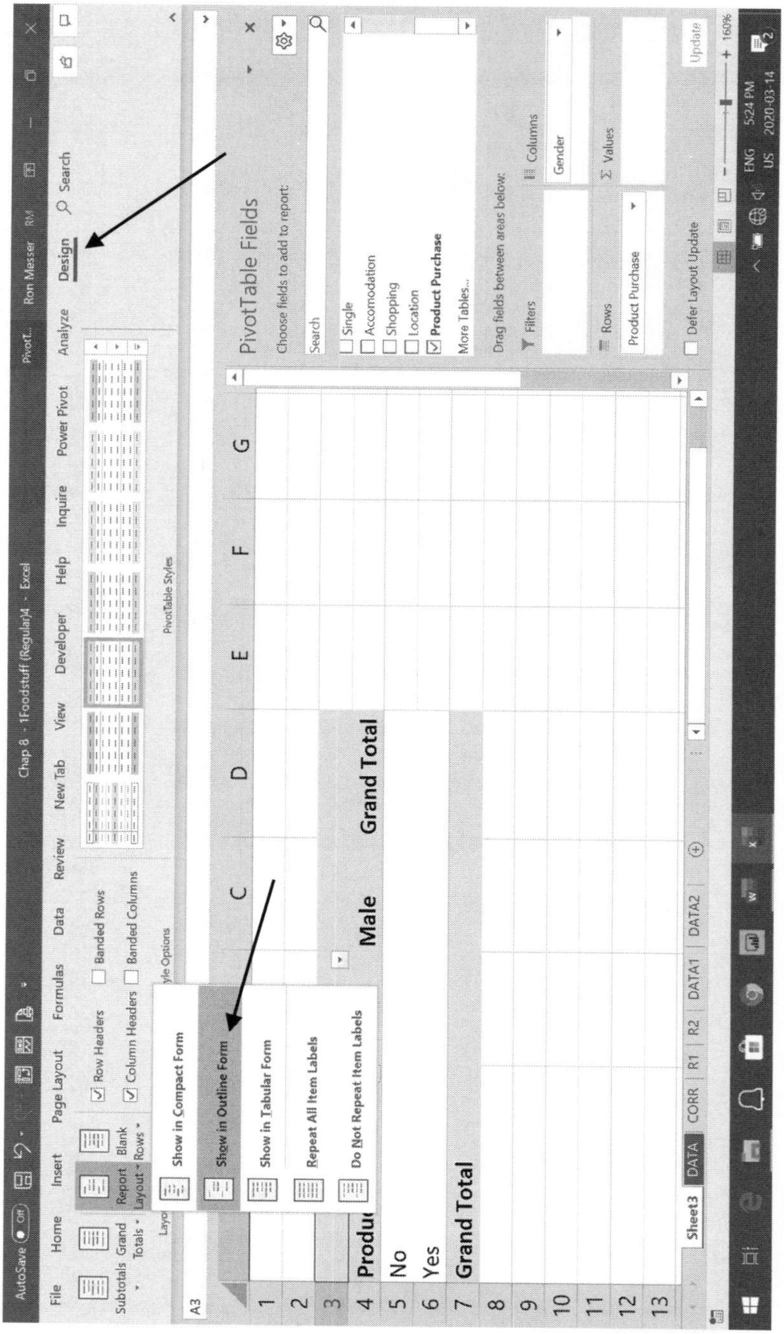

Fig. 8.8. Selecting Pivot Table Variables for Columns and Rows.

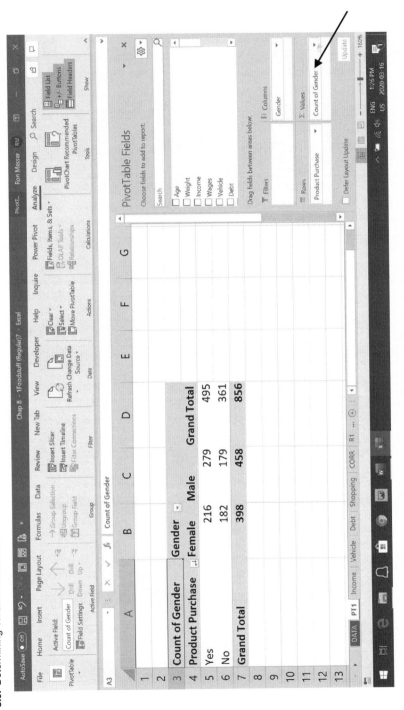

Fig. 8.9. Determining What to Calculate.

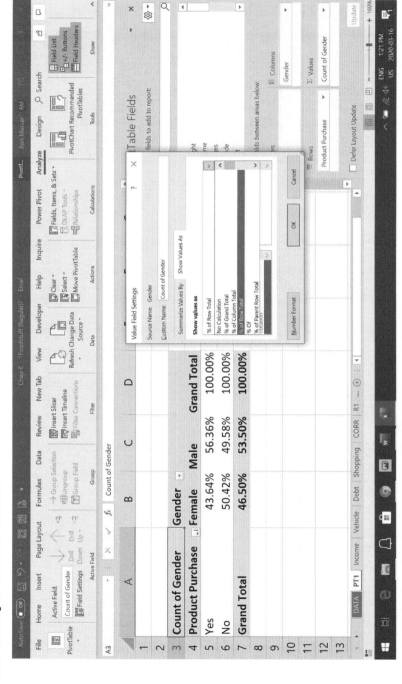

Fig. 8.10. Answering the CEO's First Question.

(3) Determine the type of values function you need to answer the question. For most questions, you will use COUNT, SUM, or AVERAGE.

(4) Select a field to count, sum, or average.

(5) Determine how to express your results, based on the question being asked – i.e., as a percentage or using another numeric format. When expressing results as a percentage, be careful to differentiate between those that are a percentage of a row, column, or grand total. Each option tells a different story. For example, consider the CEO's first question. The correct answer showed the results as a percentage of a row (see cells B5 and C5 in **Fig. 8.10**). Consider how the result for this cell would be interpreted if it were expressed differently; such as a percentage of a column (see **Fig. 8.11**).

Here the value in cell C5 tells us that 60.92% of *all males* purchased the product. If the result is expressed as a percentage of the grand total, the results appear in **Fig. 8.12**.

The value in cell C5 now shows that 32.59% of *all respondents* who bought the product were male.

To answer the CEO's second question, *how many people who purchased the product were high or low-earners*, let's use the six steps outlined.

Step 1: Identify the Fields Needed to Answer the Question
The most appropriate fields to use are "Product Purchase" and "Income" (high or low-income earners).

Step 2: Put the Fields in Rows and Columns
Because the "Product Purchase" field has only two conditions (Yes or No), we will place it in the columns and "Income" – which has more than two categories – will be situated in the rows of the pivot table. Note that when we select Income as the variable for the rows, all of the numerical values for this field appear, sorted in ascending order. We will need to group Income into a smaller number of intervals, or categories, to make the analysis easier to understand. This can be done by left clicking on any cell that contains income amounts in the pivot table and then right clicking to select "group" from the dialogue box that appears; then click OK. This is shown in **Fig. 8.13**.

Step 3: Determine the Type of Values Function
Because the CEO asks about the number of people, we can perform a simple count of the records.

Step 4: Select a Field for the Values Function
Any field can be used to perform a count. So, let's use the gender field.

Step 5: Numeric Format for Results
A number format is the most appropriate to answer this question.

Fig. 8.14 shows the pivot table that answers the CEO's second question. In the data set, only one respondent (cell C9) who was in the highest income bracket purchased the product; of the low-income people, 146 of them (cell C3) also bought the product. By activating the PIVOT CHART functionality (under PIVOT TABLE TOOLS,

Fig. 8.11. Another Answer to the Question.

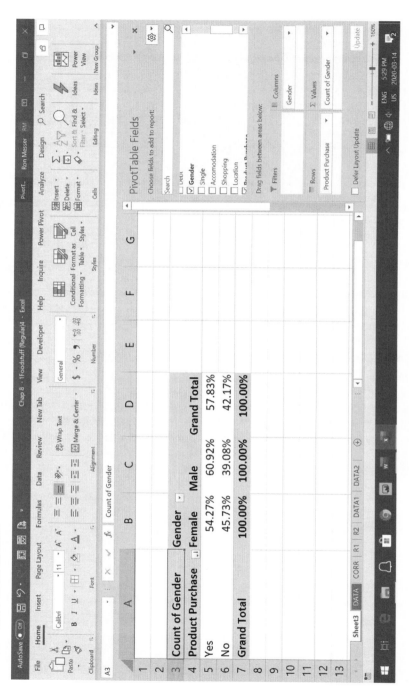

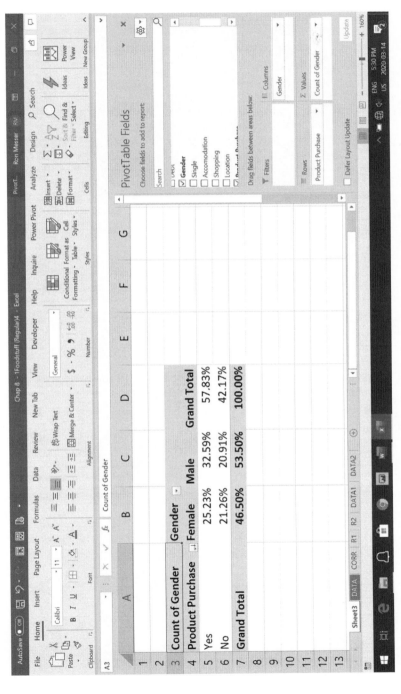

Fig. 8.12. Still Another Answer to the Question.

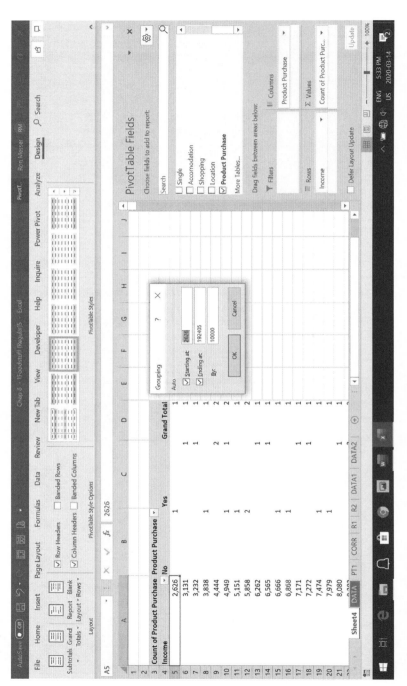

Fig. 8.13. Grouping Numeric Fields.

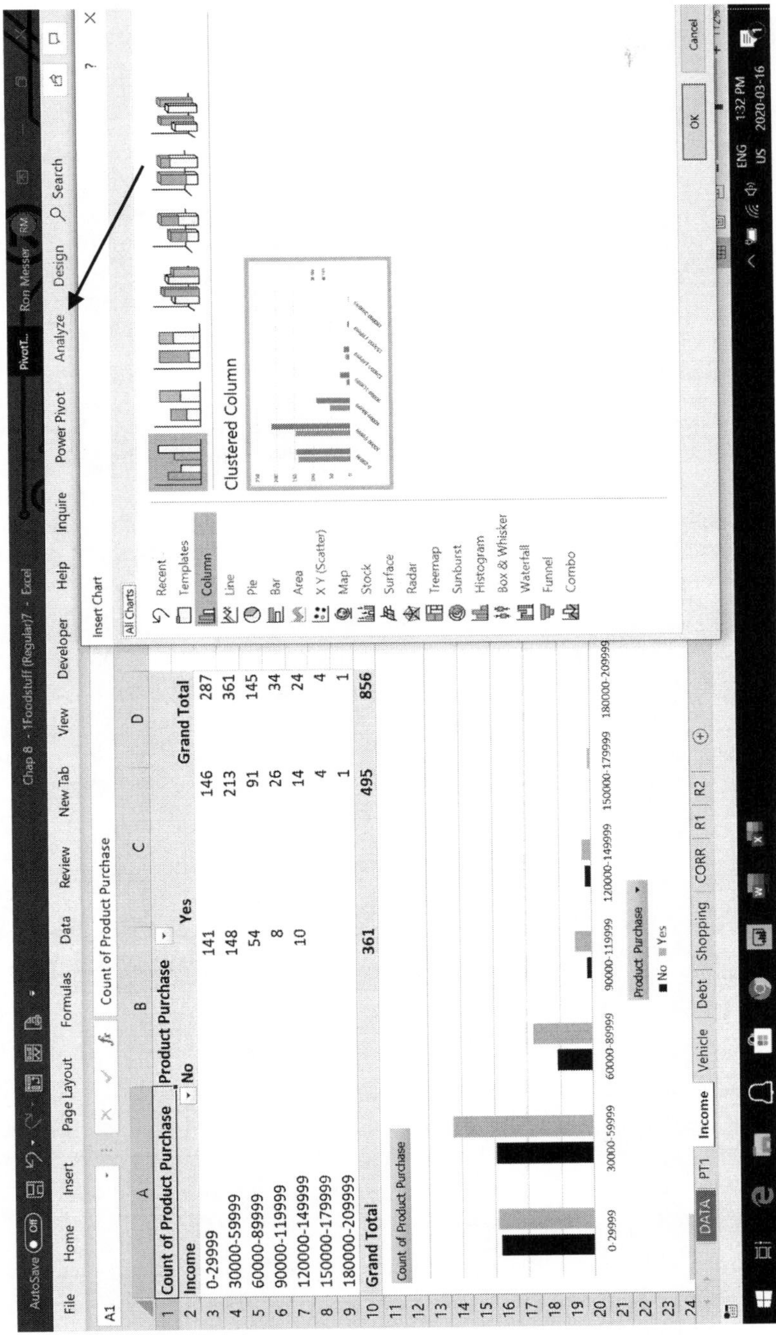

Fig. 8.14. Answering the CEO's First Question.

ANALYZE, PIVOT CHART), a simple bar chart quickly gives us the answer to the question.

The pivot chart informs us that it is primarily lower and middle-income households (earning between $30,000 to $60,000 annually) that purchased the product.

Diagnostic Analytics

Dave, the CEO of Food-stuff, also wants some more information about his prospective customers. He knows that lower and middle income earners purchased his product, but are there other factors that differentiate future buyers. The purpose of diagnostic analytics is to provide a better understanding about a business problem (in this case, who are the product's customers). In this situation there is no specific question to answer – unlike with descriptive analytics – but, familiarity with the data and professional insight will dictate the type of analysis that should be done. The CEO suspects that those who buy his product will have particular spending habits and that these will be tied to earnings. Nathan, his new analyst, identifies the fields (variables) in the data set that relate to household expenditures; these include vehicle (value of household car), debt (amount of credit card borrowing), and shopping (number of trips to the mall). All of these measures in some way represent proxies for current spending (i.e., expenditures on cars, homes, and clothing) and therefore may indicate a propensity for buying new products (like meal kits). Three pivot tables are prepared, along with accompanying charts, as shown in **Figs. 8.15–8.17**.

The pivot charts for these tables provide a consistent and convincing picture of potential users of the meal kits. Moving from left to right on each of the X-axes for the three graphs, we note an increasing preference for the meal kits. **Fig. 8.15** tells Dave that people who drive pricey cars bought the product. Also, customers who are more indebted preferred the meal kits (**Fig. 8.16**), as well as folks who shopped more frequently (**Fig. 8.17**). With this information (gleaned from the data analysis), the CEO can now target his sales toward lower and middle-income earners with bad (good?) spending habits (on cars and other consumer items).

Predictive analytics is discussed in Chapter 5, as part of the topic on regression analysis, which addresses the question: Can I predict the future? In the demonstration exercise, as a next step, Dave would use the important variables identified in the diagnostic analysis to develop a regression model that shows how customer incomes and spending habits affect product preference (i.e., "product purchase").

Some Additional Analytic Functions with Power Pivot

The process of data analytics has been greatly facilitated by the Excel add-ins: Power Query, Power Pivot, and Power BI. Each of these features provides added functionality for cleaning and managing data (Query), analyzing more complex databases (Pivot), and presenting the results to decision makers in a user-friendly way (BI).

To load Power Pivot, left click: FILE, OPTIONS, ADD-INS and the following screen appears (**Fig. 8.18**).

Select the "COM Add-ins" and press Go, and the following screen shows a series of check boxes (**Fig. 8.19**).

Fig. 8.15. Car Value and Potential Product Customers.

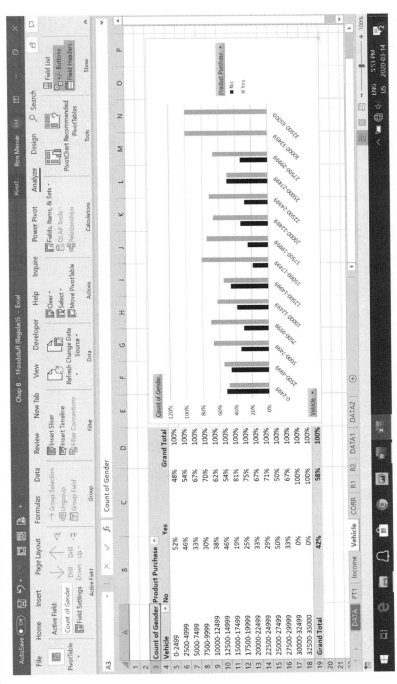

Fig. 8.16. Household Debt and Potential Product Customers.

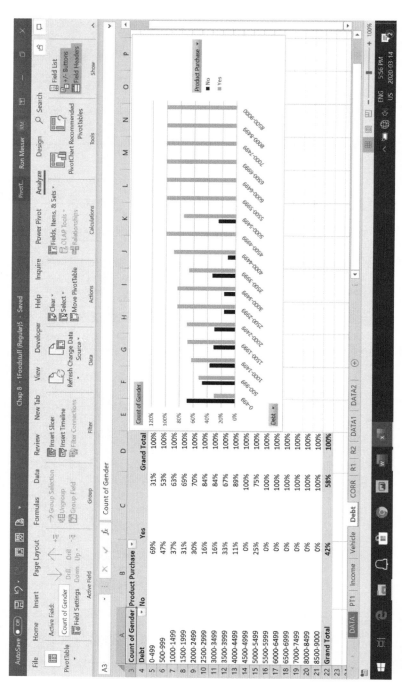

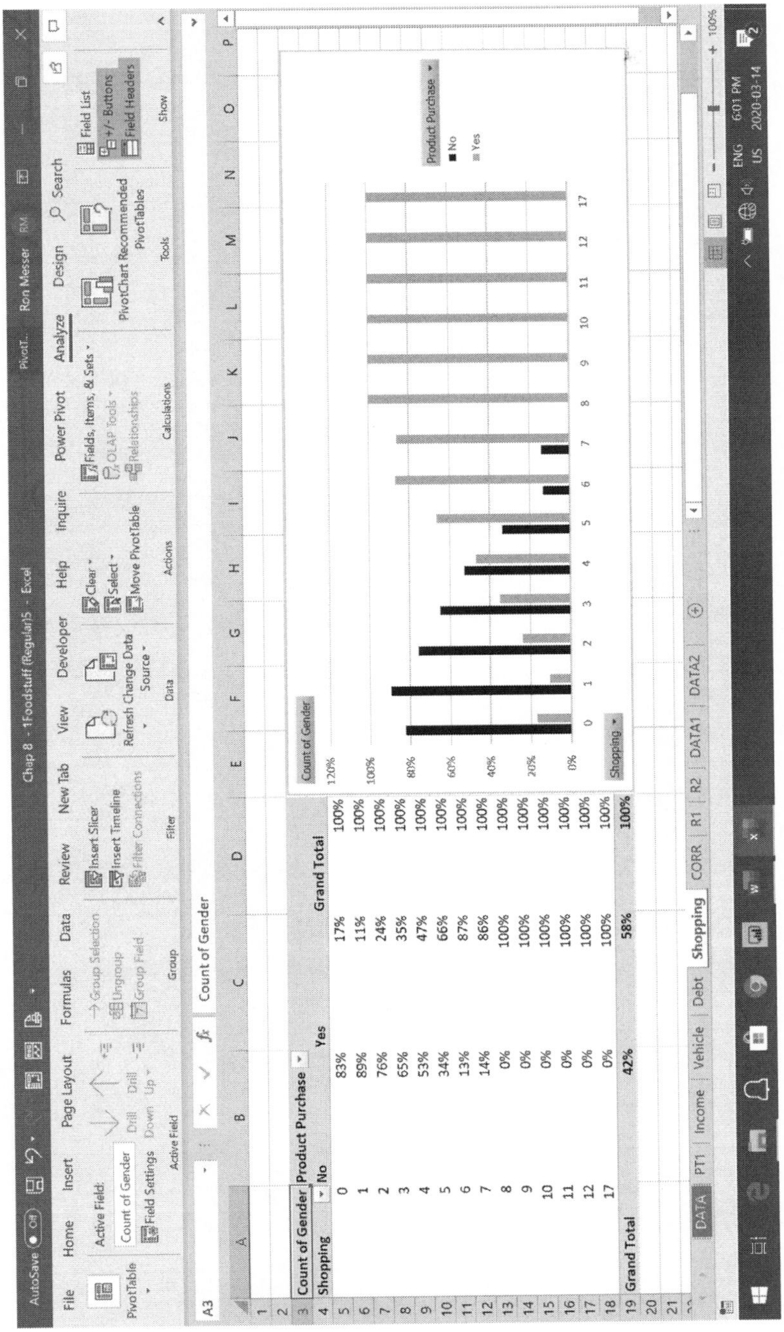

Fig. 8.17. Shopping Trips and Potential Product Customers.

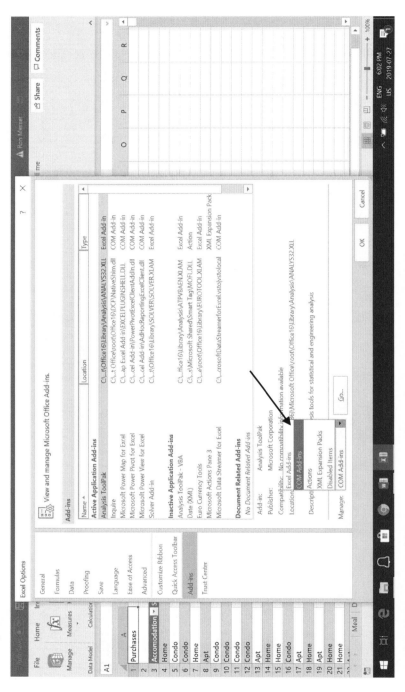

Fig. 8.18. Loading Power Pivot.

Fig. 8.19. Loading Power Pivot.

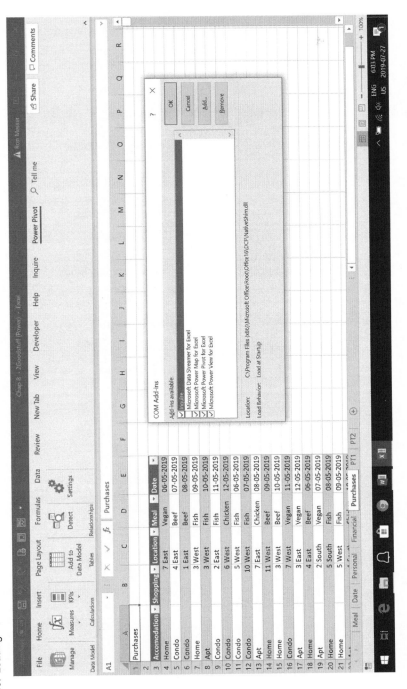

From the check box, select Power Pivot. These add-ins will now appear in the main menu of Excel.

With Power Pivot, Excel can include several tables in a database. These can be imported from external sources or incorporate existing tables. Each of the data tables that form part of the database must be linked through a "key field"; this is a variable that is common to several data tables. For example, a salesperson's name may be listed in a master table of all sales staff, which can be linked to a detailed record of sales transactions by individual salespeople.

In a database, a key field can be linked to other tables in one of three possible ways:

(1) One-to-one: where *one field* in one table is linked to a *one record* in another table.
(2) One-to-many: where *one field* in one table is linked to *many records* in another table.
(3) Many-to-many: where *many fields* in one table are linked to *many records* in another table.

Note that Power Pivot is somewhat limited with respect to the types of relationships that can be created when linking data tables, in that it only accommodates one-to-many relationships. (Excel Power BI, in addition to one-to-many relationships, also allows one-to-one relationships.)

Power Pivot will be used to gain additional insights for Food-stuff. We will revisit the company's data by incorporating several additional tables (some of this information was contained in the original data and some more information has been collected and placed in separate tables). The tables that make up the database are as follows (**Table 8.2**).

The relationships between the tables are shown in **Fig. 8.20**. (Note that the field names appear below the table names and are indented.)

The following one-to-many relationships appear in **Fig. 8.20**:

- The Meal field in the Meals table is linked to the meal field in the Personal table (one-to-many relationship).
- The Date field in the Date table is linked to the Date field in the Personal, Financial, and Purchases tables (one-to-many relationship).

Table 8.2. Creating a Database from Data Tables.

Table	Data Description
Meal	Type of meal kit by ingredients: chicken, beef, fish, vegan
Date	Date data was collected for the period May 6–12, 2019 (Monday to Sunday)
Personal	Personal information about product users: weight, gender, marital status
Financial	Financial information about product users: income, car value, personal debt
Purchases	Other information about product users: accommodation, location, shopping habits

Fig. 8.20. Data Table Relationships in Power Pivot.

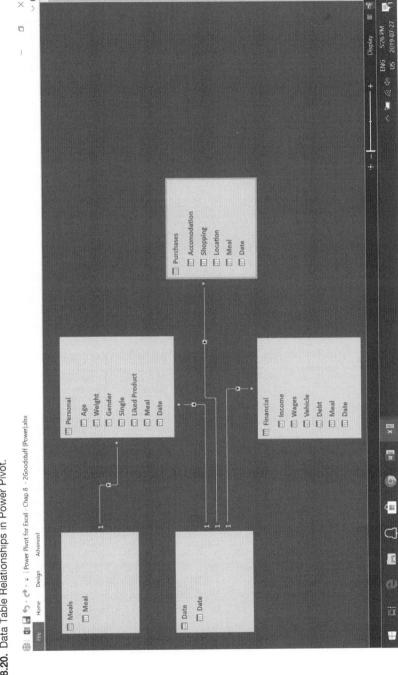

To create relationships between tables, from the main menu, left click: POWER PIVOT, ADD TO MODEL, as shown in **Figs. 8.21 and 8.22**. (Note that a separate worksheet has been created for each of the tables shown in **Fig. 8.20**.)

In this screen you can continue to add additional tables to the database. But, by using the more intuitive "Diagram View" option (which is selected in the top right section of the Power Pivot menu screen), relationships can be traced by left clicking on a field in one table (highlighted "Meal" field in the "Meals" table) and then, by holding down the left click button on the mouse, dragging the line to the relationship field in another table (highlighted "Meal" field in the "Personal" table), as shown in **Fig. 8.23**.

Once the relationships have been determined and mapped, the database can be used in Power Pivot. As an example, let's consider the following additional (diagnostic analytic) questions asked by the CEO.

(1) Is there any pattern in the type of meal kit selected based on the day of the week? (This information will be helpful for production planning, which is particularly important because of the perishable nature of the meal kits.)

(2) Is there any difference between men and women in the type of meal kit selected? (This information may influence the choice of which type of meal kit to produce, depending on whether one spouse is a homemaker, and therefore more likely to select the type of meal for the family.)

In responding to the first question, Nathan prepares the following analysis, using Power Pivot (**Fig. 8.24**).

Note that the Power Pivot dialogue box at the right – top half – shows the data tables in the database, as well as the fields included in each table. Once linked, fields in any table can be analyzed.

The pivot chart in **Fig. 8.24** shows that over the course of the week, chicken meals are preferred to beef. Fish consumption is relatively constant from Monday through Sunday, while vegan meals tend to decrease on weekends. An analysis of the second question is presented in **Fig. 8.25**.

This analysis shows that overall, males preferred the meal kits more than females and that this was true for every category of food offering (beef, chicken, fish, or vegan).

Afterthought → *considering data, information, and knowledge*

The Internet is a truly wonderful and sometimes scary thing. Web browsers helped facilitate the widespread adoption of the wired world for both storing and retrieving information. MOSAIC and Netscape were some of the first easily usable Internet search engines, which have (relatively) recently been replaced by the now dominate firm, Google. The short essay below considers Google in its historical context.

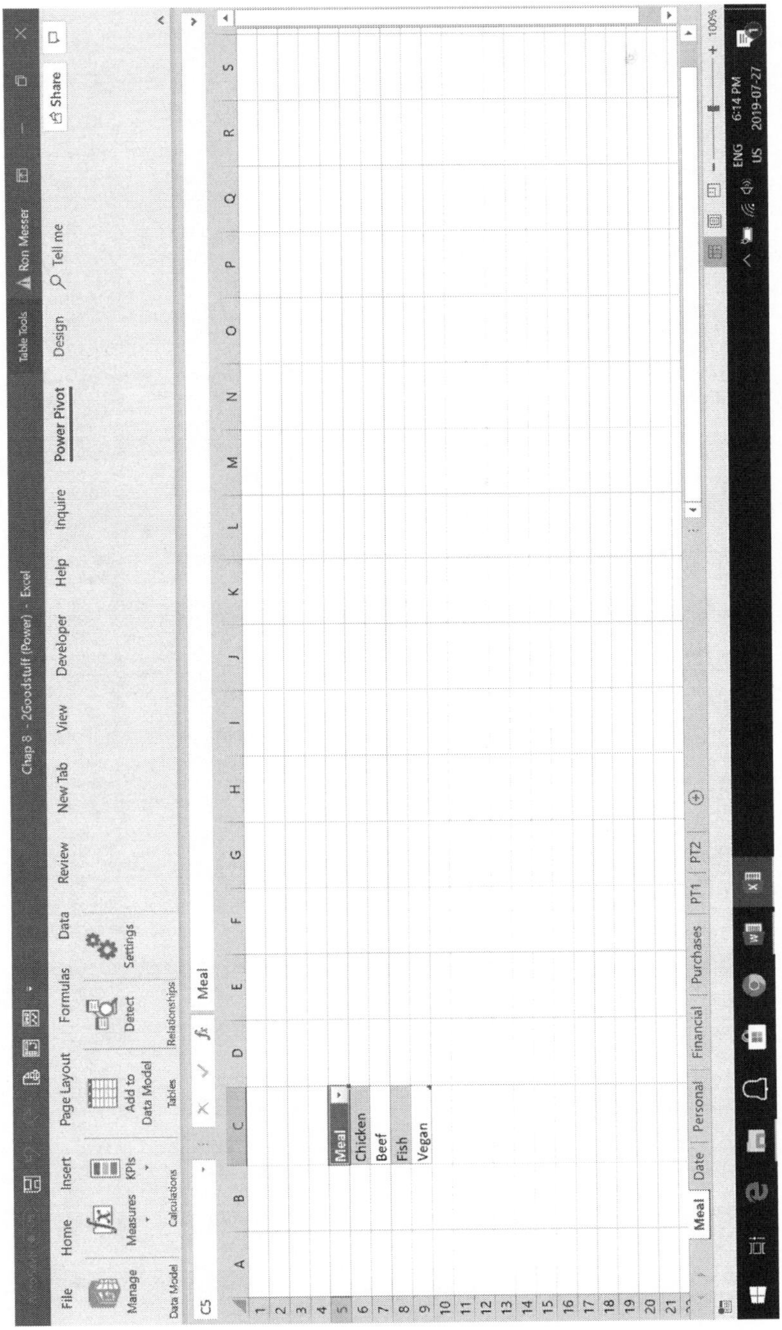

Fig. 8.21. Creating a Database Using Power Pivot.

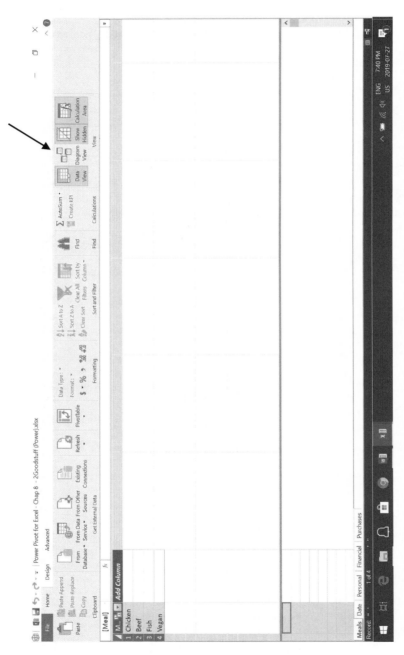

Fig. 8.22. Creating a Database Using Power Pivot.

Fig. 8.23. Creating a Database Using Power Pivot.

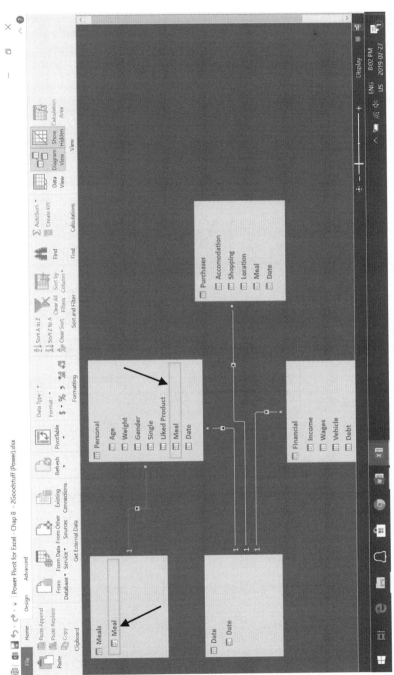

Fig. 8.24. Type of Meal Kit Selected by Day of the Week.

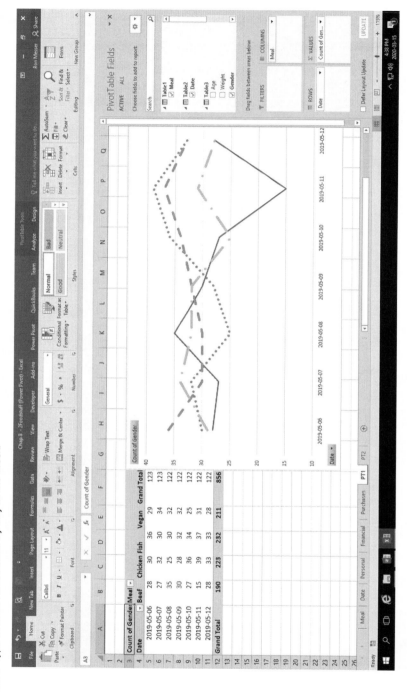

Fig. 8.25. Type of Meal Kit Selected Comparing Males and Females.

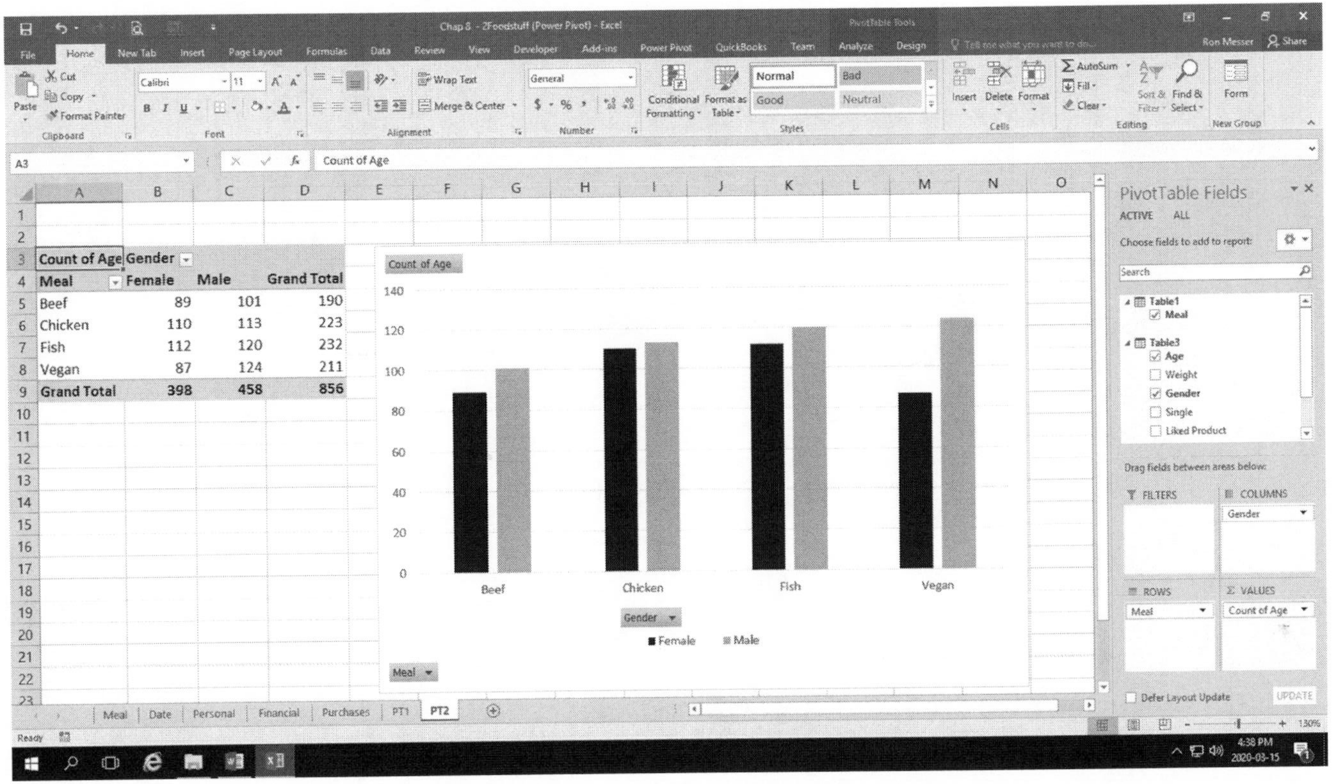

The Six Degrees of Stanley Milgram

(Googling and being googled in a small world)

Stanley Milgram was not a particularly good-looking man, but then he didn't have to be because he was famous instead. In 1967, while on the faculty of Yale University, the young professor conducted an experiment in social psychology that showed how small the planet had become. Using the US postal service as a communications channel and beginning in Omaha, Nebraska, a letter was sent to an individual selected at random from the telephone book. The letter requested that the receiver forward the correspondence to any acquaintance of theirs that may be able to connect them with an unknown stockbroker living in Massachusetts. Remarkably, after only six mailings, the letter reached its intended recipient and was then returned to an excited Stanley Milgram. He had found his six degrees of separation.

The Internet search engine, Google, has made the world a much smaller place. From the comfort of our homes we can track the lives of people we have known and they too can find out about us. I know, for example, that among the graduates of my high school class, one has become the head of surgery at a top tier medical school, another a high ranking military officer who was a star witness during the Somali inquiry, and still another is doing time in jail for being part of an underworld drug operation, with alleged mob connections. And I'm on the web too...cited for some of the things that I've written about, including the Internet.

In a recent poll, at least half of Americans surveyed indicated that they had "googled" themselves or their friends. Tracking family members through online genealogy services, powered by Google, has become tremendously popular. Professional recruiting firms regularly use the Internet to find out more about the people they are interviewing. Connecting with those we know, have known, or want to know more about, has never been easier ... or more precarious. Six degrees of separation can easily become six degrees of consternation, exasperation, or even desperation for some people, depending on whether you're googling or being googled.

For all of this, we have Stanley Milgram to thank. It was his experiment that formed the basis for the mathematical algorithm that is used today by Google (and many other Internet search engines) to perform its work on the web. Knowing that relationships create networks that have connections, it stands to reason that the greater the number of connections, the more likely it is to find out about things (like my high school acquaintance, for instance, who's cooling his heels in the Kingston penitentiary). This was the fundamental insight behind the six degrees of separation. And when you think about it, knowing that there are only six connections between you and just about anyone, anywhere, anytime – including, past friends, family members and total strangers – is both comforting and a bit creepy. Just consider this: who's googling you right now ... and why?

Part 3
Decisions Made about the Past

FEEDBACK

Chapter 9: Financial Dashboard Decisions

How has my business been doing?

Chapter 10: Budget Management Decisions

How have my managers been performing?

Chapter 11: Amortization Table Decisions

What is happening to my investments?

Chapter 9

Financial Dashboard Decisions

How has my business been doing?

Snapshot

Topic
Executive Information Systems: Key Performance Indicators and Dashboards

Subject Area
Accounting and Finance: financial statement/information analysis

Decisions Made
Key performance indicators (KPIs), including financial ratios are used to guide a company by measuring and tracking important information regarding corporate success; for example, earnings per share (EPS) or sales growth. Typically, these measures are presented in a graphical format and allow senior managers to quickly assess (typically, daily) the financial health of the company. This is facilitated by the use of executive information systems (EIS) and what has become popularly known as "dashboards."

Personal Experience
I was employed by a company in the transportation sector with over a billion dollars invested in assets, where we actively tracked passenger traffic and cargo volumes; this was because our corporate revenues were directly linked to these measures. On a monthly basis, the finance department prepared the KPIs which were reviewed by the CEO of the company. To do this, an easy to use Excel application with a graphical interface was created. It employed intuitive icons for quick navigation and was designed to visually present results on-screen. The summaries of key corporate performance metrics helped greatly in guiding the day-to-day actions of the company's executive group.

Excel Functionality

The primary Excel functions used will include simple numerical operators and variables that are input into cells through the formula bar of the worksheet. These variables can be linked to other worksheets which access the financial statements, either through cell references, or by using named ranges. The primary Excel functionality for dashboards includes the use of pivot tables and charts, slicers, spark lines, and a number of graphical displays.

Background Theory

Some Common Financial Measures

There are numerous ratios that companies can calculate to monitor their progress, including the following: (1) liquidity ratios, (2) solvency ratios, (3) activity ratios, and (4) profitability ratios.

Liquidity ratios include:

- Current ratio: Current assets (CA) relative to current liabilities (CL) = CA ÷ CL
- Quick ratio = (CA − Inventory) ÷ CL

Solvency ratios include:

- Debt to Equity = Long-term liabilities ÷ Equity
- Interest coverage ratio = Earnings before interest and taxes (EBIT) ÷ interest expense

Activity ratios include:

- Accounts receivable (A/R) turnover = Net credit sales ÷ average A/R
- Days sales in A/R = Cost of Goods Sold (COGS) ÷ Average A/R × 365 (days in a fiscal year)
- Days sales in inventory = COGS ÷ average inventory × 365 (days in a fiscal year)
- Inventory turnover = COGS ÷ average inventory

Profitability ratios include:

- Gross margin percentage = (Revenues − Cost of goods sold) ÷ Revenues
- Operating margin percentage = Operating income ÷ Revenues
- Profit margin percentage = Net income ÷ Revenues
- Return on equity (ROE) = Net income ÷ Equity
- EBIT = Net income + interest expense + taxes

This information can be extracted from the corporate financial statements, including the company's income statement and the balance sheet (aka, the Statement of Financial Position under International Accounting Standards).

Some Dashboard Principles

Two considerations are essential to creating a useful dashboard:

(1) Simplicity
(2) Significance

The information interface – i.e., what the user sees – must be easy to understand (*simplicity*) and the metrics shown, the KPIs, must be important for making decisions (*significance*). The KPIs are developed to inform and guide executive action; they allow the business to continue operating successfully, while also making future expansion possible.

Financial Management Techniques

A list of financial ratios can be found in Appendix 2 of this text. In addition, many industry-specific measures can also be calculated, such as revenue per available room, which is used by the hotel industry and revenue per available seat mile, employed by most airlines.

There are four main components in a financial model for an executive dashboard; these are created as individual worksheets, as follows:

(1) The *database*: This is where information is kept in a separate worksheet, sometimes linked to the corporate accounting system, to provide real-time data for determining important business metrics.

(2) The *pivot tables*: This is the "engine room" where the key performance indicators are calculated by referencing the database.

(3) The *references*: Based on the pivot tables, key measures are determined in a sequence that reflects the decision-making needs of the business.

(4) The *dashboard*: This is the "artistic" part of the exercise, where graphical displays are used to highlight the important metrics for decision-making.

Relevant Excel Functionality

PIVOT TABLES
CHARTS
SLICERS
SPARKLINES
TIMELINES

Demonstration Exercise

Give-it-to-me Entertainment (GIT-me) is a small company providing catering and other on-set services to movie production companies filming in Vancouver and Toronto (Excel file: GIT-me(shell).xls). It has been in business for 10 years and uses a small PC-based accounting system for its general ledger and to produce financial statements. The company's owner contributed $300,000 to start the business, which involved buying several trucks to move food and production props to movie set locations, as well as purchase portable power generators for outdoor lighting. In addition, bank financing was obtained, through a short-term loan, to pay for inventories (catering equipment and food supplies).

Because of the recent explosive growth in Internet-based content providers who are producing movies, business has been booming. The president of the company, Martin Keefer, wants to ensure that he does not become too distracted by the demand for his company's services and so, in order to make good strategic decisions, needs a summary of key metrics that will help him guide the company. You are a summer intern working for the company and have extensive experience using Excel and in particular creating dashboards.

First you need to talk with Martin, the business owner, to find out what information is important to him when making decisions. From your discussion, you learn the following.

(1) Because his bank loan includes a clause requiring him to maintain a minimum level of liquidity (i.e., a current ratio greater than 1.5), he needs to know the relationship between current assets and liabilities for GIT-me. (Note that the bank financing is short term and secured by the business's inventories and receivables.)

(2) Martin wants to know his gross margin, operating margin, and profit margin, so that he can compare these with similar companies in the entertainment industry.

He receives this competitive information on a regular basis through a subscription newsletter. (Currently, the movie production servicing sector typically achieves gross margins of 30%; operating margins of 25%, and profit margins of 10%.)

(3) The owner is concerned about having enough cash available to pay bills as they come due. For this reason, he wants to know about his cash cycle, specifically in terms of the number of days that funds are tied up in receivables and inventory.

(4) Finally, a measure of return on equity is important for him in assessing the long-term viability of the venture. He has indicated that his hurdle rate is 15%; this is the minimum return that he wants to achieve on his investment and reflects his cost of capital as well as the opportunity cost associated with operating GIT-me.

Based on further conversation with Martin, the intern learns the following information about the company's financial history (**Table 9.1**).

Table 9.1. GIT-me Financial Information History.

Financial Information (10 Years)	Amount (Average)
Annual sales growth	3%
Cost of goods sold (average % of sales)	45%
Selling, general & administration expenses (Average % of sales)	25%
Interest expense (short-term bank loan)	4%
Depreciation expense (straight line with no salvage value)	15-year life
Accounts receivable (average % of sales)	20%
Inventory (average % of sales)	10%
Accounts payable (average % of sales)	20%
Short-term bank loan (maximum line of credit used)	$100,000
Fixed assets (trucks, power generators)	$250,000
Income taxes (average rate on earnings)	20%

Step 1: Create the Database

The summer intern obtains copies of the GIT-me financial statements for the last 10 years, including the income statement and balance sheet, and hard codes the numbers into a data table in Excel (see **Fig. 9.1**). To ensure that updates to the data are captured in the pivot tables that generate the dashboard metrics, he defines the data as a table by positioning the cursor inside the data and left clicking the following: INSERT, TABLE, OK.

The intern decides that he will link the EIS-dashboard workbook to an external source (i.e., the PC-based financial statements) at a later date, so that real-time updates can occur.

Step 2: Create the Data Engine

This is accomplished by producing several pivot tables that reference the database. (Refer Chapter 8 for information about creating pivot tables). Based on the intern's conversation with Martin, pivot tables will be developed to determine the current ratio, various profitability measures, cash flows for current assets, and the ROE for GIT-me. This is shown in **Fig. 9.2**.

Fig. 9.1. The GIT-me Database.

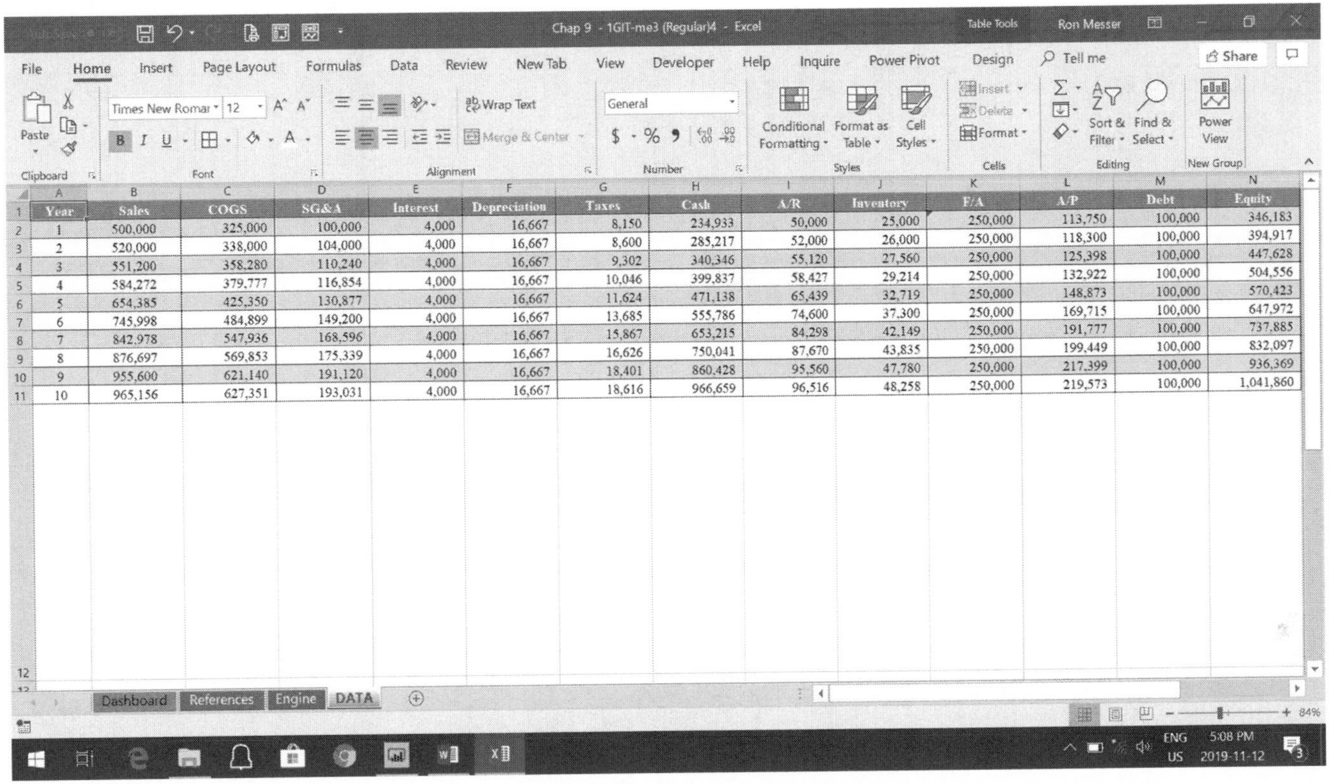

Year	Sales	COGS	SG&A	Interest	Depreciation	Taxes	Cash	A/R	Inventory	F/A	A/P	Debt	Equity
1	500,000	325,000	100,000	4,000	16,667	8,150	234,933	50,000	25,000	250,000	113,750	100,000	346,183
2	520,000	338,000	104,000	4,000	16,667	8,600	285,217	52,000	26,000	250,000	118,300	100,000	394,917
3	551,200	358,280	110,240	4,000	16,667	9,302	340,346	55,120	27,560	250,000	125,398	100,000	447,628
4	584,272	379,777	116,854	4,000	16,667	10,046	399,837	58,427	29,214	250,000	132,922	100,000	504,556
5	654,385	425,350	130,877	4,000	16,667	11,624	471,138	65,439	32,719	250,000	148,873	100,000	570,423
6	745,998	484,899	149,200	4,000	16,667	13,685	555,786	74,600	37,300	250,000	169,715	100,000	647,972
7	842,978	547,936	168,596	4,000	16,667	15,867	653,215	84,298	42,149	250,000	191,777	100,000	737,885
8	876,697	569,853	175,339	4,000	16,667	16,626	750,041	87,670	43,835	250,000	199,449	100,000	832,097
9	955,600	621,140	191,120	4,000	16,667	18,401	860,428	95,560	47,780	250,000	217,399	100,000	936,369
10	965,156	627,351	193,031	4,000	16,667	18,616	966,659	96,516	48,258	250,000	219,573	100,000	1,041,860

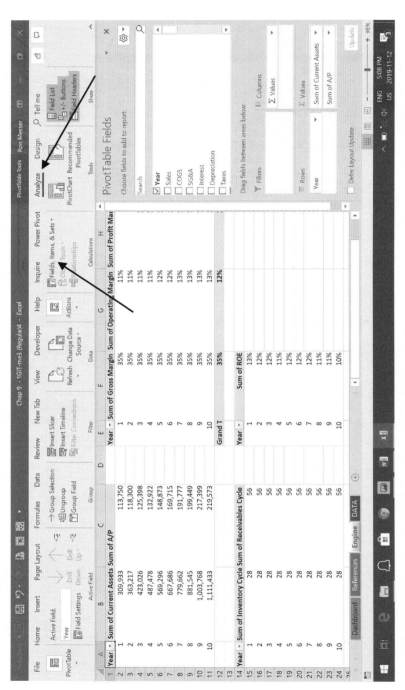

Fig. 9.2. The GIT-me Data Engine.

Note that several calculated fields were created for the pivot tables to determine the KPIs; these include calculated fields for current assets and liabilities, current ratio, gross, operating and profit margins, days sales in A/R and inventory, and the ROE. A calculated field uses existing fields in a data table and incorporates mathematical operators (such as addition, subtraction, etc.) to create at a new field, which then becomes part of the data set. It is produced by placing the cursor anywhere inside the pivot table and then left clicking ANALYZE in the main menu to select FIELD ITEMS AND SETS (see **Fig. 9.2**). Under the drop-down box, select CALCULATED FIELD. This is shown in **Fig. 9.3**, where the formula for the current ratio is created by dividing current assets into liabilities.

This process is repeated to create calculated fields for the following:

- Gross margin = (Sales − COGS) ÷ Sales
- Operating margin = (Sales − COGS − "SG&A" − Interest − Depreciation) ÷ Sales
- Profit margin = (Operating margin − Taxes) ÷ Sales
- Days sales in A/R = (A/R ÷ COGS) × 365
- Days sales in inventory = (Inventory ÷ COGS) × 365
- Return on equity = Net income ÷ Equity

Step 3: Create the References

This worksheet assembles the values needed to summarize the key decision metrics, which are made visually appealing by displaying them through conditional formatting, colorful graphics, and intuitive icons (**Fig. 9.4**).

The reference values are linked to the pivot tables in the data engine (as shown in **Fig. 9.5**).

Step 4: Create the Dashboard

Based on his interview with Martin, the intern develops charts that will quickly inform the business owner about the KPIs he needs to know about in order to operate GIT-me; these being:

(1) Current ratio metric
(2) Profitability metric
(3) Cash flows metric
(4) Return on equity metric

Charts are developed in the "references" worksheet (using INSERT, CHARTS to select from a number of chart types). A macro is also created using the Developer tab that updates the pivot tables as the table data changes (for additional data relating to the new year, for example). This is shown as a "refresh" button on the dashboard screen.

The final dashboard is shown in **Fig. 9.6**.

Observe how the dashboard is uncluttered, visually appealing and draws the observer's attention to the key measures needed to run the business – in other words, it is *simple* and at the same time *significant*. Also note these important aspects of dashboard design.

- Unnecessary visual distractions, such as row and column headings, spreadsheet gridlines, main menu items, and the formula bar have been removed from the screen. Removing these display items is done by left clicking: FILE, OPTIONS ADVANCED, and then de-selecting, using the appropriate checkboxes, "DISPLAY OPTIONS FOR THE WORKBOOK."

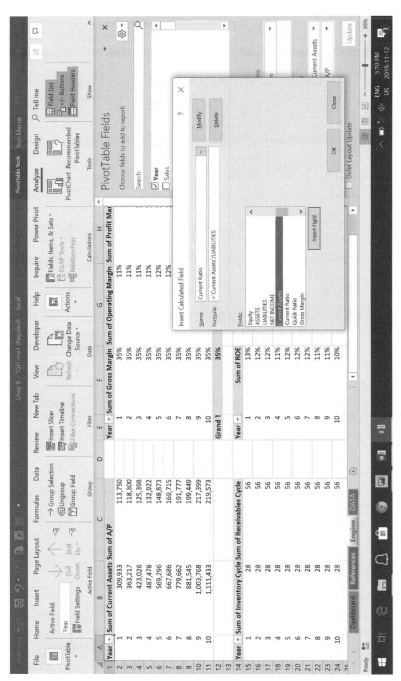

Fig. 9.3. Creating a Calculated Field.

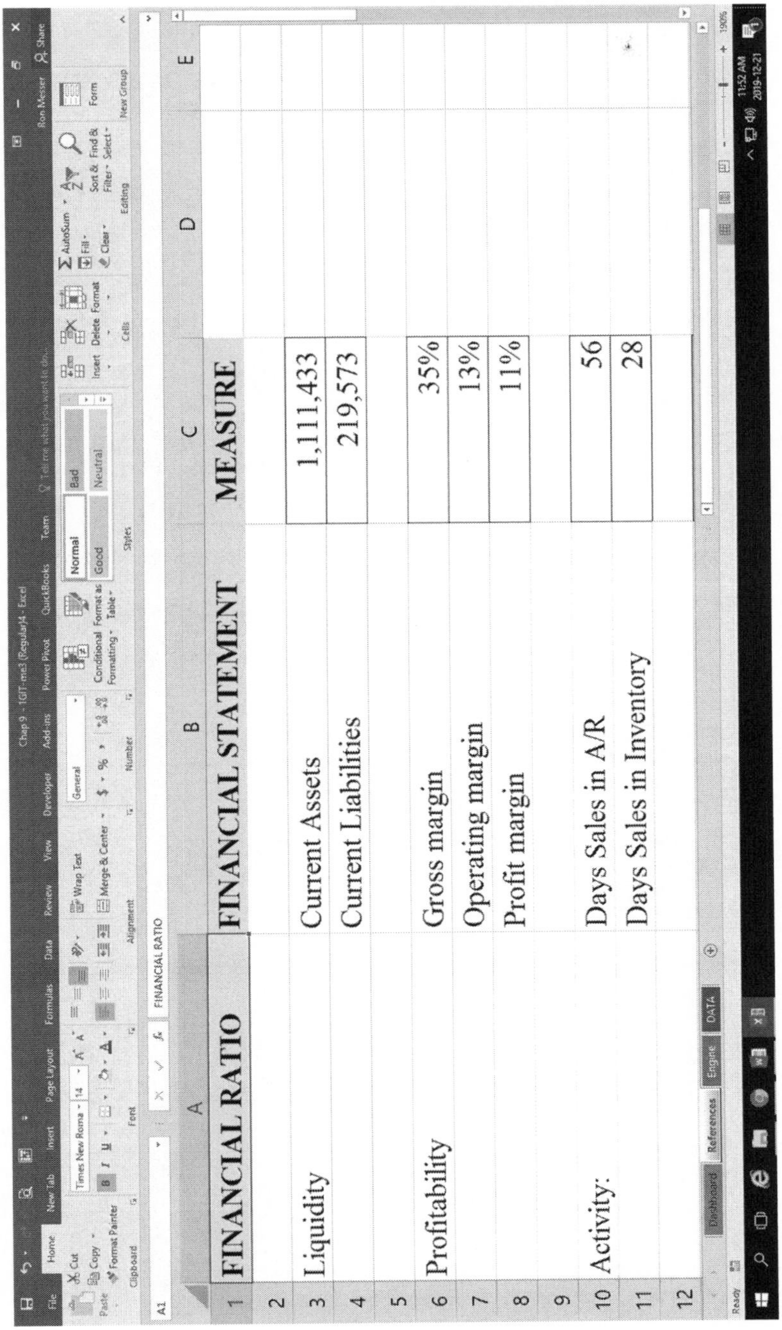

Fig. 9.4. The GIT-me References.

Fig. 9.5. Creating the References.

	FINANCIAL RATIO	FINANCIAL STATEMENT	MEASURE
Liquidity	Current Assets	=GETPIVOTDATA("Sum of Current Assets",Engine!$A$1,"Year",10)
	Current Liabilities	=GETPIVOTDATA("Sum of A/P",Engine!$A$1, "Year",10)
Profitability	Gross margin	=GETPIVOTDATA("Sum of Gross Margin",Engine!$E$1,"Year",10)
	Operating margin	=GETPIVOTDATA("Sum of Operating Margin",Engine!$E$1,"Year",10)
	Profit margin	=GETPIVOTDATA("Sum of Profit Margin",Engine!$E$1,"Year",10)
Activity:	Days Sales in A/R	=GETPIVOTDATA("Sum of Receivables Cycle",Engine!$A$14,"Year",10)
	Days Sales in Inventory	=GETPIVOTDATA("Sum of Inventory Cycle",Engine!$A$14,"Year",10)
Profitability	Return on Equity	=GETPIVOTDATA("ROE",Engine!$E$14,"Year",10)

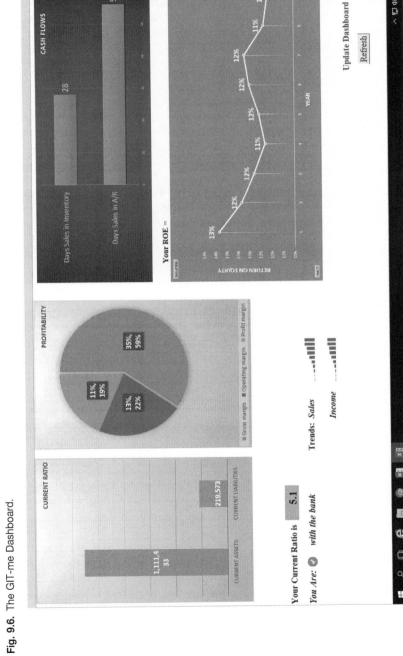

Fig. 9.6. The GIT-me Dashboard.

- The graphics used are appropriate for the measure being displayed, such as vertical bars to show the relationship between current assets and liabilities; a pie chart to illustrate the portions of income comprising gross, operating a profit margins; horizontal bars to show the number of days before current assets (inventories and A/R) turn into cash flows.
- Martin can quickly assess the financial health of his business at a glance:
  - his bankers will be happy, based on the current ratio.
  - his profit margins are reasonable when compared to industry standards.
  - he needs to improve his cash conversion time for A/R and inventory.
  - his ROE is declining and below his hurdle rate.

About Power BI (Business Intelligence)

Power BI is Microsoft's recent initiative to provide data analytic tools for the marketplace. Changes to this software package are occurring on a monthly basis, as the company responds to users' feedback. Power BI also includes as part of its functionality, Power Query, which is used for managing data.

Its key strengths are as follows:

- It can handle many different data types, from a variety of sources (such as Excel files, SQL server views, text/CSV files, web sources, access files, Oracle database, IBM DB2, SAP Business warehouse, etc.).
- It can handle a large amount of data. Whereas Excel is restricted to 1 million rows per worksheet, Power BI is not; hence the concept of "big data" really applies to this software.
- Its ability to create graphical displays for dashboards is both intuitive and easy.
- Dashboards, reports, and information can be readily shared and controlled.

Its key weaknesses (currently) include:

- Its pivot table functionality, called a "matrix," is clumsy to use. Descriptive as well as diagnostic analytics can be better handled using pivot tables or Power Pivot in MS-Excel.
- Its predictive analytics functionality uses the open source software called "R." This product, while useful, is really geared to academics and graduate students performing more advanced statistical analysis. The MS-Excel analysis tool pack works well enough for almost all accounting and finance applications. (Personally, for enhanced statistical functionality, I would recommend the software product called "Stat-tools," which can be purchased as an add-on to Excel.)
- The user interface is very crowded and requires extensive scrolling to access the required functionality. Also, the reports and visualizations created are very small on the limited screen space (called a canvas), which makes designing dashboards difficult.
- The formulas available in MS-Excel are very similar in Power BI, except they are referred to as DAX (Data Analysis Expressions) formulas. These are used mostly to create something called "measures" that generate subtotals (SUM, COUNT, AVERAGE) for data. While this occurs automatically when generating pivot tables in Excel, it must be done as a separate procedure within Power BI.

When I questioned an industry expert about the role of MS-Excel in relation to Power BI, they commented that they did not see Power BI eliminating the need for MS-Excel. They considered the two products as complimentary to each other. So, my opinion on using Power BI is that:

- It is great for producing and distributing dashboards.
- It is great for handling real life data sets, which are typically large and varied.
- It is great for managing data (by using Power Query, which is also available in MS-Excel).

However, for descriptive, diagnostic, and predictive analytics, I would recommend MS-Excel.

Demonstration Exercise

The case facts relating to GIT-me Entertainment will be used to show how Power BI can create data visualizations.

Loading Power BI

Before creating a dashboard interface, the software must be installed. For individual users, it can be downloaded free of charge from the Internet, as follows.

Google "Power BI Desktop download," or go directly to the following website: https://www.microsoft.com/en-us/download/details.aspx?id=45331.

The website will show the following:

Click the Download button.

Next, you will be asked to make a choice:

Should I download the 32-bit or 64-bit version of Windows?

The answer for most people is 64-bit, since that version can handle large amounts of memory more efficiently than 32-bit. If you don't know whether you have a 64-bit system, you can always find this information. Right click on the Windows icon in the bottom left corner of your computer screen and select SYSTEM; then you will see the following screen.

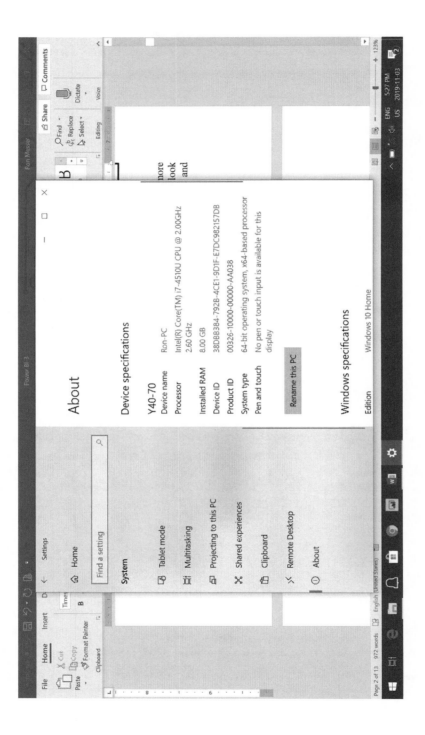

Next, you will be informed about how much space you need to install Power BI Desktop.

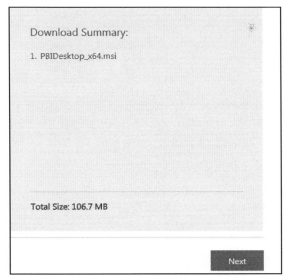

Click Next, and Power BI Desktop will be downloaded.

Open the file to start the installation process.

The installation process will start with the following window:

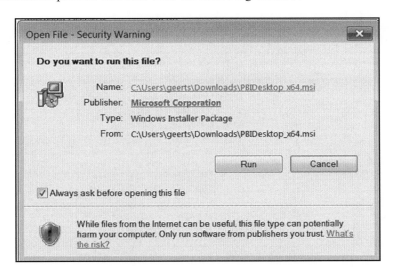

Click the Run button, and the Setup wizard will start.

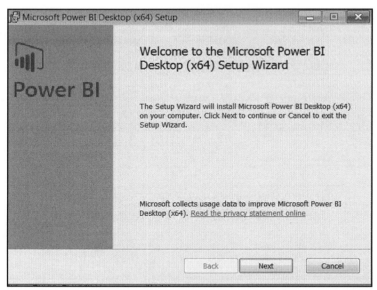

Click the Next button again. After accepting the license agreement and clicking Next, the installation wizard will ask you where the software should be installed.

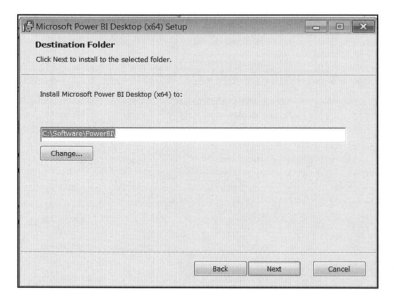

Indicate the directory where you want Power BI to be installed and then click "Next." The following screen will pop up:

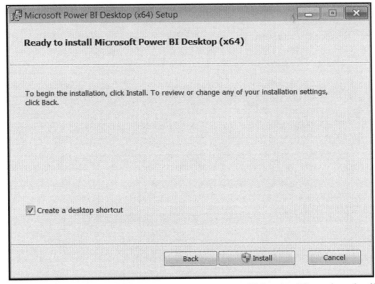

Click the Install button, and the installation process will begin. The wizard will let you know when the installation is completed.

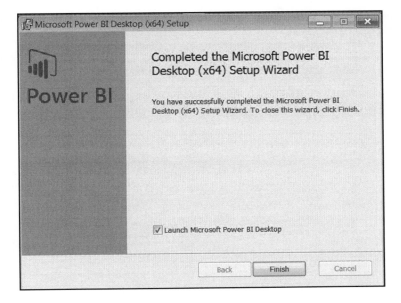

Click the Finish button and you are ready.

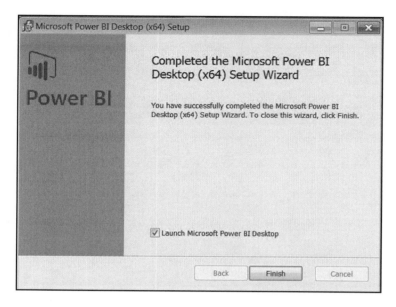

Using Power BI

To open Power BI, double left click on the icon created when the software was loaded. Note that it takes considerable time to start and so be patient. Once it opens, a screen will appear (**Fig. 9.7**).

At this stage it is best to simply left click on the "x" located in the top right corner to view the Power BI canvas, which looks like **Fig. 9.8**.

To load the data for GIT-Me, select the GET DATA drop-down arrow and choose Excel, as shown in **Fig. 9.9**.

After selecting the Excel file for the company, the following checkbox appears, which is called the "Navigator" (**Fig. 9.10**).

The Navigator screen allows you to choose the tables within the Excel file (or database) that you want to include in your visualization.

Using Power Query

At this point, you can make changes to your data by selecting a worksheet in the Excel file and choosing the TRANFORM DATA functionality, which accesses the Power Query tool. Power Query allows you to

(1) Change the data type; this is done by selecting the left-side icon in the field description (see **Fig. 9.11** that follows, which selects the "Year" field in the data table).

(2) Sort, filter, and remove empty records; this is done by selecting the right-side drop-down indicator in the field header (shown in **Fig. 9.12**, which selects the "Year" field).

(3) Remove columns and/or rows as well as split columns (as shown in the main menu ribbon in **Fig. 9.12**).

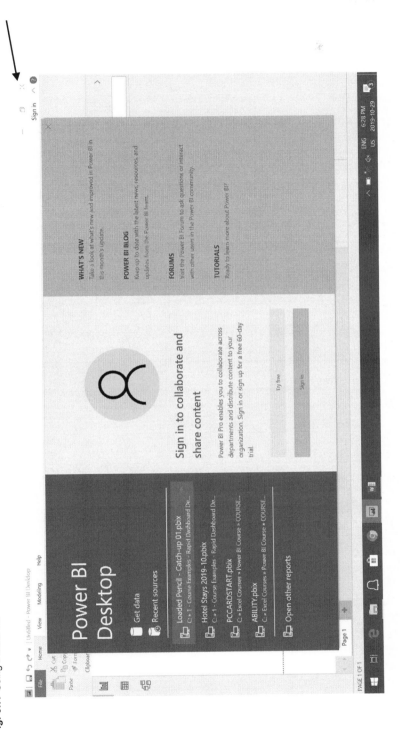

Fig. 9.7. Using Power BI.

Fig. 9.8. Using Power BI – The Canvas.

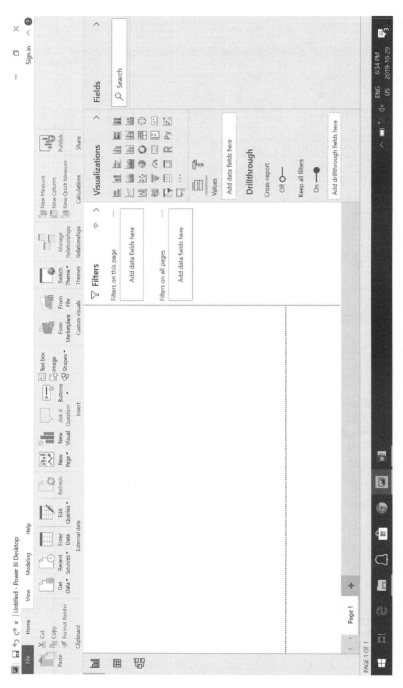

Fig. 9.9. Using Power BI – Accessing Data.

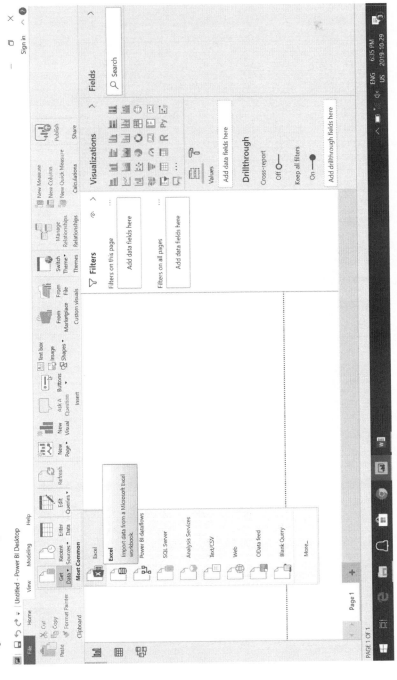

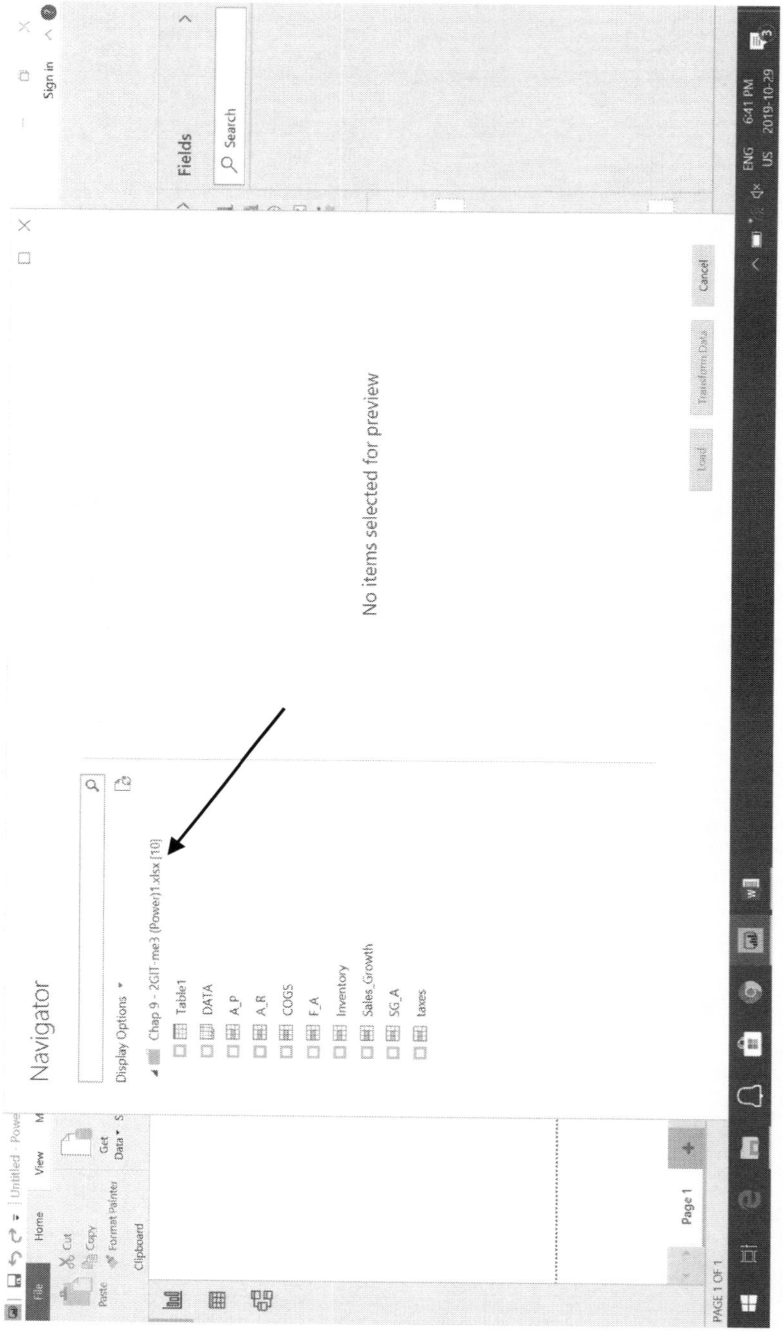

Fig. 9.10. Using Power BI – Power Query.

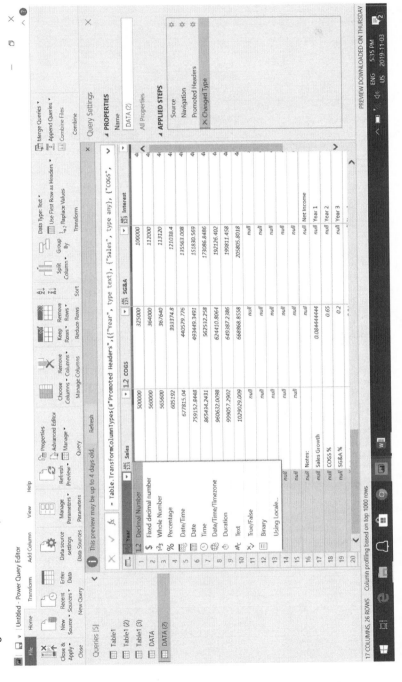

Fig. 9.11. Using Power BI – Power Query.

Fig. 9.12. Using Power BI – Power Query.

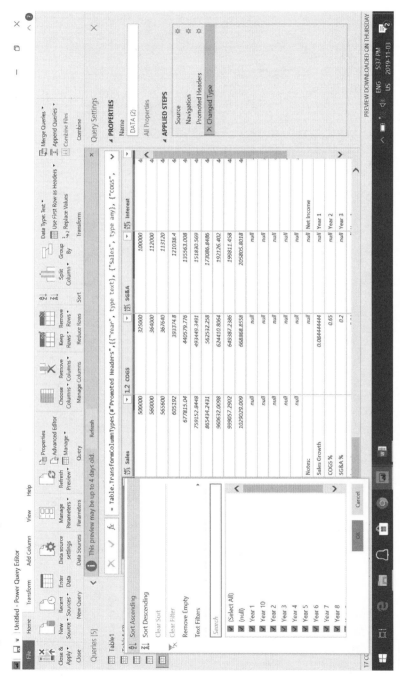

Creating Data Visualizations

After selecting the worksheet called "Data," we indicate that we want to "Transform Data" (located on the bottom right side of the Navigator dialogue box). This allows us to use Power Query to manage the data set, which appears below (**Figs. 9.13 and 9.14**).

Using Power Query, we will include only rows 1 to 10 in the data table, by left clicking on the icon in the top left corner of the Power Query dialogue box and selecting the drop-down box, as follows (**Figs. 9.15 and 9.16**).

Once done, select OK (**Fig. 9.17**).

Note that a record is kept of changes made to the data, which appears on the right side of the screen (called "APPLIED STEPS"). This will allow you to track any amendments made. Next select CLOSE AND APPLY, located in the top left corner of the screen (see **Fig. 9.17**). Once the data have been transformed and loaded, they can be used to create a dashboard (see **Fig. 9.18**).

Three icons will appear on the upper left side of the Power BI canvas, arranged vertically; their descriptions can be seen by hovering your cursor over the icon image.

- The REPORT icon (located at the top of the group) allows you to create visualizations.
- The DATA icon (located in the middle of the group), allows you to view your data table on the canvas.
- The MODEL icon (located at the bottom of the group) allows you to see the relationships in your database (i.e., the connections between the tables). In this exercise, we are only using one table (as shown in **Fig. 9.19**) and therefore no relationships exist. (Note: In Power BI, one-to-many as well as one-to-one relationships are permitted. However, these relationships must first be created in Power Pivot before being used for data visualizations in Power BI.)

To the right of the canvas, about 30 "visualization" options appear as icons that can be selected. **Fig. 9.20** shows the TABLE icon being selected for information about the A/P for GIT-me.

Recall that the owner of the company needed information about the following KPIs.

(1) Current ratio metric (current assets, current liabilities, and the ratio)
(2) Profitability metric (gross, operating and profit margin percentages)
(3) Cash flows metric (days sales in receivables and inventory)
(4) Return on equity metric (net income, equity, and the ratio, by year)
(5) Sales and income trends (for 10 years of operations)

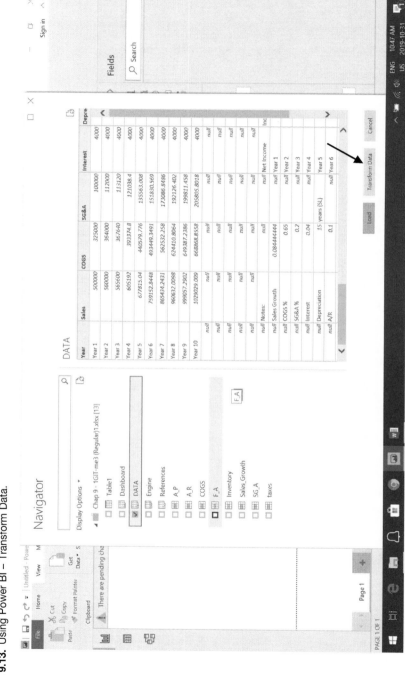

Fig. 9.13. Using Power BI – Transform Data.

Fig. 9.14. Using Power BI – Transform Data.

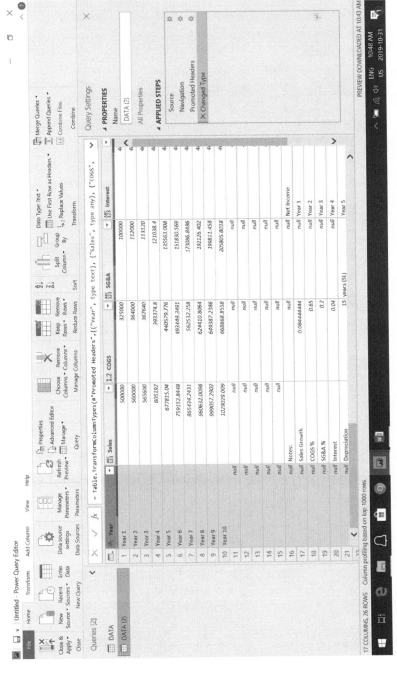

Fig. 9.15. Using Power BI – Managing Data.

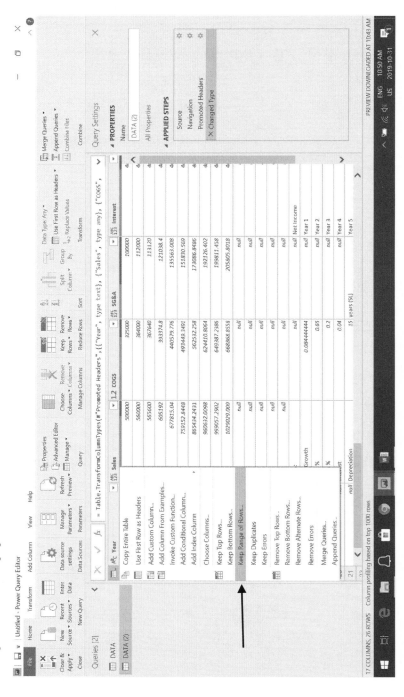

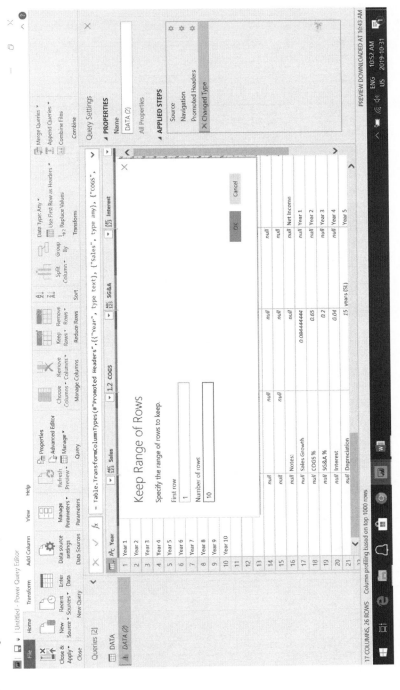

Fig. 9.16. Using Power BI – Removing Records.

Fig. 9.17. Using Power BI – Cleaned Data.

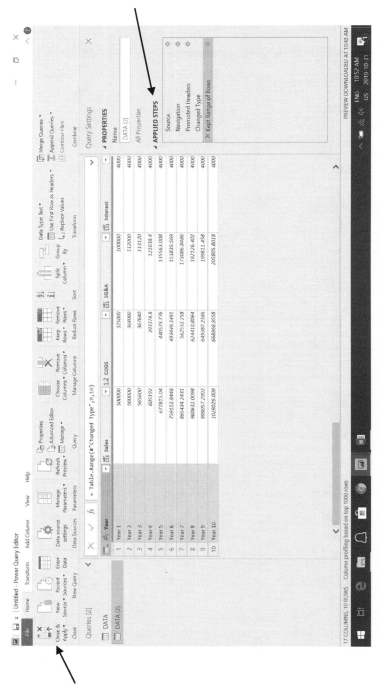

Fig. 9.18. Using Power BI – DATA, MODEL, and REPORT Functions.

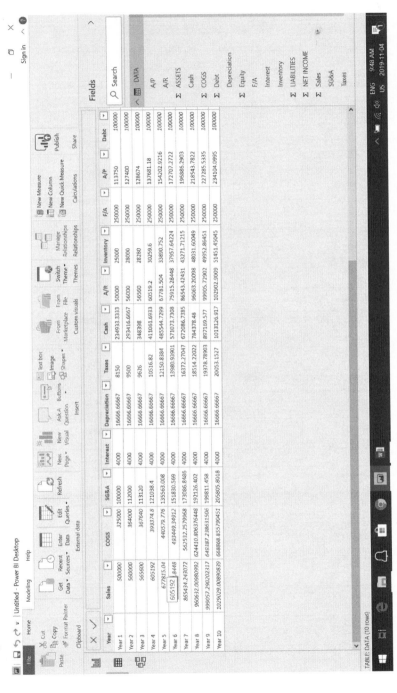

Fig. 9.19. Using Power BI – MODEL.

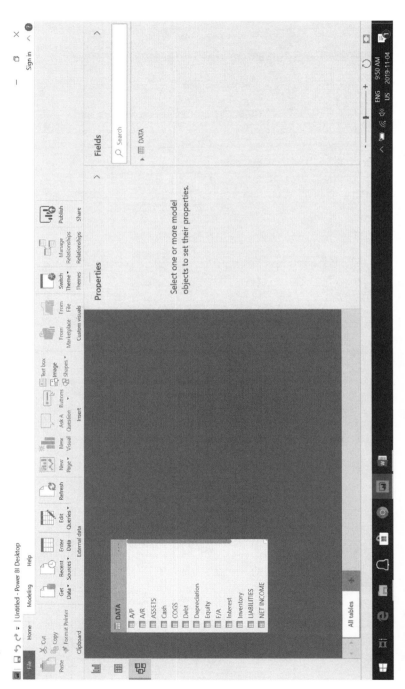

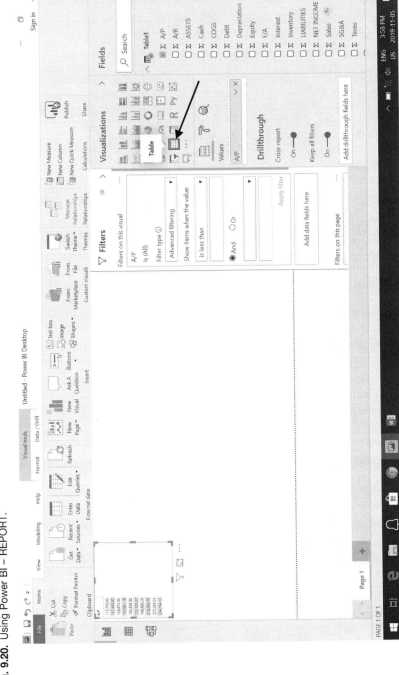

Fig. 9.20. Using Power BI – REPORT.

For each of these metrics, several "measures" must be calculated using Power BI, including:

- Current assets (metric 1)
- Current liabilities (metric 1)
- Current ratio (metric 1)
- Gross margin (metric 2)
- Operating margin (metric 2)
- Profit margin (metric 2)
- Days sales in A/R (metric 3)
- Days sales in inventory (metric 3)
- Return on equity (metric 4)

This can be done in by using DAX formulas to create new fields in the data table.

Current Ratio Metric

In the DATA screen, create a new field for "current assets" by selecting the New Column function in the main menu ribbon, as shown in **Fig. 9.21**.

Next, select the new field created and by left clicking on the ellipsis beside it, choose New Measure (see **Fig. 9.22**).

In the formula bar that appears, type the following DAX formula.

`Current Assets = Table1[Cash]+Table1[A/R]+Table1 [Inventory]`

Using this formula, for each of the records (rows) in the table, the values for Cash, A/R, and Inventory will be added together (which is, of course, the amount of current assets, by year) (**Fig. 9.23**).[1]

In the data set, current liabilities consist only of A/P and so no new field needs to be created for these amounts. But we need a formula for the current ratio, which is current assets ÷ current liabilities. This is done by again creating a new field and a related DAX formula, as follows.

`Current Ratios = Table1[Current Assets]/Table1[Current Liabilities]`

The Dax formula in the new table column is shown in **Fig. 9.24**.

We can now create a visualization for the dashboard showing the current ratio in a format like that generated using Excel and Power View. This is done as follows:

- Left click on the report icon (far left side of screen).
- Left click to select the table icon (in: Visualizations).
- Left click to select and then drag the fields for Year, Current Assets, and Current Liabilities into the "Values" box.

The report is shown in **Fig. 9.25**.

---

[1]The data can be formatted by accessing the "modeling" tab. This has been done in **Fig. 9.27** by inserting comma separators and removing decimal places from the numeric data. To format a field, simply position the cursor in the header (field) row and left click to highlight the column and then make the formatting changes.

Fig. 9.21. Using Power BI – Current Ratio.

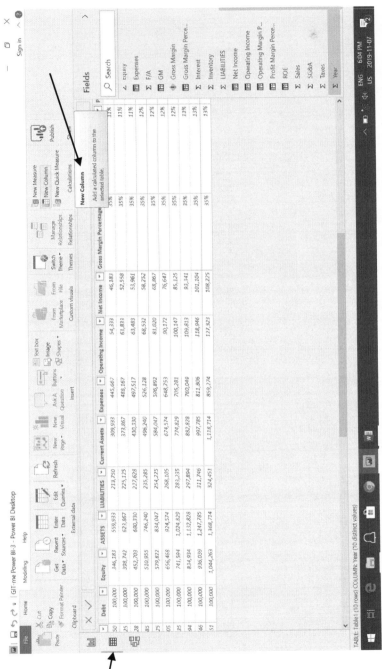

Fig. 9.22. Using Power BI – Current Ratio.

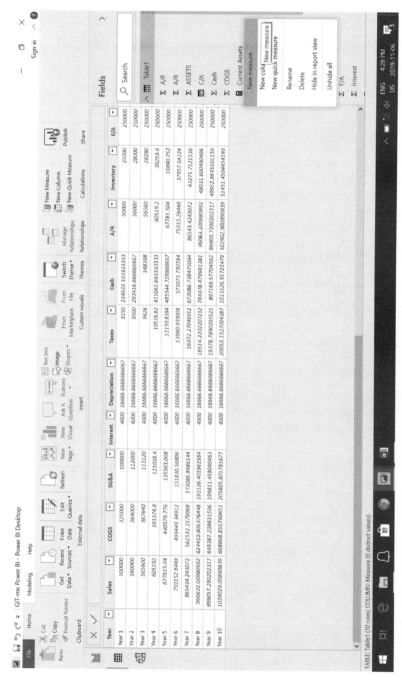

Fig. 9.23. Using Power BI – Current Ratio.

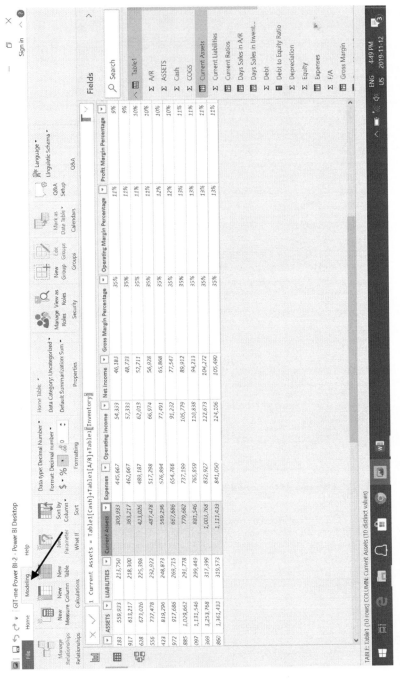

Fig. 9.24. Using Power BI – Current Ratio.

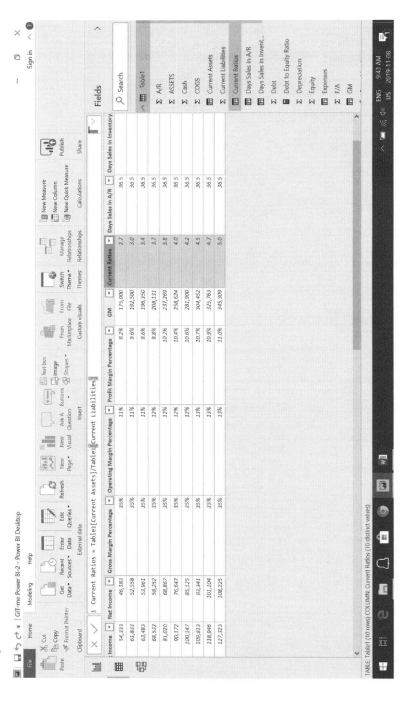

Fig. 9.25. Using Power BI – Current Ratio.

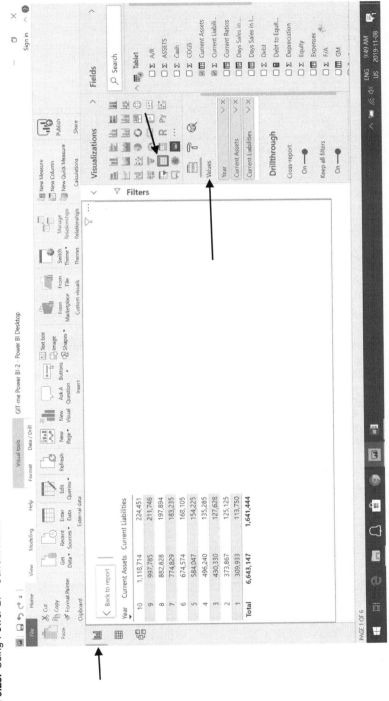

Now we need to create a vertical bar chart, which we do by selecting it from the visualizations section and including the measures for the current assets and current liabilities in the value section for the fields, as shown in **Fig. 9.26**. Note the year field has been filtered to select the most current period, year 10.

Profitability Metric

Next, we will create the pie chart showing the profitability for the company, including gross, operating and profit margins for year 10. To create this visualization, we will do the following.

    (1) Add new columns to the table for:
- gross margin
- gross margin percentage
- operating income
- operating margin percentage
- net income
- profit margin percentage

    (2) Create DAX formulas for each of the new columns
    (3) Generate a pie chart showing the respective profit margins for year 10

Fig. 9.27 shows the new columns (fields) that have been created in the table.

In each of these columns the following DAX formulas have been used (step 2):

- Gross Margin = Table1[Sales]-Table1[COGS]
- Gross Margin Percentage = Table1[Gross Margin]/Table1[Sales]
- Operating Income = (Table1[Sales])-(Table1[Expenses])
- Operating Margin Percentage = Table1[Operating Income]/Table1[Sales]
- Net Income = Table1[Operating Income]-Table1[Taxes]
- Profit Margin Percentage = Table1[Net Income]/Table1[Sales]

Next, left click on the REPORT icon and choose the pie chart visualization. Include the following fields in the values box: Gross Margin Percentage, Operating Profit percentage, Profit margin Percentage. Filter on year 10 (**Fig. 9.28**).

Cash Flow Metric

We will now create a horizontal bar chart for the days sales in A/R and Inventory for year 10. To create this visualization, do the following:

    (1) Add new columns to the table for:
- days sales in A/R
- days sales in inventory
    (2) Create DAX formulas for each of these new columns (**Fig. 9.29**)
    (3) Generate a horizontal bar chart showing the respective cash flows for year 10

In each of these columns, the following DAX formulas have been used (Step 2):

Days Sales in A/R = Table1[A/R]/Table1[Sales]*365
Days Sales in Inventory = Table1[Inventory]/Table1[COGS]*365

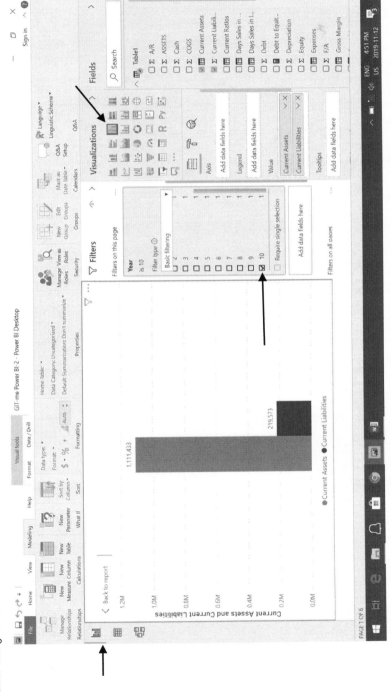

Fig. 9.26. Using Power BI – Current Ratio.

Fig. 9.27. Using Power BI – Profitability Measures, Steps 1 and 2.

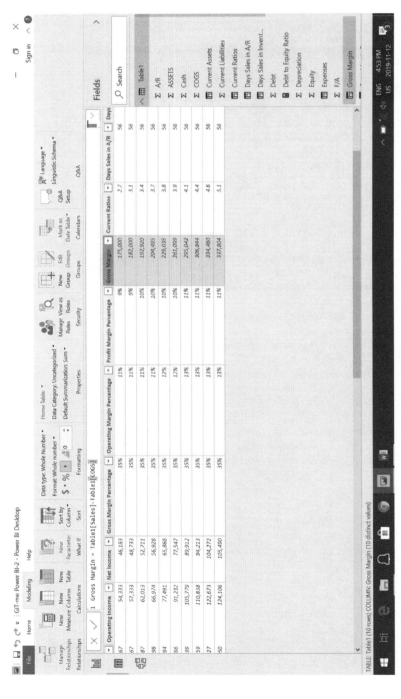

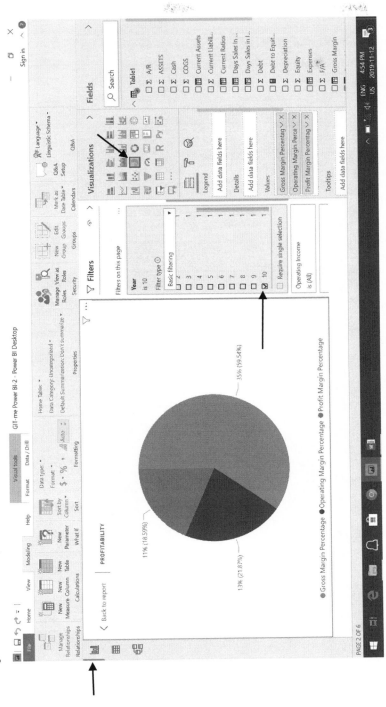

Fig. 9.28. Using Power BI – Profitability Measures, Step 3.

Fig. 9.29. Using Power BI – Cash Flows Measures, Steps 1 and 2.

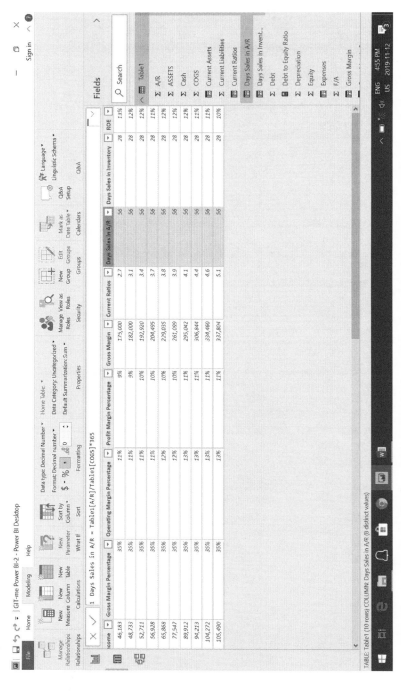

Next, left click on the REPORT icon and choose the horizontal bar chart visualization. Include the following fields in the values box: days sales in A/R and days sales in inventory. Filter on year 10, as shown in **Fig. 9.30**.

Return on Equity Metric

We will now create a line chart for the return on equity for all 10 years. To create this visualization, do the following:

(1) Add new columns to the table for:
   - ROE
(2) Create DAX formulas for each of these new columns (**Fig. 9.31**)
(3) Generate a line chart showing the ROE for all 10 years

In each of these columns the following DAX formulas have been used (Step 2):

```
ROE = Table1[Net Income]/Table1[Equity]
```

Next, left click on the REPORT icon and choose the line chart visualization. Include the ROE field in the values box. (Note that no filtering is required, as we want to include all 10 years of data (**Fig. 9.32**).)

Sales and Income Trends

To create a visualization for sales and income trends, select the bar chart icon, add the "year" field to the axis box and the "sales" field to the values box (see **Fig. 9.33**).

Repeat this process, but instead use the net income field in the values box, as shown in **Fig. 9.34**.

Afterthought → *Can you handle the truth?*

Making decisions based on historical information is sometimes tricky. But what else is there on which to base a plan about the future other than what has already happened. Yet, is this the best guide for executives tasked with captaining the corporate ship? Consider as an alternative the wisdom of large groups.

Fig. 9.30. Using Power BI –Cash Flows Measures, Step 3.

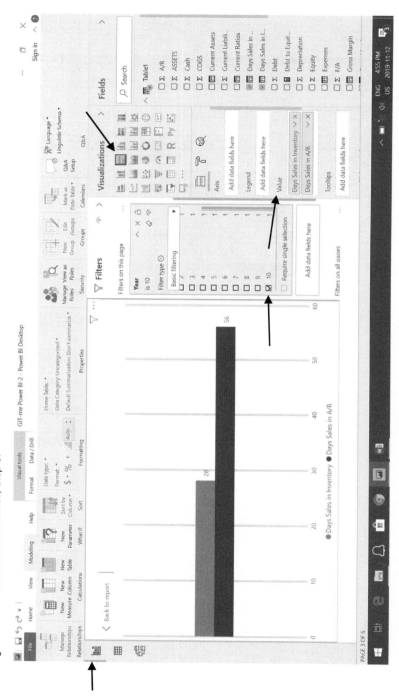

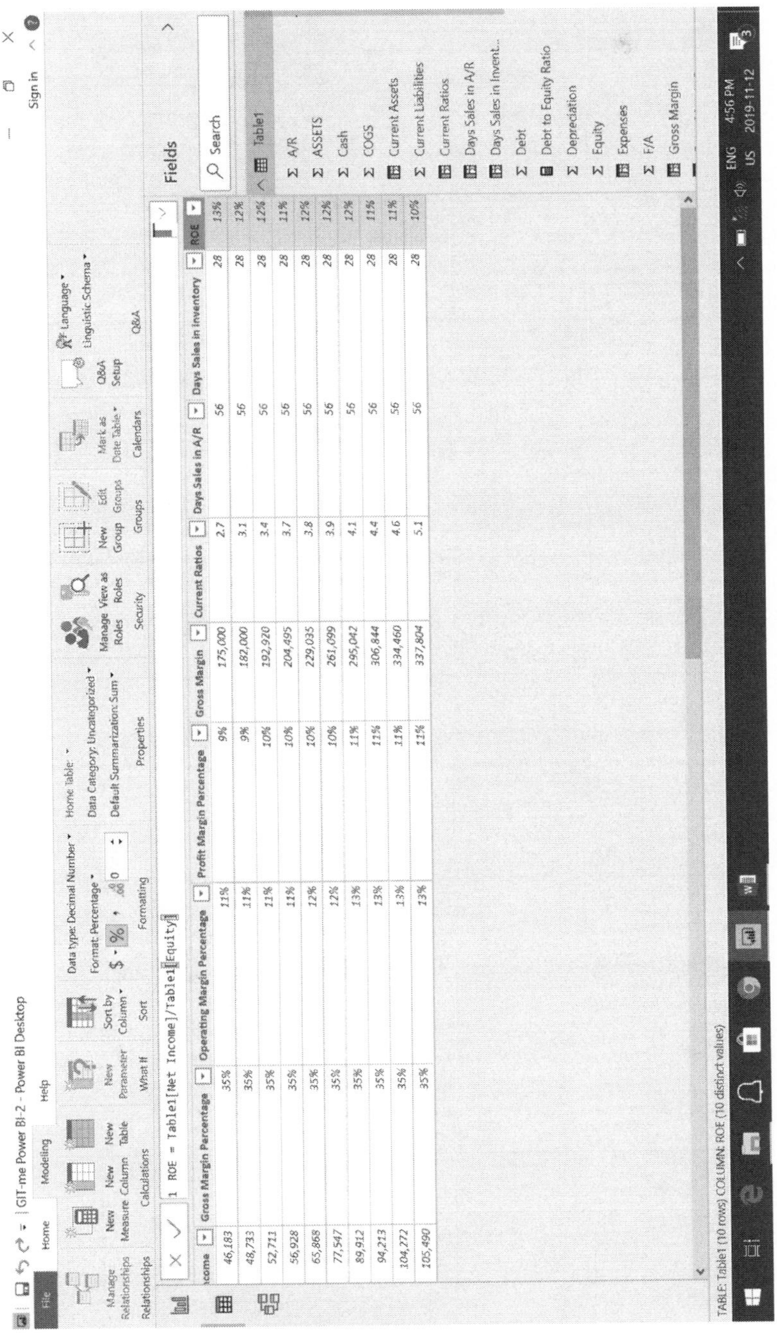

Fig. 9.31. Using Power BI – ROE Measures, Steps 1 and 2.

Income	Gross Margin Percentage	Operating Margin Percentage	Profit Margin Percentage	Gross Margin	Current Ratios	Days Sales in A/R	Days Sales in Inventory	ROE
46,183	35%	11%	9%	175,000	2.7	56	28	13%
48,733	35%	11%	9%	182,000	3.1	56	28	12%
52,711	35%	11%	10%	192,920	3.4	56	28	12%
56,928	35%	11%	10%	204,495	3.7	56	28	11%
65,868	35%	12%	10%	229,035	3.8	56	28	12%
77,547	35%	12%	10%	261,099	3.9	56	28	12%
89,912	35%	13%	11%	295,042	4.1	56	28	12%
94,213	35%	13%	11%	306,844	4.4	56	28	11%
104,272	35%	13%	11%	334,460	4.6	56	28	11%
205,490	35%	13%	11%	337,804	5.1	56	28	10%

Fig. 9.32. Using Power BI – ROE Measures, Step 3.

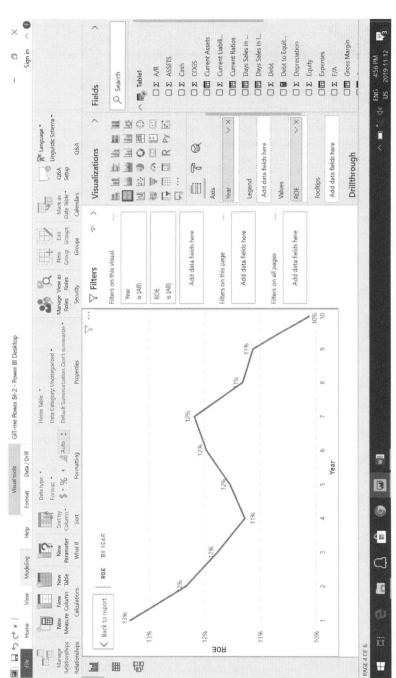

Fig. 9.33. Using Power BI – Sales Trend Measure.

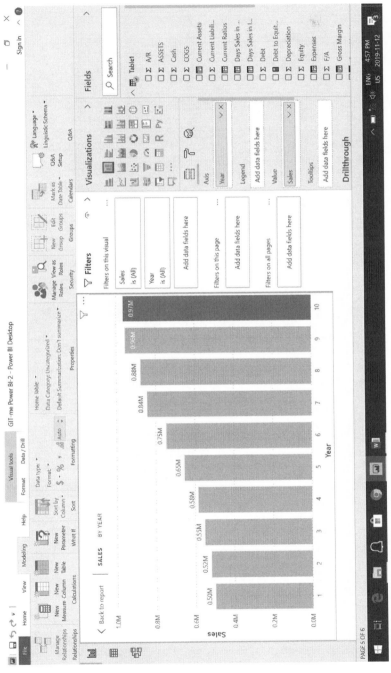

Fig. 9.34. Using Power BI – Income Trend Measure.

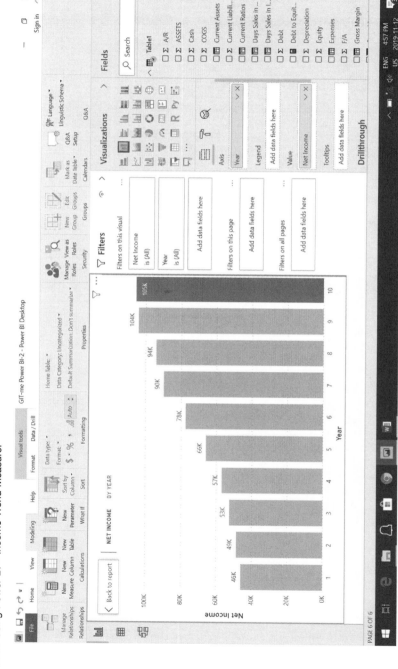

The Truth Is Out There

*(What do the Internet, some Iowa University students,
and large crowds have in common?)*

A revolution is taking place which few people have noticed but that is definitely affecting all of us. Social networking is a popular buzzword that refers to Internet websites where information is shared among a community of like-minded users. Think of the Wiki movement, Myspace.com, or any blogs that you may frequent as examples of this phenomenon. Aside from the billions of dollars that have been paid to the creators of some of these otherwise pedestrian web-based enterprises, an unexpected and at the same time invaluable contribution has resulted because of them.

The University of Iowa is pioneering the concept of the elections stock market. This is a forum where votes for presidential and congressional elections in the US are exchanged – bought and sold – by the students of the university. It was created by professors in the business school to gauge how accurately a relatively well-informed community of users could predict a future outcome. The initial results were not so much surprising as they were startling; the elections stock market outperformed professional pollsters, political pundits, and an assortment of prognosticators both in terms of the actual election results and the margin of win/loss achieved by the various candidates.

The notion of the "wisdom of crowds" is the latest business concept that has become popularized as a result of both social networking and the work done at the University of Iowa. Using the Internet as a medium for exchanging information among a community of reasonably well-informed users, a variety of issues about future events can be predicted with uncanny accuracy. Companies are now asking their customers, suppliers, and complete strangers to vote online about important strategic decisions, such as which new products to launch, what prices to charge for their current offerings, and what features to include with new and existing models. The wisdom of crowds has proven a powerful decision-making tool for some companies.

To illustrate how large crowds can make good predictions about the future, the next time you are reading an online newspaper think about some of the polls being run that concern future events, such as the recent Quebec provincial election. Prior to the final votes being tallied, approximately 80% of the roughly 7,000 readers polled by the *Globe and Mail* said that a minority government would be elected in the province. (Consider too that Quebec has not had a minority government for more than 100 years.) With remarkable accuracy, this bold prediction came true, which suggests infinite possibilities.

With a computer screen as a window into the future, the truth is out there for anyone who wants to find it; all that is required is starting an online poll on a personal blog and asking a question. What do the Internet, some Iowa University students, and large crowds have in common? They are all *"out there"* and waiting to lead us to the truth.

Chapter 10

Budget Management Decisions

How have my managers been performing?

Snapshot

Topic
Budgets and Variance Analysis

Subject Area
Management accounting

Decisions Made
Budgets represent the financial plans of the organization and are used to implement its strategic goals and objectives. Analyzing deviations from plans, through variances, facilitates management control.

Personal Experience
I was at one time employed as a budget analyst and then subsequently as a manger of financial services, where my duties included both developing and managing budgets for a number of responsibility centers. In every organization where I have worked, budgets and variance analysis are used to monitor and control corporate performance. Both favorable and unfavorable variances are calculated and tracked as responsibility is assigned to managers. This is typically done every month, and the differences between planned and actual results are presented to senior management for review. The process allows for timely corrective action if the variances are significant and also assigns responsibility to specific individuals.
Part of my job duties included managing a cash budget, which because of seasonal patterns in our business, resulted in significant surpluses during certain times of the year. Through a practice of prudent, but effective placement of funds, we were able to generate an important revenue stream for the organization with the excess cash amounts.

Excel Functionality

Financial modeling for budgeting involves a number of sequential steps, including:

- Creating the annual income statement budget
- Developing monthly budgets from the annual plan
- Making a cash budget for inflows and outflows each month
- Calculating detailed variances between actual and budget results

These calculations are not especially difficult but they are numerous and therefore good modeling practices are important (refer to Chapter 1 in this regard). These practices include creating and using named ranges, providing comments for cell information and ensuring that models are dynamic, allowing users to quickly assess the impact of changes in key variables (using sensitivity analysis), such as various assumptions about sales growth.

Variances are generally simple calculations of differences between two amounts. They can also represent a more complex exercise, when (for example) determining the material price variance, which is the difference between the standard and actual price for material purchases multiplied by the actual quantity purchased.

Background Theory

Budgeting involves two separate phases, based on timing: budgeted development comes first, where the financial plan for the organization is created, and is followed by budget management, where a comparison of the budget to actual results is done. This comparison generates variances that must be analyzed and explained. The feedback loop is completed when corrective action is taken to address deviations from the approved plan.

In summary, the budget management cycle involves

- planning = budget development
- control = variance analysis
- feedback = corrective action

Budget Development

On an annual basis, budgets are created for a company's income statement as well as its cash position. There are a number of budget development methodologies used, but the most popular is the incremental approach, where the prior year's actual results form the basis for the current year's financial plan. Other budget development methods include:

- Zero-based budgeting—where each and every expenditure (and revenue stream) must be fully explained and justified to senior management every year.
- Top-down budgeting—where senior managers dictate the budget for the year (including plans for both sales and spending) and responsibility centers managers must comply with these directives. When this approach is used, the budget amounts are commonly referred to as a "standards", since they are imposed on those responsible, rather than negotiated with them.

- Participative budgeting—where everyone who has responsibility for a budget has input into developing it, in this way soliciting acceptance of the process as well as the company's financial objectives.
- Balanced scorecard budgeting—where budgets address other factors that directly impact the financial results (which are considered a lagging indicator), such as improving business processes, supporting employee development and ensuring customer satisfaction. This methodology is linked to specific measures that form the basis for evaluating manager's performance.
- Activity-based budgeting—where spending on indirect costs (i.e., overhead) is planned based on activity cost drivers. This method uses the principles of activity-based costing, or ABC, to plan for the quantity of the cost driver—for example, the number of machine hours used—for each activity.
- Strategic budgeting—where the key business drivers determine the level of planned revenues and spending for the organization.

Budget planning covers only the next fiscal year (i.e., a 12-month period) and differs from a forecast, which can relate to as many as 20 years into the future.

Budget Management
Comparing budgeted amounts with actual operating results is an important part of the management control function—known as variance analysis. In a manufacturing environment, there are several commonly calculated variances, including,

- Materials Price Variance, which compares the budgeted with actual prices for materials bought.
- Materials Efficiency Variance, which compares the budgeted with actual usage of material in production.
- Labor Price Variance, which compares the budgeted with actual hourly rates paid for labor.
- Labor Efficiency Variance, which compares the budgeted with actual labor hours used in production.

Revenue variances are also determined; for example, comparing the budgeted with actual amounts for product prices and mix. These differences relate to the sales price variance and the product mix variance.

Cash Flow Budgets
The cash budget tracks the receipts and disbursements of cash, by month. This is done to prepare for periods of net cash outflows (deficits) as well as inflows (surpluses). When deficits are anticipated, a borrowing facility must be arranged, such as a standby line of credit, with a bank. With excess cash, an investment plan is required to ensure that funds earn a good return and do not sit idle. Monthly cash budgets show both incremental and cumulative cash balances for the year.

Financial Management Techniques
When developing a master budget for earnings, a number of steps are involved that proceed in sequence, following the format of the income statement from top to bottom. This means that the revenue budget is prepared first, based on sales estimates,

followed by the production plan, which includes an inventory cushion to address stock outs and to prevent loss of market share. Based on the planned production, resources are then budgeted for materials, labor and indirect costs (overhead). Finally, non-manufacturing expenses are determined, typically based on a percentage of manufacturing costs.

After the budget for the income statement is completed, the monthly allocations are determined; these are usually based on the previous year's sales pattern. Once completed, the annual financial plan, broken down by month, is compared to actual results taken from the corporate accounting system. A detailed analysis of variances related to expenses and revenues is completed for each month and the year-to-date.

Finally, the monthly income statement budget is adjusted to reflect cash inflows net of outflows to predict periods of cash surpluses and deficits.

Relevant Excel Functionality

Budget development with Excel is primarily formula driven and relies of prior years' trends and the relationship of revenues and expenses to the organization's key drivers. While incremental budgeting is the norm, current management thinking is moving to creating budgets based on business drivers and in this way more closely linking financial plans to corporate strategy.

Once the income statement master budget has been created, it must be converted into monthly budgets to facilitate timely feedback about performance and to provide control. It is at this time that variances are calculated for both the current month and for the period to date. These differences from plan will be classified as favorable (F) or unfavorable (U), depending on their effect on operating income. Favorable variances result in increased income relative to budget, while unfavorable variances show less income than planned.

Demonstration Exercise

Snowboarding has become very popular and is rapidly replacing skiing as the number one winter sports activity. This exercise relates to a manufacturer of customized snowboards for the hard-core outdoor enthusiast (Excel file: Chill-Dude(shell).xls).

Case Facts

Michelle Yung has been tasked with developing the income statement budget for her company, CHILL-DUDE, which makes snowboards for the local, as well as tourist population in Whistler BC, Canada. Her company is a small manufacturer that specializes in the production of customized boards that are built according to buyer's preferences. This can include specialized materials (such as different species of wood), lengths, shapes, finishes and waxes. As a boutique operation, they have carved (pun intended) a unique segment in the booming winter sport market. Michelle wants to base her budget on the key drivers of her company's success, which she has found include the following:

- World GDP (gross domestic product), which is a proxy measure for consumer prosperity and the amount of potential disposable income available for vacations and recreational activity. This means that as global GDP increases, people are more likely to take ski vacations.

- Canadian Forex, which is the foreign exchange rate relative to the domestic currency, particularly for the US dollar and the Euro, as Americans and Europeans comprise the bulk of the customer base. This means that as the Canadian dollar depreciates relative to these other currencies, ski vacations become less expensive and therefore more desirable.

By analyzing historical data, Michelle has determined that sales volumes are correlated with both GDP and Forex (see Chapter 5 on regression analysis and how this technique can be used to make predictions about future events). World GDP is expected to grow by 2% next year, and US and Euro forex rates (based on estimates provided by futures markets for these currencies) indicate a decline of 1% in the value of the Canadian dollar relative to these monies. Using a regression model, she has found a high degree of correspondence between these two predictors of sales (based on a significant r^2), such that the combined impact will result in an expected increase of 3% in demand for snowboards compared to last year.

Preparing the Income Statement Budget

Table 10.1 gives information that Michelle has compiled to prepare the annual budget.

Other assumptions:

- Because production is customized, the manufacture and sale of snowboards is assumed to occur in the same month. They are produced during the fall and winter, which is from September through March every year. There is no work in process or ending inventory.
- Stocks of wood and fiberglass are purchased, in bulk, at the beginning of the year in order to take advantage of volume discounts and also to ensure adequate supply.

Preparing the Monthly Income Statement Budget

Prior year sales, by month, were as follows (**Table 10.2**):

Preparing the Cash Flow Budget

Because the snowboards are custom built, payment is received in advance, in the month they are produced. All boards ordered in a month are manufactured in that month. Cash disbursements for materials (wood and fiberglass) are made in the month following purchase (i.e., net 30 days), while workers are paid in the month of production. Employees making snowboards are hired on contract, based on confirmed sales, which means that the factory labor force is only paid when orders are received. Administrative disbursements are incurred evenly throughout the year and relate primarily to salaries for staff, which are paid on a bimonthly basis, as well as other fixed costs for leased space, office equipment, insurance, and property taxes.

Preparing the Analysis of Variances

Actual results for the year are shown in **Table 10.3**.

The next figure shows the worksheet used to develop the annual income statement master budget, which incorporates the expected sales volume increases based on the key business drivers (which are world GDP and the US/Euro forex) (**Fig. 10.1**).

Table 10.1. Income Statement Budget Assumptions.

Income Statement	Price/Cost	Quantity	Notes
Sales	$500 per snowboard	1,580 snowboards	While prices can vary depending on customer specifications, the average amount charged for a custom snowboard is about $500. The quantity is based on last year's actual sales, adjusted for the expected increase predicted by the regression model (i.e., using predictive analytics).
Materials: Wood, in board feet (bf) Fiberglass, in yards (yd)	$25.00/bf $6.50/yd	5 bf per snowboard 8,000 bf purchased 6 yd per snowboard 9,500 yd purchased	The cost of wood can vary, depending on the type selected, but the average price is $25 per board foot. The quantity of wood purchased is based on the expected demand. Extra material is not bought, as the boards are manufactured to customer specification.
Labor	$30/hr	5 hrs	The hourly rate includes all employee benefits (CPP, EI and medical).
Overhead: per direct labor hour (DLH)	$5/DLH	1,580 snowboards × 5 hrs = 7,900 DLH	As the manufacturing process is primarily manual, labor hours is the most suitable cost driver to allocate overhead, which includes costs for utilities, property taxes, insurance, and amortization of building and equipment.
SG&A	10%	10% of COGM	Historically, nonmanufacturing costs have been about 10% of the cost of producing the snowboards.

Table 10.2. Prior Year Monthly Sales Volume in Dollars.

Month	Sales ($)
January	78,999
February	19,750
March	6,583
April	–
May	–
June	–
July	–
August	–
September	46,083
October	105,332
November	171,165
December	230,414
TOTAL	**658,326**

Table 10.3. Actual Results Compared to Budget.

Item	Actual	Budget
Sales price	$510.00	$500.00
Sales Volume	1,620 snowboards	1,580 snowboards
Wood cost	$24.50/bf	$25.00/bf
Wood usage	5.25 bf/board	5 bf/board
Fiberglass cost	$6.00/yd	$6.50/yd
Fiberglass usage	6 yd/board	6 yd/board
Labor rate	$32.00/hr	$30.00/hr
Labor usage	4.75 hrs/board	5 hrs/board
Overhead	$45,250	$39,500

A one-way data table tests the sensitivity of changes to the base case assumption of 3% sales growth (using amounts that are both less than and greater than 3%).

The assumptions presented in **Table 10.1** are shown as decision variables (light gray–shaded cells) so that important sensitivities can be tested, such as changes in the assumed sales volume and how this will affect profits. The figure that follows shows the formulas used in the financial model for the income statement (**Fig. 10.2**).

To effectively manage the budget, the annual amounts must be converted into monthly figures. This is done by analyzing the prior year's sales volumes and pro-rating the annual budget based on this historical experience, as shown in the figures below (**Figs. 10.3 and 10.4**).

Fig. 10.1. CHILL-DUDE Income Statement Budget.

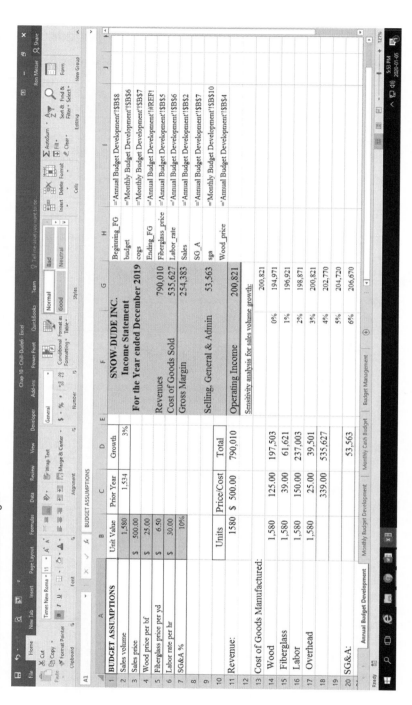

Fig. 10.2. CHILL-DUDE Income Statement Budget (Formulas).

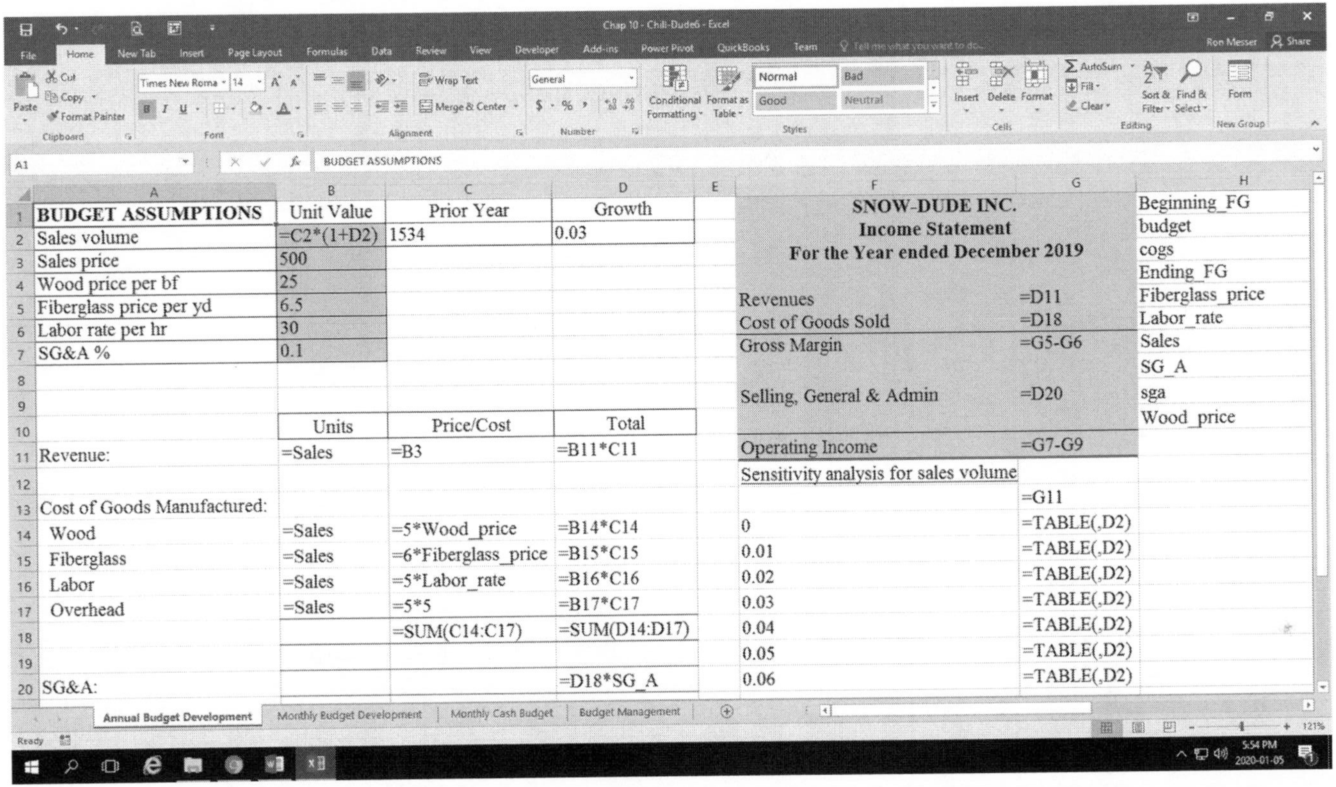

	A	B	C	D	F	G	H
1	BUDGET ASSUMPTIONS	Unit Value	Prior Year	Growth	SNOW-DUDE INC. Income Statement For the Year ended December 2019		Beginning_FG
2	Sales volume	=C2*(1+D2)	1534	0.03			budget
3	Sales price	500	=B3				cogs
4	Wood price per bf	25			Revenues	=D11	Ending_FG
5	Fiberglass price per yd	6.5			Cost of Goods Sold	=D18	Fiberglass_price
6	Labor rate per hr	30			Gross Margin	=G5-G6	Labor_rate
7	SG&A %	0.1					Sales
8							SG_A
9					Selling, General & Admin	=D20	sga
10		Units	Price/Cost	Total			Wood_price
11	Revenue:	=Sales	=B3	=B11*C11	Operating Income	=G7-G9	
12					Sensitivity analysis for sales volume		
13	Cost of Goods Manufactured:					=G11	
14	Wood	=Sales	=5*Wood_price	=B14*C14	0	=TABLE(,D2)	
15	Fiberglass	=Sales	=6*Fiberglass_price	=B15*C15	0.01	=TABLE(,D2)	
16	Labor	=Sales	=5*Labor_rate	=B16*C16	0.02	=TABLE(,D2)	
17	Overhead	=Sales	=5*5	=B17*C17	0.03	=TABLE(,D2)	
18			=SUM(C14:C17)	=SUM(D14:D17)	0.04	=TABLE(,D2)	
19					0.05	=TABLE(,D2)	
20	SG&A:			=D18*SG_A	0.06	=TABLE(,D2)	

Fig. 10.3. CHILL-DUDE Income Statement Monthly Budget.

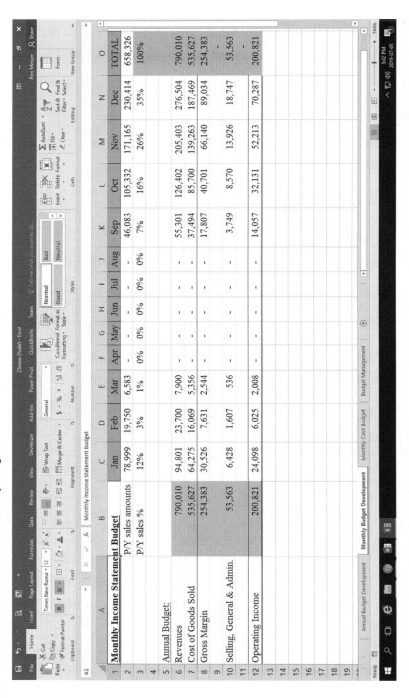

Fig. 10.4. CHILL-DUDE Income Statement Monthly Budget (Formulas).

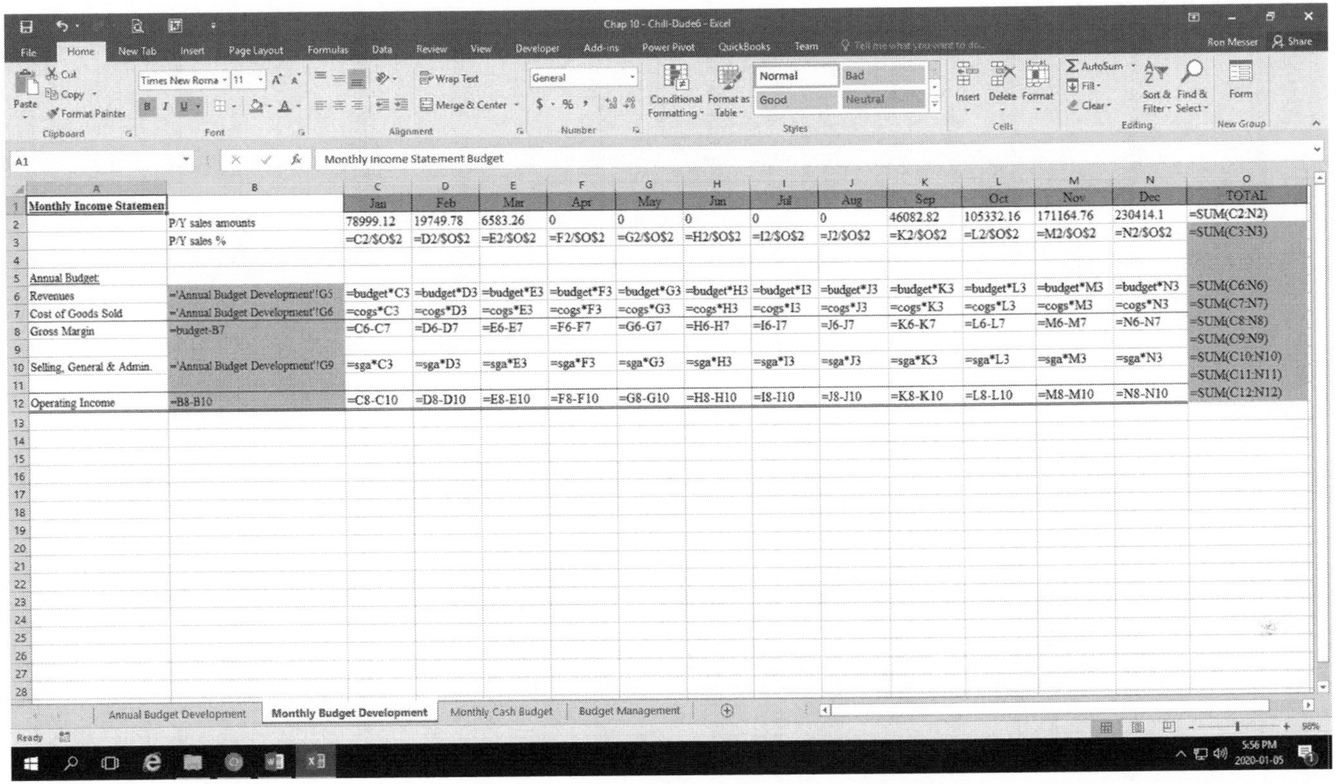

	A / B	C Jan	D Feb	E Mar	F Apr	G May	H Jun	I Jul	J Aug	K Sep	L Oct	M Nov	N Dec	O TOTAL
1	Monthly Income Statement													
2	P/Y sales amounts	78999.12	19749.78	6583.26	0	0	0	0	0	46082.82	105332.16	171164.76	230414.1	=SUM(C2:N2)
3	P/Y sales %	=C2/$O$2	=D2/$O$2	=E2/$O$2	=F2/$O$2	=G2/$O$2	=H2/$O$2	=I2/$O$2	=J2/$O$2	=K2/$O$2	=L2/$O$2	=M2/$O$2	=N2/$O$2	=SUM(C3:N3)
4														
5	Annual Budget													
6	Revenues ='Annual Budget Development'!G5	=budget*C3	=budget*D3	=budget*E3	=budget*F3	=budget*G3	=budget*H3	=budget*I3	=budget*J3	=budget*K3	=budget*L3	=budget*M3	=budget*N3	=SUM(C6:N6)
7	Cost of Goods Sold ='Annual Budget Development'!G6	=cogs*C3	=cogs*D3	=cogs*E3	=cogs*F3	=cogs*G3	=cogs*H3	=cogs*I3	=cogs*J3	=cogs*K3	=cogs*L3	=cogs*M3	=cogs*N3	=SUM(C7:N7)
8	Gross Margin =budget-B7	=C6-C7	=D6-D7	=E6-E7	=F6-F7	=G6-G7	=H6-H7	=I6-I7	=J6-J7	=K6-K7	=L6-L7	=M6-M7	=N6-N7	=SUM(C8:N8)
9														
10	Selling, General & Admin. ='Annual Budget Development'!G9	=sga*C3	=sga*D3	=sga*E3	=sga*F3	=sga*G3	=sga*H3	=sga*I3	=sga*J3	=sga*K3	=sga*L3	=sga*M3	=sga*N3	=SUM(C10:N10)
11														=SUM(C11:N11)
12	Operating Income =B8-B10	=C8-C10	=D8-D10	=E8-E10	=F8-F10	=G8-G10	=H8-H10	=I8-I10	=J8-J10	=K8-K10	=L8-L10	=M8-M10	=N8-N10	=SUM(C12:N12)

Annual Budget Development   Monthly Budget Development   Monthly Cash Budget   Budget Management

Using the pattern of sales in the monthly income statement budget and following the "rules" concerning the timing and amount of cash receipts and disbursements, the monthly cash budget appears below (**Figs. 10.5 and 10.6**).

The cash budget clearly shows that the company must arrange short-term financing for three fiscal quarters (January through September) as net cash flows are not positive until toward the end of the fiscal year. The excess cash at the year-end can then be used to pay off the line of credit.

The variances between actual and budget are shown in the figures that follow (**Figs. 10.7 and 10.8**).

The detailed variances show that the average selling price was better than expected and total sales volume was above the budgeted amount. Materials cost more than planned for wood but savings were achieved on purchases of fiberglass. More wood was used than budgeted but less fiberglass was needed. Paying their workers somewhat less than planned probably explains the extra time required to manufacture snowboards.

Afterthought → *liar, liar... finances so dire*

Budgeting just refuses to go away. It is a time-consuming and frequently frustrating exercise that has been analyzed in the academic and popular press for many years. At its heart, the problem with financial planning is the lack of honesty of those participating in the process; everyone wants more than the company is willing to give. Consider, therefore, whether an alternative exists.

Fig. 10.5. CHILL-DUDE Monthly Cash Budget.

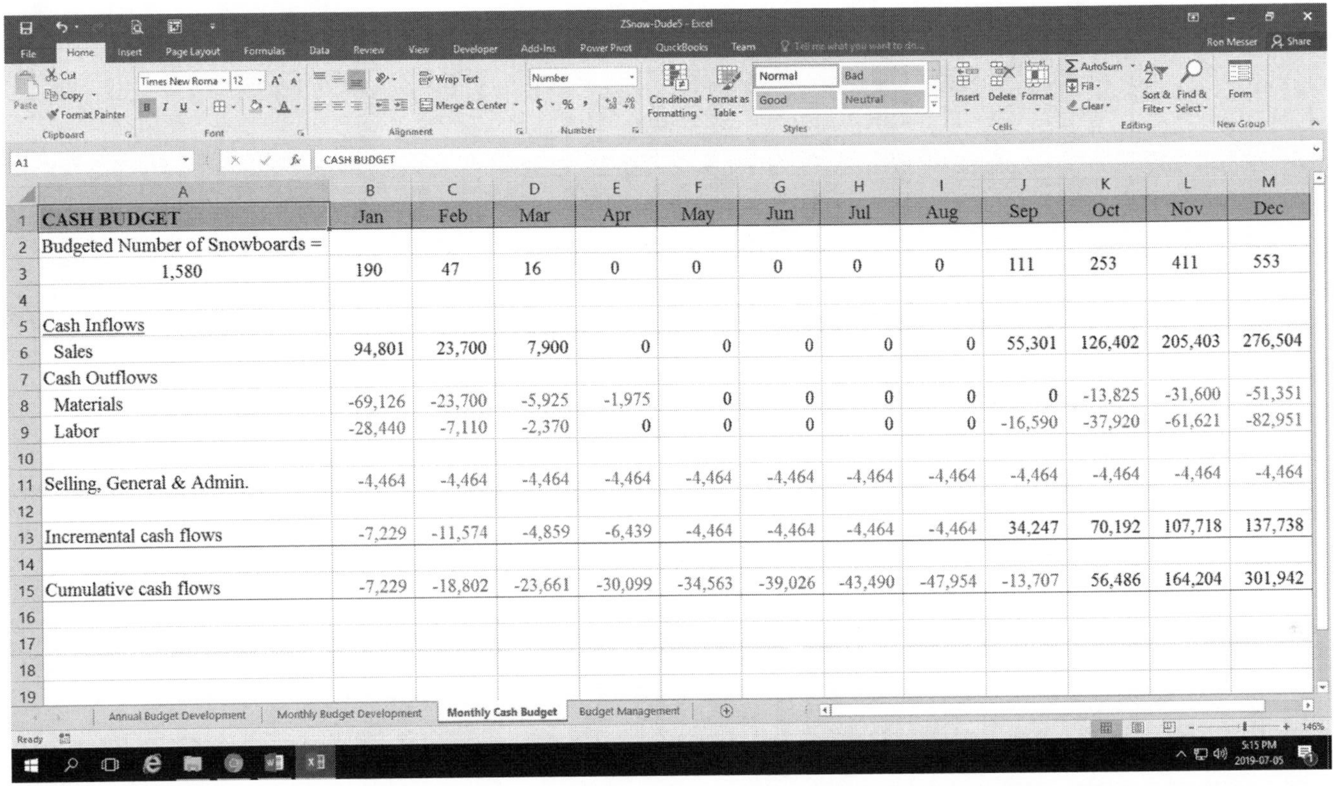

CASH BUDGET

Budgeted Number of Snowboards = 1,580

	Jan	Feb	Mar	Apr	May	Jun	Jul	Aug	Sep	Oct	Nov	Dec
	190	47	16	0	0	0	0	0	111	253	411	553
Cash Inflows												
Sales	94,801	23,700	7,900	0	0	0	0	0	55,301	126,402	205,403	276,504
Cash Outflows												
Materials	-69,126	-23,700	-5,925	-1,975	0	0	0	0	0	-13,825	-31,600	-51,351
Labor	-28,440	-7,110	-2,370	0	0	0	0	0	-16,590	-37,920	-61,621	-82,951
Selling, General & Admin.	-4,464	-4,464	-4,464	-4,464	-4,464	-4,464	-4,464	-4,464	-4,464	-4,464	-4,464	-4,464
Incremental cash flows	-7,229	-11,574	-4,859	-6,439	-4,464	-4,464	-4,464	-4,464	34,247	70,192	107,718	137,738
Cumulative cash flows	-7,229	-18,802	-23,661	-30,099	-34,563	-39,026	-43,490	-47,954	-13,707	56,486	164,204	301,942

Fig. 10.6. CHILL-DUDE Monthly Cash Budget (Formulas).

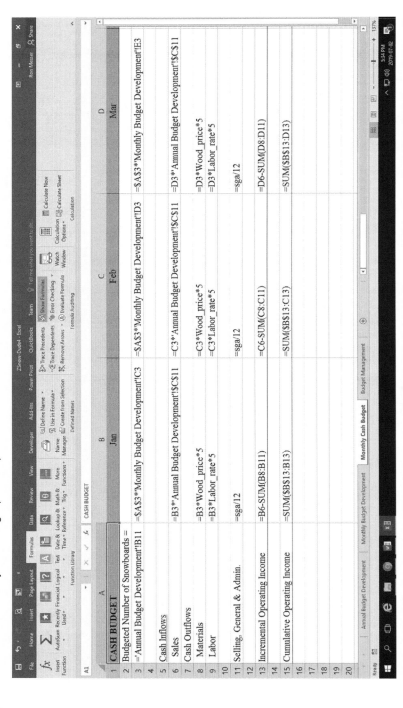

Fig. 10.7. CHILL-DUDE Variance Calculations.

Item	Actual	Budget
Sales price	$510.00	$500.00
Sales volume	1,620	1,580
Wood cost	$25.50	$25.00
Wood purchased, in bf	8,000	7,900
Wood usage, in bf	8,100	7,900
Fiberglass cost	$6.00	$6.50
Fiberglass purchased, in yds	9,300	9,480
Fiberglass usage, in yds	9,300	9,480
Labor cost	$32.00	$30.00
Labor usage, in hrs	7,450	7,900
Overhead rate	$6.07	$5.00

Variance Component	Actual Price	Budget Price	Actual Quantity	Budget Quantity
Sales	$510.00	$500.00	1,620	1,580
Wood	$25.50	$25.00	8,100	7,900
Fibreglass	$6.00	$6.50	9,300	9,480
Labor	$32.00	$30.00	7,450	7,900
Overhead (based on Labor Hrs.)	45,250	39,500	7,450	7,900

Detailed Variances	Amount	F/U
Sales Price Variance	$16,200	Favorable
Sales Volume Variance	$20,000	Favorable
Materials Price Variance:		
Wood	-$4,050	Unfavorable
Fiberglass	$4,650	Favorable
Materials Usage Variance:		
Wood	-$5,000	Unfavorable
Fiberglass	$1,170	Favorable
Labor Price Variance	-$14,900	Unfavorable
Labor Usage Variance	$13,500	Favorable
Overhead Spending Variance	-$5,750	Unfavorable
Overhead Efficiency Variance	$2,250	Favorable

Fig. 10.8. CHILL-DUDE Variance Calculations (Formulas).

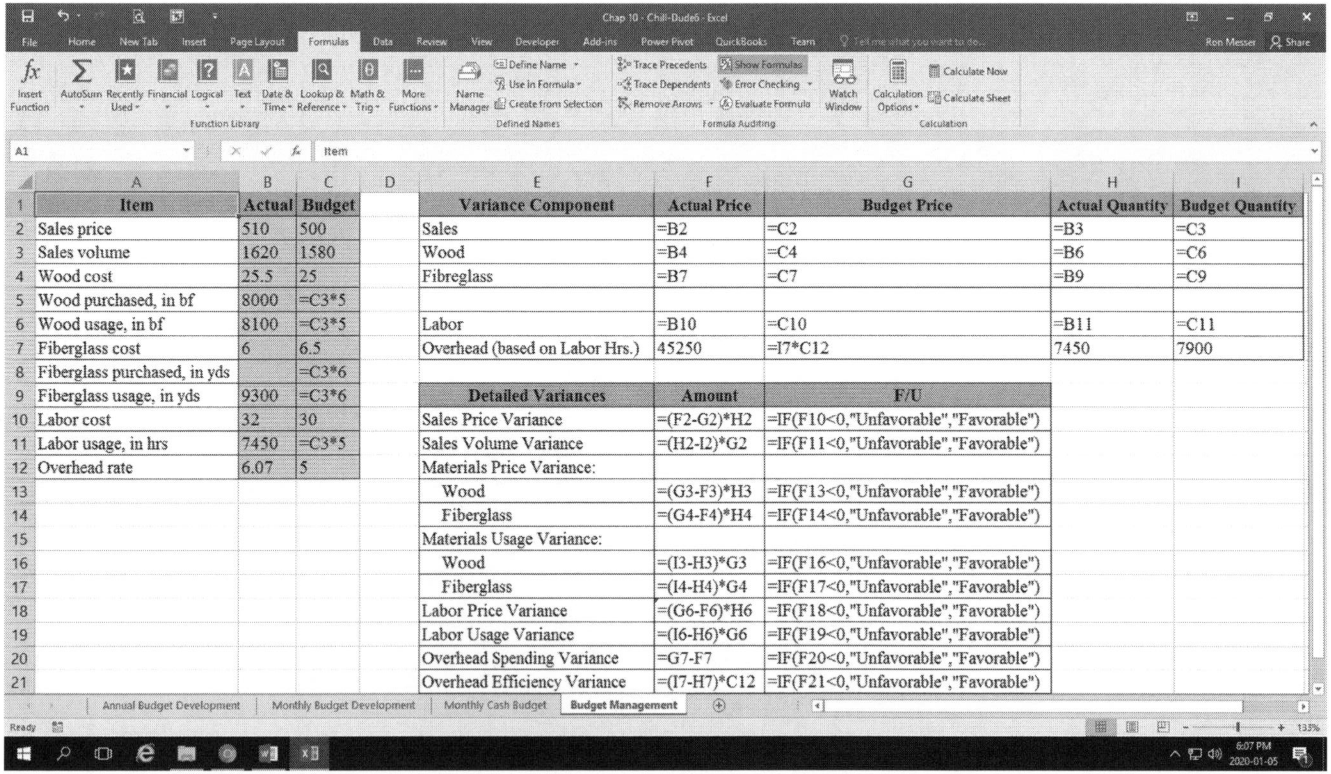

	A	B	C	D	E	F	G	H	I
	Item	Actual	Budget		Variance Component	Actual Price	Budget Price	Actual Quantity	Budget Quantity
2	Sales price	510	500		Sales	=B2	=C2	=B3	=C3
3	Sales volume	1620	1580		Wood	=B4	=C4	=B6	=C6
4	Wood cost	25.5	25		Fibreglass	=B7	=C7	=B9	=C9
5	Wood purchased, in bf	8000	=C3*5						
6	Wood usage, in bf	8100	=C3*5		Labor	=B10	=C10	=B11	=C11
7	Fiberglass cost	6	6.5		Overhead (based on Labor Hrs.)	45250	=I7*C12	7450	7900
8	Fibreglass purchased, in yds		=C3*6						
9	Fibreglass usage, in yds	9300	=C3*6		Detailed Variances	Amount	F/U		
10	Labor cost	32	30		Sales Price Variance	=(F2-G2)*H2	=IF(F10<0,"Unfavorable","Favorable")		
11	Labor usage, in hrs	7450	=C3*5		Sales Volume Variance	=(H2-I2)*G2	=IF(F11<0,"Unfavorable","Favorable")		
12	Overhead rate	6.07	5		Materials Price Variance:				
13					Wood	=(G3-F3)*H3	=IF(F13<0,"Unfavorable","Favorable")		
14					Fiberglass	=(G4-F4)*H4	=IF(F14<0,"Unfavorable","Favorable")		
15					Materials Usage Variance:				
16					Wood	=(I3-H3)*G3	=IF(F16<0,"Unfavorable","Favorable")		
17					Fiberglass	=(I4-H4)*G4	=IF(F17<0,"Unfavorable","Favorable")		
18					Labor Price Variance	=(G6-F6)*H6	=IF(F18<0,"Unfavorable","Favorable")		
19					Labor Usage Variance	=(I6-H6)*G6	=IF(F19<0,"Unfavorable","Favorable")		
20					Overhead Spending Variance	=G7-F7	=IF(F20<0,"Unfavorable","Favorable")		
21					Overhead Efficiency Variance	=(I7-H7)*C12	=IF(F21<0,"Unfavorable","Favorable")		

Budgets and Other Lies

(Or, how do you do the things you do)

There are few things more certain in business than budgets and taxes. Some companies don't pay taxes (for those of you who didn't know, nonprofits are tax exempt) but nevertheless, we certainly do a lot of budgeting. A budget is many different things, depending on your perspective. Some see it as a tedious chore that needs to be done (or else nothing will get done because there won't be any money to do it). Others see it as an opportunity to plan and prioritize their activities for the coming year. In my view, at its most basic level, a budget is tool for modifying behavior. Think about it! A budget tells people important information about you, like where you spend your money and how much you have to spend. By monitoring and controlling someone's spending, you can influence not only what they do, but how they do it.

Budgets are also a bunch of lies. Don't misunderstand what I'm saying. Budgets are lies because no one can know with certainty what they'll be spending next year or even tomorrow for that matter. For this reason, people make an educated guess (i.e. tell a lie) about how much they'll need to do the things they have to do. Folks usually know that their guess will be wrong and consequently add a little extra...just to be sure. In this way, confusion arises about what they *expect* to happen and what's most *likely* to happen. For example, simply saying that you expect inflation to increase your operating costs doesn't mean that this is likely (or even probable).

Since budgets tell others so much about us—and because we all want to look good—we stretch the truth (i.e. tell a bigger lie), which creates a huge problem. If an organization uses its budget for business planning, then its usefulness is seriously eroded if the information is, at the outset, (knowingly) incorrect. If bad information goes in, then bad information (and decisions) comes out. But, what's the alternative?

There is growing opposition to traditional budgeting, mostly among European businesses. These companies have done away with the budget process entirely and instead are focusing on business planning, formulating strategy and long-term forecasts. Operating managers are informed of corporate goals and objectives and then left to sort out how they will help achieve these. It's simple, it saves time, and it lets people do the things they have to do without having to lie.

Chapter 11

Amortization Table Decisions

What is happening to my investments?

Snapshot

Topic
Amortizations

Subject Area
Financial accounting: corporate bonds; bank borrowing; property, plant, and equipment (PP&E)

Decisions Made
Amortization relates to the usage, with the passage of time, of an item in the financial statements (such as investing in an asset or incurring a liability). It is intended to match the cost of the item with the company's ability to earn income. In other words, PP&E is acquired to generate revenues, and borrowed funds enable the company to acquire PP&E.

Some common amortizations include the following:

- Debt and interest charges related to corporate bonds
- Loan and mortgage payments associated with bank borrowings
- Recognizing the usage of productive assets through amortization

Personal Experience
When working as a senior manager for an energy company, it was my job to review the interest expense on the income statement. Our organization was heavily financed by debt (in the amount of several billion dollars), through sales of corporate bonds. As part of our bond indenture agreement, we were required to maintain a predetermined interest coverage ratio (which is calculated as net income plus interest expense divided by interest expense). For this reason, it was critical to correctly determine interest charges. As these bonds were sold over many years, we had to calculate the annual interest expense using the effective interest rate method (following International Financial Reporting Standards – IFRS), which amortized the bond discounts and premiums over the term of the

debt. Bonds sold at a discount incurred additional interest expense, while those sold at a premium represented reduced interest charges. This was an extremely complex and important calculation, as we typically had as many as 100 bond series outstanding at any time.

Excel Functionality
NPV
IRR
RATE
PMT

Background Theory

Corporate Bonds

Bonds will sell at a discount when the market rate of interest exceeds that of the bond coupon payment (also referred to as the stated value). This should make sense because if the bond is paying less than the current market rate of interest, to entice buyers to purchase these securities they must sell for an amount below their face value. Conversely, if the bond coupon is paying more than the current market rate it will sell for a premium, which means that the issuing company will receive more money than they are required to pay back at a later date. Both bond discounts and premiums must be recognized over the term of the bond as an increase (discount) or decrease (premium) in interest expense.

A bond that sells at its face value is said to have sold at par, or 100. A bond selling at a discount is described based on a percentage of par (or 100), such as 98 – this means that the bond sold for 98% of its face value (or a 2% discount). A bond that sells at a premium has a selling price in excess of 100, for example, 102, which means that the bond was sold for 102% of its face value (or, a 2% premium).

Bank Borrowing

Amounts borrowed from third-party lenders come in many forms: from standby credit facilities to long-term loans. Typically, the term of the loan will be matched to the life of the asset – i.e., long-term assets will be financed with long-term debt and short-term assets with short-term borrowing. Excel can be used to generate amortization tables for these loans as well as to determine some of the critical variables associated with deciding how much to borrow, such as the periodic payments required to service the borrowing.

Property, Plant, and Equipment

Capital assets are noncurrent and according to GAAP must be recognized in the earnings process by matching their consumption, on a reasonable basis, with revenues generated. This can include straight line amortization, several accelerated methods or based on the number of units produced. Excel can be used to create such amortization schedules. For greater clarity, the term *amortization* generally describes the consumption of intangible assets over time, such as patents and copyrights. *Depreciation* refers to tangible assets, including machinery and equipment. *Depletion* addresses the consumption of natural resources to earn income, such as timber harvesting or mineral extraction. For simplicity and consistency, the term amortization will be used synonymously with these other measures.

Financial Management Techniques

According to IFRS (international GAAP), bond discounts and premiums must be amortized over the life of the bond by using the effective interest rate method. This approach calculates the interest expense at every interest payment date (for example, annually or semi-annually), based on the carrying value of the bond at that time. Its purpose is to match the cost of the financing (interest expense) with the time period receiving the benefits, including the capital necessary to operate a business.

Repayments on bank borrowing represent blended payments, where the periodic amounts remitted pay down both principal and interest over time. During the earlier periods, payments relate primarily to interest on outstanding amounts and later, mostly to the principal owing.

PP&E can be amortized using either a straight line method (with equal annual amounts), an accelerated approach (with higher amortization in the early years), or based on actual usage (such as the number of units of produced).

Using MS-Excel Functionality

Financial models for bond pricing and amortization are primarily formula driven. This means that the cells in the Excel worksheet contain numerous calculations. (Remember when using formulas to be aware of the correct order of operation – i.e., power function; multiply/divide; add/subtract.) The Excel functions employed for this exercise include NPV, IRR, RATE, PMT.

Demonstration Exercise

Geezer Incorporated is an old, well-established company operating in the extractive industries sector. As a producer of commodities, it is a price-taker, whose revenues depend on worldwide demand and supply for its output. As a result, cost control is vital to corporate profitability. The company's major expenses include payments made on corporate bonds and bank loans, as well as purchases of capital assets. Geezer has developed several models to help it manage its financial affairs; these address on the impact of interest expense and depreciation on the bottom line. (Excel file: Geezer(shell).xls.)

Corporate Bonds

The financial model shown in **Fig. 11.1** includes input parameters for calculating the price of a bond (shown as light gray cells in the worksheet), which are described in **Table 11.1**.

For this exercise, assume the following case facts:

- PAR = $1,000,000
- MARKET = 11.5%
- COUPON = 9.5%
- TERM = 10 years
- PAYMENT = semi-annually

Fig. 11.1. Bond Interest Expense Amortization.

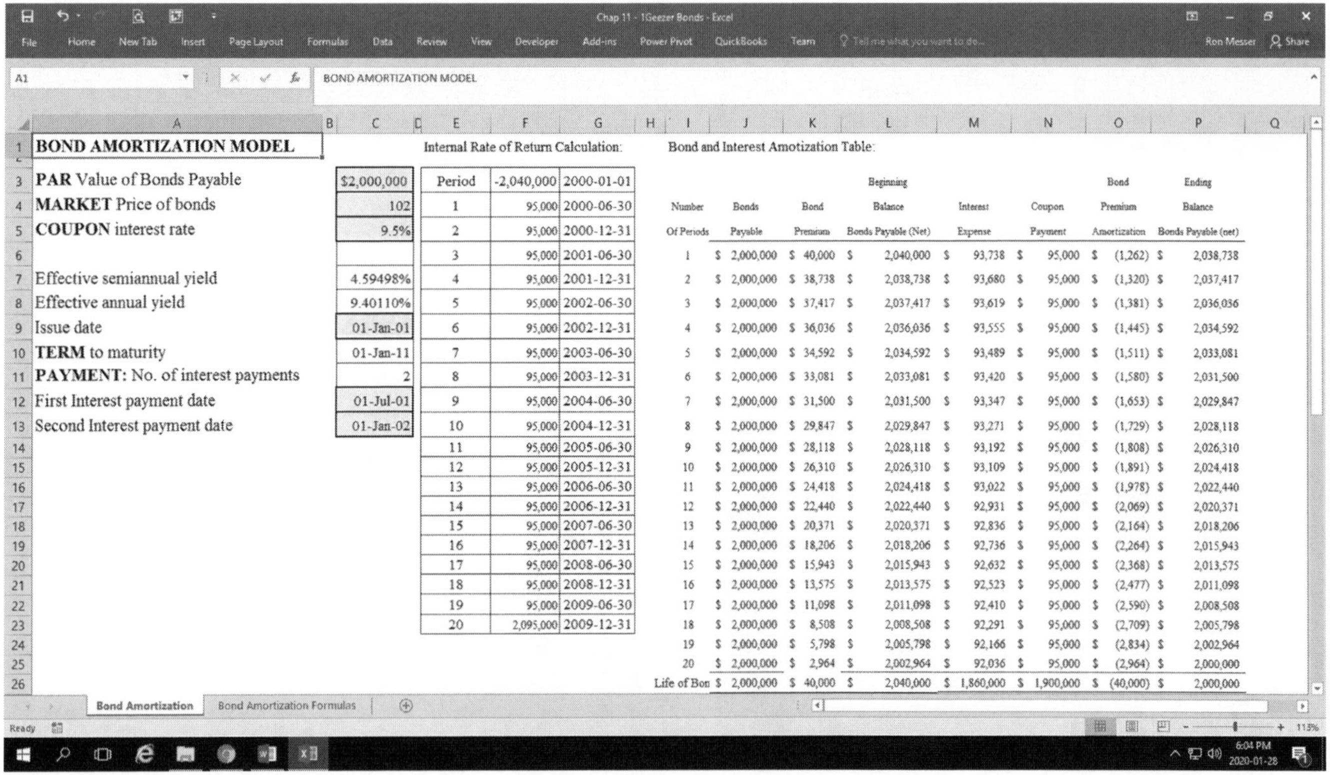

BOND AMORTIZATION MODEL

PAR Value of Bonds Payable	$2,000,000
MARKET Price of bonds	102
COUPON interest rate	9.5%
Effective semiannual yield	4.59498%
Effective annual yield	9.40110%
Issue date	01-Jan-01
TERM to maturity	01-Jan-11
PAYMENT: No. of interest payments	2
First Interest payment date	01-Jul-01
Second Interest payment date	01-Jan-02

Internal Rate of Return Calculation:

Period		
	-2,040,000	2000-01-01
1	95,000	2000-06-30
2	95,000	2000-12-31
3	95,000	2001-06-30
4	95,000	2001-12-31
5	95,000	2002-06-30
6	95,000	2002-12-31
7	95,000	2003-06-30
8	95,000	2003-12-31
9	95,000	2004-06-30
10	95,000	2004-12-31
11	95,000	2005-06-30
12	95,000	2005-12-31
13	95,000	2006-06-30
14	95,000	2006-12-31
15	95,000	2007-06-30
16	95,000	2007-12-31
17	95,000	2008-06-30
18	95,000	2008-12-31
19	95,000	2009-06-30
20	2,095,000	2009-12-31

Bond and Interest Amortization Table:

Number Of Periods	Bonds Payable	Bond Premium	Beginning Balance Bonds Payable (Net)	Interest Expense	Coupon Payment	Bond Premium Amortization	Ending Balance Bonds Payable (net)
1	2,000,000	40,000	2,040,000	93,738	95,000	(1,262)	2,038,738
2	2,000,000	38,738	2,038,738	93,680	95,000	(1,320)	2,037,417
3	2,000,000	37,417	2,037,417	93,619	95,000	(1,381)	2,036,036
4	2,000,000	36,036	2,036,036	93,555	95,000	(1,445)	2,034,592
5	2,000,000	34,592	2,034,592	93,489	95,000	(1,511)	2,033,081
6	2,000,000	33,081	2,033,081	93,420	95,000	(1,580)	2,031,500
7	2,000,000	31,500	2,031,500	93,347	95,000	(1,653)	2,029,847
8	2,000,000	29,847	2,029,847	93,271	95,000	(1,729)	2,028,118
9	2,000,000	28,118	2,028,118	93,192	95,000	(1,808)	2,026,310
10	2,000,000	26,310	2,026,310	93,109	95,000	(1,891)	2,024,418
11	2,000,000	24,418	2,024,418	93,022	95,000	(1,978)	2,022,440
12	2,000,000	22,440	2,022,440	92,931	95,000	(2,069)	2,020,371
13	2,000,000	20,371	2,020,371	92,836	95,000	(2,164)	2,018,206
14	2,000,000	18,206	2,018,206	92,736	95,000	(2,264)	2,015,943
15	2,000,000	15,943	2,015,943	92,632	95,000	(2,368)	2,013,575
16	2,000,000	13,575	2,013,575	92,523	95,000	(2,477)	2,011,098
17	2,000,000	11,098	2,011,098	92,410	95,000	(2,590)	2,008,508
18	2,000,000	8,508	2,008,508	92,291	95,000	(2,709)	2,005,798
19	2,000,000	5,798	2,005,798	92,166	95,000	(2,834)	2,002,964
20	2,000,000	2,964	2,002,964	92,036	95,000	(2,964)	2,000,000
Life of Bon	2,000,000	40,000		1,860,000	1,900,000	(40,000)	2,000,000

Bond Amortization | Bond Amortization Formulas

Table 11.1. Bond Input Parameters.

Input	Parameter Description
PAR	Par value of the bond (also known as its "face" value) is the issue amount shown on the bond certificate.
MARKET	Market rate of interest (also known as the bond yield, which is either more, or less than, the par value).
COUPON	Coupon interest rate, which is the periodic interest payment made to bond holders and is stated on the bond certificate.
TERM	Issue date and term of bond (i.e., the number of periods – usually in years – before the bond matures).
PAYMENT	Periodic payments made, which is the schedule of interest payments (typically annually, semi-annually, or quarterly) to bondholders.

Note that in this example, the bond is sold at a 2% premium (i.e., 102, as shown in cell C4). For this reason, the amortization table shows the interest expense as being less than the semi-annual coupon payment of \$47,500 (i.e., $9.5\% \times \frac{1}{2} \times 1,000,000 = 47,500$). The market rate of interest is the coupon rate of 9.5%, plus the 2% premium (i.e., 102, or $9.5\% + 2.0\% = 11.5\%$).

Figs. 11.2 and 11.3 show the formulas used in the amortization schedule.

Note the following:

- Effective semi-annual yield uses the IRR function to determine the yield based on the coupon and the amortization of the bond premium.
- Effective annual yield converts the semi-annual to an annual effective yield.

Bank Borrowing

Almost all companies have bank loans as part of their short-, or long-term liabilities. These can include everything from a standby line of credit to multiyear business borrowing. For these financing arrangements, an amortization schedule is indispensable when recording the annual interest expense. **Fig. 11.4** shows the completed amortization schedule for a bank loan. The decision variable in this financial model is the amount of the loan (cell D1 – medium gray cell color) and the objective function is the amount of the monthly payment (cell D5 – dark gray cell color).

Note how the interest portion of the payments is gradually reducing over time. The PMT function calculates the effective monthly interest rate by taking one-twelfth of the annual rate; it determines the number of payments based on 12 periods for 5 years – i.e., 60 payments. **Fig. 11.5** shows the formulas used in the worksheet.

Property, Plant, and Equipment[1]

The financial model shown below (**Fig. 11.6**) tracks asset utilization based on the date of acquisition and records the amortization, based on the expected useful life; this amount appears on the company's income statement.

---

[1] This model was developed based on training I received at a professional development session offered by the Chartered Accountants of British Columbia (Canada).

Fig. 11.2. Bond Interest Expense Amortization (Formulas – Part 1).

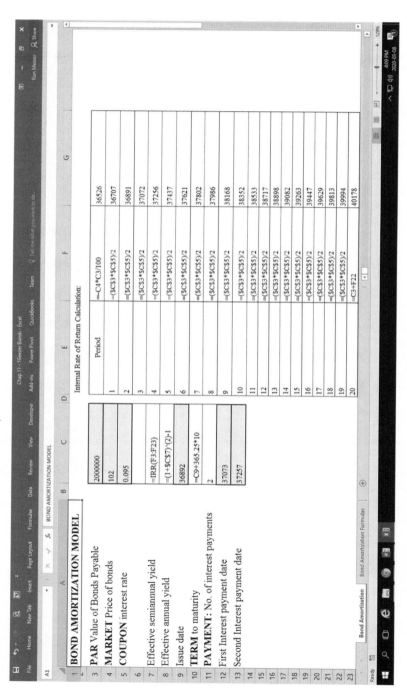

Fig. 11.3. Bond Interest Expense Amortization (Formulas – Part 2).

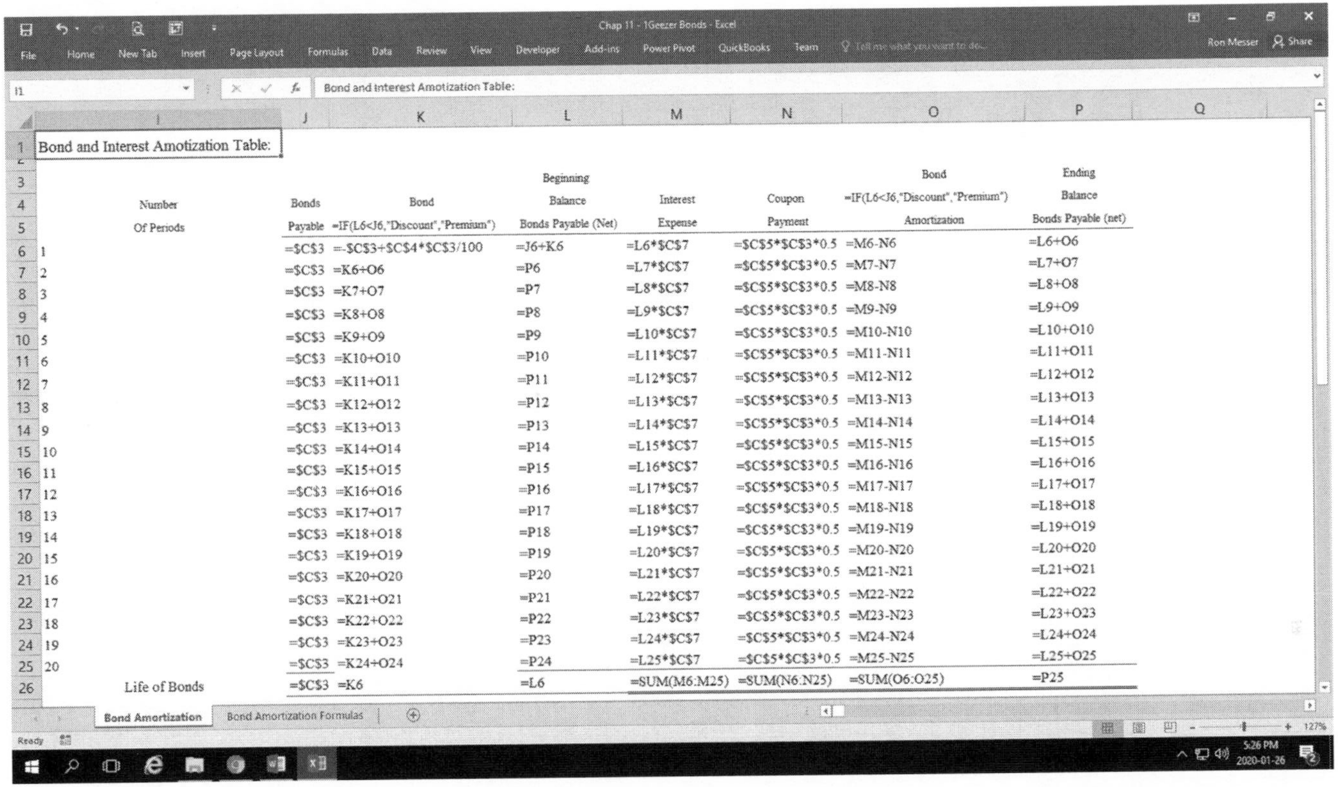

Bond and Interest Amortization Table:

Bond and Interest Amortization Table:

Number Of Periods	Bonds Payable	Bond =IF(L6<J6,'Discount','Premium')	Beginning Balance Bonds Payable (Net)	Interest Expense	Coupon Payment	Bond Amortization =IF(L6<J6,'Discount','Premium')	Ending Balance Bonds Payable (net)
	=$C$3	=$C$4*$C$3*$C$3/100	=J6+K6	=L6*$C$7	=$C$5*$C$3*$C$7*0.5	=M6-N6	=L6+O6
	=$C$3	=K6+O6	=P6	=L7*$C$7	=$C$5*$C$3*$C$7*0.5	=M7-N7	=L7+O7
	=$C$3	=K7+O7	=P7	=L8*$C$7	=$C$5*$C$3*$C$7*0.5	=M8-N8	=L8+O8
	=$C$3	=K8+O8	=P8	=L9*$C$7	=$C$5*$C$3*$C$7*0.5	=M9-N9	=L9+O9
	=$C$3	=K9+O9	=P9	=L10*$C$7	=$C$5*$C$3*$C$7*0.5	=M10-N10	=L10+O10
	=$C$3	=K10+O10	=P10	=L11*$C$7	=$C$5*$C$3*$C$7*0.5	=M11-N11	=L11+O11
	=$C$3	=K11+O11	=P11	=L12*$C$7	=$C$5*$C$3*$C$7*0.5	=M12-N12	=L12+O12
	=$C$3	=K12+O12	=P12	=L13*$C$7	=$C$5*$C$3*$C$7*0.5	=M13-N13	=L13+O13
	=$C$3	=K13+O13	=P13	=L14*$C$7	=$C$5*$C$3*$C$7*0.5	=M14-N14	=L14+O14
	=$C$3	=K14+O14	=P14	=L15*$C$7	=$C$5*$C$3*$C$7*0.5	=M15-N15	=L15+O15
	=$C$3	=K15+O15	=P15	=L16*$C$7	=$C$5*$C$3*$C$7*0.5	=M16-N16	=L16+O16
	=$C$3	=K16+O16	=P16	=L17*$C$7	=$C$5*$C$3*$C$7*0.5	=M17-N17	=L17+O17
	=$C$3	=K17+O17	=P17	=L18*$C$7	=$C$5*$C$3*$C$7*0.5	=M18-N18	=L18+O18
	=$C$3	=K18+O18	=P18	=L19*$C$7	=$C$5*$C$3*$C$7*0.5	=M19-N19	=L19+O19
	=$C$3	=K19+O19	=P19	=L20*$C$7	=$C$5*$C$3*$C$7*0.5	=M20-N20	=L20+O20
	=$C$3	=K20+O20	=P20	=L21*$C$7	=$C$5*$C$3*$C$7*0.5	=M21-N21	=L21+O21
	=$C$3	=K21+O21	=P21	=L22*$C$7	=$C$5*$C$3*$C$7*0.5	=M22-N22	=L22+O22
	=$C$3	=K22+O22	=P22	=L23*$C$7	=$C$5*$C$3*$C$7*0.5	=M23-N23	=L23+O23
	=$C$3	=K23+O23	=P23	=L24*$C$7	=$C$5*$C$3*$C$7*0.5	=M24-N24	=L24+O24
	=$C$3	=K24+O24	=P24	=L25*$C$7	=$C$5*$C$3*$C$7*0.5	=M25-N25	=L25+O25
Life of Bonds	=$C$3	=K6	=L6	=SUM(M6:M25)	=SUM(N6:N25)	=SUM(O6:O25)	=P25

Bond Amortization | Bond Amortization Formulas

Fig. 11.4. Bank Borrowing Amortization Schedule.

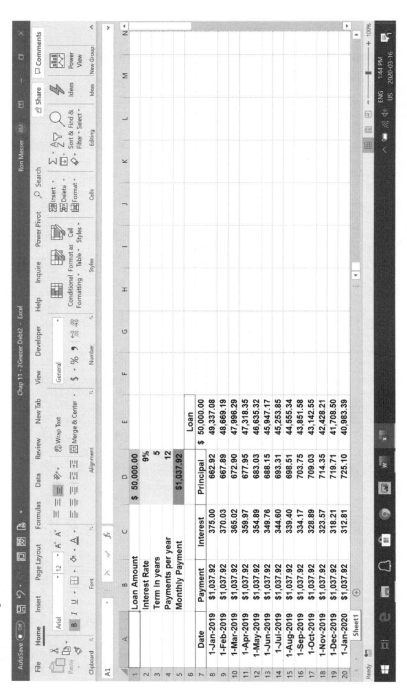

Fig. 11.5. Bank Borrowing Amortization Schedule (Formulas).

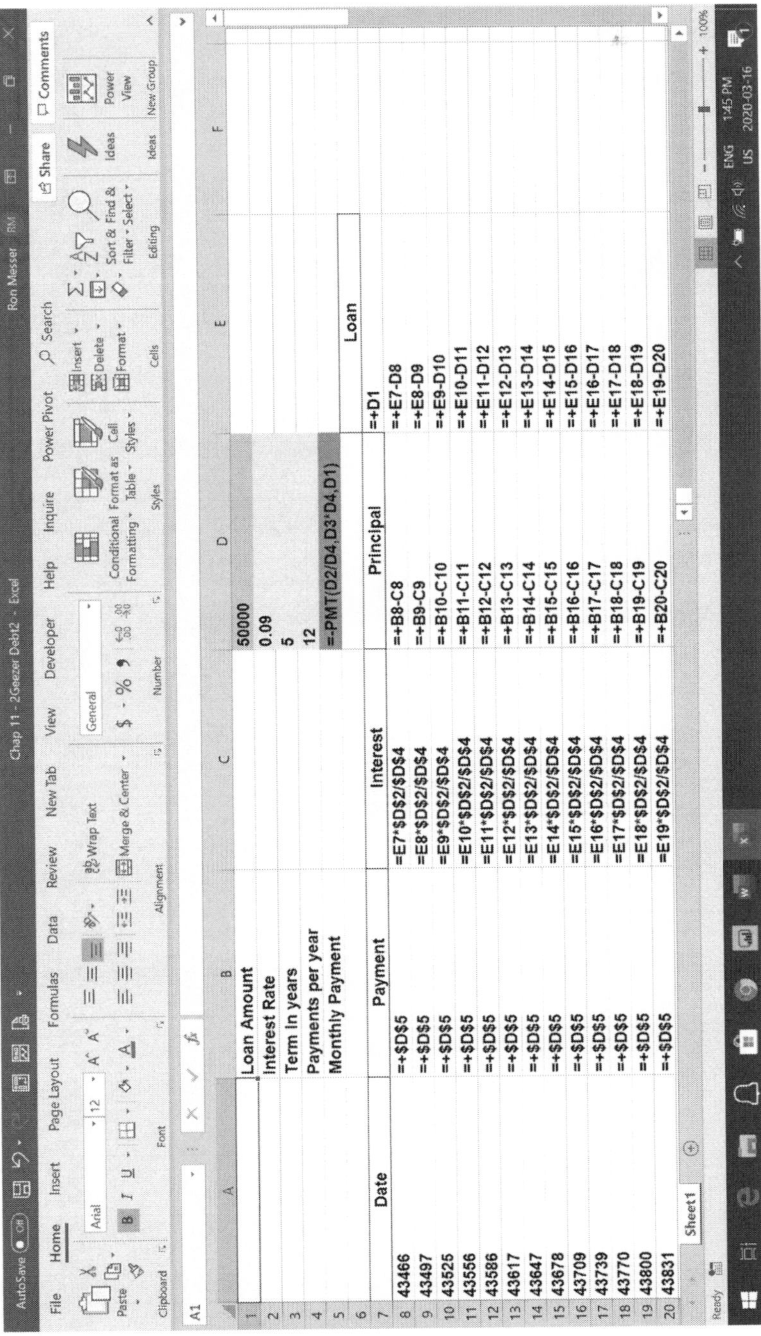

	A	B	C	D	E	F
1		Loan Amount		50000		
2		Interest Rate		0.09		
3		Term In years		5		
4		Payments per year		12		
5		Monthly Payment		=-PMT(D2/D4,D3*D4,D1)		
6					Loan	
7	Date	Payment	Interest	Principal	=+D1	
8	43466	=+$D$5	=E7*$D$2/$D$4	=+B8-C8	=+E7-D8	
9	43497	=+$D$5	=E8*$D$2/$D$4	=+B9-C9	=+E8-D9	
10	43525	=+$D$5	=E9*$D$2/$D$4	=+B10-C10	=+E9-D10	
11	43556	=+$D$5	=E10*$D$2/$D$4	=+B11-C11	=+E10-D11	
12	43586	=+$D$5	=E11*$D$2/$D$4	=+B12-C12	=+E11-D12	
13	43617	=+$D$5	=E12*$D$2/$D$4	=+B13-C13	=+E12-D13	
14	43647	=+$D$5	=E13*$D$2/$D$4	=+B14-C14	=+E13-D14	
15	43678	=+$D$5	=E14*$D$2/$D$4	=+B15-C15	=+E14-D15	
16	43709	=+$D$5	=E15*$D$2/$D$4	=+B16-C16	=+E15-D16	
17	43739	=+$D$5	=E16*$D$2/$D$4	=+B17-C17	=+E16-D17	
18	43770	=+$D$5	=E17*$D$2/$D$4	=+B18-C18	=+E17-D18	
19	43800	=+$D$5	=E18*$D$2/$D$4	=+B19-C19	=+E18-D19	
20	43831	=+$D$5	=E19*$D$2/$D$4	=+B20-C20	=+E19-D20	

Fig. 11.6. Property, Plant, and Equipment Amortization.

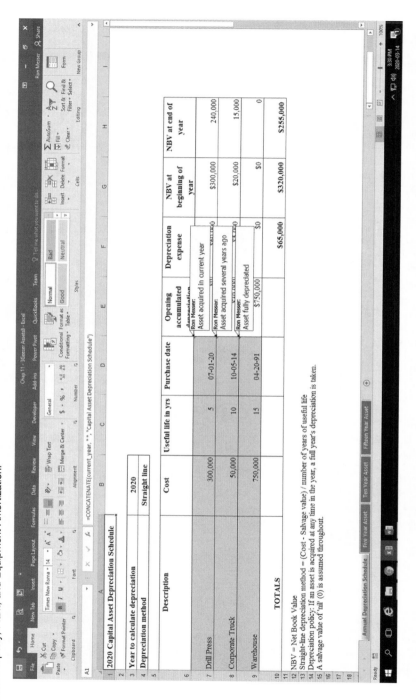

The following formulas (with nested IF statements) are used to calculate the field values shown under the table headings in **Fig. 11.6**, as follows:

Formula for opening accumulated depreciation (cell E7):

$$= \textbf{IF}(\textbf{current\_year} - \textbf{YEAR}(\textbf{D7}) = \textbf{0}, \textbf{0}, \textbf{IF}(\textbf{YEAR}(\textbf{D7}) < \textbf{current\_year}, \textbf{IF}(\textbf{current\_}$$
$$\textbf{year} - \textbf{YEAR}(\textbf{D7}) > \textbf{C7}, \textbf{B7}, \textbf{B7}/\textbf{C7} * (\textbf{current\_year} - \textbf{YEAR}(\textbf{D7})))))$$

This formula tests the year of the asset's acquisition in relation to the current year, as well as whether the asset is fully depreciated. It then deducts the accumulated depreciation to date from the asset's acquisition cost. More specifically:

$$= \textbf{IF}(\textbf{current\_year} - \textbf{YEAR}(\textbf{D7}) = \textbf{0}, \textbf{0}$$

This part of the formula tests whether this is a newly acquired asset and if so, assigns an opening value of zero (0).

$$\textbf{IF}(\textbf{YEAR}(\textbf{D7}) < \textbf{current\_year}, \textbf{IF}(\textbf{current\_year} - \textbf{YEAR}(\textbf{D7}) > \textbf{C7}, \textbf{B7}$$

This part of the formula tests whether this is an asset that was previously depreciated and if so, whether it is fully depreciated; if it is fully depreciated, the capital cost is the value assigned for the opening accumulated depreciation.

$$\textbf{B7}/\textbf{C7} * (\textbf{current\_year} - \textbf{YEAR}(\textbf{D7})))))$$

Finally, the FALSE condition in the nested IF statement indicates that if (1) this is not a newly acquired asset and (2) it has not been fully depreciated, the accumulated depreciation is calculated by dividing the cost of the asset by its useful life in years and multiplying the result by the years elapsed since the date of acquisition.

Formula for depreciation expense (cell F7):

$$= \textbf{IF}(\textbf{E7} = \textbf{B7}, \textbf{0}, \textbf{B7}/\textbf{C7})$$

This formula calculates the straight line depreciation (assuming zero salvage value) up to the maximum amount of the asset's cost.

Formula for NBV at beginning of year (cell G7):

This is the difference between the cost of the asset and the opening accumulated depreciation.

Formula for NBV at end of year (cell H7):

This is the difference between the NBV at the beginning of the year and the depreciation expense for the year.

The drill press asset, which is amortized on a straight line basis over 5 years, is shown below. The detailed calculations are illustrated in the worksheet labeled "Five year Asset" in **Fig. 11.7**.

The formulas for the detailed amortization calculations are shown in **Fig. 11.8**.

Afterthought → *nothing ventured, nothing gained*

Fig. 11.7. Property, Plant, and Equipment Amortization – Drill Press.

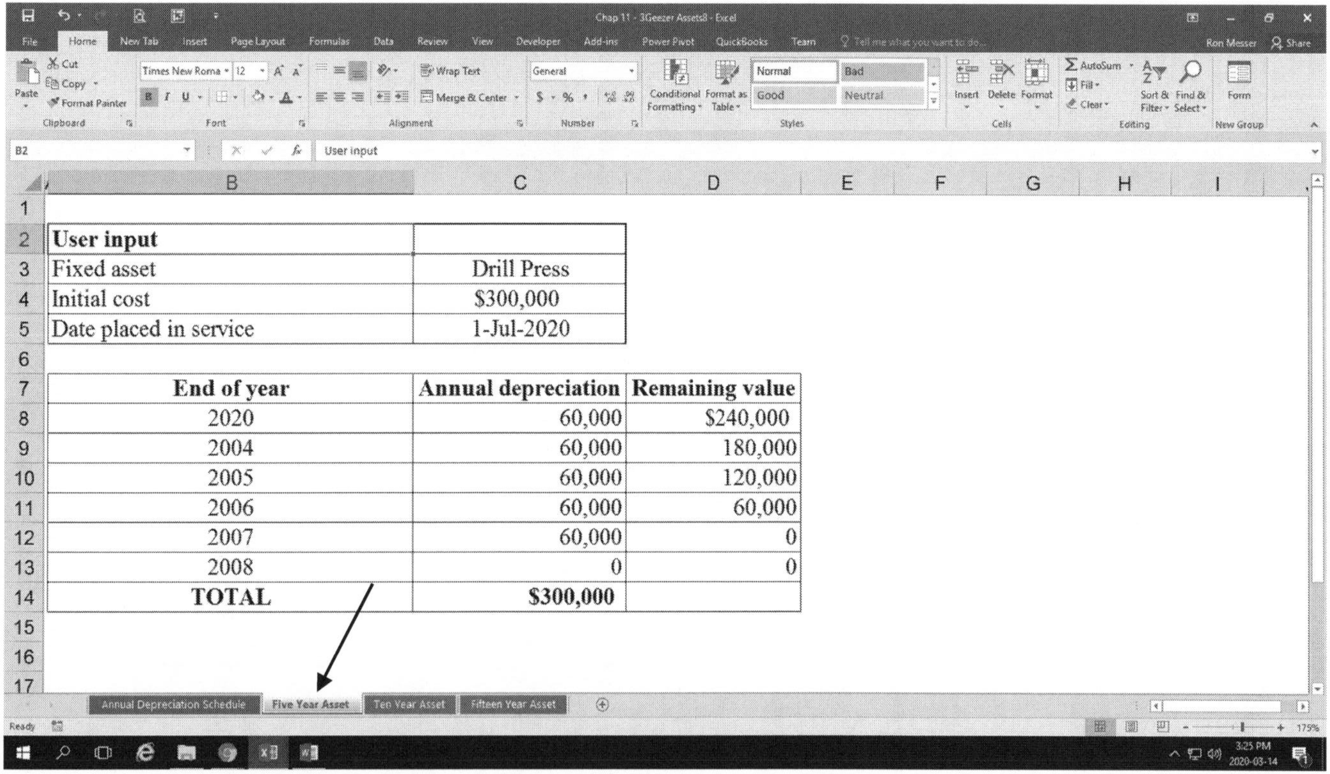

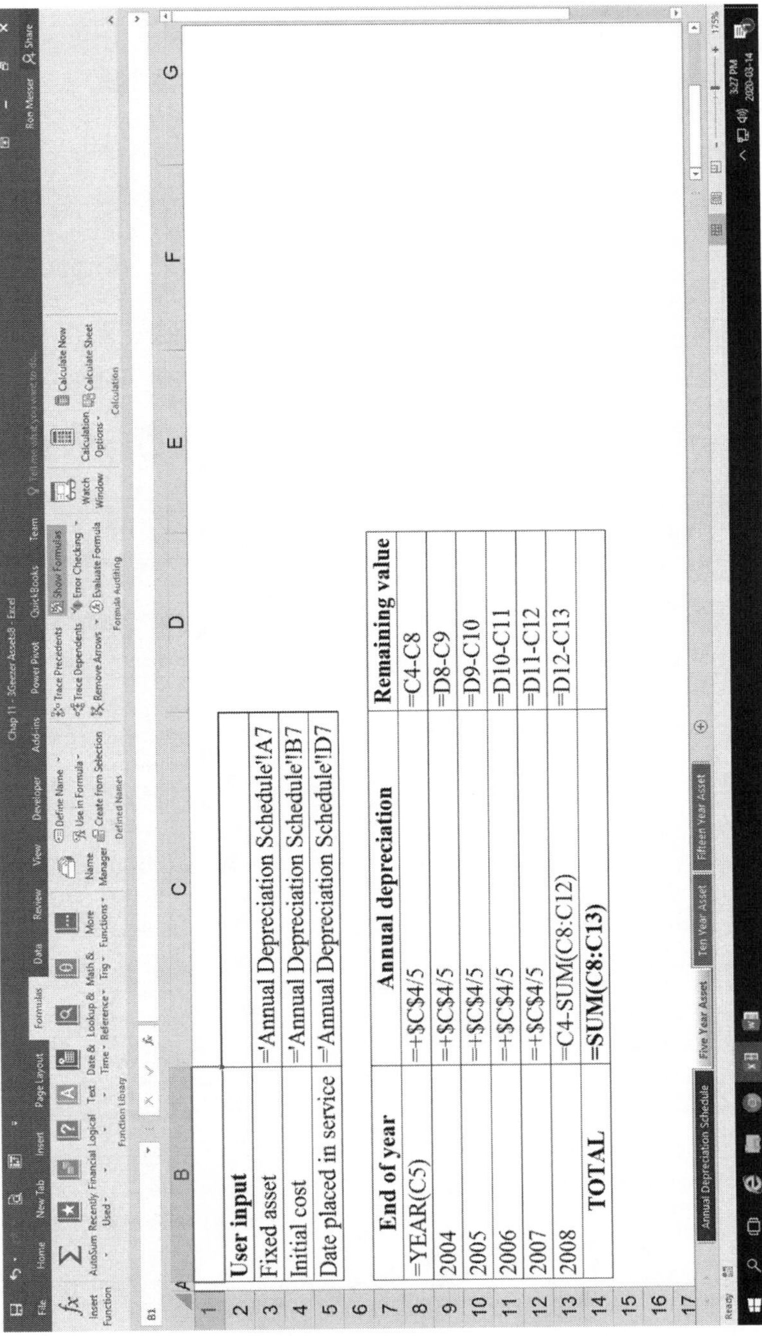

Fig. 11.8. Property, Plant, and Equipment Amortization – Drill Press (Formulas).

	B	C	D
1			
2	**User input**		
3	Fixed asset	='Annual Depreciation Schedule'!A7	
4	Initial cost	='Annual Depreciation Schedule'!B7	
5	Date placed in service	='Annual Depreciation Schedule'!D7	
6			
7	**End of year**	**Annual depreciation**	**Remaining value**
8	=YEAR(C5)	=+$C$4/5	=C4-C8
9	2004	=+$C$4/5	=D8-C9
10	2005	=+$C$4/5	=D9-C10
11	2006	=+$C$4/5	=D10-C11
12	2007	=+$C$4/5	=D11-C12
13	2008	=C4-SUM(C8:C12)	=D12-C13
14	**TOTAL**	=SUM(C8:C13)	
15			
16			
17			

The long-term decisions that a business makes are extremely important in determining its future wealth. These include how much debt it will incur (which measures its degree of *financial* leverage, based on usage of corporate bonds or bank borrowing) and how much capital it plans to acquire (which is its degree of *operating* leverage, created through purchases of property, plant, and equipment). Does it take a genius to make these decisions? Maybe or, maybe not. Think about this ...

Mine's Bigger than Yours

(Taking chances...)

At a wealth management conference in the United States that was attended by academics and successful business owners, a well-known scholar from an Ivy League school was challenged during his presentation by a wealthy entrepreneur. The well-to-do businessman wanted to know why, if the speaker claimed to be so smart, he wasn't also rich. To this, the scholar retorted: "If you're so rich, why aren't you smart?" (Oh ... snap!)

While his rebuke must have stung – and certainly caused some amusement among the conference attendees – the question still remains: Why are the world's smartest people not also its wealthiest? If it is true that we live in a knowledge economy, then those with the highest IQs should, presumably, also be the most affluent. Arguably this is true in some cases (think of Bill Gates), but it is not universally valid (consider, for example, the many poorly paid professors toiling to publish original research for little economic gain; on the flip-side, consider the cases of certain wealthy, but not-too-bright, heirs and heiresses in the public eye). All of which begs the question: What came first, an oversized intelligence or a fat bank account?

In a fascinating study on communities of business owners, researchers at the Wharton Business School in Philadelphia analyzed how wealth accumulated among families in a number of countries. They discovered that business success was directly related (not surprisingly) to the number of attempts made at starting new ventures. The salient points in the authors' investigation were that (1) there was always someone willing to accept the risk involved in starting a new business and (2) inevitably, one of these new ventures succeeded, with some becoming extremely prosperous. However, success or failure in these endeavors was not predicated on the amount of education possessed by the company's founder. In fact, it was found that intelligence was neither causative, nor predictive, of great wealth.

Simply put, what this study demonstrated is that you don't have to be smart to be rich – all you need is some luck. And luck is nothing other than a statement about probabilities – in other words, if you keep trying long enough, you (or at least someone) will sooner or later succeed. As long as enough folks are trying to be rich, some of them will eventually (and inevitably) make it. Also, because there are only a limited number of smart people in the world, the chances that they will become wealthy are (statistically) less likely than for the average (but more numerous) risk-taking Joe and Jane.

Therefore, in response to the academic's (perhaps rhetorical) question about why someone who is wealthy isn't also smart, the explanation is that the odds of being rich are probably in favor of the less intelligent, simply because there are more of them. But, the scholar can take comfort in the knowledge that, while his savings account may be smaller, his IQ is undoubtedly bigger. Now, what are the chances of that?

Part 4
Decisions Made in Time

PUTTING IT ALL TOGETHER

Chapter 12: Making a Lot of Decisions

Help ... What should I do?

Chapter 12

Making a Lot of Decisions

Help ... What should I do?

Background Theory

It is both useful and convenient to think about business decisions based on four key variables: cost, expense, price, and value.

(1) *Cost* represents the resources consumed to produce a good or service. It is important in:

- break-even analysis when defining fixed and variable costs.
- linear programing for product mix/scheduling, based on unit costs.
- regression analysis when allocating indirect costs.

(2) *Expense* is the non–production-related costs incurred to run a business. It is important in:

- business valuation models for determining cash outflows.
- budget management when analyzing variances related to business expenses.
- amortizing corporate debt and assets as interest and depreciation expense.

(3) *Price* is what someone is willing to pay for what you are selling. It is important in:

- capital budgeting for determining cash inflows.
- business valuation models for determining cash inflows.

(4) *Value* represents how someone perceives what you are selling. It is important in:

- time series forecasting for product sales demand.
- developing dashboards to monitor KPIs in strategic planning.

Note that these concepts are interrelated; for example, costs represent assets, while expenses relate to assets consumed during a period. Cost forms the basis for pricing decisions and value is foundational to effective pricing (i.e., the price of something cannot exceed its value). Financial models used to make business decisions will include some, or all, of these variables.

(Capstone) Demonstration Exercise

As a final exercise, the following case facts both combine and integrate the financial modeling decisions that were covered in previous chapters. This is done through a comprehensive business situation, which takes an enterprise from its initial inception to mature operations. The exercise involves making decisions about production (costs), spending (expenses), revenues (prices), and sales (value). (Excel file: Omega Corp (shell).xls.)

Case Facts

Omega Corporation is Bob's latest venture (remember our budding entrepreneur from Chapter 1). He has started several businesses since his high school days – with lack-luster results – and thinks that his latest idea has some potential for success. Realizing that his past mistakes resulted from poor choices, Bob wants to develop models for all the decisions he has to make now and, as his company evolves, in the future. In this regard, he will need to address the following concerns.

Planning Decisions:

    (1) Is the new business viable – break-even decision
    (2) How much demand will there be for the product – times series forecasting decision
    (3) Should major investments be made – capital budgeting decision
    (4) How should product costs be allocated – regression analysis decision
          Control Decisions:
    (5) Which products should be produced – product mix decision
    (6) How should the company's shares be priced – corporate valuation decision
    (7) How to interpret customer buying behavior – data analytics decision
          Feedback Decisions:
    (8) Which KPIs should guide the company – dashboard decisions
    (9) How to measure financial performance – budget management decisions
  (10) How to track utilization of assets and liabilities – amortization decisions

Omega Corp. is a manufacturer of high-tech, desktop pencil holders (Bob, just can't let go of his original idea). But these are not ordinary executive ornaments. In addition to holding writing instruments, they also have a monitor and keyboard that can be used to access the Internet, a voice over IP device to allow phone calls, and a camera for taking pictures. There are three models available, called Omega 1, 2, and 3. To decide whether the business is viable, Bob has assembled the following data (**Table 12.1**).

The selling prices are intended to achieve a 10% profit margin per unit, based on a recovery of all manufacturing-related costs (i.e., using absorption costing). Similar products are offered by Bob's nemesis, Rob, who is the head of Zulu Inc., which has been in business for a number of years and also manufactures three varieties of high-tech pencil holders.[1] However, Zulu's prices differ from those of Omega. Bob is curious about this pricing discrepancy, as both companies utilize identical production methods and technologies.

Sales volumes were determined based on a time series forecast using exponential smoothing, with the dampening factor optimized to minimize the MAPE (see **Fig. 12.2**). Prior sales volumes were obtained from data gleaned from Zulu's annual reports. The sales percentages, by product type, are also based on Zulu's sales volumes for each of its three products.

---

[1]Rob was a one-time friend of Bob, who stole his idea of producing pencil holders (remember Alpha Co. from the first chapter) when he founded his own, similarly named, Junior Achievement company (which he called, Alfa Co.) many years ago. Bob claims that this is the reason his original firm did not fare as well as it should have and now it is time for Bob to take his revenge.

Table 12.1. Omega Corp. Financial Data.

Item	Omega 1	Omega 2	Omega 3
Selling price (per unit)	$1,056	$1,117	$1,178
Sales volume (total units)	4,500	3,000	2,500
Sales mix (of total units sold)	45%	30%	25%
Unit variable costs:			
Material	300	330	360
Labor	250	275	300
Overhead	300	300	300
Total unit costs	850	905	960
Fixed costs	$1,000,000		

Fixed costs relate to the annual amortization of capital assets acquired to produce the Omega products. This represents an investment in property, plant, and equipment for a fully automated production line and assumes a 10-year useful life with no residual value. The total planned investment in capital assets is $10,000,000. The Omega facility uses robots to perform assembly, while humans conduct quality control through product testing. Because of the robust economy, it has been difficult to recruit workers.

Planning Decisions
Decision 1: Considering business risk in relation to product price and cost

Fig. 12.1 shows the break-even volume in units and sales dollars for the three products.[2]

The formulas used in the break-even model, are shown in **Fig. 12.2**.

In order to cover his annual fixed costs, Bob must sell 4,744 units, in total. Each of the break-even sales volumes for the individual products is well below the forecast sales, and therefore, Omega is confident that it can cover the downside risk associated with this business venture. In other words, the business is viable.

Decision 2: Considering how customers perceive product value

The estimated demand for the products is 9,863 total units, per **Fig. 12.3** – which has been rounded to the nearest 1,000 – or 10,000 units, as shown in cell E4 in **Fig. 12.1**. The forecast sales for both the individual products and the entire line of Omegas show a significant margin of safety (which is the difference between the break-even and expected sales).

The formulas used in the forecasting model, are shown in **Fig. 12.4**. (Refer Chapter 3 for details on how to use exponential smoothing for forecasting, including a discussion on incorporating Solver to optimize the dampening factor so that the MAPE is minimized.)

---

[2]In this multiproduct situation, the break-even sales volume uses an average unit contribution margin based on the product mix percentages – i.e., BE = FC ÷ (45% of 206 + 30% of 212 + 25% of 218).

Fig. 12.1. Omega Break-even Decision Model.

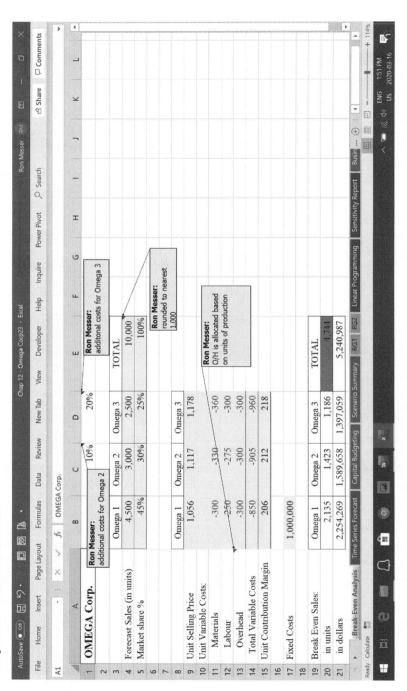

Fig. 12.2. Omega Break-even Decision Model (Formulas).

	A	B	C	D	E
1	OMEGA Corp.		0.1	0.2	
2					
3		Omega 1	Omega 2	Omega 3	TOTAL
4	Forecast Sales (in units)	=B5*$E$4	=C5*$E$4	=D5*$E$4	10000
5	Market share %	0.45	0.3	0.25	=E4/$E$4
6					
7					
8		Omega 1	Omega 2	Omega 3	
9	Unit Selling Price	1055	1116	1177	
10	Unit Variable Costs:				
11	Materials	-300	=B11*(1+$C$1)	=B11*(1+$D$1)	
12	Labour	-250	=B12*(1+$C$1)	=B12*(1+$D$1)	
13	Overhead	-300	-300	-300	
14	Total Variable Costs	=SUM(B11:B13)	=SUM(C11:C13)	=SUM(D11:D13)	
15	Unit Contribution Margin	=B9+B14	=C9+C14	=D9+D14	
16					
17	Fixed Costs	1000000			
18					
19	Break Even Sales:	Omega 1	Omega 2	Omega 3	TOTAL
20	in units	=$E$20*B5	=$E$20*C5	=$E$20*D5	=B17/(B5*B15+C5*C15-D5*D15)
21	in dollars	=B20*B9	=C20*C9	=D20*D9	=SUM(B21:D21)

Tabs: Break Even Analysis | Time Series Forecast | Capital Budgeting | Linear Programming | Sensitivity Report | Business Valuation

Fig. 12.3. Omega Time Series Forecasting Decision Model.

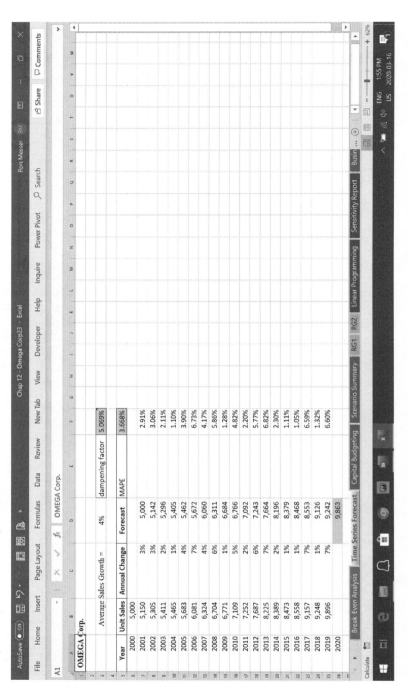

Year	Unit Sales	Annual Change	Forecast		
		Average Sales Growth =	4%	dampening factor	5.069%
			Forecast	MAPE	3.668%
2000	5,000				
2001	5,150	3%	5,000		2.91%
2002	5,305	3%	5,142		3.06%
2003	5,411	2%	5,296		2.11%
2004	5,465	1%	5,405		1.10%
2005	5,683	4%	5,462		3.90%
2006	6,081	7%	5,672		6.73%
2007	6,324	4%	6,060		4.17%
2008	6,704	6%	6,311		5.86%
2009	6,771	1%	6,684		1.28%
2010	7,109	5%	6,766		4.82%
2011	7,252	2%	7,092		2.20%
2012	7,687	6%	7,243		5.77%
2013	8,225	7%	7,664		6.82%
2014	8,389	2%	8,196		2.30%
2015	8,473	1%	8,379		1.11%
2016	8,558	1%	8,468		1.05%
2017	9,157	7%	8,553		6.59%
2018	9,248	1%	9,126		1.32%
2019	9,896	7%	9,242		6.60%
2020			9,863		

Decision 3: Considering cost (cash outflows) and price (cash inflows) when investing

Having decided that the business opportunity is viable, Bob now needs to assess the return on investment for capital expenditures. To do this, he must determine the NPV, IRR, and payback period for the projected future cash flows of Omega. Using the expected sales mix, unit prices, and variable costs (which represent reasonable approximations of cash flows, as they are not accrual based), along with an average sales growth of 4% (taken from the forecast data, shown in cell D3 of **Fig. 12.3**), a capital budgeting model is prepared, along with base-case, best-case, and worst-case scenarios (**Fig. 12.5**). Bob's cost of capital is 10%.[3]

The formulas used in the capital budgeting model, as shown in **Fig. 12.6**.

With a positive NPV, the investment is justified for the base case. In the best-case situation, Omega will have an even larger, positive NPV of $7,221,834, and in the worst case the NPV still remains positive, at $3,264,895 (see **Fig. 12.7**).

The scenario summary appears in **Fig. 12.8**.

Decision 4: Considering costs and how they affect product prices

Bob notes that indirect costs comprise about 40% of the total manufacturing costs, which is significant.[4] For this reason, predictive models, using regression techniques will be helpful in determining the appropriate cost driver(s) to use for allocating these amounts.[5] Omega is currently using units of production for this purpose; however, a correlation table showing the relationships between overhead spending and several cost drivers – including machine hours, labor hours, and production runs – shows a very strong relationship between indirect costs and machine hours, which has an $r =$ 0.9945, as shown in cell H13 below (**Fig. 12.9**). (Refer Chapter 5 for details on using the Analysis Tool-pack to produce correlation tables.)

The regression report using machine hours as the explanatory variable appears in **Fig. 12.10**.

Bob observes that the r^2 (i.e., the coefficient of determination) is almost 99% (cell B5), which means that machine hours explain virtually all of the variation in overhead costs. Also, the p-value (cell E18) indicates that there is virtually no risk of incorrectly using machine hours to allocate overhead costs. **Table 12.2** compares the current method for charging indirect costs to the three products with the revised allocation rate, based on machine hours.

With this information, Bob is now able to review his product prices and revise them accordingly. **Table 12.3** shows the original selling prices for Omega 1, 2, and 3 and the revised prices when machine hours are used as the cost driver to allocate overhead.

---

[3]The cost of capital is based on the company's borrowing costs of 5% and an assumed long-term equity premium of 5% (which approximates the opportunity cost associated with this investment).
[4]The variable indirect costs are $300 and the fixed overhead costs are $100 (per unit). The average total manufacturing costs are $1,005; this means that overhead is about 40% of production costs.
[5]Determining strong cause and effect relationships between costs and cost drivers is the process prescribed by activity-based costing (ABC), first articulated by Robert Kaplan and Robin Cooper in 1988.

Fig. 12.4. Omega Time Series Forecasting Decision Model (Formulas).

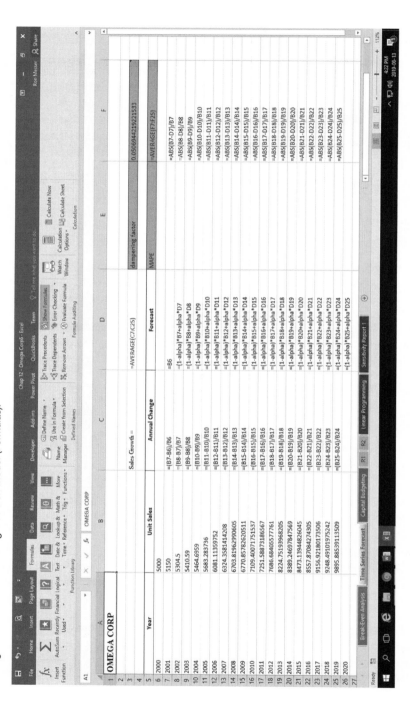

Fig. 12.5. Omega Capital Budgeting Decision Model.

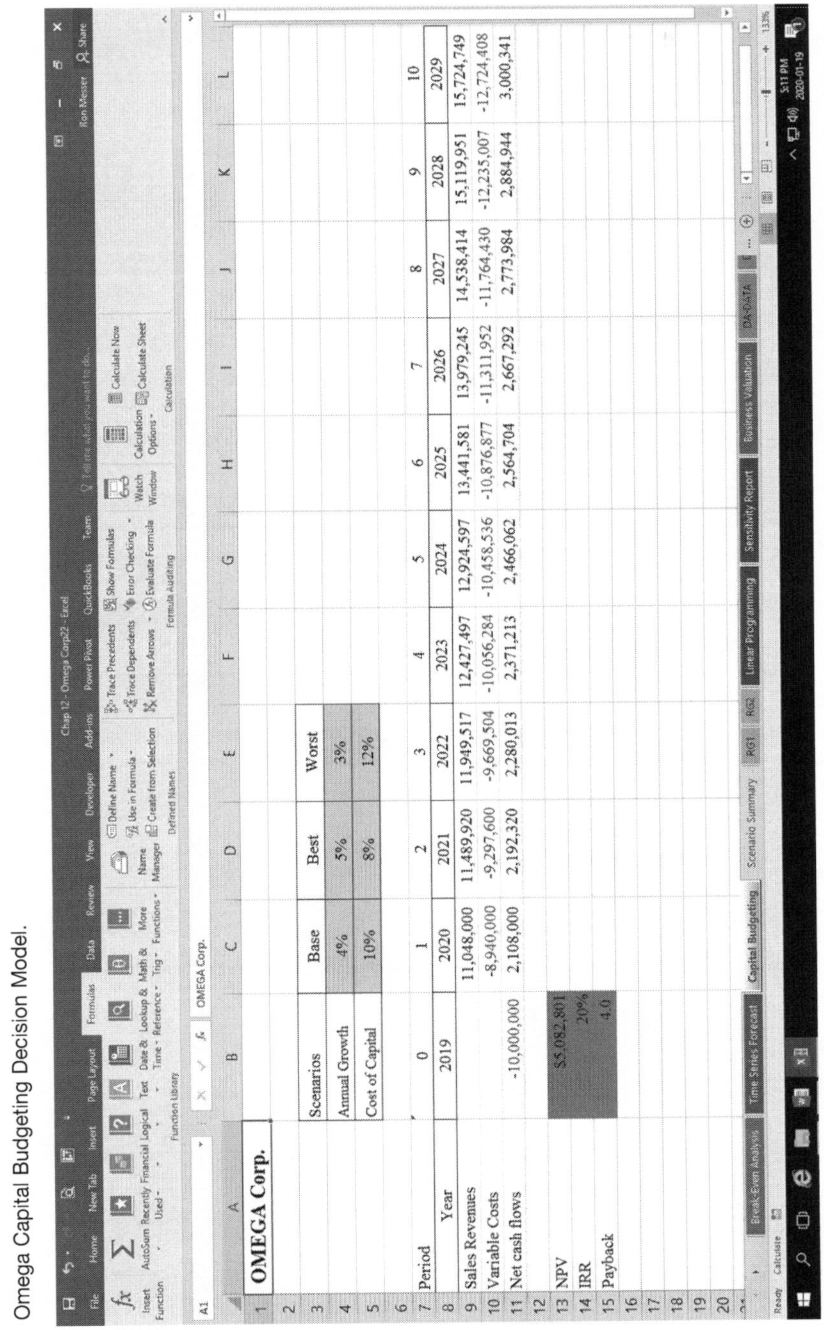

OMEGA Corp.

		Base	Best	Worst
Scenarios				
Annual Growth		4%	5%	3%
Cost of Capital		10%	8%	12%

Period	0	1	2	3	4	5	6	7	8	9	10
Year	2019	2020	2021	2022	2023	2024	2025	2026	2027	2028	2029
Sales Revenues		11,048,000	11,489,920	11,949,517	12,427,497	12,924,597	13,441,581	13,979,245	14,538,414	15,119,951	15,724,749
Variable Costs		-8,940,000	-9,297,600	-9,669,504	-10,056,284	-10,458,536	-10,876,877	-11,311,952	-11,764,430	-12,235,007	-12,724,408
Net cash flows	-10,000,000	2,108,000	2,192,320	2,280,013	2,371,213	2,466,062	2,564,704	2,667,292	2,773,984	2,884,944	3,000,341

NPV	$5,082,801
IRR	20%
Payback	4.0

Fig. 12.6. Omega Capital Budgeting Decision Model (Formulas).

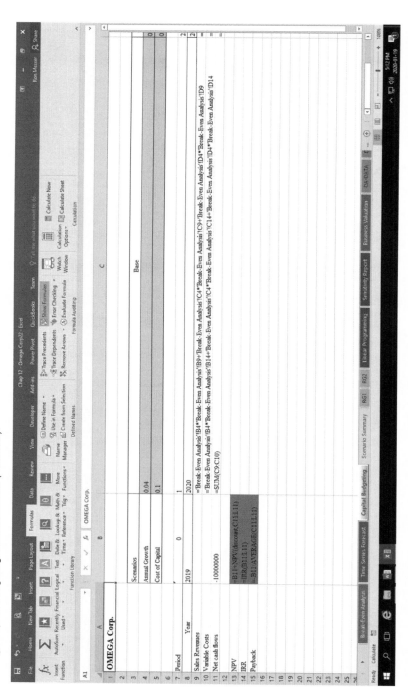

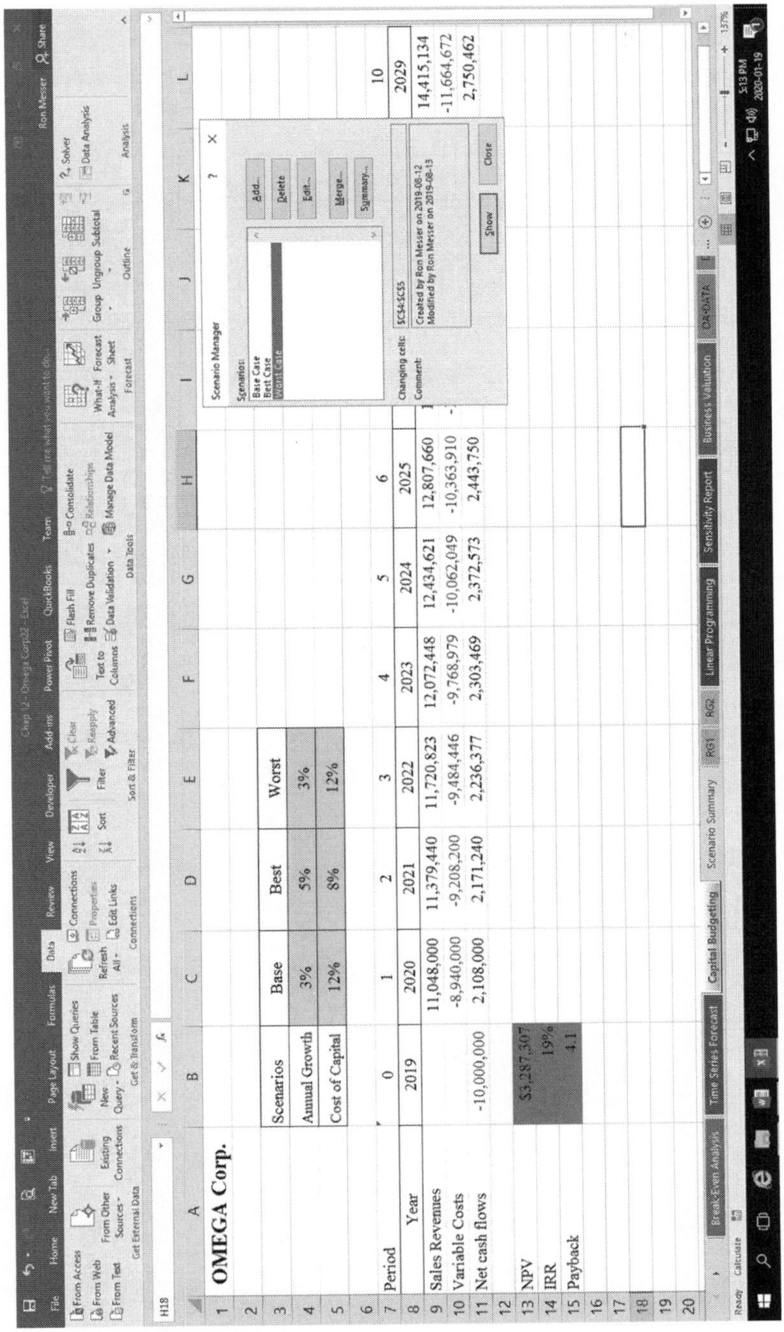

Fig. 12.7. Omega Scenario Analysis.

Fig. 12.8. Omega Scenario Summary.

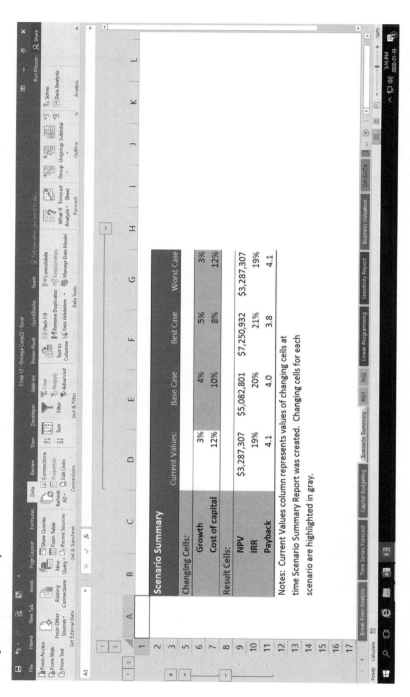

Scenario Summary					
		Current Values:	Base Case	Best Case	Worst Case
Changing Cells:					
	Growth	3%	4%	5%	3%
	Cost of capital	12%	10%	8%	12%
Result Cells:					
	NPV	$3,287,307	$5,082,801	$7,250,932	$3,287,307
	IRR	19%	20%	21%	19%
	Payback	4.1	4.0	3.8	4.1

Notes: Current Values column represents values of changing cells at time Scenario Summary Report was created. Changing cells for each scenario are highlighted in gray.

Fig. 12.9. Omega Overhead Cost Allocation (Correlation Table).

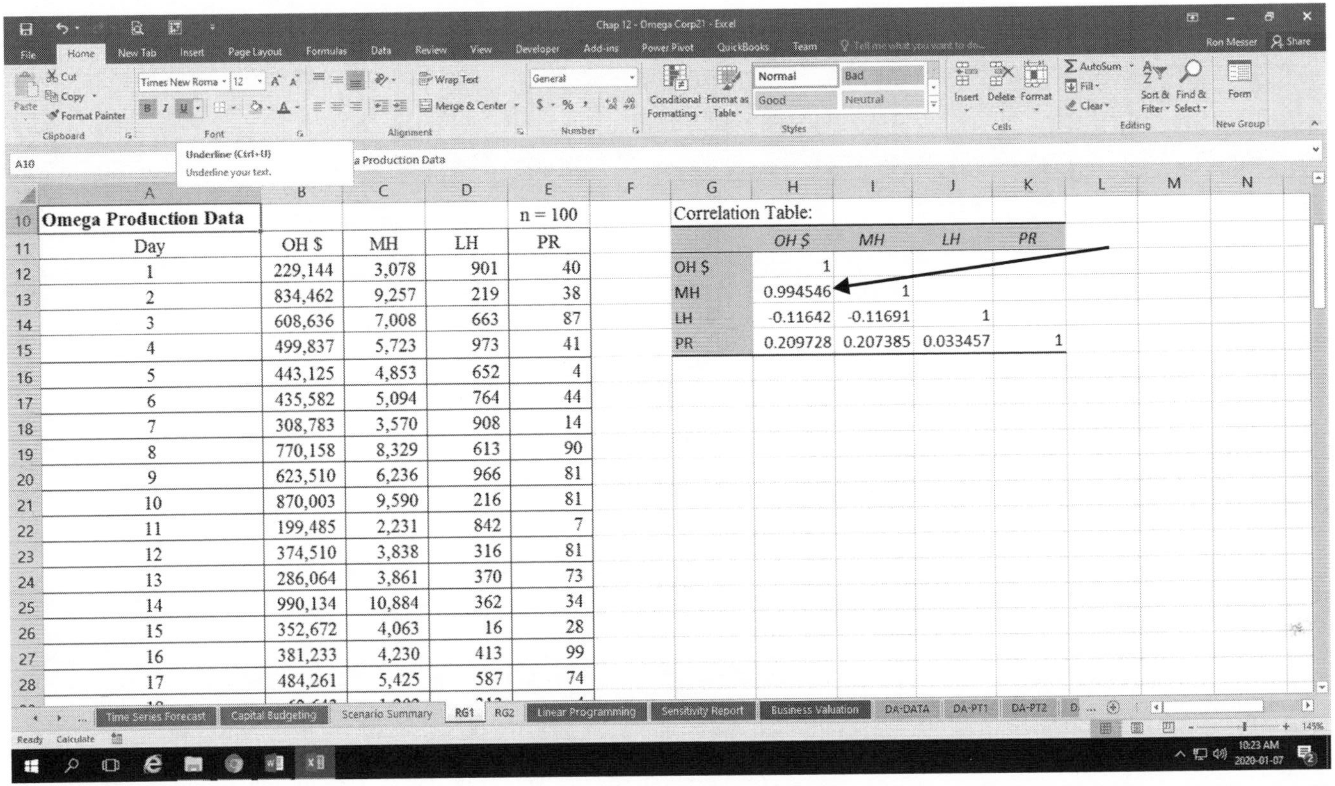

Fig. 12.10. Omega Overhead Cost Allocation (Regression Analysis).

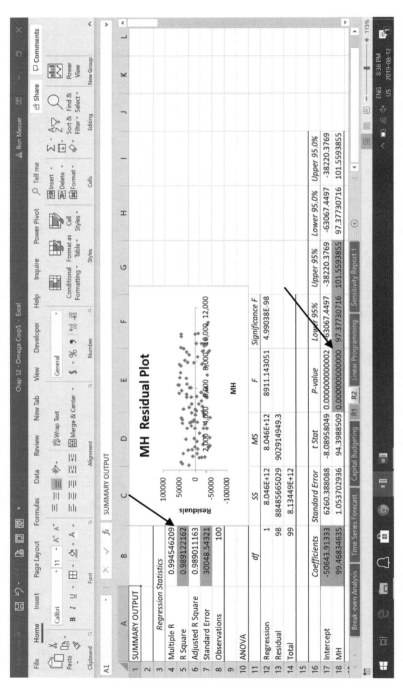

Table 12.2. Allocating Overhead.

Unit Cost	Traditional Allocation ($ per Production Unit)	ABC Allocation ($ per Machine Hour)
Variable	$300	$21
Fixed	$100	$7
Total	$400	$29

Perhaps not surprisingly, the revised product prices are very similar to those of his competitor, Zulu Inc. With the new pricing structure, Omega finds that it is able to sell more of its products and seriously erode his nemesis's market share.

Control Decisions
Decision 5: Considering constraints and their effect on product prices and costs

But now, Bob must address the decision about product mix. In this regard, his company is dealing with two production constraints:

- Constraint on labor hours: There are only 50 workers available for testing the products and assuming a 2,000-hour work-year (i.e., 50 workers × (52 weeks per year − 2 weeks' vacation) × 40 hours per week = 2,000 hours per worker per year); this means that there are only 100,000 labor hours available.
- Constraint on product demand: The maximum demand for the products is 10,000 units in total, consisting of 4,500 Omega 1, 3,000 Omega 2, and 2,500 Omega 3.

To make the decision about how much of each product to produce when constraints exist, a linear programming model, using Solver, was developed. This is shown in **Fig. 12.11**.

The formulas used in the linear programming model are shown in **Fig. 12.12**.

Note that the objective is to maximize profitability (cell J27), subject to labor constraints (cell H29), and demand limitations (cells G24 to I24), by determining the appropriate production mix (which is shown as the decision variables in cells G22 to I22). The completed Solver dialogue box appears in **Fig. 12.13**.

The optimal mix that maximizes profitability will be to produce all of the units demanded for Omega 1 and 2, but only 500 units of Omega 3. **Fig. 12.14** shows the sensitivity report for this product mix decision.

Table 12.3. Revised Product Selling Prices.

Prices	Omega 1	Omega 2	Omega 3
Original price	1,056	1,117	1,178
Revised price	929	1,148	1,368
Price change ($)	(127)	31	190
Price change (%)	(12%)	3%	16%

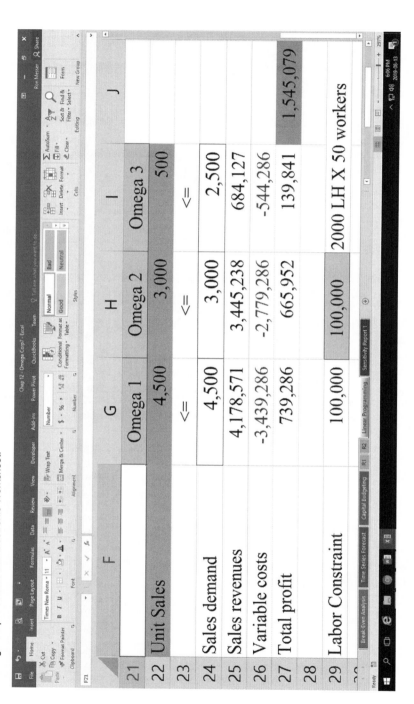

Fig. 12.11. Omega Corp. Product Mix Electronic Worksheet.

	G	H	I	J
	Omega 1	Omega 2	Omega 3	
22 Unit Sales	4,500	3,000	500	
23	<=	<=	<=	
24 Sales demand	4,500	3,000	2,500	
25 Sales revenues	4,178,571	3,445,238	684,127	
26 Variable costs	-3,439,286	-2,779,286	-544,286	
27 Total profit	739,286	665,952	139,841	1,545,079
28				
29 Labor Constraint	100,000	100,000	2000 LH X 50 workers	

Fig. 12.12. Omega Corp. Product Mix Electronic Worksheet (Formulas).

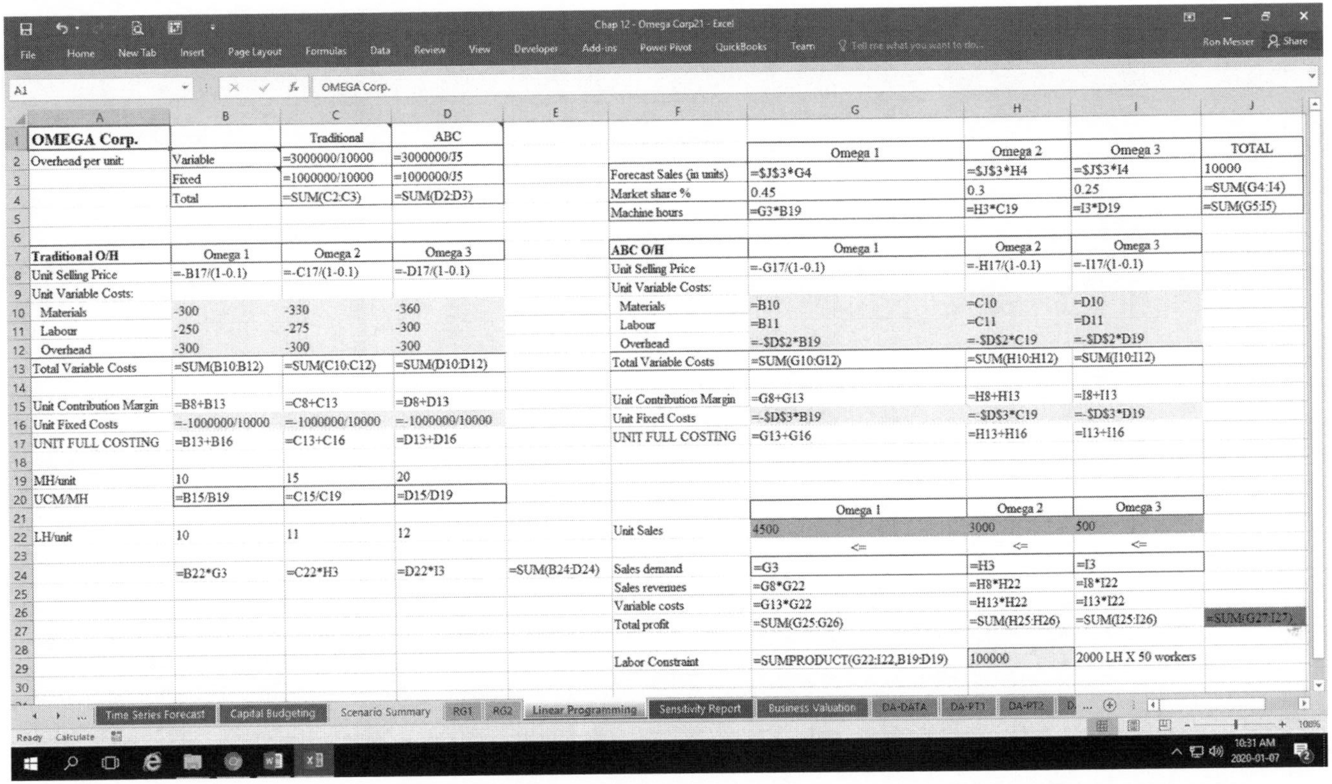

	A	B	C (Traditional)	D (ABC)	E	F	G (Omega 1)	H (Omega 2)	I (Omega 3)	J (TOTAL)
1	OMEGA Corp.									
2	Overhead per unit	Variable	=300000/10000	=300000/.035		Forecast Sales (in units)	=$J$3*G4	=$J$3*H4	=$J$3*I4	10000
3		Fixed	=1000000/10000	=1000000/.035		Market share %	0.45	0.3	0.25	=SUM(G4:I4)
4		Total	=SUM(C2:C3)	=SUM(D2:D3)		Machine hours	=G3*B19	=H3*C19	=I3*D19	=SUM(G5:I5)
5										
6										
7	Traditional O/H	Omega 1	Omega 2	Omega 3		ABC O/H	Omega 1	Omega 2	Omega 3	
8	Unit Selling Price	=B17/(1-0.1)	=C17/(1-0.1)	=D17/(1-0.1)		Unit Selling Price	=G17/(1-0.1)	=H17/(1-0.1)	=I17/(1-0.1)	
9	Unit Variable Costs:					Unit Variable Costs:				
10	Materials	-300	-330	-360		Materials	=B10	=C10	=D10	
11	Labour	-250	-275	-300		Labour	=B11	=C11	=D11	
12	Overhead	-300	-300	-300		Overhead	=$D$2*B19	=$D$2*C19	=$D$2*D19	
13	Total Variable Costs	=SUM(B10:B12)	=SUM(C10:C12)	=SUM(D10:D12)		Total Variable Costs	=SUM(G10:G12)	=SUM(H10:H12)	=SUM(I10:I12)	
14										
15	Unit Contribution Margin	=B8+B13	=C8+C13	=D8+D13		Unit Contribution Margin	=G8+G13	=H8+H13	=I8+I13	
16	Unit Fixed Costs	=-1000000/10000	=-1000000/10000	=-1000000/10000		Unit Fixed Costs	=$D$3*B19	=$D$3*C19	=$D$3*D19	
17	UNIT FULL COSTING	=B13+B16	=C13+C16	=D13+D16		UNIT FULL COSTING	=G13+G16	=H13+H16	=I13+I16	
18										
19	MH/unit	10	15	20						
20	UCM/MH	=B15/B19	=C15/C19	=D15/D19						
21							Omega 1	Omega 2	Omega 3	
22	LH/unit	10	11	12		Unit Sales	4500 <=	3000 <=	500 <=	
23										
24		=B22*G3	=C22*H3	=D22*I3	=SUM(B24:D24)	Sales demand	=G3	=H3	=I3	
25						Sales revenues	=G8*G22	=H8*H22	=I8*I22	
26						Variable costs	=G13*G22	=H13*H22	=I13*I22	
27						Total profit	=SUM(G25:G26)	=SUM(H25:H26)	=SUM(I25:I26)	=SUM(G27:I27)
28						Labor Constraint	=SUMPRODUCT(G22:I22,B19:D19)	100000	2000 LH X 50 workers	
29										

Fig. 12.13. Omega Corp. Product Mix Solver Dialogue Box.

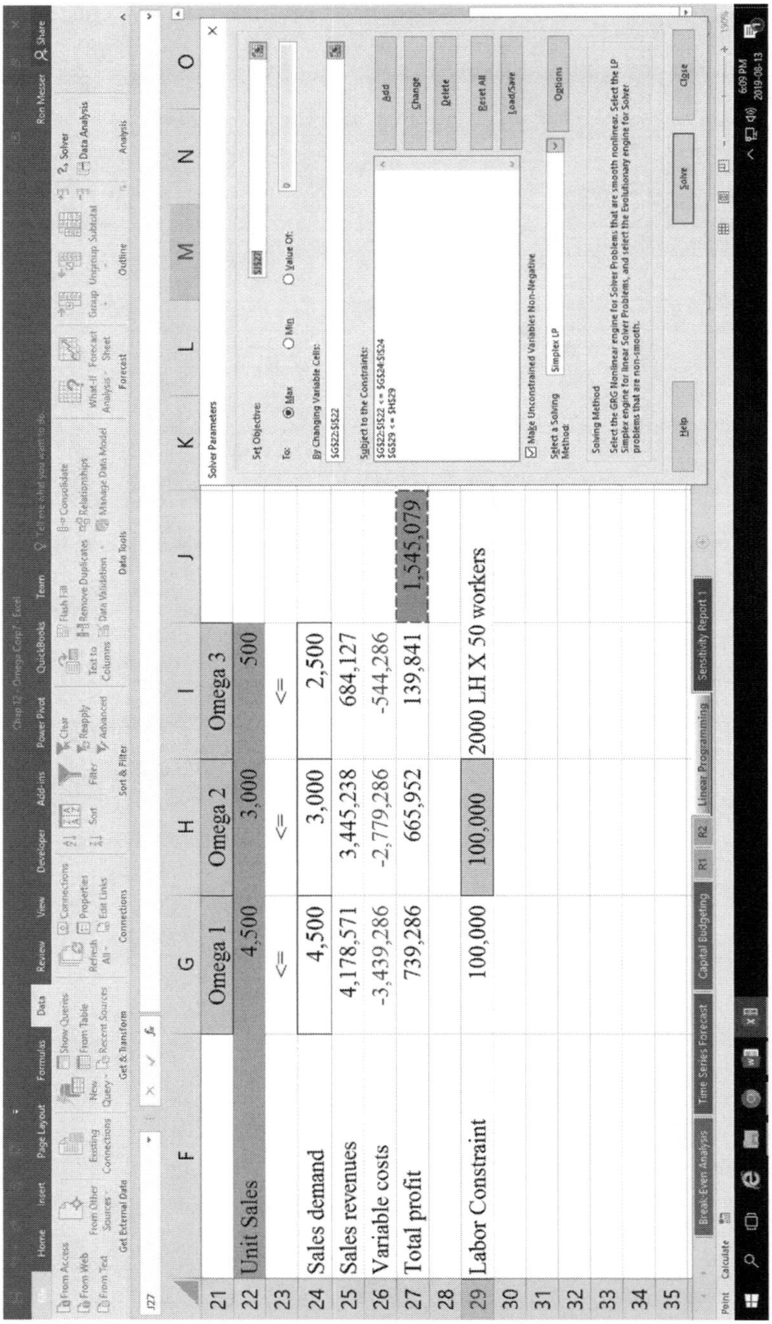

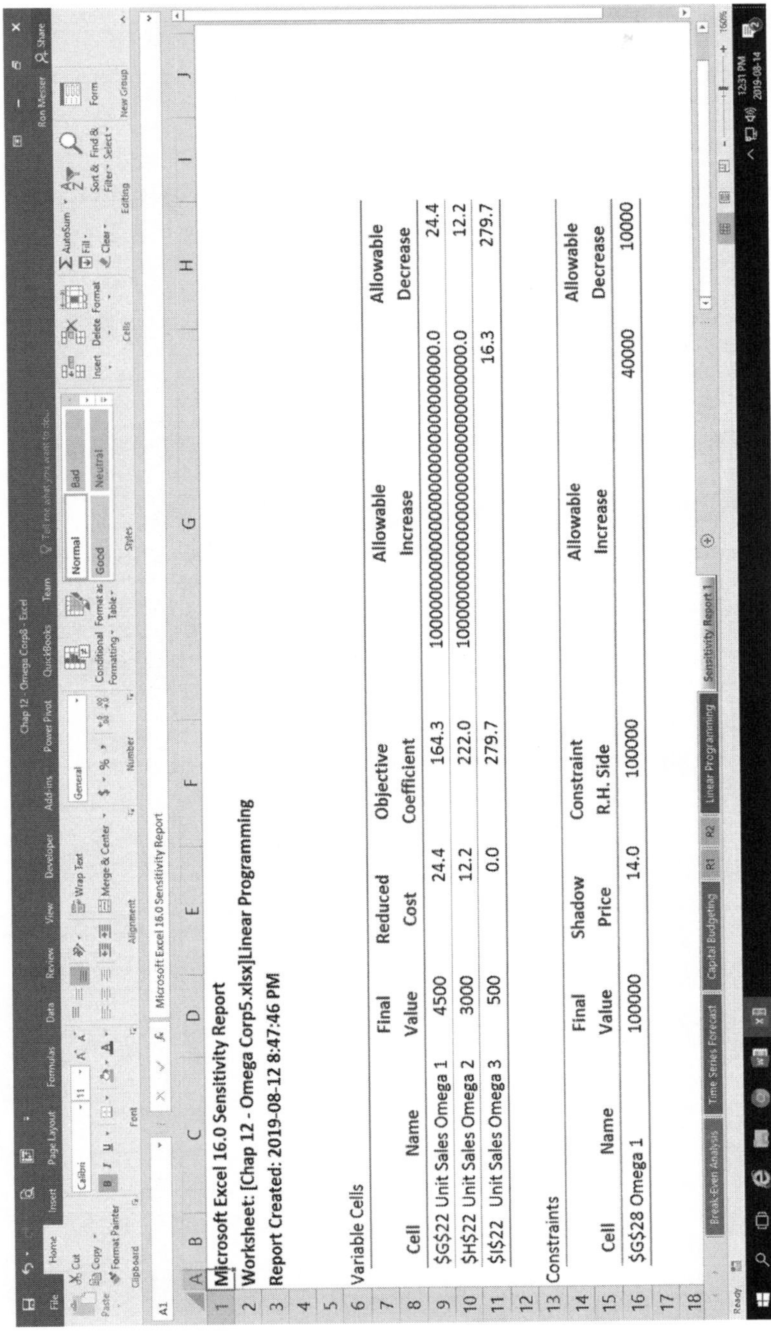

Fig. 12.14. Omega Corp. Product Mix Sensitivity Report.

Microsoft Excel 16.0 Sensitivity Report

Worksheet: [Chap 12 - Omega Corp5.xlsx]Linear Programming

Report Created: 2019-08-12 8:47:46 PM

Variable Cells

Cell	Name	Final Value	Reduced Cost	Objective Coefficient	Allowable Increase	Allowable Decrease
$G$22	Unit Sales Omega 1	4500	24.4	164.3	100000000000000000000000000.0	24.4
$H$22	Unit Sales Omega 2	3000	12.2	222.0	100000000000000000000000000.0	12.2
$I$22	Unit Sales Omega 3	500	0.0	279.7	16.3	279.7

Constraints

Cell	Name	Final Value	Shadow Price	Constraint R.H. Side	Allowable Increase	Allowable Decrease
$G$28	Omega 1	100000	14.0	100000	40000	10000

The shadow price indicates that labor hours are fully utilized (i.e., it is a binding constraint), since the "final value" is equal to the "constraint R.H. side." It also informs Bob that for each additional labor hour acquired, his profits will increase by $14.00 (cell E16). With this information, he may want to consider increasing his wage rate to attract more workers from other companies.

The reduced cost gives us information about the changes necessary to the unit contribution margins that would result in a revised production plan; for example, if the profitability of the Omega 1 were to decrease by $24.40 (cell H9), then fewer than 4,500 units would be produced. Bob can use this information to make decisions about product pricing and cost control.

Decision 6: Considering the value of a business when selling shares

As a result of the changes made to product prices, Omega Corp. sales have boomed. Corporate executives have fallen in love with Bob's version of high-tech, desktop pencil holders. But, as demand has increased, the company has been hard pressed to match supply for the popular devices. Strategically, therefore, it is time to consider expanding capacity to better compete with Zulu Inc. However, Bob does not want to take on any more debt and so he approaches an investment bank about proceeding with an initial public offering (IPO) to raise equity capital.

The following financial statements (**Tables 12.4 and 12.5**) show the results of Omega's first year of operations.

To determine the current value of Omega, the investment banker needs to forecast future earnings. He does this by using the assumptions in **Table 12.6**. (Refer Chapter 7 for a more detailed discussion on how to create models for making business valuation decisions.).

Figs. 12.15–12.18 show the pro-forma Income Statement and Balance Sheet for Omega Corp. for the 5-year period from 2021 to 2025, based on these assumptions.

Table 12.4. Omega Corp. Year 1 Operating Results.

Omega Corp.	Actual
Income Statement:	2020
Sales	11,044,444
Cost of goods sold	−8,940,000
Depreciation	−1,000,000
Interest payments on debt	−200,000
Interest earned on cash	7,383
Profit before tax	2,586,286
Taxes (40%)	−1,034,514
Profit after tax	1,551,772
Dividends	−512,085
Retained earnings	1,039,687

Table 12.5. Omega Corp. Year 1 Operating Results.

Omega Corp.	Actual
Balance Sheet:	**2020**
Cash	369,165
A/R and inventory	1,100,000
Fixed assets	
Fixed assets at cost	10,000,000
Accumulated depreciation	−1,000,000
Net fixed assets	9,000,000
Total assets	**10,469,165**
Current liabilities	1,100,000
Debt	4,000,000
Owner's equity	3,000,000
Retained earnings	2,369,165
Total liabilities and equity	**10,469,165**

Table 12.6. Forecast Assumptions for Valuing Omega Corp. − 2021 to 2025.

Annual Changes to Financial Information	Assumption
Growth in sales revenue	10%
COGS/Sales	60%
Depreciation rate	10 year life, SL
Interest on debt	5%
Interest earned on cash balances	2%
Tax rate	20%
Dividend payout ratio	33%
Current assets/sales	10%
Current liabilities/sales	10%
Cost of capital	10%
Terminal value future growth	2%
Number of common shares issued	1,000,000

Using the net income from the pro-forma income statement, the investment banker then calculates the estimated future cash flows (**Figs. 12.19 and 12.20**).

Using the discounted future cash flows and terminal value, the share price is determined (**Figs. 12.21 and 12.22**).

Fig. 12.15. Omega Corp. Pro-forma Income Statement.

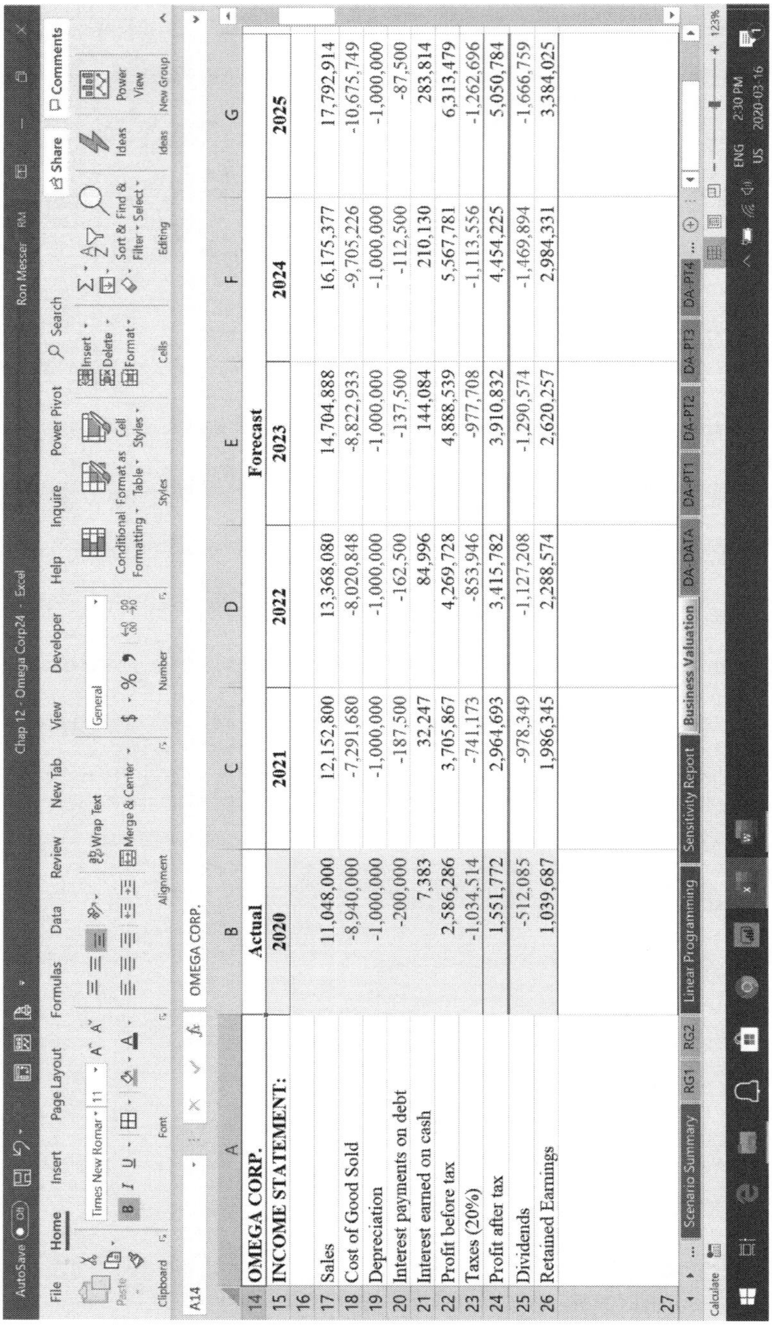

	A	B	C	D	E	F	G
14	OMEGA CORP.	Actual			Forecast		
15	INCOME STATEMENT:	2020	2021	2022	2023	2024	2025
16							
17	Sales	11,048,000	12,152,800	13,368,080	14,704,888	16,175,377	17,792,914
18	Cost of Good Sold	-8,940,000	-7,291,680	-8,020,848	-8,822,933	-9,705,226	-10,675,749
19	Depreciation	-1,000,000	-1,000,000	-1,000,000	-1,000,000	-1,000,000	-1,000,000
20	Interest payments on debt	-200,000	-187,500	-162,500	-137,500	-112,500	-87,500
21	Interest earned on cash	7,383	32,247	84,996	144,084	210,130	283,814
22	Profit before tax	2,586,286	3,705,867	4,269,728	4,888,539	5,567,781	6,313,479
23	Taxes (20%)	-1,034,514	-741,173	-853,946	-977,708	-1,113,556	-1,262,696
24	Profit after tax	1,551,772	2,964,693	3,415,782	3,910,832	4,454,225	5,050,784
25	Dividends	-512,085	-978,349	-1,127,208	-1,290,574	-1,469,894	-1,666,759
26	Retained Earnings	1,039,687	1,986,345	2,288,574	2,620,257	2,984,331	3,384,025
27							

Fig. 12.16. Omega Corp. Pro-forma Balance Sheet.

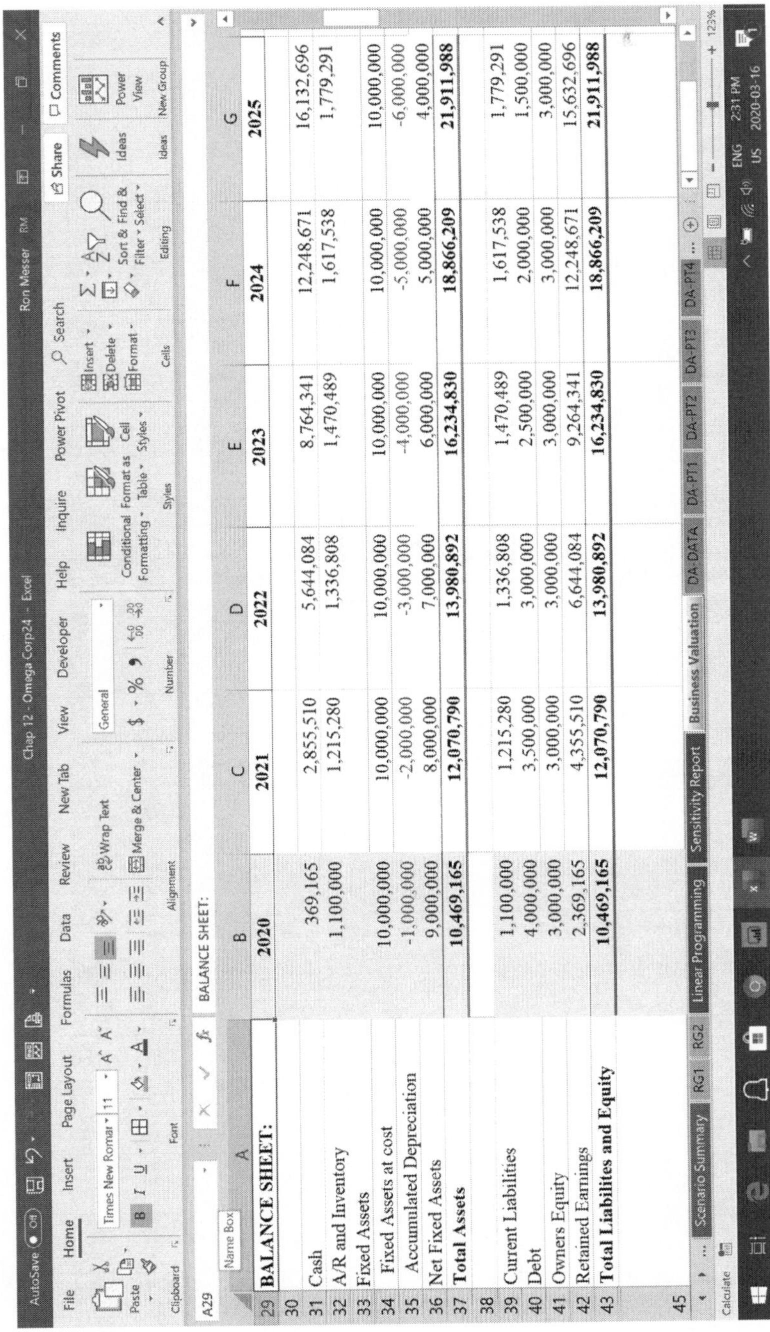

BALANCE SHEET:	2020	2021	2022	2023	2024	2025
Cash	369,165	2,855,510	5,644,084	8,764,341	12,248,671	16,132,696
A/R and Inventory	1,100,000	1,215,280	1,336,808	1,470,489	1,617,538	1,779,291
Fixed Assets						
Fixed Assets at cost	10,000,000	10,000,000	10,000,000	10,000,000	10,000,000	10,000,000
Accumulated Depreciation	-1,000,000	-2,000,000	-3,000,000	-4,000,000	-5,000,000	-6,000,000
Net Fixed Assets	9,000,000	8,000,000	7,000,000	6,000,000	5,000,000	4,000,000
Total Assets	10,469,165	12,070,790	13,980,892	16,234,830	18,866,209	21,911,988
Current Liabilities	1,100,000	1,215,280	1,336,808	1,470,489	1,617,538	1,779,291
Debt	4,000,000	3,500,000	3,000,000	2,500,000	2,000,000	1,500,000
Owners Equity	3,000,000	3,000,000	3,000,000	3,000,000	3,000,000	3,000,000
Retained Earnings	2,369,165	4,355,510	6,644,084	9,264,341	12,248,671	15,632,696
Total Liabilites and Equity	10,469,165	12,070,790	13,980,892	16,234,830	18,866,209	21,911,988

Fig. 12.17. Omega Corp. Pro-forma Income Statement (Formulas).

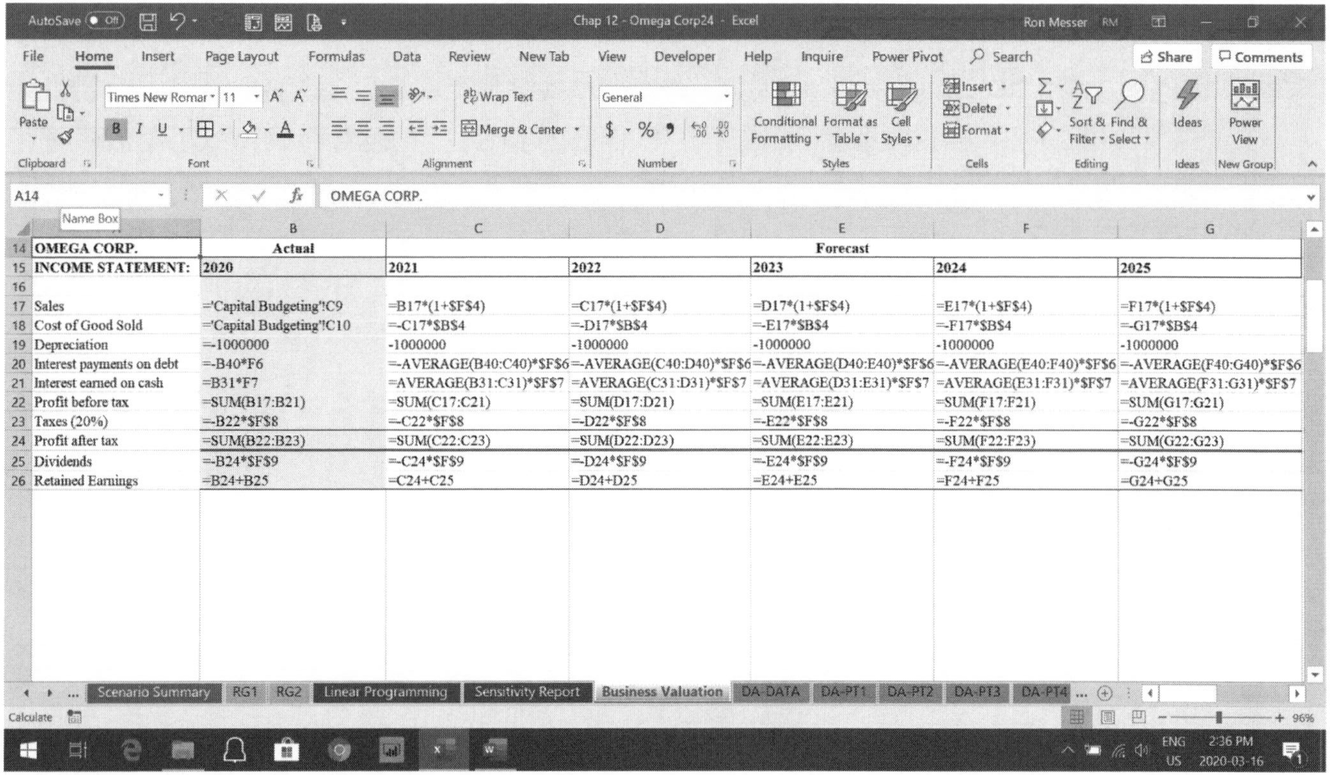

	A	B	C	D	E	F	G
14	OMEGA CORP.	Actual	Forecast				
15	INCOME STATEMENT:	2020	2021	2022	2023	2024	2025
16							
17	Sales	='Capital Budgeting'!C9	=B17*(1+$F$4)	=C17*(1+$F$4)	=D17*(1+$F$4)	=E17*(1+$F$4)	=F17*(1+$F$4)
18	Cost of Good Sold	='Capital Budgeting'!C10	=-C17*$B$4	=-D17*$B$4	=-E17*$B$4	=-F17*$B$4	=-G17*$B$4
19	Depreciation	=-1000000	-1000000	-1000000	-1000000	-1000000	-1000000
20	Interest payments on debt	=-B40*F6	=-AVERAGE(B40:C40)*$F$6	=-AVERAGE(C40:D40)*$F$6	=-AVERAGE(D40:E40)*$F$6	=-AVERAGE(E40:F40)*$F$6	=-AVERAGE(F40:G40)*$F$6
21	Interest earned on cash	=B31*F7	=AVERAGE(B31:C31)*$F$7	=AVERAGE(C31:D31)*$F$7	=AVERAGE(D31:E31)*$F$7	=AVERAGE(E31:F31)*$F$7	=AVERAGE(F31:G31)*$F$7
22	Profit before tax	=SUM(B17:B21)	=SUM(C17:C21)	=SUM(D17:D21)	=SUM(E17:E21)	=SUM(F17:F21)	=SUM(G17:G21)
23	Taxes (20%)	=-B22*$F$8	=-C22*$F$8	=-D22*$F$8	=-E22*$F$8	=-F22*$F$8	=-G22*$F$8
24	Profit after tax	=SUM(B22:B23)	=SUM(C22:C23)	=SUM(D22:D23)	=SUM(E22:E23)	=SUM(F22:F23)	=SUM(G22:G23)
25	Dividends	=-B24*$F$9	=-C24*$F$9	=-D24*$F$9	=-E24*$F$9	=-F24*$F$9	=-G24*$F$9
26	Retained Earnings	=B24+B25	=C24+C25	=D24+D25	=E24+E25	=F24+F25	=G24+G25

Fig. 12.18. Omega Corp. Pro-forma Balance Sheet (Formulas).

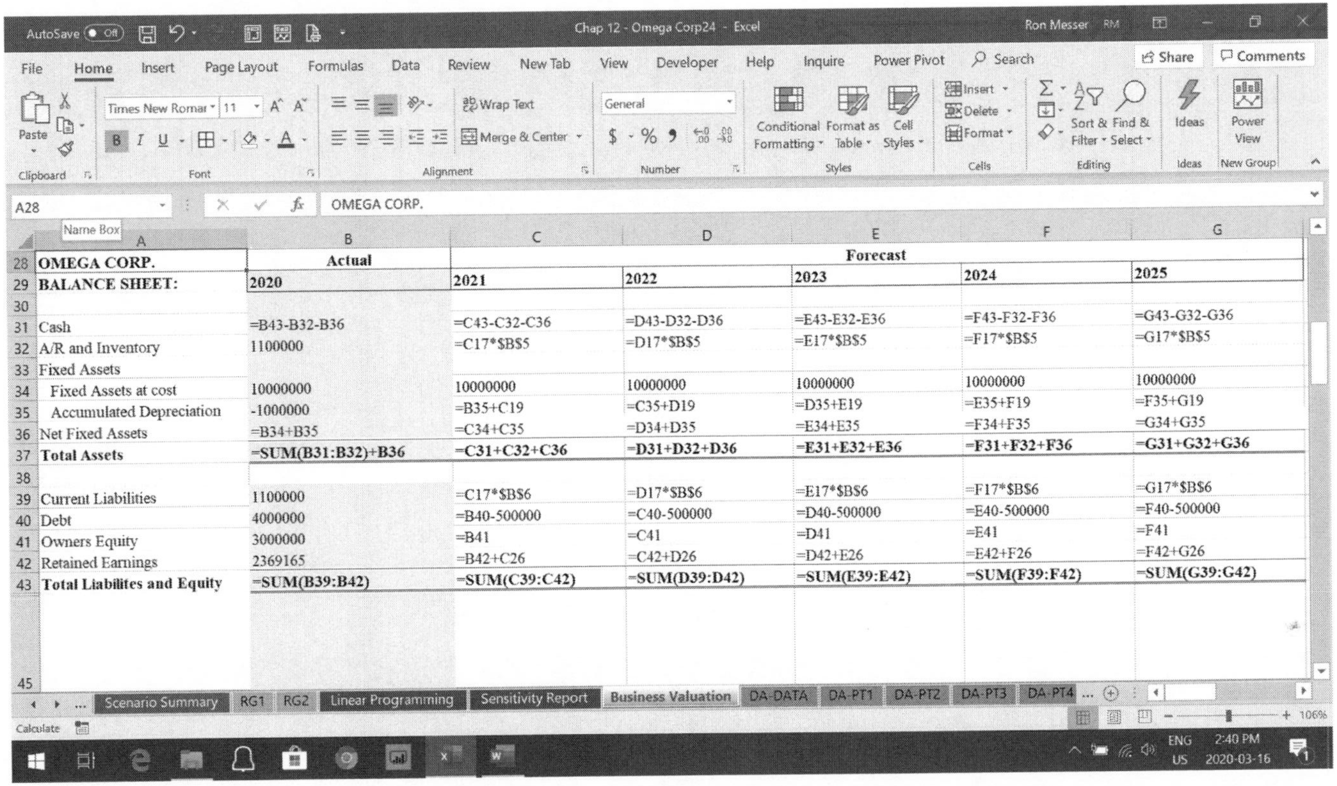

Name Box: A28 — OMEGA CORP.

	Actual			Forecast		
OMEGA CORP.	2020	2021	2022	2023	2024	2025
BALANCE SHEET:						
Cash	=B43-B32-B36	=C43-C32-C36	=D43-D32-D36	=E43-E32-E36	=F43-F32-F36	=G43-G32-G36
A/R and Inventory	1100000	=C17*$B$5	=D17*$B$5	=E17*$B$5	=F17*$B$5	=G17*$B$5
Fixed Assets						
Fixed Assets at cost	10000000	10000000	10000000	10000000	10000000	10000000
Accumulated Depreciation	-1000000	=B35+C19	=C35+D19	=D35+E19	=E35+F19	=F35+G19
Net Fixed Assets	=B34+B35	=C34+C35	=D34+D35	=E34+E35	=F34+F35	=G34+G35
Total Assets	=SUM(B31:B32)+B36	=C31+C32+C36	=D31+D32+D36	=E31+E32+E36	=F31+F32+F36	=G31+G32+G36
Current Liabilities	1100000	=C17*$B$6	=D17*$B$6	=E17*$B$6	=F17*$B$6	=G17*$B$6
Debt	4000000	=B40-500000	=C40-500000	=D40-500000	=E40-500000	=F40-500000
Owners Equity	3000000	=B41	=C41	=D41	=E41	=F41
Retained Earnings	2369165	=B42+C26	=C42+D26	=D42+E26	=E42+F26	=F42+G26
Total Liabilities and Equity	=SUM(B39:B42)	=SUM(C39:C42)	=SUM(D39:D42)	=SUM(E39:E42)	=SUM(F39:F42)	=SUM(G39:G42)

Scenario Summary   RG1   RG2   Linear Programming   Sensitivity Report   Business Valuation   DA-DATA   DA-PT1   DA-PT2   DA-PT3   DA-PT4

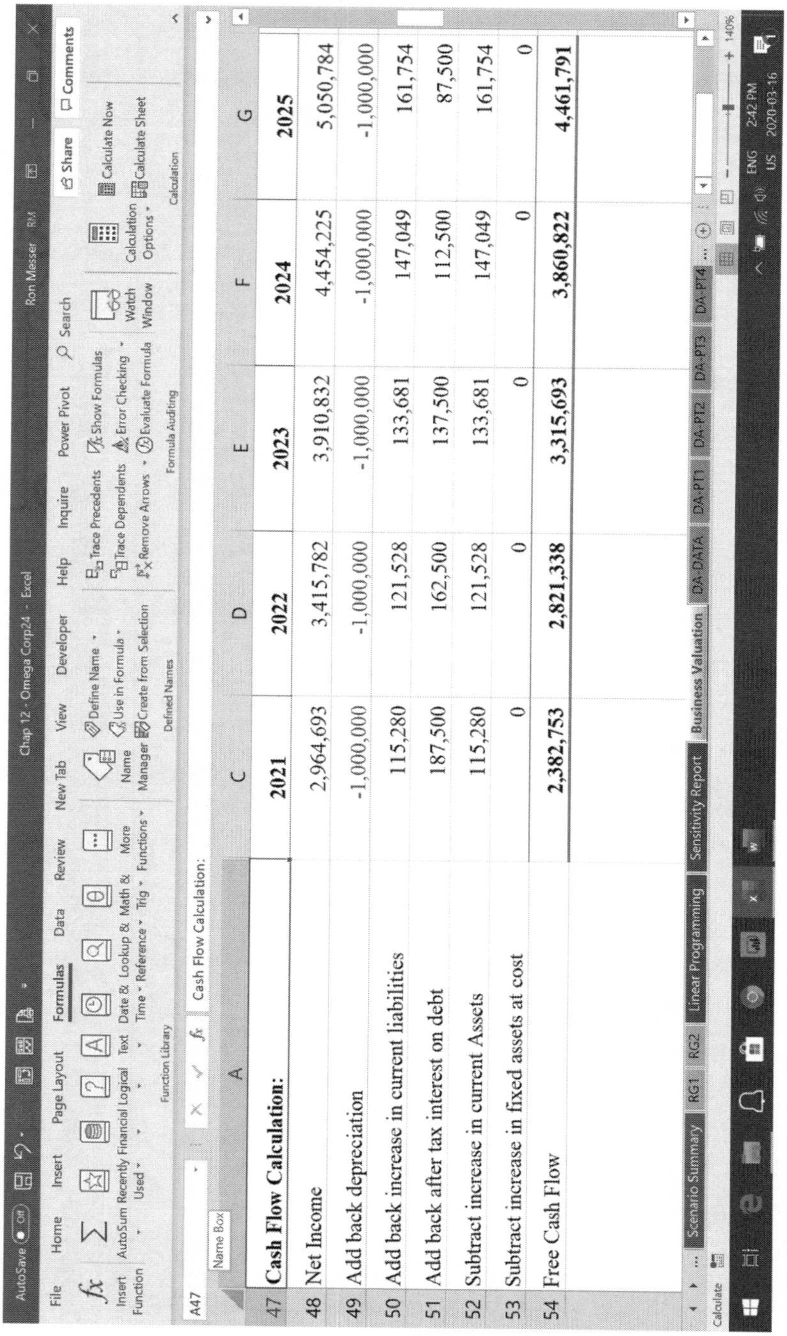

	A	C	D	E	F	G
47	Cash Flow Calculation:	2021	2022	2023	2024	2025
48	Net Income	2,964,693	3,415,782	3,910,832	4,454,225	5,050,784
49	Add back depreciation	-1,000,000	-1,000,000	-1,000,000	-1,000,000	-1,000,000
50	Add back increase in current liabilities	115,280	121,528	133,681	147,049	161,754
51	Add back after tax interest on debt	187,500	162,500	137,500	112,500	87,500
52	Subtract increase in current Assets	115,280	121,528	133,681	147,049	161,754
53	Subtract increase in fixed assets at cost	0	0	0	0	0
54	Free Cash Flow	2,382,753	2,821,338	3,315,693	3,860,822	4,461,791

Fig. 12.19. Omega Corp. Free Cash Flows.

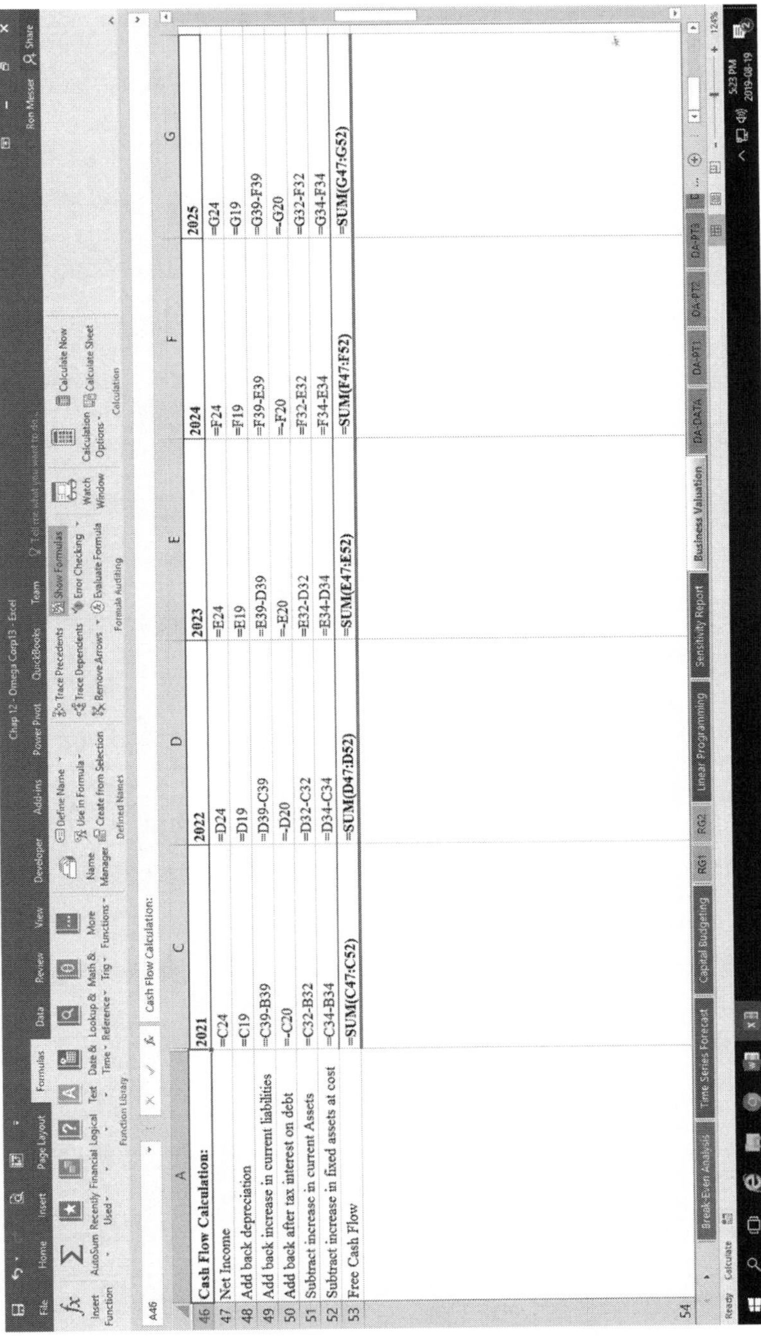
Chap 12 - Omega Corp13 - Excel
Cash Flow Calculation:
Cash Flow Calculation:
2021
2022
2023
2024
2025
Net Income
=C24
=D24
=E24
=F24
=G24
Add back depreciation
=C19
=D19
=E19
=F19
=G19
Add back increase in current liabilities
=C39-B39
=D39-C39
=E39-D39
=F39-E39
=G39-F39
Add back after tax interest on debt
=-C20
=-D20
=-E20
=-F20
=-G20
Subtract increase in current Assets
=C32-B32
=D32-C32
=E32-D32
=F32-E32
=G32-F32
Subtract increase in fixed assets at cost
=C34-B34
=D34-C34
=E34-D34
=F34-E34
=G34-F34
Free Cash Flow
=SUM(C47:C52)
=SUM(D47:D52)
=SUM(E47:E52)
=SUM(F47:F52)
=SUM(G47:G52)
Break-Even Analysis
Time Series Forecast
Capital Budgeting
RG1
RG2
Linear Programming
Sensitivity Report
Business Valuation
DA-DATA
DA-PT1
DA-PT2
DA-PT3

Fig. 12.20. Omega Corp. Free Cash Flows (Formulas).

Fig. 12.21. Omega Corp. Share Value.

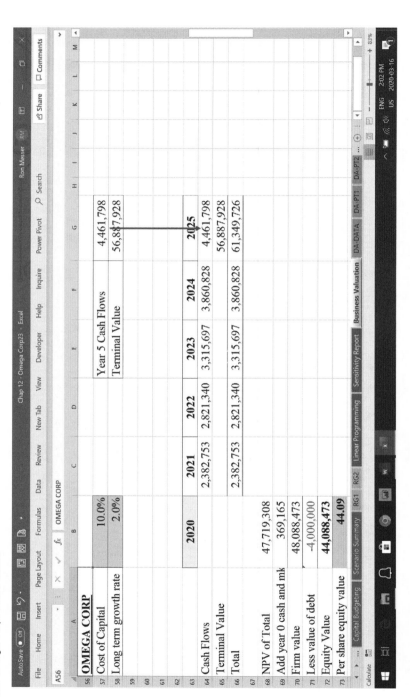

Fig. 12.22. Omega Corp. Share Value (Formulas).

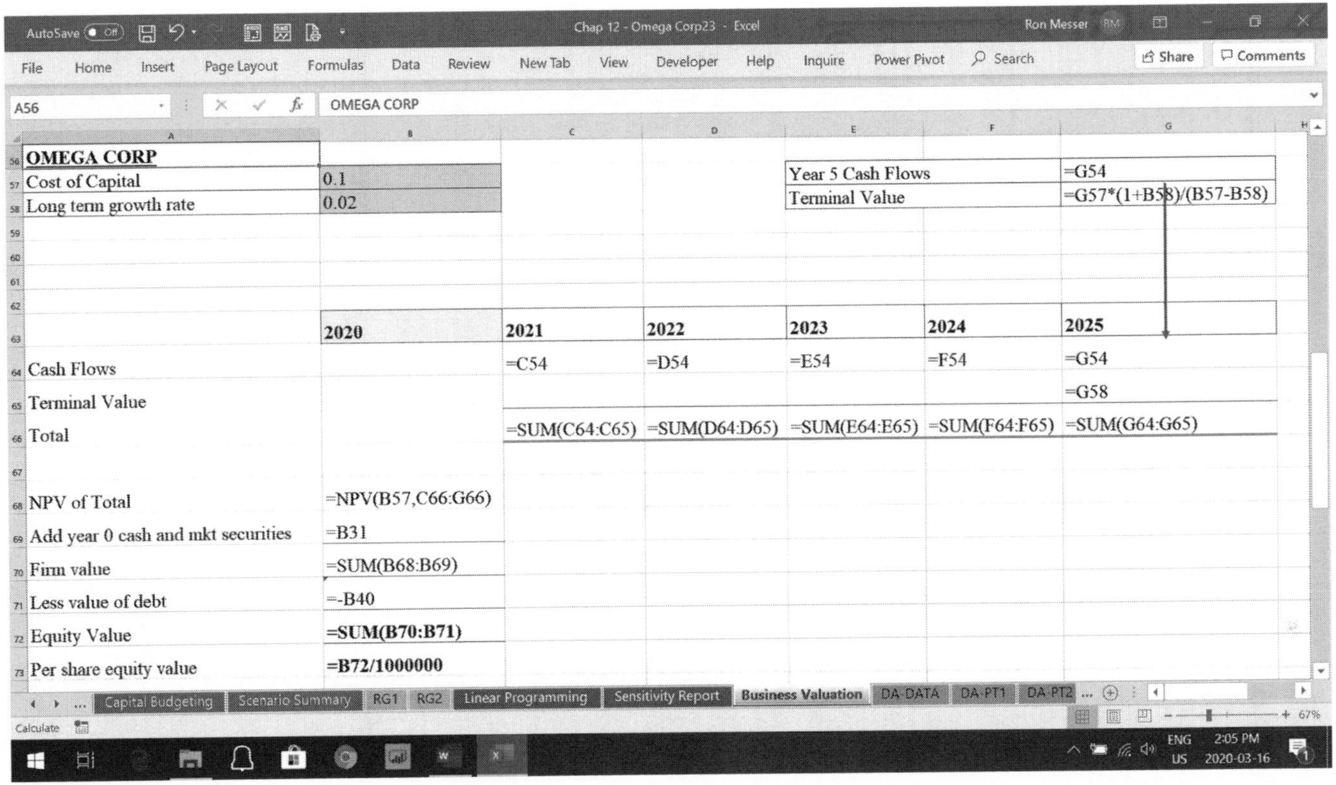

	A	B	C	D	E	F	G
56	**OMEGA CORP**						
57	Cost of Capital	0.1		Year 5 Cash Flows			=G54
58	Long term growth rate	0.02		Terminal Value			=G57*(1+B58)/(B57-B58)
63		2020	2021	2022	2023	2024	2025
64	Cash Flows		=C54	=D54	=E54	=F54	=G54
65	Terminal Value						=G58
66	Total		=SUM(C64:C65)	=SUM(D64:D65)	=SUM(E64:E65)	=SUM(F64:F65)	=SUM(G64:G65)
68	NPV of Total	=NPV(B57,C66:G66)					
69	Add year 0 cash and mkt securities	=B31					
70	Firm value	=SUM(B68:B69)					
71	Less value of debt	=-B40					
72	Equity Value	=SUM(B70:B71)					
73	Per share equity value	=B72/1000000					

The company can sell its shares for $44.07, based on the valuation model, which will generate approximately $44 million in additional financing and allow Omega Corp. to increase its productive capacity.

Decision 7: Considering customer perceptions of product value

Bob has experienced success in his first year of running the business and is now flush with cash from selling Omega shares. Before proceeding with expansion, he wants to gain some more insight into his customers and their perceptions of the company's products. For this reason, he has asked for a record of past sales, by product type, as well as additional information about the purchasers; this was obtained through a series of confidential feedback surveys conducted during the company's initial period of operations. **Table 12.7** shows the information collected, along with a description of each item of data.

A series of pivot tables was constructed from these data to analyze the relationships between buying behavior and customer characteristics. These are shown in **Figs. 12.23–12.28**.

Analysis of the pivot tables suggests that the customers who liked the products were primarily males (**Fig. 12.23**), in their 50s (**Fig. 12.24**) who worked for small- and medium-sized organizations (**Fig. 12.25**), mostly in the retail and government sectors (**Fig. 12.26**). Of the different product types available, the Omega 3 was the preferred type of pencil holder (**Fig. 12.27**). With this type of descriptive information, Bob can make the appropriate adjustments to his corporate strategy.

Feedback Decisions
Decision 8: Considering performance indicators for product price, cost, and value

After a highly successful first year resulting from sound business decisions about product prices (based on better cost allocations) and mix, and after obtaining additional financing

Table 12.7. Omega Corp. Customer Profiles.

Field Name	Data Collected
Month	Month when product was purchased (1 = Jan to 12 = Dec)
Gender	Male or female (M/F)
Age	30s (young), 40s, 50s, 60s (old)
Company size	Approximate annual sales of the company buying the product: Small: sales < $10 million annually Medium: sales $>$10 million & < $100 million annually Large: sales > $100 million & < $500 million annually
Industry	Primary revenue source for the company buying the product: Retail Food and beverage Manufacturing Government Energy Mining
Omega product	Sales by product type: Omega 1, 2, or 3
Liked product	Yes or No

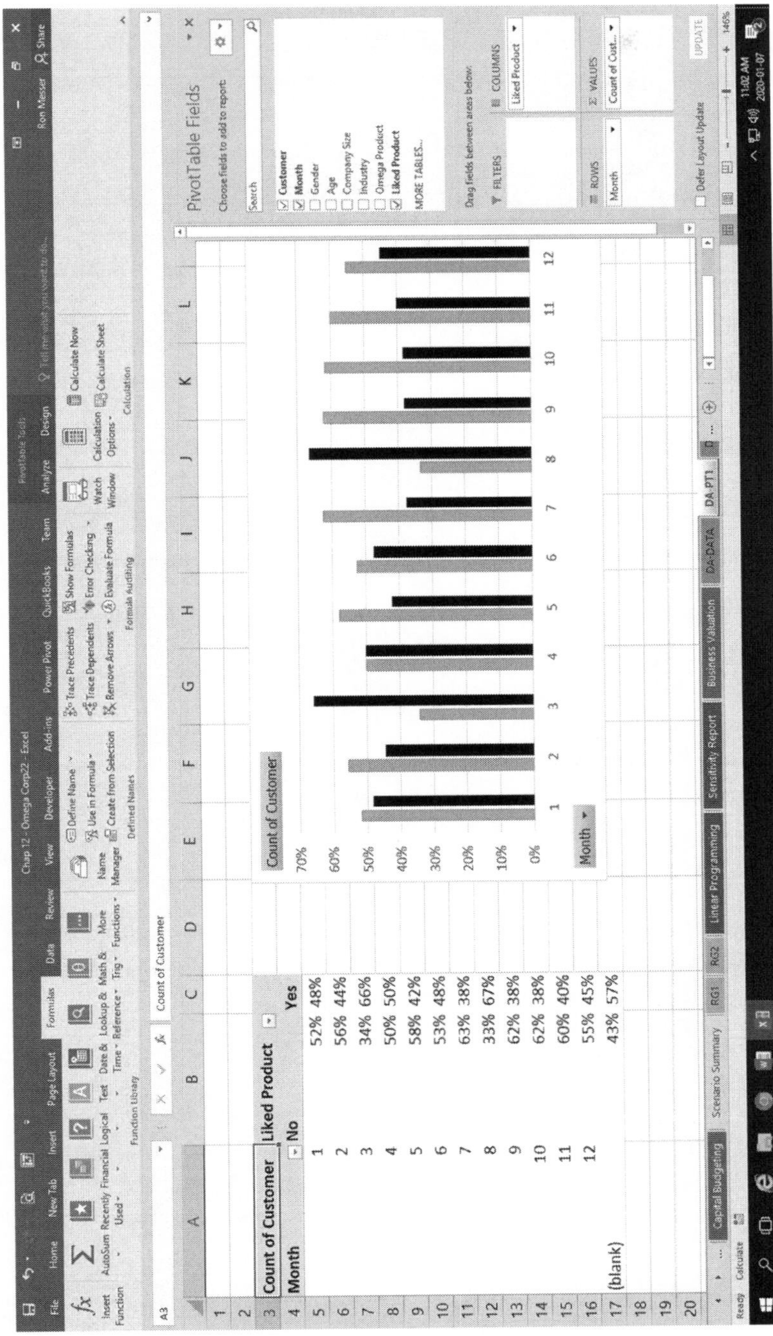

Fig. 12.23. Omega Corp. Product Purchases by Month.

Fig. 12.24. Omega Corp. Product Purchases by Gender.

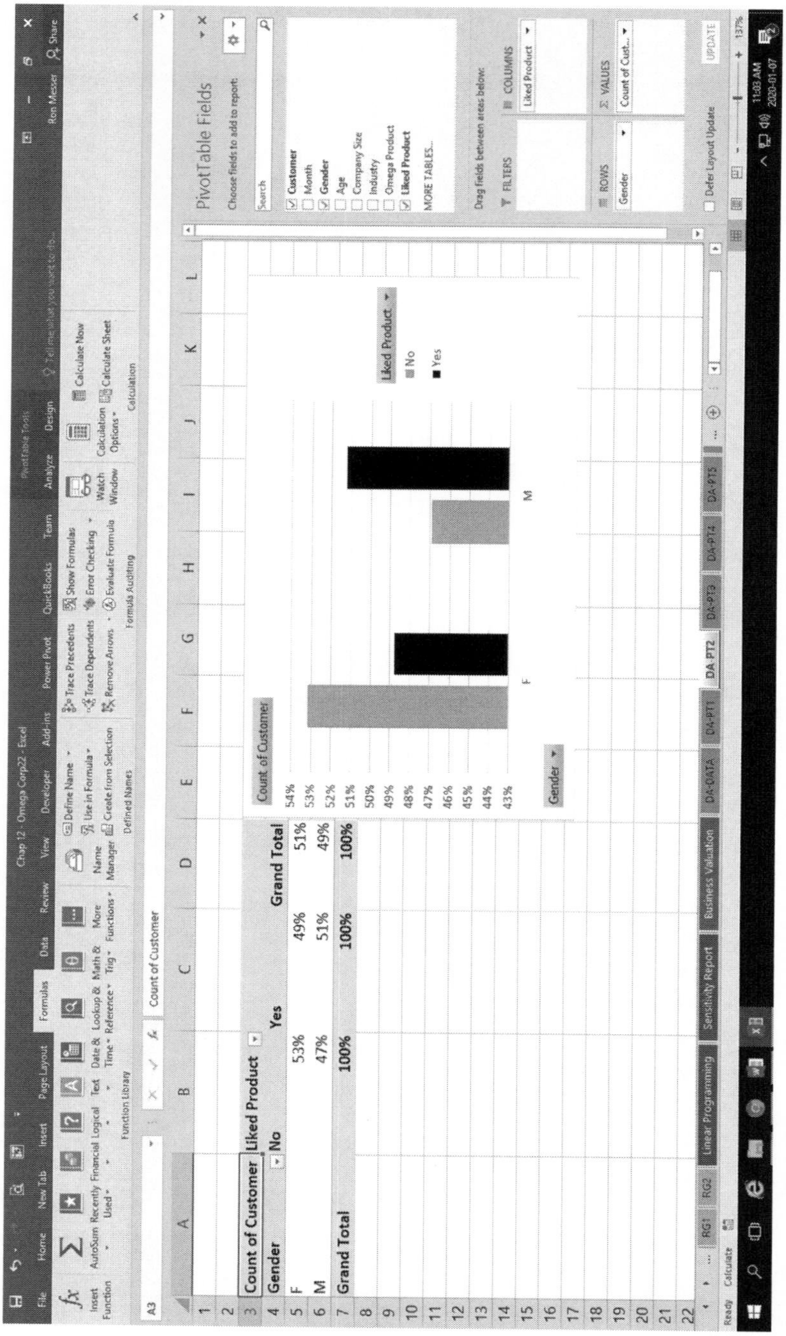

Fig. 12.25. Omega Corp. Product Purchases by Age.

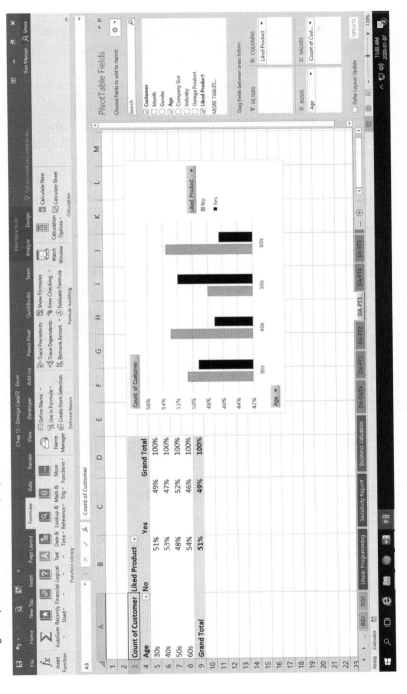

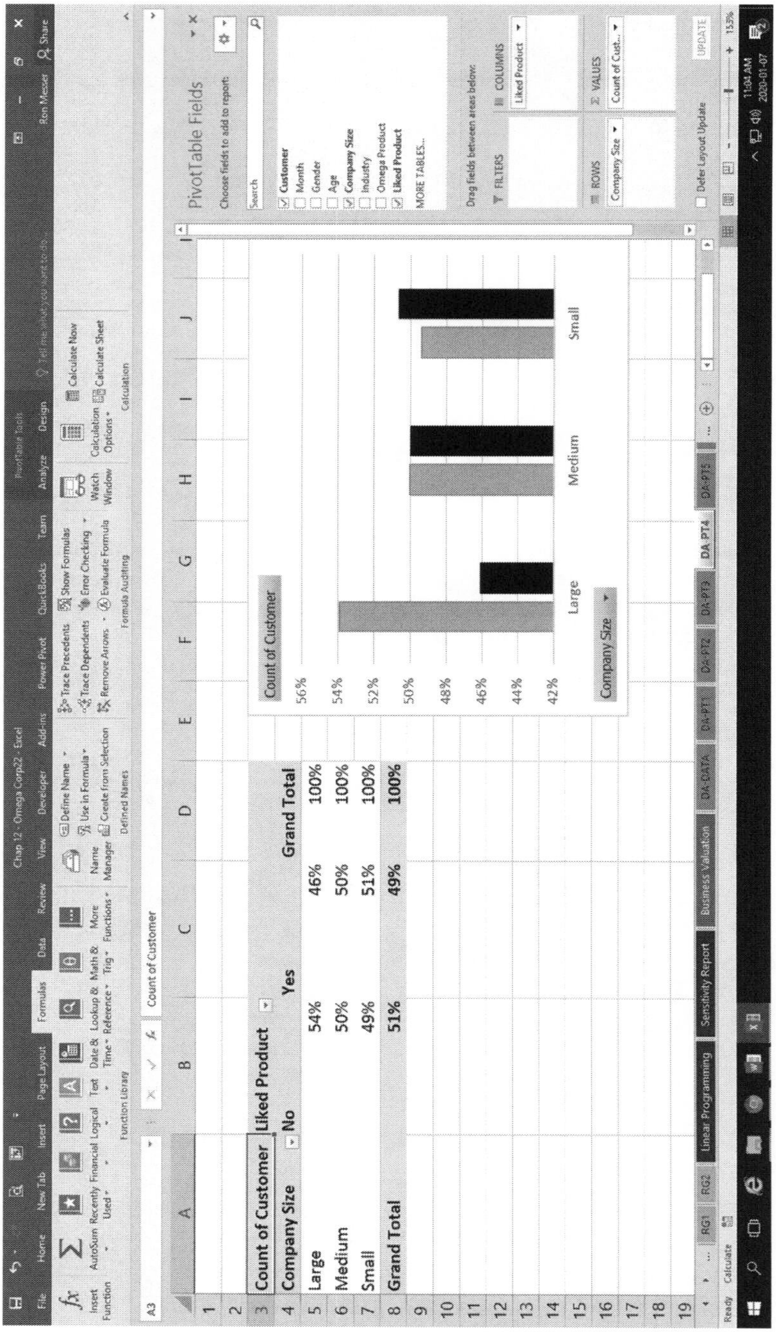

Fig. 12.26. Omega Corp. Product Purchases by Company Size.

Fig. 12.27. Omega Corp. Product Purchases by Industry.

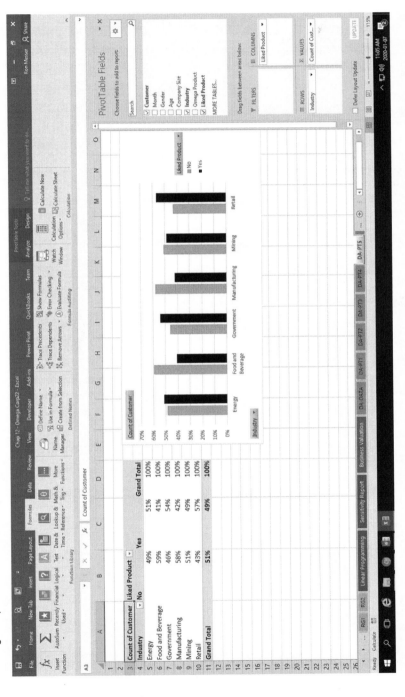

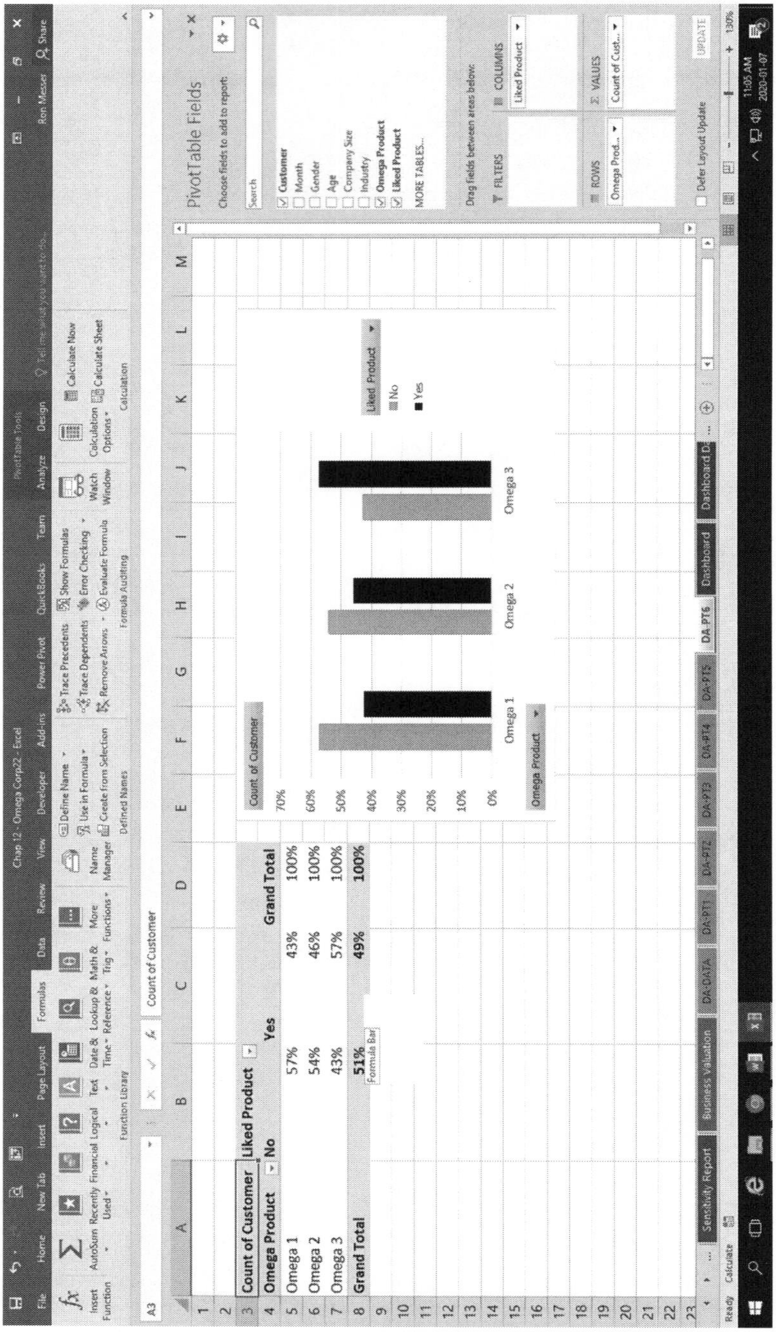

Fig. 12.28. Omega Corp. Product Purchases by Type.

to expand capacity, Bob wants to ensure that he is informed about the company's oper-ations in a timely manner. This will include knowing about Omega sales, corporate profits, and working capital. More specifically, on a monthly basis, he wants to know: (1) sales volume by product type (activity metric); (2) income and return on equity (profit-ability metric); (3) current assets and liabilities (liquidity metric).

To this end, a dashboard was designed that provides these *significant* measures in a *simple* format; this is shown for the month of March (along with February comparatives), in **Fig. 12.29**. (Note that the scales used in the comparative graphs are the same, which allows for more accurate comparisons of period-over-period operating results.)

Bob observes a significant decline in sales for Omega 3 in March (which is his most profitable product) and a consequent drop in income and ROE. However, the current ratio has improved for the period. With this information, he can take appropriate corrective action.

Decision 9: Considering budgets for prices, costs, and expenses

Using its first year financial results, Omega Corp. can develop an income statement master budget, based on the following assumptions (**Tables 12.8 and 12.9**).

Using prior year sales, the monthly income statement budget is prepared, as shown in **Fig. 12.30**.

Table 12.8. Assumptions Used to Develop the Income Statement Budget.

Income Statement Item	Assumption
Sales revenue growth	10%
Cost of goods sold relative to sales revenues	60%
Depreciation expense	10 year, SL
Interest expense	5%
Interest revenue	2%
Tax rate	20%

Table 12.9. Budgeted Income Statement.

Income Statement:	2021
Sales revenue	12,141,800
Interest revenue	32,223
Cost of goods sold	−7,285,080
Depreciation expense	−1,000,000
Interest expense	−187,500
Operating income	3,701,443
Tax expense	−740,289
Net income	2,961,154

Fig. 12.29. Omega Corp. KPI Dashboard.

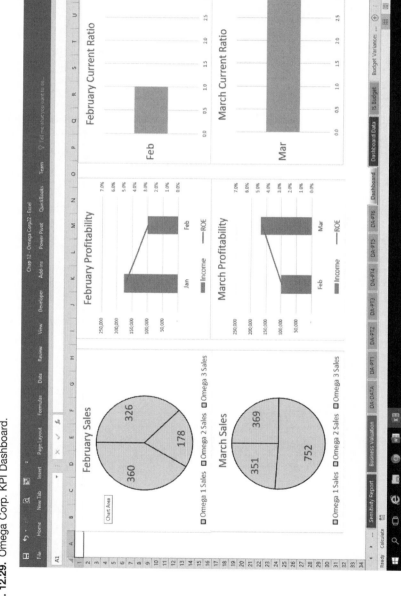

Fig. 12.30. Omega Corp. Monthly Income Statement Budget.

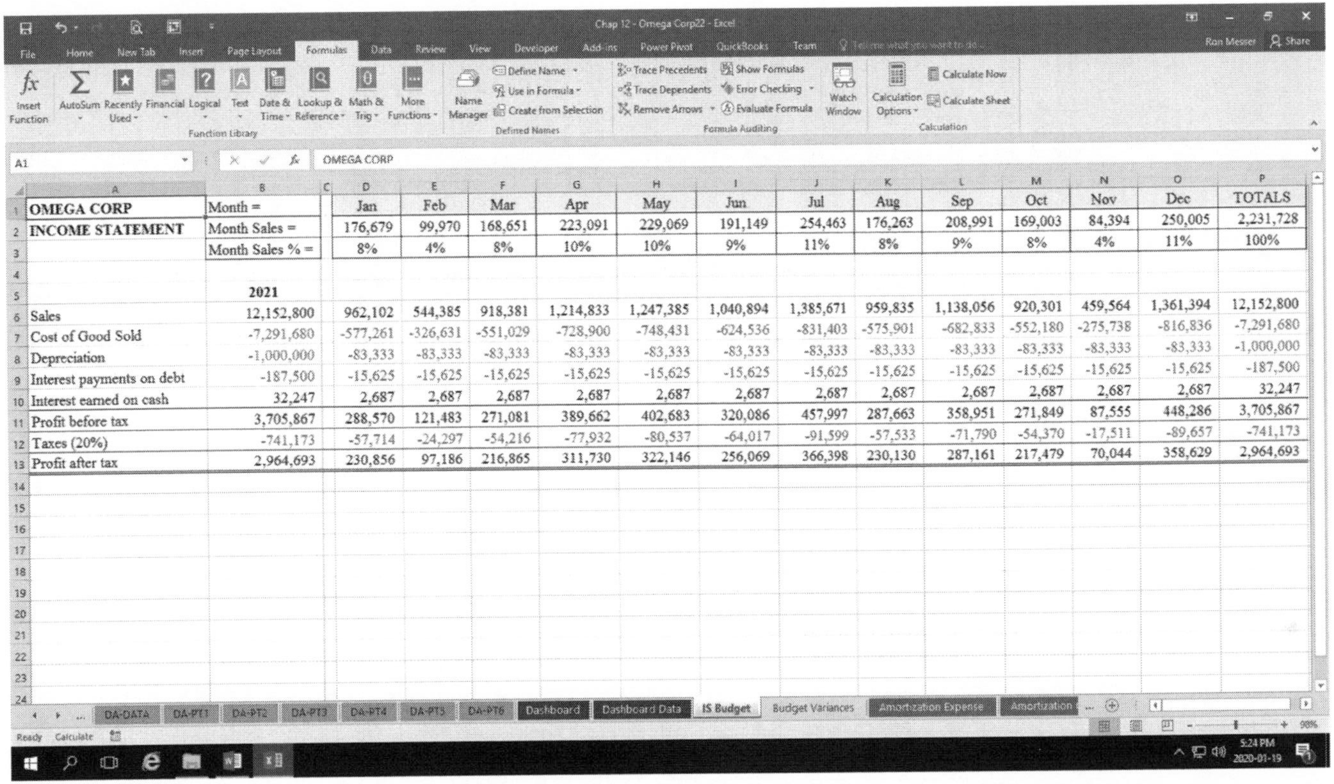

OMEGA CORP	Month =	Jan	Feb	Mar	Apr	May	Jun	Jul	Aug	Sep	Oct	Nov	Dec	TOTALS
INCOME STATEMENT	Month Sales =	176,679	99,970	168,651	223,091	229,069	191,149	254,463	176,263	208,991	169,003	84,394	250,005	2,231,728
	Month Sales % =	8%	4%	8%	10%	10%	9%	11%	8%	9%	8%	4%	11%	100%
	2021													
Sales	12,152,800	962,102	544,385	918,381	1,214,833	1,247,385	1,040,894	1,385,671	959,835	1,138,056	920,301	459,564	1,361,394	12,152,800
Cost of Good Sold	-7,291,680	-577,261	-326,631	-551,029	-728,900	-748,431	-624,536	-831,403	-575,901	-682,833	-552,180	-275,738	-816,836	-7,291,680
Depreciation	-1,000,000	-83,333	-83,333	-83,333	-83,333	-83,333	-83,333	-83,333	-83,333	-83,333	-83,333	-83,333	-83,333	-1,000,000
Interest payments on debt	-187,500	-15,625	-15,625	-15,625	-15,625	-15,625	-15,625	-15,625	-15,625	-15,625	-15,625	-15,625	-15,625	-187,500
Interest earned on cash	32,247	2,687	2,687	2,687	2,687	2,687	2,687	2,687	2,687	2,687	2,687	2,687	2,687	32,247
Profit before tax	3,705,867	288,570	121,483	271,081	389,662	402,683	320,086	457,997	287,663	358,951	271,849	87,555	448,286	3,705,867
Taxes (20%)	-741,173	-57,714	-24,297	-54,216	-77,932	-80,537	-64,017	-91,599	-57,533	-71,790	-54,370	-17,511	-89,657	-741,173
Profit after tax	2,964,693	230,856	97,186	216,865	311,730	322,146	256,069	366,398	230,130	287,161	217,479	70,044	358,629	2,964,693

With the benefit of hindsight, monthly differences between planned and actual results can be analyzed to evaluate management performance and take corrective action. As an example, **Table 12.10** shows the budgeted and actual unit costs for materials and labor for each of the three products, along with the variances.

The material variances for Omega 1 and 2 are unfavorable (gray shaded area) and should be investigated to determine whether they are caused by problems with price (i.e., purchase cost) or efficiency (i.e., excess usage).

Decision 10: Considering the effects of amortization expense

With equity capital now available, Bob wants to review how acquisitions of additional equipment will affect his bottom line. Productive capacity costs $10,000,000 for each fully automated assembly line, which can be used to manufacture any of the three Omega products. In its first year, the company used straight line depreciation, but wants to know how other GAAP methods would affect net income. This is shown in **Fig. 12.31**.

Bob notes that over the 10-year productive life of an assembly line, there are significant differences in annual depreciation charges. Because Omega is now publicly traded, he knows that he has to provide shareholders with increasing net income. The accelerated approaches (which include double declining, declining balance, and sum-of-the-years digits) charge larger amounts to the earlier – lower revenue – years, and thus negatively impact earnings. The current straight line method expenses equal

Table 12.10. Variance Analysis of Production Inputs.

March			
Budget			
Unit Costs	**Omega 1**	**Omega 2**	**Omega 3**
Materials	−300.00	−330.00	−360.00
Labor	−250.00	−275.00	−300.00
Actual			
Unit Costs	**Omega 1**	**Omega 2**	**Omega 3**
Materials	−301.00	−332.00	−357.00
Labor	−249.00	−274.00	−299.00
$ Variances per Unit			
Unit Costs	**Omega 1**	**Omega 2**	**Omega 3**
Materials	−1.00	−2.00	3.00
Labor	1.00	1.00	1.00
$ Variances in Total			
Unit Costs	**Omega 1**	**Omega 2**	**Omega 3**
Volumes	369	752	351
Materials	−369.00	−1,504.00	1,053.00
Labor	369.00	752.00	351.00

Fig. 12.31. Alternative Depreciation Methods.

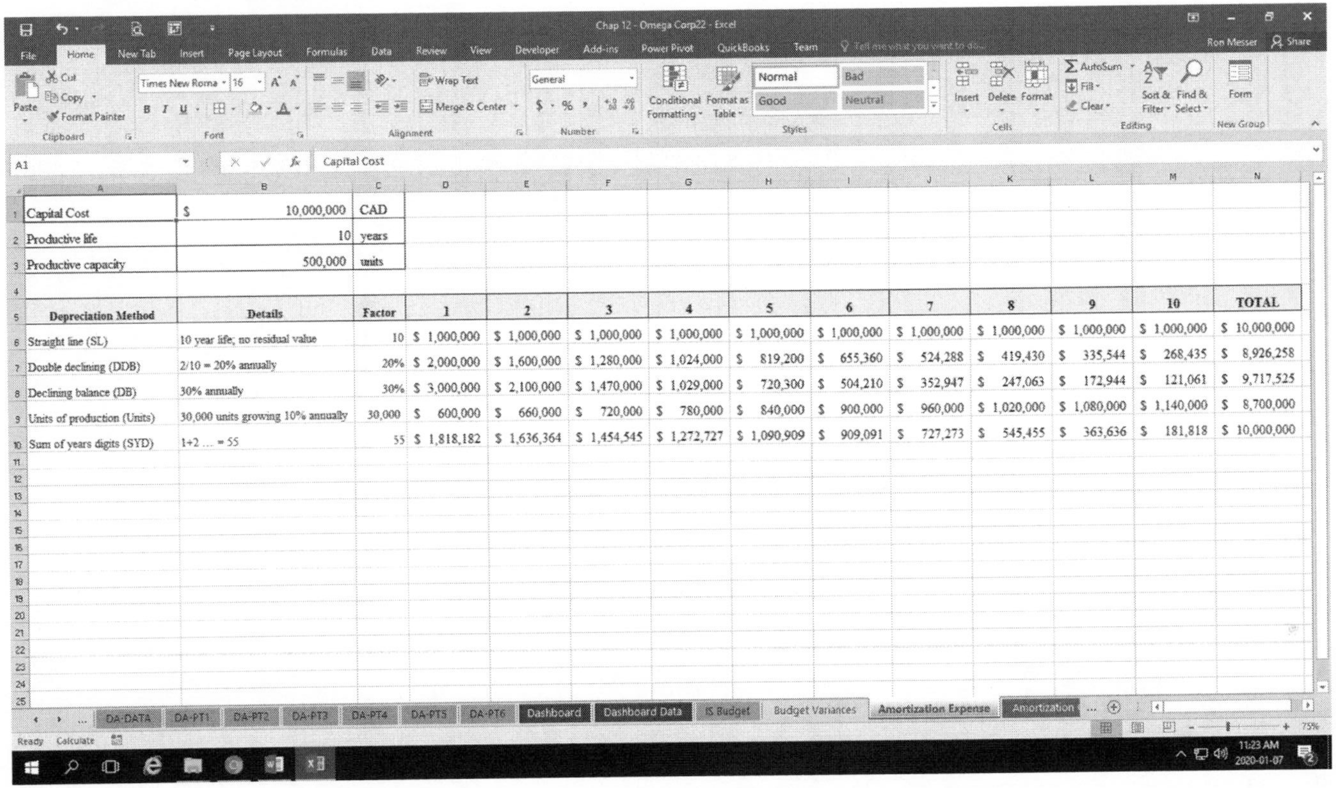

Capital Cost	$	10,000,000	CAD
Productive life		10	years
Productive capacity		500,000	units

Depreciation Method	Details	Factor	1	2	3	4	5	6	7	8	9	10	TOTAL
Straight line (SL)	10 year life, no residual value	10	$ 1,000,000	$ 1,000,000	$ 1,000,000	$ 1,000,000	$ 1,000,000	$ 1,000,000	$ 1,000,000	$ 1,000,000	$ 1,000,000	$ 1,000,000	$ 10,000,000
Double declining (DDB)	2/10 = 20% annually	20%	$ 2,000,000	$ 1,600,000	$ 1,280,000	$ 1,024,000	$ 819,200	$ 655,360	$ 524,288	$ 419,430	$ 335,544	$ 268,435	$ 8,926,258
Declining balance (DB)	30% annually	30%	$ 3,000,000	$ 2,100,000	$ 1,470,000	$ 1,029,000	$ 720,300	$ 504,210	$ 352,947	$ 247,063	$ 172,944	$ 121,061	$ 9,717,525
Units of production (Units)	30,000 units growing 10% annually	30,000	$ 600,000	$ 660,000	$ 720,000	$ 789,000	$ 840,000	$ 900,000	$ 960,000	$ 1,020,000	$ 1,080,000	$ 1,140,000	$ 8,700,000
Sum of years digits (SYD)	1+2 … = 55	55	$ 1,818,182	$ 1,636,364	$ 1,454,545	$ 1,272,727	$ 1,090,909	$ 909,091	$ 727,273	$ 545,455	$ 363,636	$ 181,818	$ 10,000,000

amounts every period. Assuming that there will be increasing annual sales, the best matching of revenues with asset usage will be the units of production method.

Fig. 12.32 illustrates the trends in annual depreciation expense, based on the different methods described.

Afterthought → *mission impossible(?)*

While this book has focused primarily on the technical aspects of making good business decisions, every enterprise must ultimately ask the bigger question about its reason for existence ... in other words, what is its purpose, or raison d'etre?

Fig. 12.32. Effects of Alternative Depreciation Methods.

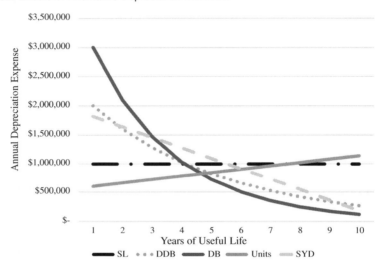

The Unbearable Importance of Being

(To be or not to be – but what's the question?)

Ontology is one of those odd words in the English language that means both a lot and not very much at all. Simply put, ontology is the study of "*being.*" It addresses the question of what it means when we say that something – a person or an object – exists, or "is" *something.* As Hamlet famously quipped: "to be or not to be...."

Business organizations have an ontology, too, that is captured in their mission statement. These formal expressions of "being" articulate a purpose – such as, to *be* the best railway in North America or to *be* the number one soft drink maker in the world. To "be" something both to itself, and in relation to other businesses, provides meaning to those who work for these companies.

Futurists and human resource professionals tell us that in the coming decade, employees will become increasingly concerned about working for organizations that have a purpose that provides them with meaning. The Coca Cola company's mission includes being a "*world citizen*" that "*improves the countries where it operates.*" Conversely, beating Coke, the stated goal of its main competitor Pepsi, will probably not inspire commitment among today's workers. However, saying that Pepsi promotes third world development may invite others to join the cause – being socially responsible, while earning a profit too.

But, before a company can "be" it must ask itself what it "is" and, more importantly, what it wants to become. The reason why the US rail barons stopped prospering at the turn of the last century was because they too narrowly defined themselves as being in charge of railroads. They failed to understand that people were not asking how they could travel by train; rather, they wanted to know how they could be transported from one place to another, opening the way for automobiles and airplanes. The question for Pepsi may not be: "Who do we need to beat," but instead how can we do a better job than our competitors at meeting the public's desire for refreshment and at the same time contribute to the greater good.

For many companies, the issue of what "to be" or "not to be" will become more important as they try to attract their share of a dwindling supply of workers and compete in a more global, socially conscious world. These businesses will have to ask themselves some hard questions, such as, if I am, what am I, and if I must be, what's the question I need to answer – for example, am I running a railroad or providing transportation. While Shakespeare's Hamlet anguished over this conundrum – with tragic consequences – most companies can change who they are by coming to a clearer appreciation of the nature of their business and its mission. Struggling with mission statements is sometimes unbearable, but also undeniably important. Remember this the next time someone asks the question: Will that be Coke or Pepsi?

Appendix 1

Excel Shortcut Keys

Table A1.I. Navigating Shortcuts.

Keystroke	Action
Alt + Tab	Toggle between programs
Ctrl + Esc	Show the Windows Start menu
Ctrl + Tab	Toggle between open Excel files
Ctrl + Page Up (Page Down)	Move between worksheets within the active file
Shift + Ctrl + Page Up (Page Down)	Select multiple worksheets within the active file
Home	Move to the beginning of the line
Ctrl + Home	Move to the beginning of the worksheet
Ctrl + End	Move to the last cell on the worksheet
End (press and release) + Arrow Keys	Move by one block of data within a row or column
Ctrl + Arrow Keys	Move by one block of data within a row or column
Ctrl + [/ Ctrl +]	Jump to precedent cells/jump to dependent cells
F5 (Go To) and then Enter	Return to the last cell visited
Ctrl +\	In a selected row, select the cells that don't match the formula in the active cell

Table A1.II. Function Keys.

Keystroke	Action
F1	Display Help
Alt + F4	Close Help (or any window)
F2	Edit the active cell
F4 or (Ctrl + Y)	Repeat the last action
F4	Absolute referencing
F5 or (Ctrl + G)	Go To
F7	Spell check
F9	Calculate (manual)

Table A1.III. Function Shortcuts.

Keystroke	Action
Ctrl + N	Create a new file
Ctrl + O	Open an existing file
Ctrl + p	Print
Ctrl + S	Save
Ctrl + W	Close the existing file
Alt + =	Sum a column
Shift + F2	Insert a comment
Ctrl + Shift + A	Prompts to edit a formula

Table A1.IV. Formatting Shortcuts.

Keystroke	Action
Ctrl + 1	Display the Cells command
Ctrl + B	Apply bold formatting
Ctrl + i	Apply italic formatting
Ctrl + U	Underline cells
Ctrl + ;	Enter the date
Ctrl + Shift + ;	Enter the time
Ctrl + Shift + !	Apply the number format
Ctrl + Shift + #	Apply the date format
Ctrl + Shift + $	Apply currency format
Ctrl + Shift + %	Apply percent format
Ctrl + Shift + &	Apply an outline border
Ctrl + Shift + _	Remove an outline border
Ctrl + O	Hide selected column(s)
Ctrl + Shift + O	Unhide selected column(s)
Ctrl + 9	Hide selected row(s)
Ctrl + Shift + 9	Unhide selected row(s)
Ctrl + ~	View cell formulas

Table A1.V. Editing Shortcuts.

Keystroke	Action
F2	Edit the active cell
Ctrl + C	Copy
Ctrl + D	Copy down
Ctrl + F	Find
Ctrl + G	Go to
Ctrl + H	Replace
Ctrl + R	Copy right
Ctrl + V	Paste
Ctrl + Alt + V	Paste Special
Ctrl + X	Cut
Ctrl + Y	Repeat last action
Ctrl + Z	Undo last action
Alt + Enter	Start new line in same cell
Alt + down-arrow	Open a filter drop down box
Ctrl + Delete	Delete text to end of line
Ctrl + '	Copy formula from cell above
Ctrl + Shift + '	Copy value from cell above

Table A1.VI. Selecting Cells.

Keystroke	Action
Ctrl + A	Select entire sheet
Ctrl + Spacebar	Select the column
Shift + Spacebar	Select the row
Alt + Shift + Rt (Lt) Arrow	Group (ungroup) selected rows or columns
Shift + End + Arrow Keys	Extend the selection to the last nonblank cell in the same row or column

Appendix 2
Common Financial Ratios

Table A2.I. Activity, Liquidity, Solvency, and Profitability Measures.

Type	Ratio	Formula
Activity	A/R Turnover	Net Credit Sales ÷ Average A/R
Activity	Inventory Turnover	Sales ÷ Average Inventory
Activity	Days Sales on A/R	Average A/R ÷ Credit Sales × 365
Activity	Days Sales in Inventory	Inventory ÷ Cost of Goods Sold × 365
Liquidity	Current Ratio	Current Assets ÷ Current Liabilities
Liquidity	Quick Ratio	(Current Assets − Inventories) ÷ Current Liabilities
Solvency	Debt-to-Equity Ratio	Total Liabilities ÷ Shareholders Equity
Solvency	Solvency Ratio	Net Income ÷ Total debt
Solvency	Interest Coverage Ratio	Earnings Before Interest and Taxes ÷ Interest Expense
Profitability	Return on Equity (ROE)	Net Income ÷ Shareholder's Equity
Profitability	Net Profit Margin	Net Income ÷ Net Sales
Profitability	Return on Total Assets	Net Income ÷ Average Total Assets
Profitability	Earnings per Share (EPS)	(Net Income − P/S Dividends) ÷ Average Common Shares
Profitability	P/E (the multiple)	Market Price of C/S ÷ EPS

Index